JOHN

ANNA LAETITI.

EVENINGS AT HOME

OR

THE JUVENILE BUDGET OPENED

CORRECTED AND REVISED

BY CECIL HARTLEY

Elibron Classics
www.elibron.com

Elibron Classics series.

© 2005 Adamant Media Corporation.

ISBN 1-4021-6975-2 (paperback)
ISBN 1-4021-0672-6 (hardcover)

This Elibron Classics Replica Edition is an unabridged facsimile
of the edition published in 1863 by Routledge, Warne, and Routledge,
London.

Already was I bound, and just ready to be set a sailing, when the schoolmaster, taking a walk that way, obliged the boys to set me at liberty.   P. 64.

EVENINGS AT HOME;

OR,

THE JUVENILE BUDGET OPENED.

BY

DR. AIKIN & MRS. BARBAULD.

CORRECTED AND REVISED

BY CECIL HARTLEY, M.A.
AUTHOR OF "PRINCIPLES OF THE SCIENCES," ETC.

A New Edition, Illustrated with Fine Engravings.

LONDON:
ROUTLEDGE, WARNE, & ROUTLEDGE,
FARRINGDON STREET;
NEW YORK: 56, WALKER STREET.
1863.

PREFACE.

No apology is necessary for presenting a new, revised, and improved edition of Dr. AIKIN and Mrs. BARBAULD's *Evenings at Home*. The well-earned and long-established popularity of the work has entitled it to every attention on the part of the publisher; and so far as regards paper and print, binding and pictorial illustration, he is happy in the opportunity of offering to his young friends a *Gift-Book for the Season*—for ANY season—worthy of their acceptance.

In bringing the present edition before the world, the advance of time, and the consequent advance of literature, science, and the arts, called for some editorial application. Accordingly, obsolete and rugged expressions have been modernised or polished; and, wherever it may have been judged necessary, new and useful information has been inserted. With the original plan or tendency of the work, however, not the slightest liberty has been taken. All that has been attempted is to render it more in accordance with the general and improved taste of the age.

Thus, happily interspersing and blending instruction with amusement, *Evenings at Home* will, under the present form of arrangement, be found to contain an almost exhaustless store of interesting material for the unfatiguing exercise of mind, from the state of infancy to that of adolescence. In the perusal of this volume, brothers and sisters may ·alike aid each other and facilitate their mental studies; and with yet greater advantage, by a little occasional assistance from Papa or Mamma, the Tutor or the Governess.

The new and beautiful series of illustrations cannot fail to prove additionally attractive to all.

CONTENTS.

EVENINGS AT HOME.

INTRODUCTION.

THE mansion-house of the pleasant village of *Beech-grove* was inhabited by the family of FAIRBORNE, consisting of the master and mistress, and a numerous progeny of children, boys and girls. Of these, some were educated at home under their parents' care, and some were sent out to school. The house was seldom unprovided with visitors, the intimate friends or relations of the owners, who were entertained with cheerfulness and hospitality, free from ceremony and parade. They formed, during their stay, part of the family, and were ready to concur with Mr. and Mrs. Fairborne in any little domestic plan for varying their amusements, and particularly for promoting the instruction and entertainment of the younger part of the household. As some of them were accustomed to writing, they would frequently produce a fable, a story, or dialogue, adapted to the age and understanding of the young people. It was always considered as a high favour when they would so employ themselves; and when the pieces had been once read over, they were carefully deposited by Mrs. Fairborne in a box, of which she kept the key. None of these were allowed to be taken out again till all the children were assembled in the holidays. It was then made one of the evening amusements of the family to *rummage the budget*, as their phrase was. One of the youngest children was sent to the box, who, putting in its little hand, drew out the paper that came next, and brought

B

it into the parlour. This was then read distinctly by one of the older ones; and after it had undergone sufficient consideration, another little messenger was despatched for a fresh supply; and so on, till as much time had been spent in this manner as the parents thought proper. Other children were admitted to these readings; and as the *Budget of Beechgrove Hall* became somewhat celebrated in the neighbourhood, its proprietors were at length urged to lay it open to the public. They were induced to comply; and thus, without further preface, begins the

FIRST EVENING.

THE YOUNG MOUSE.

A Fable.

A YOUNG Mouse lived in a cupboard where sweetmeats were kept: she dined every day upon biscuit, marmalade, or fine sugar. Never any little Mouse had lived so well. She had often ventured to peep at the family while they sat at supper; nay, she had sometimes stolen down on the carpet, and picked up the crumbs, and nobody had ever hurt her. She would have been quite happy, but that she was sometimes frightened by the cat, and then she ran trembling to the hole behind the wainscot. One day she came running to her mother in great joy, "Mother!" said she, "the good people of this family have built me a house to live in; it is in the cupboard: I am sure it is for me, for it is just big enough; the bottom is of wood, and it is covered all over with wires; and I dare say they have made it on purpose to screen me from that terrible cat, which has run after me so often: there is an entrance just big enough for me, but puss cannot follow; and they have been so good as to put in some toasted cheese, which smells so deliciously, that I should have run in directly and taken possession-of my new house, but I thought I would tell you first, that we might go in together, and both lodge there to-night, for it will hold us both."

"My dear child," said the old Mouse, "it is most happy that you did not go in, for this house is called a trap, and you would never have come out again, except to be devoured, or put to death in some way or other. Though man has not so fierce a look as a cat, he is as much our enemy, and has still more cunning."

THE WASP AND THE BEE.

A Fable.

A WASP met a Bee, and said to him, "Pray can you tell me what is the reason that men are so ill-natured to me, while they are so fond of you? We are very much alike, only that the broad golden rings about my body make me much handsomer than you are: we are both winged insects, we both love honey, and we both sting people when we are angry; yet men always hate me, and try to kill me, though I am much more familiar with them than you are, and pay them visits in their houses, and at their tea-tables, and at all their meals: while you are very shy, and hardly ever come near them: yet they build you curious houses thatched with straw, and take care of and feed you in the winter very often. I wonder what is the reason."

The Bee said, "Because you never do them any good, but, on the contrary, are very troublesome and mischievous; therefore they do not like to see you; but they know that I am busy all day long in making them honey. You had better pay them fewer visits, and try to be useful."

THE GOOSE AND THE HORSE.

A Fable.

A GOOSE, who was plucking grass upon a common, thought herself affronted by a Horse who fed near her, and in hissing accents thus addressed him: "I am certainly a more noble and perfect animal than you, for the whole range and extent of your faculties is confined to one element. I can walk upon the ground, as well as you: I have, besides, wings, with which I can raise myself in the air; and, when I please, I can sport in ponds and lakes, and refresh myself in the cool waters: I enjoy the different powers of a bird, a fish, and a quadruped."

The Horse, snorting somewhat disdainfully, replied, " It is true you inhabit three elements, but you make no very distinguished figure in any one of them. You fly, indeed; but your flight is so heavy and clumsy, that you have no right to put yourself on a level with the lark or the swallow. You can swim on the surface of the waters, but you cannot live in them as fishes do; you cannot find much of your food in that element, nor glide smoothly along the bottom of the waves. And when you walk, or rather waddle, upon the ground, with your broad feet, and your long neck stretched out, hissing at every one who passes by, you bring upon yourself the derision of all beholders. I confess that I am formed only to move upon the ground; but how graceful is my make! how well turned my limbs! how highly finished my whole body! how great my strength! how astonishing my speed! I had far rather be confined to one element, and be admired in that, than be a Goose in all."

THE FLYING FISH.

THE Flying Fish, says the Fable, had originally no wings, but being of an ambitious and discontented temper, she repined at always being confined to the waters, and wished to soar in the air. " If I could fly like the birds," said she, " I should not only see more of the beauties of nature, but I should be able to escape from those fish which are continually pursuing me, and which render my life miserable." She therefore petitioned Jupiter for a pair of wings : and immediately she perceived her fins to expand. They suddenly grew to the length of her whole body, and became at the same time so strong as to do the office of pinions. She was at first much pleased with her new powers, and looked with an air of disdain on all her former companions ; but she soon perceived herself exposed to new dangers. When flying in the air, she was incessantly pursued by the tropic bird and the albatross ; and when, for safety, she dropped into the water, she was so fatigued with her flight, that she was less able than ever to escape from her old enemies, the fish. Finding herself more unhappy than before, she now begged of Jupiter to recall his present ; but Jupiter said to her, " When I gave you your wings, I well knew they would prove a curse ; but your proud and restless disposition deserved this disappointment. Now, therefore, what you begged as a favour, keep as a punishment ! "

THE LITTLE DOG.
A Fable.

" WHAT shall I do," said a very little dog one day to his mother, " to show my gratitude to our good master, and make myself of some value to him ? I cannot draw or carry burdens, like the horse ; nor give him milk, like the cow; nor lend him my covering for his clothing, like the sheep; nor produce him eggs, like the poultry; nor catch mice and rats so well as the cat. I cannot divert him with singing, like the canaries and linnets; nor can I defend him against robbers, like our relation Towzer; I should not be of use to him even if I were dead, as the hogs are. I am a poor, insignificant creature, not worth the cost of keeping; and I don't see that I can do a single thing to entitle me to his regard." So saying, the poor little dog hung down his head in silent despondency.

"My dear pet," replied his mother, "though your abilities are but small, yet a hearty goodwill is sufficient to supply all defects. Do but love your master dearly, and prove your love by all the means in your power, and you will not fail to please him."

The little dog was comforted with this assurance, and, on his master's approach, ran to him, licked his feet, gambolled before him, and every now and then stopped, wagging his tail, and looking up to him with expressions of the most humble and affectionate attachment. The master observed him. "Ah! little Fido," said he, "you are an honest, good-natured little fellow!"—and stooped down to pat his head. Poor Fido was ready to go out of his wits for joy.

Fido was now his master's constant companion in his walks, playing and skipping around him, and amusing him by a thousand sportive tricks. He took care, however, not to be troublesome by leaping on him with dirty paws, nor would he follow him into the parlour, unless invited. He also attempted to make himself useful by a number of little services. He would drive away the sparrows, as they were stealing the chickens' meat; and would run and bark with the utmost fury at any strange pigs or other animals that offered to come into the yard. He kept the poultry, geese, and pigs from straying beyond their bounds, and particularly from doing mischief in the garden. He was always ready to alarm Towzer if there were any suspicious noise about the house, day or night. If his master pulled off his coat in the field to help his workmen, as he would sometimes do, Fido always sat by it, and would not suffer either man or beast to touch it. By this means he came to be considered as a very trusty protector of his master's property.

His master was once confined to his bed with a dangerous illness. Fido planted himself at the chamber-door, and could not be persuaded to leave it, even to take food; and as soon as his master had so far recovered as to sit up, Fido, being admitted into the room, ran up to him with such marks of excessive joy and affection as would have melted any heart to behold. This circumstance wonderfully endeared him to his master; and some time after he had an opportunity of doing him a very important service. One hot day, after dinner, his master was sleeping in a summer-house with Fido by his side. The building was old and crazy; and the dog, who was faithfully watching his master, perceived the wall shake, and pieces of mortar fall from the ceiling. He comprehended the danger, and began barking to awake his master; and this not sufficing, he jumped up, and gently bit his finger. The master upon this started up, and had just time to get out of the door before the whole building fell down. Fido, who was behind, got hurt by some rubbish which fell upon him; on which his master had him taken care of with the utmost tenderness, and ever after acknowledged his obligation to this little animal as the preserver of his life. Thus his love and fidelity had their full reward.

Moral. The poorest man may repay his obligations to the richest and greatest by faithful and affectionate service—the meanest creature may obtain the favour and regard of the Creator himself, by humble gratitude, and steadfast obedience.

TRAVELLERS' WONDERS.

ONE winter's evening, as Captain Compass was sitting by the fireside with his children all around him, little Jack said to him, "Papa, pray tell us some stories about what you have seen in your voyages. I have been vastly entertained whilst you were abroad, with Gulliver's Travels, and the Adventures of Sinbad the Sailor; and I think, as you have gone round and round the world, you must have met with things as wonderful as they did."—"No, my dear," said the Captain, "I never met with Lilliputians, or Brobdignagians, I assure you, nor ever saw the black loadstone mountain, or the valley of diamonds; but, to be sure, I have seen a great variety of people, and their different manners and ways of living; and if it will be any entertainment to you, I will tell you some curious particulars of what I observed."—"Pray do, Papa," cried Jack and all his brothers and sisters; so they drew close around him, and he began as follows :—

"Well then—I was once, about this time of the year, in a country where it was very cold, and the poor inhabitants had much ado to keep themselves from starving. They were clad partly in the skins of beasts, made smooth and soft by a particular art, but chiefly in garments made from the outer covering of a middle-sized quadruped, which they were so cruel as to strip off his back while he was alive. They dwelt in habitations, part of which was sunk under-ground. The materials were either stones, or earth hardened by fire; and so violent in that country were the storms of wind and rain, that many of them covered their roofs all over with stones. The walls of their houses had holes to let in the light; but to prevent the cold air and wet from coming in, they were faced by a sort of transparent stone, made artificially of melted sand or flints. As wood was rather scarce, I know not what

they would have done for firing, had they not discovered in the bowels of the earth a very extraordinary
kind of stone, which, when put among burning wood,
caught fire and flamed like a torch."

"Dear me," said Jack, "what a wonderful stone!
I suppose it was somewhat like what we call fire-stones,
that shine so when we rub them together."—"I don't
think they would burn," replied the Captain; "besides, these are of a darker colour."

"Well—but their diet too was remarkable. Some
of them ate fish that had been hung up in the smoke
till they were quite dry and hard; and along with it
they ate either the roots of plants, or a sort of coarse
black cake made of powdered seeds. These were the
poorer class; the richer had a whiter kind of cake,
which they were fond of daubing over with a greasy
matter that was the product of a large animal among
them. This grease they used, too, in almost all their
dishes, and when fresh, it really was not unpalatable.
They also devoured the flesh of many birds and beasts
when they could get it; and ate the leaves and other
parts of a variety of vegetables growing in the country,
some absolutely raw, others variously prepared by the
aid of fire. Another great article of food was the curd
of milk, pressed into a hard mass and salted. This
had so rank a smell, that persons of weak stomachs
often could not bear to come near it. For drink,
they made great use of the water in which certain
dry leaves had been steeped. These leaves, I was
told, came from a great distance. They had also a
method of preparing a liquor of the seeds of a grass-
like vegetable steeped in water, with the addition of
the flower of a bitter plant, and then set to work or
ferment. I was prevailed upon to taste it, and thought
it at first nauseous enough; but in time I liked it
pretty well. When a large quantity of the ingredients
is used, it becomes perfectly intoxicating. But what
astonished me most, was their use of a liquor so excessively hot and pungent, that it seems like liquid fire.

I once got a mouthful of it by mistake, taking it for water, which it resembles in appearance; but I thought it would instantly have taken away my breath. Indeed, people are not unfrequently killed by it; and yet many of them will swallow it greedily whenever they can get it. This, too, is said to be prepared from the seeds above mentioned, which are innocent and even salutary in their natural state, though made to yield such a pernicious juice. The strangest custom that I believe prevails in any nation, I found here, which was, that some take a mighty pleasure in filling their mouths full of stinking smoke; and others, in thrusting a dirty powder up their nostrils."

"I should think it would choke them," said Jack. "It almost did me," answered his father, "only to stand by while they did it—but use, it is truly said, is second nature."

"I was glad enough to leave this cold climate; and about half a year after, I fell in with a people enjoying a delicious temperature of air, and a country full of beauty and verdure. The trees and shrubs were furnished with a great variety of fruits, which, with other vegetable products, constituted a large part of the food of the inhabitants. I particularly relished certain berries growing in bunches, some white and some red, of a very pleasant sourish taste, and so transparent that one might see the seeds at their very centre. Here were whole fields full of extremely odoriferous flowers; which they told me were succeeded by pods bearing seeds, that afforded good nourishment to man and beast. A great variety of birds enlivened the groves and woods; among which I was entertained with one, that without any teaching spoke almost as articulately as a parrot, though indeed it was all the repetition of a single word. The people were tolerably gentle and civilized, and possessed many of the arts of life. Their dress was very various. Many were clad only in a thin cloth made of the long fibres of the stalk of a plant cultivated for the purpose, which they prepared by soaking in water, and then beating with large mallets. Others wore cloth woven from a sort of vegetable wool, growing in pods upon bushes. But the most singular material was a fine glossy stuff, used chiefly by the richer classes, which, as I was credibly informed, is manufactured out of the webs of caterpillars—a most wonderful circumstance, if we consider the immense number of caterpillars necessary to the production of so large a quantity of the stuff as I saw used. This people are very fantastic in their dress, especially the women, whose apparel consists of a great number of articles impossible to be described, and strangely disguising the natural form of the body. In some instances they seem very cleanly; but in others the Hottentots can hardly go beyond them; particularly in the management of their hair, which is all matted and stiffened with the fat of swine and other animals, mixed up with powders of various colours and ingredients. Like most Indian nations, they use feathers in the head-dress. One thing surprised me much, which was, that they bring up in their houses an animal of the tiger kind, with formidable teeth and claws, which, notwithstanding its natural ferocity, is played with and caressed by the most timid and delicate of their women."

" I am sure I would not play with it," said Jack. " Why, you might chance to get an ugly scratch if you did," said the Captain.

" The language of this nation seems very harsh and unintelligible to a foreigner, yet they converse among one another with great ease and quickness. One of the oddest customs is that which men use on saluting each other. Let the weather be what it will, they uncover their heads, and remain uncovered for some time, if they mean to be extraordinarily respectful."

" Why, that's like pulling off our hats," said Jack. " Ah! ah! Papa," cried Betsey, " I have found you out. You have been telling us of our own country, and what is done at home all this while." " But," said

Jack, "we don't burn stones, or eat grease and powdered seeds, or wear skins and caterpillars' webs, or
play with tigers." "No," said the Captain—" pray
what are coals but stones; and is not butter, grease;
and corn, seeds; and leather, skins; and silk, the web
of a kind of caterpillar; and may we not as well call
a cat an animal of the tiger kind, as a tiger an animal
of the cat kind? So, if you recollect what I have
been describing, you will find, with Betsey's help, that
all the other wonderful things I have told you of are
matters familiar among ourselves. But I meant to
show you, that a foreigner might easily represent everything as equally strange and wonderful among us, as
we could do with respect to his country; and also to
make you sensible that we daily call a great many
things by their names, without ever inquiring into
their nature and properties; so that, in reality, it is
only their names, and not the things themselves, with
which we are acquainted."

*** The passage about the management of hair, in
the preceding page, refers to the period when ladies—
and gentlemen also—used vast quantities of powder,
pomatum, &c. in their head-dress. Happily, for clean-
liness, beauty, and good taste, those times are past,
never, it is hoped, to return.—EDITOR.

***

THE DISCONTENTED SQUIRREL.

In a pleasant wood, on the western side of a ridge
of mountains, lived a Squirrel, who had passed two or
three years of his life very happily. At length he
began to grow discontented, and one day fell into the
following soliloquy :—

" What, must I spend all my time in this spot, running up and down the same trees, gathering nuts and
acorns, and dozing away months together in a hole!
I see a great many of the birds who inhabit this wood
ramble about to a distance wherever their fancy leads

them, and at the approach of winter, set out for some remote country, where they enjoy summer weather all the year round. My neighbour Cuckoo tells me he is just going; and even little Nightingale will soon follow. To be sure, I have not wings like them, but I have legs nimble enough; and if one do not use them, one might as well be a mole or a dormouse. I dare say I could easily reach that blue ridge which I see from the tops of the trees; which no doubt must be a fine place, for the sun comes directly from it every morning, and it often appears all covered with red and yellow, and the finest colours imaginable. There can be no harm, at least, in trying, for I can soon get back again if I don't like it. I am resolved to go, and I will set out to-morrow morning."

When Squirrel had taken this resolution, he could not sleep all night for thinking of it; and at peep of day, prudently taking with him as much provision as he could conveniently carry, he began his journey in high spirits. He presently got to the outside of the wood, and entered upon the open moors that reached to the foot of the hills. These he crossed before the sun had got high; and then, having eaten his breakfast with an excellent appetite, he began to ascend. It was heavy, toilsome work scrambling up the steep sides of the mountains; but Squirrel was accustomed to climbing; so for a while he proceeded expeditiously. Often, however, was he obliged to stop and take breath; so that it was a good deal past noon before he had arrived at the summit of the first cliff. Here he sat down to eat his dinner; and looking back, was wonderfully pleased with the fine prospect. The wood in which he lived lay far beneath his feet; and he viewed with scorn the humble habitation in which he had been born and bred.

When he looked forward, however, he was somewhat discouraged to observe that another eminence rose above him, full as distant as that to which he had already reached; and he now began to feel stiff and fatigued. However, after a little rest, he set out again, though not so briskly as before. The ground was rugged, brown, and bare; and to his great surprise, instead of finding it warmer as he got nearer the sun, he felt it grow colder and colder. He had not travelled two hours before his strength and spirits were almost spent; and he seriously thought of giving up the point, and returning before night should come on. While he was thus deliberating with himself, clouds began to gather round the mountain, and to take away all view of distant objects. Presently a storm of mingled snow and hail came down, driven by a violent wind, which pelted poor Squirrel most pitifully, and made him quite unable to move forward or backward. Besides, he had completely lost his road, and did not know which way to turn towards that despised home, which it was now his only desire again to reach. The storm lasted till the approach of night; and it was as much as he could do, benumbed and weary as he was, to crawl to the hollow of a rock at some distance, which was the best lodging he could find for the night. His provisions were spent; so that, hungry and shivering, he crept into the furthest corner of the cavern, and rolling himself up, with his bushy tail over his back, he got a little sleep, though disturbed by the cold, and the shrill whistling of the wind amongst the stones.

The morning broke over the distant tops of the mountains, when Squirrel, half-frozen and famished, came out of his lodging, and advanced, as well as he could, towards the brow of the hill, that he might discover which way to take. As he was slowly creeping along, a hungry kite, soaring in the air above, descried him, and making a stoop, carried him off in her talons. Poor Squirrel, losing his senses with the fright, was borne away with vast rapidity, and seemed inevitably doomed to become food for the kite's young ones; when an eagle, who had seen the kite seize her prey, pursued her in order to take it from her; and overtaking her, gave her such a buffet as caused her to drop the Squirrel in order to defend herself. The poor animal kept falling through the air a long time, till at last he alighted in the midst of a thick tree, the leaves and tender boughs of which so broke his fall, that, though stunned and breathless, he escaped without material injury, and after lying awhile, came to himself again. But what were his pleasure and surprise to find himself in the very tree which contained his nest. "Ah!" said he, "my dear native place and peaceful home! if ever I am again tempted to leave you, may I undergo a second time all the miseries and dangers from which I have now so wonderfully escaped."

SECOND EVENING.

ON THE MARTIN.

"LOOK up, my dear," said his papa to little William, "at those birds' nests above the chamber windows, beneath the eaves of the house. Some, you see, are just begun,—nothing but a little clay stuck against the wall. Others are half-finished; and others are quite built—close and tight—leaving nothing but a small hole for the birds to come in and go out at."

"What nests are they?" said William.

"They are Martins' nests," replied his father: "and there you see the owners. How busily they fly backwards and forwards, bringing clay and earth in their bills, and laying it upon their work, forming it into shape with their bills and feet! The nests are built very strong and thick, like a mud wall, and are lined with feathers to make a soft bed for the young. Martins are a kind of swallows. They feed on flies, gnats, and other insects; and always build in towns and villages about the houses. People do not molest them, for they do good rather than harm; and it is very amusing to view their manners and actions. See how swiftly they skim through the air in pursuit of their prey! In the morning they are up by daybreak, and twitter about your window while you are asleep in bed; and all day long they are upon the wing, getting food for themselves and their young. As soon as they have caught a few flies, they hasten to their nests, pop into the hole, and feed their little ones. I'll tell you a story about the great care they take of their young. A pair of Martins once built their nest in a porch; and when they had young ones, it happened that one of them climbing up to the hole before he was fledged, fell out, and alighting upon the stones, was killed. The old birds perceiving this accident, went and got short bits of strong straw, and stuck them with mud, like palisades, all round the hole of the nest, in order to keep the other little ones from tumbling after their poor brother."

"How sagacious that was!" cried William.

"Yes," said his father; "and I can tell you another story of their sagacity, and also of their disposition to help one another. A saucy cock-sparrow (you know what impudent rogues sparrows are!) had got into a Martin's nest whilst the owner was abroad; and when he returned, the sparrow put his head out of the hole, and pecked at the Martin with open bill as he attempted to enter his own house. The poor Martin was sadly provoked at this injustice, but was unable by his own strength to right himself. So he flew away and gathered a number of his companions, who all came with bits of clay in their bills, with which they plastered up the hole of the nest, and kept the sparrow in prison, who died miserably for want of food and air."

"He was rightly served," said William.

"So he was," rejoined his papa. "Well; I have more to say about the sagacity of these birds. In autumn, when it begins to be cold weather, the Martins and other swallows assemble in great numbers upon the roofs of high buildings, and prepare for their departure to a warmer country; for, as all the insects here die in the winter, they would have nothing to live on if they were to stay. They take several short flights in flocks round and round, in order to try their strength, and then, on some fine calm day, they set out together for a long journey southwards, over sea and land, to a very distant country."

"But how do they find their way?" said William.

"We say," answered his father, "that they are taught by *instinct;* that is, God has implanted in their minds a desire of travelling at the season which he knows to be proper, and has also given them an impulse to take the right road. They steer their course through the wide air, directly to the proper spot. Sometimes, however, storms and contrary winds meet them, and drive the poor birds about till they are quite spent, and fall into the sea, unless they happen to meet with a ship, on which they can alight and rest themselves. The swallows from this country are supposed to go as far as the middle of Africa to spend the winter, where the weather is always warm, and insects are to be met with all the year. In spring, they take another long journey back again to these northern countries. Sometimes, when we have fine weather very early, a few of them come too soon; for when it changes to frost and snow again, the poor creatures are starved for want of food, or perish from the cold. Hence arises the proverb,

One swallow does not make a summer.

But when a great many of them are come, we may be sure that winter is over, so that we are always very glad to see them again. The Martins find their way back over a great length of sea and land to the very same villages and houses where they were bred. This has been discovered by catching some of them, and marking them. They repair their old nests, or build new ones, and then set about laying eggs and hatching their young. Pretty things! I hope you will never knock down their nests, or take their eggs or young ones! for as they come such a long way to visit us, and lodge in our houses without fear, we ought to use them kindly."

MOUSE, LAPDOG, AND MONKEY.
A Fable.

A POOR little Mouse, being half-starved, ventured one day to steal from behind the wainscot while the family were at dinner, and, trembling all the while, picked up a few crumbs which were scattered on the floor. She was soon observed, however: everybody was immediately alarmed; some called for the cat; others took up whatever was at hand, and endeavoured to crush her to pieces; and the poor terrified animal was driven round the room in an agony of terror. At length, however, she was fortunate enough to gain her hole, where she sat panting with fatigue. When the family were again seated, a Lapdog and a Monkey came into the room. The former jumped into the lap of his mistress, fawned upon every one of the children, and made his court so effectually, that he was rewarded with some of the best morsels of the entertainment. The Monkey, on the other hand, forced himself into notice by his grimaces. He played a thousand little mischievous tricks, and was regaled, at the appearance of the dessert, with plenty of nuts and apples. The unfortunate little Mouse, who saw from her hiding-place everything that passed, sighed, in anguish of heart, and said to herself, "Alas! how ignorant was I, to imagine that poverty and distress were sufficient recommendations to the charity of the opulent. I now find, that whoever is not master of fawning and buffoonery, is but ill qualified for a dependant, and will not be suffered even to pick up the crumbs that fall from the table."

ANIMALS AND THEIR COUNTRIES.

O'ER Afric's sand the tawny Lion stalks:
On Phasis' banks the graceful Pheasant walks:
The lonely Eagle builds on Kilda's shore:
Germania's forests feed the tusky Boar!
From Alp to Alp the sprightly Ibex bounds:
With peaceful lowings Britain's isle resounds:
The Lapland peasant o'er the frozen meer
Is drawn in sledges by the swift Rein-Deer:
The River-Horse and scaly Crocodile
Infest the reedy banks of fruitful Nile:
Dire Dipsas hiss o'er Mauritania's plain:
And Seals and spouting Whales sport in the Northern
    Main.

THE MASQUE OF NATURE.

WHO is this beautiful Virgin that approaches, clothed in a robe of light green? She has a garland of flowers on her head, and flowers spring up whorever she sets her foot. The snow which covered the fields, and the ice, which was in the rivers, melt away when she breathes upon them. The young lambs frisk about her, and the birds warble in their little throats to welcome her coming; and when they see her, they begin to choose their mates, and to build their nests. Youths and maidens, have ye seen this beautiful Virgin? If ye have, tell me who she is, and what is her name.

Who is this that cometh from the south, thinly clad in a light transparent garment? her breath is hot and sultry; she seeks the refreshment of the cool shade; she seeks the clear streams, the crystal brooks, to bathe her languid limbs. The brooks and rivulets fly from her, and are dried up at her approach. She cools her parched lips with berries, and the grateful

c 2

acid of all fruits; the seedy melon, the sharp apple, and the red pulp of the juicy cherry, which are poured out plentifully around her. The tanned haymakers welcome her coming; and the sheep-shearer, who clips the fleeces off his flock with his sounding shears. When she cometh, let me lie under the thick shade of a spreading beech-tree,—let me walk with her in the early morning, when the dew is yet upon the grass,— let me wander with her in the soft twilight, when the shepherd shuts his fold and the star of evening appears. Who is she that cometh from the south? Youths and maidens, tell me, if you know, who is she, and what is her name?

Who is he that cometh with sober pace, stealing upon us unawares? His garments are red with the blood of the grape, and his temples are bound with a sheaf of ripe wheat. His hair is thin, and begins to fall; and the auburn is mixed with mournful grey. He shakes the brown nuts from the tree. He winds the horn, and calls the hunters to their sport. The gun sounds. The trembling partridge and the beautiful pheasant flutter, bleeding in the air, and fall dead at the sportsman's feet. Who is he that is crowned with the wheat-sheaf? Youths and maidens, tell me, if ye know, who is he, and what is his name?

Who is he that cometh from the north, clothed in furs and warm wool? He wraps his cloak close about him. His head is bald; his beard is formed of sharp icicles. He loves the blazing fire high piled upon the hearth, and the wine sparkling in the glass. He binds skates to his feet, and skims over the frozen lakes. His breath is piercing and cold, and no little flower dares to peep above the surface of the ground, when he is by. Whatever he touches turns to ice. If he were to stroke you with his cold hand, you would be quite stiff and dead, like a piece of marble. Youths and maidens, do you see him? He is coming fast upon us, and soon he will be here. Tell me, if you know, who he is, and what is his name?

THE FARM-YARD JOURNAL.

DEAR TOM,—Since we parted at the breaking-up, I have been most of the time at a pleasant farm in Hertfordshire, where I have employed myself in rambling about the country, and assisting, as well as I could, in the work going on at home and in the fields. On wet days, and in the evenings, I have amused myself with keeping a journal of all the great events that have happened among us; and, hoping that when you are tired of the bustle of your busy town, you may receive some entertainment from comparing our transactions with yours, I have copied out for your perusal one of the days in my memorandum-book.

Pray let me know, in return, what you are doing, and believe me,

Your very affectionate friend,
RICHARD MARKWELL.

Hazel-Farm.

JOURNAL.

June 10th. Last night we had a dreadful alarm. A violent scream was heard from the hen-roost; the geese all set up a cackle, and the dogs barked. Ned, the boy who lies over the stable, jumped up and ran into the yard, when he observed a fox galloping away with a chicken in his mouth, and the dogs in full chase after him. They could not overtake him, and soon returned. Upon further examination, the large white cock was found lying on the ground, all bloody, with his comb torn almost off, and his feathers all ruffled, and the speckled hen and three chickens lay dead beside him. The cock recovered, but appeared terribly frightened. It seems that the fox had jumped over the garden hedge, and then, crossing part of the yard behind the straw, had crept into the hen-roost through a broken pale. John the carpenter was sent for, to make all fast, and prevent the like mischief again.

Early this morning the brindled cow was delivered of a fine bull-calf. Both are likely to do well. The calf is to be fattened for the butcher.

The duck-eggs that were sitten upon by the old black hen were hatched this day, and the ducklings all directly ran into the pond, to the great terror of the hen, who went round and round, clucking with all her might, in order to call them out; but they did not regard her. An old drake took the little ones under his care, and they swam about very merrily.

As Dolly this morning was milking the new cow that was bought at the fair, she kicked with her hind-legs, and threw down the milk-pail, at the same time knocking Dolly off her stool into the dirt. For this offence the cow was sentenced to have her head fastened to the rack, and her legs tied together.

A kite was observed to hover a long while over the yard, with an intention of carrying off some of the young chickens; but the hens called their broods together under their wings, and the cocks put themselves in order of battle, so that the kite was disappointed. At length, one chicken, not minding its mother, but straggling heedlessly to a distance, was descried by the kite, who made a sudden swoop, and seized it in his talons. The chicken cried out, and the cocks and hens all screamed; when Ralph, the farmer's son, who saw the attack, snatched up a loaded gun, and, just as the kite was flying off with his prey, fired, and brought him dead to the ground, along with the poor chicken, who was killed in the fall. The dead body of the kite was nailed up against the wall, by way of warning to his savage comrades.

In the forenoon we were alarmed with strange noises approaching us, and looking out, we saw a number of people with frying-pans, warming-pans, tongs, and pokers, beating, ringing, and making all possible din. We soon discovered them to be our neighbours of the next farm, in pursuit of a swarm of bees, which was hovering in the air over their heads. The bees

We soon discovered them to be our neighbours of the next farm, in pursuit of a swarm of bees which was hovering in the air over their heads.   P. 22.

at length alighted on the tall pear-tree in our orchard, and hung in a bunch from one of the boughs. A ladder was got, and a man ascending, with gloves on his hands and an apron tied over his head, swept them into a hive, rubbed on the inside with honey and sweet herbs. But, as he was descending, some bees that had got under his gloves, stung him so severely, that he hastily threw down the hive, upon which the greater part of the bees fell out, and began in a rage to fly among the crowd, and sting all upon whom they alighted. Away scampered the people, the women shrieking, the children roaring; and poor Adam, who had held the hive, was assailed so furiously, that he was obliged to throw himself on the ground, and creep under the gooseberry bushes. At length the bees began to return to the hive, in which the queen bee had remained; and after a while, all being quietly settled, a cloth was thrown over it, and the swarm was carried home.

About noon, three pigs broke into the garden, where they were rioting upon the carrots and turnips, and doing a great deal of mischief by trampling the beds, and rooting up the plants with their snouts, when they were spied by old Towzer, the mastiff, who ran among them, and laying hold of their long ears with his teeth, made them squeal most dismally, and get out of the garden as fast as they could.

Roger, the ploughman, when he came for his dinner, brought word that he had discovered a patridge's nest with sixteen eggs in the Home Field. Upon which, the farmer went out and broke them all; saying, that he did not choose to rear birds upon his corn which he was not allowed to catch, but must leave to some qualified sportsman, who would besides break down his fences in the pursuit. [This was a very unjustifiable act on the part of the farmer.]

A sheep-washing was held this day at the millpool, when seven score were well washed, and then penned in the High Meadow, to dry. Many of them made great resistance at being thrown into the water; and the old ram, being dragged to the brink by a boy at each horn, and a third pushing behind, by a sudden spring threw two of them into the water, to the great diversion of the spectators.

Towards the dusk of the evening, the squire's mongrel greyhound, which had been long suspected of worrying sheep, was caught in the fact. He had killed two lambs, and was making a hearty meal upon one of them, when he was disturbed by the approach of the shepherd's boy, and directly leaped the hedge and made off. The dead bodies were taken to the squire's, with an indictment of wilful murder against the dog. But, when they came to look for the culprit, he was not to be found in any part of the premises, and is supposed to have fled his country, through consciousness of his heinous offence.

Joseph, who sleeps in the garret at the old end of the house, after having been some time in bed, came down stairs in his shirt, as pale as ashes, and frightened the maids, who were going up. It was some time before he could tell what was the matter; at length, he said he had heard some dreadful noises over-head, which he was sure must be made by some ghost or evil spirit; nay, he thought he had seen something moving, though he owned he durst hardly lift up his eyes. He concluded with declaring, that he would rather sit up all night in the kitchen than go to his room again. The maids were almost as much alarmed as he, and did not know what to do; but the master overhearing their talk, came out, and insisted upon their accompanying him to the spot, in order to search into the affair. They all went into the garret, and for a while heard nothing; when the master ordered the candle to be taken away, and every one to keep quite still. Joseph and the maids stuck close to each other, and trembled every limb. At length a kind of groaning or snoring began to be heard, which grew louder and louder, with intervals of a strange sort of hissing.

" That's it !" whispered Joseph, drawing back towards the door—the maids were ready to sink; and even the farmer himself was a little disconcerted. The noise seemed to come from the rafters, near the thatch. In a while, a glimpse of moonlight shining through a hole at the place, plainly discovered the shadow of something stirring; and, on looking intently, something like feathers were perceived. The farmer now began to suspect what the case was; and ordering up a short ladder, bade Joseph climb to the spot, and thrust his hand into the hole. This he did rather unwillingly, and soon drew it back, crying loudly that it was bitten. However, gathering courage, he put it in again, and pulled out a large white owl, another at the same time being heard to fly away. The cause of the alarm was now made clear enough; and poor Joseph, after being heartily jeered by the maids, though they had been as much frightened as he, sneaked into bed again, and the house soon became quiet.

THE PRICE OF PLEASURE.

" I THINK I will take a ride," said the little Lord Linger, after breakfast; " bring me my boots, and let my horse be brought to the door."

The horse was saddled, and his lordship's spurs were putting on.

" No," said he, " I'll have my low chair and the ponies, and take a drive round the park."

The horse was led back, and the ponies were almost harnessed, when his lordship sent his valet to countermand them. He would walk into the corn-field, and see how the new pointer hunted.

" After all," says he, " I think I will stay at home and play a game or two at billiards."

He played half a game, but could not make a stroke to please himself. His tutor, who was present, now thought it a good opportunity to ask his lordship if he would read a little.

"Why—I think—I will—for I am tired of doing nothing. What shall we have?"

"Your lordship left off last time in one of the finest passages of the Æneid. Suppose we finish it."

"Well—ay! But—no—I had rather go on with Hume's history. Or, suppose we do some geography?"

"With all my heart. The globes are upon the study table."

They went to the study; and the little lord, leaning upon his elbows, looked at the globe—then twirled it round two or three times—and then listened patiently while the tutor explained some of its parts and uses. But whilst he was in the midst of a problem, "Come," said his lordship, "now for a little Virgil."

The book was brought; and the pupil, with a good deal of help, got through twenty lines.

"Well," said he, ringing the bell, "I think we have done a good deal. Tom! bring my bow and arrows."

The fine, London-made bow, in its green case, and the quiver, with all its appurtenances, were brought, and his lordship went down to the place where the shooting-butts were erected. He aimed a few shafts at the target, but not coming near it, he shot all the remainder at random, and then ordered out his horse.

He sauntered, with a servant at his heels, for a mile or two through the lanes, and came, just as the clock struck twelve, to a village green, close by which a school was kept. A door flew open, and out burst a shoal of boys, who, spreading over the green, with immoderate vociferation, instantly began a variety of sports. Some fell to marbles—some to trap-ball—some to leap-frog. In short, not one of the whole crew but was eagerly employed. Everything was noise, motion, and pleasure. Lord Linger, riding slowly up, espied one of his tenant's sons, who had been formerly admitted as a playfellow of his, and called him from the throng.

"Jack," said he, "how do you like school?"

" O—pretty well, my lord."

" What—have you a good deal of play ? "

" O no! We have only from twelve to two for playing and eating our dinners; and then an hour before supper."

" That is very little, indeed!"

" But *we play heartily when we do play, and work when we work.* Good bye, my lord! It is my turn to go in at trap."

So saying, Jack ran off.

" I wish I were a schoolboy!" cried the little lord to himself.

THE RAT WITH A BELL.

A Fable.

A LARGE old house in the country was so extremely infested with rats, that nothing could be secured from their depredations. They scaled the walls to attack flitches of bacon, though hung as high as the ceiling. Hanging shelves afforded no protection to the cheese and pastry. They penetrated by sap into the store-room, and plundered it of preserves and sweetmeats. They gnawed through cupboard-doors, undermined floors, and ran races behind the wainscots. The cats could not get at them; they were too cunning and too well fed to meddle with poison; and traps only now and then caught a heedless straggler. One of these, however, on being taken, was the occasion of practising a new device. This was, to fasten a collar with a small bell about the prisoner's neck, and then turn him loose again.

Overjoyed at the recovery of his liberty, the rat ran into the nearest hole, and went in search of his companions. They heard at a distance the bell tinkle, tinkle, through the dark passages, and, suspecting some enemy had got among them, away they scoured, some one way, and some another. The bell-bearer pursued; and soon guessing the cause of their flight, he was greatly amused by it. Wherever he approached, it was all hurry-scurry, and not a tail of one of them was to be seen. He chased his old friends from hole to hole, and room to room, laughing all the while at their fears, and increasing them by all the means in his power. Presently he had the whole house to himself. "That's right (quoth he)—the fewer, the better cheer." So he rioted alone among the good things, and stuffed till he could hardly walk.

For two or three days this course of life went on very pleasantly. He ate, and ate, and played the bugbear to perfection. At length he grew tired of this lonely condition, and longed to mix with his companions again upon the former footing. But the difficulty was, how to get rid of his bell. He pulled and tugged with his fore feet, and almost wore the skin off his neck in the attempt, but all in vain. The bell was now his plague and torment. He wandered from room to room, earnestly desiring to make himself known to one of his companions, but they all kept out of his reach. At last, as he was moping about disconsolate, he fell in puss's away, and was devoured in an instant.

He who is raised so much above his fellow-creatures as to be the object of their terror, must suffer for it in losing all the comforts of society. He is a solitary being in the midst of crowds. He keeps them at a distance, and they equally shun him. Dread and affection cannot subsist together.

THE DOG BAULKED OF HIS DINNER.
A Tale.

Think yourself sure of nothing till you've got it :
This is the lesson of the day,
In metaphoric language I might say,
Count not your bird before you've shot it.
Quoth Proverb, " 'Twixt the cup and lip,
There's many a slip."

Not every guest invited sits at table,
   So says *my* fable.

    A man once gave a dinner to his friend ;
His friend !—his patron I should rather think,
By all the loads of meat and drink,
    And fruits and jellies without end,
    Sent home the morning of the feast.
    Jowler, his dog, a social beast,
Soon as he smelt the matter out, away
Scampers to old acquaintance Tray,
    And, with expressions kind and hearty,
    Invites him to the party.

Tray wanted little pressing to a dinner ;
He was, in truth, a gormandizing sinner,
    He lick'd his chops and wagg'd his tail ;
    "Dear friend !" he cried, "I will not fail :
      But what's your hour ?"
      " We dine at four ;
But, if you come an hour too soon,
You'll find there's something to be done."

His friend withdrawn, Tray, full of glee,
As blithe as blithe could be,
   Skipp'd, danced, and play'd full many an antic,
    Like one half frantic,
   Then sober in the sun lay winking,
    But could not sleep for thinking.
   He thought on every dainty dish,
    Fried, boil'd, and roast,
   Flesh, fowl, and fish,
    With tripes and toast,
    Fit for a dog to eat ;
And in his fancy made a treat,
    Might grace a bill of fare
    For my Lord Mayor.

    At length, just on the stroke of three,
      Forth sallied he ;

And, through a well-known hole,
  He slily stole,
  Pop on the scene of action.
Here he beheld, with wondrous satisfaction,
All hands employ'd, in drawing, stuffing,
  Skewering, spitting, and basting,
The red-faced cook, perspiring, puffing,
  Chopping, mixing, and tasting.
Tray skulk'd about, now here, now there,
  Peep'd into this, and smelt at that,
  And lick'd the gravy and the fat,
And cried, " O rare ! how I shall fare !"

  But Fortune, spiteful as Old Nick,
  Resolved to play our dog a trick ;
    She made the cook
    Just cast a look
  Where Tray, beneath the dresser lying,
  His promised bliss was eyeing.

A cook, while cooking, is a sort of fury ;—
A maxim worth rememb'ring, I assure ye.
    Tray found it true,
    And so may you,
  If e'er you choose to try.
" How now !" quoth she, " what's this I spy ?
A nasty cur ! who let him in ?
Would he were hang'd, with all his kin !
A pretty kitchen guest, indeed !
But I shall pack him off with speed !"

  So saying, on poor Tray she flew,
  And dragg'd the culprit forth to view ;
Then, to his terror and amazement,
Whirl'd him like lightning through the casement.

THIRD EVENING.

THE KID.

ONE bleak day in March, Sylvia, returning from a visit to the sheepfold, met with a young kidling deserted by its dam on the naked heath. It was bleating piteously, and was so benumbed with the cold, that it could hardly stand. Sylvia took it up in her arms, and pressed it close to her bosom. She hastened home, and showing her little foundling to her parents, begged she might rear it for her own. They consented; and Sylvia immediately got a basket full of clean straw, and made a bed for him on the hearth. She warmed some milk, and held it to him in a platter. The poor creature drank it up eagerly, and then licked her hand for more. Sylvia was delighted. She chafed his tender legs with her warm hands, and soon saw him jump out of his basket, and frisk across the room. When full, he lay down again and took a comfortable nap.

The next day, the kid had a name bestowed upon him. As he gave tokens of being an excellent jumper, it was Capriole. He was introduced to all the rest of the family, and the younger children were allowed to stroke and pat him; but Sylvia would let nobody be intimate with him but herself. The great mastiff was charged never to hurt him, and, indeed, he had no intention to do it.

Within a few days, Capriole followed Sylvia all about the house; trotted by her side into the yard; ran races with her in the Home Field; fed out of her hand, and was a declared pet and favourite. As the spring advanced, Sylvia roamed in the fields and gathered wild flowers, with which she wove garlands, and hung them round her kid's neck. He could not be kept, however, from munching his finery, when he could reach it with his mouth. He was also rather troublesome in thrusting his nose into the meal-tub and flour-box, and following people into the dairy, and sipping the milk that was set for cream. He now and then got a blow for his intrusion; but his mistress always took his part, and indulged him in every liberty.

Capriole's horns now began to bud, and a little white beard sprouted at the end of his chin. He grew bold enough to put himself into a fighting posture whenever he was offended. He butted down little Colin into the dirt; quarrelled with the geese for their allowance of corn; and held many a stout battle with the old turkey-cock. Everybody said, " Capriole is growing too saucy, he must be sent away, or taught better manners." But Sylvia still stood his friend, and he repaid her love with many tender caresses.

The farm-house where Sylvia lived was situated in a sweet valley, by the side of a clear stream, bordered with trees. Above the house rose a sloping meadow, and beyond that was an open common, covered with purple heath and yellow furze. Farther on, at some distance, rose a steep hill, the summit of which was a bare, craggy rock, hardly accessible to human feet. Capriole, ranging at his pleasure, often got upon the common, and was pleased with browsing the short grass and wild herbs which grew there. Still, however, when his mistress came to see him, he would run, bounding at her call, and accompany her back to the farm.

One fine summer's day, Sylvia, after having finished the business of the morning, wanted to play with her kid; and missing him, she went to the side of the common, and called aloud, " Capriole! Capriole!" expecting to see him come running to her, as usual. No Capriole came. She went on and on, still calling her kid with the most endearing accents, but nothing was to be seen of him. Her heart began to flutter. " What can have become of him? Surely somebody must have stolen him,—or perhaps the neighbours' dogs have worried him. Oh, my poor Capriole! my dear Capriole! I shall never see you again!"—and Sylvia began to weep.

She still went on, looking wistfully all around, and making the place echo with "Capriole! Capriole! where are you, my Capriole?" till at length she came to the foot of the steep hill. She climbed up its sides, to get a better view. No kid was to be seen. She sat down, and wept, and wrung her hands. After a while, she fancied she heard a bleating like the well-known voice of her Capriole. She started up, and looked towards the sound, which seemed a great way overhead. At length she spied, just on the edge of a steep crag, her Capriole peeping over. She stretched out her hands to him, and began to call, but with a timid voice, lest in his impatience to return to her, he should leap down and break his neck. But there was no such danger. Capriole was inhaling the fresh breeze of the mountains, and enjoying with rapture the scenes for which nature designed him. His bleating was the expression of joy, and he bestowed not a thought on his kind mistress, nor paid the least attention to her call. Sylvia ascended as high as she could towards him, and called louder and louder, but all in vain. Capriole leaped from rock to rock, cropped the fine herbage in the clefts, and was quite lost in the pleasure of his new existence.

Poor Sylvia stayed till she was tired, and then returned disconsolate to the farm, to relate her misfortune. She got her brothers to accompany her back to the hill, and took with her a slice of white bread and some milk, to tempt the little wanderer home. But he had mounted still higher, and had joined a herd of companions of the same species, with whom he was frisking and sporting. He had neither eyes nor ears for his old friends of the valley. All former habits were broken at once, and he had commenced free commoner of nature. Sylvia came back crying, as much from vexation as sorrow. "The little ungrateful thing!" said she—"so well as I loved him, and so kindly as I treated him, to desert me in this way at last!—But he was always a rover!"

"Take care then, Sylvia," said her mother, "how you set your heart upon *rovers* again!"

HOW TO MAKE THE BEST OF IT.

ROBINET, a peasant of Lorraine, after a hard day's work at the next market-town, was returning home with a basket in his hand. "What a delicious supper shall I have!" said he to himself. "This piece of kid, well stewed down, with my onions sliced, thickened with my meal, and seasoned with my salt and pepper, will make a dish fit for the bishop of the diocese. Then I have a good piece of barley-loaf at home to finish with. How I long to be at it!"

A noise in the hedge now attracted his notice, and he spied a squirrel nimbly running up a tree, and popping into a hole between the branches. "Ha!" thought he, "what a nice present a nest of young squirrels will be to my little master! I'll try if I can get it." Upon this, he set down his basket in the road, and began to climb up the tree. He had half ascended, when, casting a look at his basket, he saw a dog with his nose in it, ferreting out the piece of kid's flesh. He made all possible speed down, but the dog was too quick for him, and ran off with the meat in his mouth. Robinet looked after him—"Well," said he, "then I must be content with soup-maigre—and no bad thing neither."

He travelled on, and came to a little public-house by the road side, where an acquaintance of his was sitting on a bench drinking. He invited Robinet to take a draught. Robinet seated himself by his friend, and set his basket on the bench close by him. A tame raven, kept at the house, came slily behind him, and, perching on the basket, stole away the bag in which the meal was tied up, and hopped off with it to his hole. Robinet did not perceive the theft till he had got on his way again. He returned, to search for his bag, but could hear no tidings of it. "Well," says he, "my soup will be the thinner; but I will boil a slice of bread with it, and that will do it some good, at least."

He went on again, and arrived at a little brook, over which was laid a narrow plank. A young woman coming up to pass at the same time, Robinet gallantly offered her his hand. As soon as she had got to the middle, either through fear or sport, she shrieked out, and cried she was falling. Robinet, hastening to support her with his other hand, let his basket drop into the stream. As soon as she was safe over, he jumped in and recovered it, but when he took it out, he perceived that all the salt was melted, and the pepper washed away. Nothing was now left but the onions. "Well!" says Robinet, "then I must sup to-night upon roasted onions and barley bread. Last night I had the bread alone. To-morrow morning it will not signify what I had." So saying, he trudged on, singing as before.

ORDER AND DISORDER.
A Fairy Tale.

JULIET was a clever, well-disposed girl, but apt to be heedless. She could do her lessons very well, but commonly as much time was taken up in getting her things together as in doing what she was set about. If she were to work, there was generally the housewife to seek in one place, and the thread-papers in another. The scissors were left in her pocket up stairs, and the thimble was rolling about the floor. In writing, the copy-book was generally missing, and the ink dried up, and the pens, new and old, all tumbled about the cupboard. The slate and slate-pencil were never found together. In making her exercises, the English dictionary always came to hand instead of the French grammar; and when she was to read a chapter, she usually got hold of Robinson Crusoe, or the World Displayed, instead of the Testament.

Juliet's mamma was almost tired of teaching her, so she sent her to make a visit to an old lady in the country, a very good woman, but rather strict with young folk. Here she was shut up in a room above stairs by herself after breakfast every day, till she had quite finished the tasks set her. This house was one of the very few that are still haunted by fairies. One of these, whose name was Disorder, took a pleasure in plaguing poor Juliet. She was a frightful figure to look at; being crooked and squint-eyed, with her hair hanging about her face, and her dress put on all awry, and full of rents and tatters. She prevailed on the old lady to let her set Juliet her tasks; so one morning she came up with a work-bag full of threads of silk of all sorts of colours, mixed and entangled together, and a flower, very nicely worked, to copy. It was a pansy, and the gradual melting of its hues into one another was imitated with great accuracy and beauty. "Here, Miss," said she, "my mistress has sent you a piece of work to do, and she insists upon having it done before you come down to dinner. You will find all the materials in this bag."

Juliet took the flower and the bag, and turned out all the silks upon the table. She slowly pulled out a red, and a purple, and a blue, and a yellow, and at length fixed upon one to begin working with. After taking two or three stitches, and looking at her model, she found another shade was wanted. This was to be hunted out from the bunch, and a long while it took her to find it. It was soon necessary to change it for another. Juliet saw that, in going on at this rate, it would take days instead of hours to work the flower, so she laid down the needle and fell a-crying. After this had continued some time, she was startled at the sound of some one stamping on the floor;

and taking her handkerchief from her eyes, she spied a neat diminutive figure advancing towards her. She was as upright as an arrow, and had not so much as a hair out of its place, or the least article of her dress rumpled or discomposed. When she came up to Juliet, " My dear," said she, " I heard you crying, and knowing you to be a good girl in the main, I am come to your assistance. My name is Order; your mamma is well acquainted with me, though this is the first time you ever saw me. But I hope we shall know one another better for the future." She then sprang upon the table, and with a wand gave a tap upon the heap of entangled silk. Immediately the threads separated, and arranged themselves in a long row consisting of little skeins, in which all of the same colour were collected together, those approaching nearest in shade being placed next each other. This done, she disappeared. Juliet, as soon as her surprise was over, resumed her work, and found it to go on with ease and pleasure. She finished the flower by dinner-time, and obtained great praise for the neatness of the execution.

The next day, the ill-natured fairy came up with a great book under her arm. " This," said she, "is my mistress's house-book, and she says you must draw out against dinner an exact account of what it has cost her last year in all the articles of housekeeping, including clothes, rent, taxes, wages, and the like. You must state separately the amount of every article, under the heads of baker, butcher, milliner, shoemaker, and so forth, taking special care not to miss a single thing entered down in the book. Here is a quire of paper and a parcel of pens." So saying, with a malicious grin, she left her.

Juliet turned pale at the very thought of the task she had to perform. She opened the great book and saw all the pages closely written, but in the most confused manner possible. Here was, " Paid Mr. Crusty for a week's bread and baking, so much."—

Then, " Paid Mr. Pinchtoe for shoes, so much."—
" Paid half a year's rent, so much." Then came a
butcher's bill, succeeded by a milliner's, and that by a
tallow-chandler's. "What shall I do?" cried poor
Juliet—" where am I to begin, and how can I possibly
pick out all these things? Was ever such a tedious
perplexing task? O that my good little creature were
here again with her wand!"

She had but just uttered the words, when the fairy
Order stood before her. "Don't be startled, my
dear," said she; "I knew your wish, and made haste
to comply with it. Let me see your book." She
turned over a few leaves, and then cried, "I see my
cross-grained sister has played you a trick; she has
brought you the day-book, instead of the ledger; but
I will set the matter to rights instantly." She va-
nished, and presently returned with another book, in
which she showed Juliet every one of the articles
required standing at the tops of the pages, and all the
particulars entered under them from the day-book;
so that there was nothing for her to do but cast up
the sums, and copy out the heads with their amount
in single lines. As Juliet was a ready accountant,
she was not long in finishing the business, and produced her account, neatly written on one sheet of
paper, at dinner.

The next day Juliet's tormentor brought her up a
large box full of letters stamped upon small bits of
ivory, capitals and common letters of all sorts, but
jumbled together promiscuously, as though they had
been shaken in a bag. "Now, Miss," said she,
" before you come down to dinner, you must exactly
copy out this poem in these ivory letters, placing them
line by line on the floor of your room."

Juliet thought at first that this task would be pretty
sport enough; but, when she set about it, she found
such trouble in hunting out the letters she wanted,
every one seeming to come to hand before the right
one, that she proceeded very slowly; and the poem

" Oh that my good little creature were here again with her wand!" She had but just uttered the words when the fairy Order stood before her.

P. 38.

being a long one, it was plain that night would come before it was finished. Sitting down, and crying for her kind friend, was therefore her only resource.

Order was not far distant, for, indeed, she had been watching her proceedings all the while. She made herself visible, and, giving a tap on the letters with her wand, they immediately arranged themselves alphabetically in little double heaps, the small in one, and the great in the other. After this operation, Juliet's task went on with such expedition, that she called up the old lady an hour before dinner to be witness to its completion.

The good lady kissed her, and told her that as she hoped she was now made fully sensible of the benefits of order, and the inconveniences of disorder, she would not confine her any longer to work by herself at set tasks, but she should come and sit with her. Juliet took such pains to please her, by doing everything with the greatest neatness and regularity, and reforming all her careless habits, that when she was sent back to her mother, the following presents were made her, in order constantly to remind her of the beauty and advantage of order.

A cabinet of English coins, in which all the gold and silver money of our kings was arranged in the order of their reigns.

A set of plaster casts of the Roman emperors.

A cabinet of beautiful shells, displayed according to the most approved system.

A very complete box of water-colours, and another of crayons, sorted in all the shades of the primary colours.

And, a very nice housewife, with all the implements belonging to a sempstress, and good store of the best needles, in sizes.

LIVE DOLLS.

" I WISH very much, mamma," said a little girl as she was walking one fine spring morning, with her doll in her arms, " that my doll could breathe, and speak, and tell me how she loves these sweet and bright little flowers, that are coming up all over the banks and hedge-rows." As she said this, she turned her eyes first upon the pretty but inanimate little figure she had pressed to her bosom, and then upon the fair and sunshiny scene that lay all around her. Everything appeared to have had a fresh life given.

The trees, and flowers, and sparkling rivulets looked so gay, that one might almost fancy them to be really rejoicing that the summer was coming again ; and as for the birds and the young lambs, with which the soft green fields were full, the one sang so sweetly and cheerily, and the others did so sport about in the sunshine, that our little girl could not contain herself for delight. But when she looked at her doll again, her eyes ceased to sparkle, for there it was, with its painted cheeks, and its moveless lips and eyes, a thing more without life than any other object near her. It had been her companion in the winter, when the cold winds and the snow had kept her shut up in the house, and she had amused herself tolerably well, in making it frocks and hats, of all variety of fashions ; but she had not once thought then about its having no life, or feeling like herself, and she was contented with it, merely because nothing led her to reflect, that her care and labour about it were useless.

But everything now reminded her, that there was a vast difference between the gayest toy-shop and the beautiful country dressed up by the returning spring ; and she could not but think that the very best plaything which her mamma could buy her, was not so really worth possessing as the flowers that were growing wild but fragrantly on the hedges. Before, therefore, she had long continued her walk, her doll was entirely neglected, and it lay upon her arm as though it were a burden. She began gathering some of the prettiest of the wild geraniums, and the sweet little blue harebells, that peeped and smiled from among the dewy grass, and having formed them into a wreath, she felt for a short time as though she possessed something that she could love much better than a doll, that had no sense of the happy spring-time.

" Are they not beautiful, mamma ?" said she, holding them up with delight. " They are, indeed, dear Ellen," said her mamma, " and they ought to make you love that great Creator, who, while he had the power to make this world, and the sun, and the stars, has also had the benevolence to adorn the earth so beautifully, to make it the pleasant abode of the young and innocent."

Little Ellen understood and felt the truth of her mamma's observation, and she never afterwards looked upon the lovely scenes which every season of the year in turn produces, without recalling it to her thoughts. But scarcely had she ceased expressing her pleasure at the sight of her spring-flowers, when their heads began to droop, their leaves to grow flaccid, and all their brightness to fade away. " What a sad thing it is, mamma," exclaimed the disappointed little girl, " that we should not be able longer to preserve such beautiful things."

" It would, indeed, be sad," was the answer, "if they had not been intended only to bloom in a particular situation, and then for a short time only. But you must learn to observe, Ellen, that all these beautiful little objects are ornaments to the earth, which can be easily destroyed, while things more necessary to our comfort are better defended, or by nature different."

Ellen looked vexed when she found it would be of no use to carry the flowers any farther, and she was again without anything to pet and love. To her

great delight, however, on passing a small green recess
on one side of the road, they saw a man sitting and
employing his skill in making captives of many of the
sweet little birds, whose songs she had listened to with
such pleasure. If she had reflected a moment on the
real cruelty of this occupation, she would not have
observed the birdcatcher with such feelings of gratification; but she was intent on nothing but the pleasure
she should have in possessing one of the little warblers,
and she forgot the barbarity of making it a prisoner,
in the thoughts of what care she would take to feed it,
and make it lie in her bosom, and sleep there when
the weather was again very cold. One of the birds,
therefore, was bought, and the man lent her one of his
small cages to carry it home in.

Overjoyed at possessing such a dear little creature,
so gentle and pretty, and, what was still more in her
thoughts, a real living being that would in time know
her and sing to her, Ellen carried the cage as the
greatest treasure that could have been given her; and
so delighted was she, that she could not help stopping
every now and then to look at the bird, and she every
time expressed more fondness for it. But at last, not
satisfied with these momentary glances, she begged
her mamma to rest a few minutes, and she sat down on
a bank to enjoy more leisurely the sight of her new
companion. The birds in the trees and hedges were
all singing loudly and joyfully, and they flew from
bough to bough, flitting their gay wings in the air, and
chasing each other, for the very pleasure of floating
on the pleasant breeze. " Oh how delightful!" said
Ellen, " to possess one of these pretty, happy things;"
and she looked at her little bird in the cage.—Alas!
there it sat, up at one end of the perch, its head drooping, its wings folded to its sides, but rough and broken,
and its eyes half-covered with a thick film. Ellen
spoke to it, but the poor little creature was not to be
so cheered, and she looked at her mamma, more grieved
than ever.

"Yes," said the latter, smiling, "I had no doubt you would soon discover your error, or I should not have so readily agreed to your wishes. I had no doubt you would be very kind to the bird, but your kindness could not supply the place either of its liberty, or of the pleasure it doubtless has among its own proper companions in the woods. Besides, Ellen, though you might love it very much, you would never feel great satisfaction in attending to a thing which would have no reason to thank you for your pains, and could never talk with you!"

"No, indeed, mamma," said Ellen, and she hung down her head, looked again at the bird, and, after playing a few moments with the door of the cage, continued, "Well, I am sure you are right, and it would be very useless and very cruel to keep a thing a prisoner only for my own satisfaction, and it would be a bad companion after all." So saying, she opened the door, the bird put its head at first fearfully out, and then, shaking its wings, darted out, and was soon perched and singing on one of the trees hard by. Ellen looked again at her doll, and began almost to think that she must be contented with her playthings, which could neither fade nor feel it cruel to be locked up. But this thought continued only a moment, and as they passed through a field where several lambs were lying about, she made another attempt at finding something which she might play with and love at the same time. But she was again disappointed; a lamb was very pretty, very gentle, and very playful; but after she had succeeded in getting near one, and had spoken to it very kindly, and called it by a hundred tender names, it looked at her for an instant, and then bounding away, could not be induced to return by all the persuasion she could employ.

The walk was now nearly at an end, and the sweet spring morning had only made Ellen dissatisfied with her senseless and inanimate doll. Before, however, reaching home, her mamma had to call at the cottage

of one of the villagers, and thither they now went. A
neat little garden before the door was smelling sweetly
with some carefully-cultivated plants, and everything
about the place bore an air of great neatness. But
what struck Ellen the most were three or four children
who were playing among the flowers, the youngest of
which was nursed by a girl about seven years old

"Oh, what a dear little baby," said she, going up
to it, and at the moment it stretched out its arms, and
laughing in her own smiling face, put its little flaxen
head against her bosom. "Indeed, indeed, mamma,"
said she, "it is a live doll;" and she gave her own
painted one to the young nurse, and took the infant,
all joy and innocence, in her arms.

Ellen had now found something which was as beautiful as the spring-flowers, as gentle and happy as the
free birds, as gay as the sportive little lambs, and,
which was better still, endowed with a mind and reason like her own to rejoice in all that is bright, and
beautiful, and good upon the earth. The thoughts
with which she returned home, led her ever afterwards
to employ her summer days and winter evenings in
more profitable occupations than formerly ; and there
was many a live doll in the neighbourhood, whose little
lips soon began to lisp its thanks for the pretty presents or the warm clothing with which her industry
furnished it.

THE HOG, AND OTHER ANIMALS.

A DEBATE once arose among the animals in a farm-
yard, which of them was most valued by their common
master. After the horse, the ox, the cow, the sheep,
and the dog, had stated their several pretensions, the
hog took up the discourse.

"It is plain," said he, "that the greatest value must
be set upon that animal which is kept most for his
own sake, without expecting from him any return of

use and service. Now which of you can boast so much in that respect as I can?

"As for you, Horse, though you are very well fed and lodged, and have servants to attend upon you and make you sleek and clean, yet all this is for the sake of your labour. Do not I see you taken out early every morning, put in chains, or fastened to the shafts of a heavy cart, and not brought back till noon; when, after a short respite, you are taken to work again till late in the evening? I may say just the same to the Ox, except that he works for poorer fare.

"For you, Mrs. Cow, who are so dainty over your chopped straw and grains, you are thought worth keeping only for your milk, which is drained from you twice a day, to the last drop, while your poor young ones are taken from you, and sent I know not whither.

"You, poor innocent Sheep, who are turned out to shift for yourselves upon the bare hills, or penned upon the fallows, with now and then a withered turnip or some musty hay, you pay dearly enough for your keep, by resigning your warm coat every year, for want of which you are liable to be starved to death on some of the cold nights, before summer.

"As for the Dog, who prides himself so much on being admitted to our master's table, and made his companion, that he will scarcely condescend to reckon himself one of us, he is obliged to do all the offices of a domestic servant by day, and to keep watch during the night, while we are quietly asleep.

"In short, you are all of you creatures maintained for use—poor subservient things, made to be enslaved or pillaged. I, on the contrary, have a warm stye and plenty of provisions all at free cost. I have nothing to do but to grow fat and follow my amusement; and my master is best pleased when he sees me lying at ease in the sun, or gratifying my appetite for food."

Thus argued the Hog, and put the rest to silence

by so much logic and rhetoric. This was not long
before winter set in. It proved a very scarce season
for fodder of all kinds; so that the farmer began to
consider how he was to maintain all his live stock till
spring. " It will be impossible for me," thought he,
"to keep them all; I must therefore part with those I
can best spare. As for my horses and working oxen,
I shall have business enough to employ them; they
must be kept, cost what it will. My cows will not
give me much milk in the winter, but they will calve
in the spring, and be ready for the new grass. I must
not lose the profit of my dairy. The sheep, poor
things, will take care of themselves as long as there is
a bite upon the hills; and should deep snow come, we
must do with them as well as we can, by the help of a
few turnips and some hay; for I must have their wool
at shearing-time, to make out my rent with. But my
hogs will eat me out of house and home, without doing
me any good. They must go to pot, that's certain;
and the sooner I get rid of the fat ones, the better."

So saying, he singled out the orator, as one of the
prime among them, and sent him to the butcher the
very next day.

FOURTH EVENING.

THE BULLIES.

As young Francis was walking through a village
with his tutor, they were annoyed by two or three cur
dogs that come running after them with looks of the
utmost fury, snarling and barking as though they
would tear their throats, and seeming every moment
ready to fly upon them. Francis every now and then
stopped, and shook his stick at them, or stooped down
to pick up a stone, upon which the curs retreated as
fast as they came; but as soon as he turned about,
they were after his heels again. This lasted till they

came to a farm-yard, through which their road lay.
A large mastiff was lying down in it, at his ease in the
sun. Francis was almost afraid to pass him, and kept
as close to his tutor as possible. However, the dog
took not the least notice of them.

Presently they came upon a common, where, going
near a flock of geese, they were assailed with hissings,
and pursued some way by these foolish birds, which,
stretching out their long necks, made a very ridi-
culous figure. Francis only laughed at them, though
he was tempted to give the foremost a switch across
his neck. A little further, was a herd of cows, with a
bull among them, upon which Francis looked with
some degree of apprehension; but they kept quietly
grazing, and did not take their heads from the ground
as he passed.

"It is a lucky thing," said Francis to his tutor,
"that mastiffs and bulls are not so quarrelsome as
curs and geese; but what can be the reason of it?"

"The reason," replied his tutor, "is, that paltry
and contemptible animals, possessing no confidence in
their own strength and courage, and knowing themselves liable to injury from most of those that come
in their way, think it safest to act the part of bullies,
and to make a show of attacking those of whom in
reality they are afraid. Whereas animals which are
conscious of force sufficient for their own protection,
suspecting no evil designs from others, entertain none
themselves, but maintain a dignified composure.

"Thus you will find it among mankind. Weak,
mean, petty characters are suspicious, snarling,
and petulant. They raise an outcry against their
superiors in talents and reputation, of whom they
stand in awe, and put on airs of defiance and inso-
lence through mere cowardice. But the truly great
are calm and inoffensive. They fear no injury, and
offer none. They even suffer slight attacks to go
unnoticed, conscious of their power to right themselves whenever the occasion shall seem to require it."

THE TRAVELLED ANT.

THERE was a garden enclosed with high brick walls, and laid out somewhat in the old fashion. Under the walls were wide beds, planted with flowers, garden-stuff, and fruit-trees. Next to them, was a broad gravel walk running round the garden, and the middle was laid out in grass-plots, and beds of flowers and shrubs, with a fishpond in the centre.

Near the root of one of the wall-fruit-trees, a numerous colony of ants was established, which had extended its subterraneous works over great part of the bed in its neighbourhood. One day, two of the inhabitants, meeting in a gallery under-ground, fell into the following conversation:—

"Ha! my friend," said the first, "is it you? I am glad to see you. Where have you been this long time? All your acquaintance have been in pain about you, lest you should have met with some accident."

"Why," replied the other, "I am, indeed, a sort of stranger; for you must know I am but just returned from a long journey."

"A journey! whither, pray, and on what account?"

"A tour of mere curiosity. I had long felt dissatisfied with knowing so little about this world of ours, so at length I took a resolution to explore it. And I may now boast that I have gone round its utmost extremities, and that no considerable part of it has escaped my researches."

"Wonderful! What a traveller you have been, and what sights you must have seen!"

"Why, yes, I have seen more than most ants, to be sure; but it has been at the expense of so much toil and danger, that I know not whether it were worth the pains"

"Will you oblige me with some account of your adventures ?"

"Willingly. I set out, then, early one sunshiny morning; and, after crossing our territory and the line of plantation by which it is bordered, I came upon a wide, open plain, where, as far as the eye could reach, not a single green thing was to be descried, but the hard soil was everywhere covered with huge stones, which made travelling equally painful to the eye and the feet. As I was toiling onwards, I heard a rumbling noise behind me, which became louder and louder. I looked back, and with the utmost horror beheld a prodigious rolling mountain approaching me so fast, that it was impossible to get out of the way. I threw myself flat on the ground, behind a stone, and lay expecting nothing but instant death. The mountain soon passed over me; and I continued, I know not how long, in a state of insensibility. When I recovered, I began to stretch my limbs one by one, and to my surprise found myself not in the least injured ; but the stone beside me was almost buried in the earth by the crash!"

"What an escape!"

"A wonderful one, indeed. I journeyed on over the desert, and at length came to the end of it, and entered upon a wide, green tract, consisting chiefly of tall, narrow-pointed leaves, which grew so thick and entangled, that it was with the greatest difficulty I could make my way between them ; and I should continually have lost my road, had I not taken care to keep the sun in view before me. When I had got near the middle of this region, I was startled with the sight of a huge four-legged monster, with a yellow speckled skin, which took a flying leap directly over me. Somewhat further, before I was aware, I ran upon one of those long, round, crawling creatures, without head, tail, or legs, which we sometimes meet with under-ground, near our settlement.

E

As soon as he felt me upon him, he drew back into his hole so swiftly, that he was near drawing me in along with him. However, I jumped off, and proceeded on my way.

"With much labour, I got at last to the end of this perplexed tract, and came to an open space, like that in which we live, in the midst of which grew trees so tall that I could not see to their tops. Being hungry, I climbed up the first I came to, in expectation of finding some fruit; but, after a weary search, I returned empty. I tried several others with no better success. There were, indeed, leaves and flowers in plenty, but nothing of which I could make a meal; so that I might have been famished, had I not found some sour, harsh berries upon the ground, on which I made a poor repast. While I was doing this, a greater danger than any of the former befel me. One of those two-legged feathered creatures, which we often see to our cost, jumped down from a bough, and picked up in his enormous beak the very berry on which I was standing. Luckily, he did not swallow it immediately, but flew up again with it to the tree; and in the mean time I disengaged myself, and fell from a vast height to the ground, but received no hurt.

"I crossed this plantation, and came to another entangled green like the first. After I had laboured through it, I came suddenly to the side of a vast glittering plain, the nature of which I could not possibly guess at. I walked along a fallen leaf which lay on the side, and, coming to the farther edge of it, I was greatly surprised to see another ant coming from below to meet me. I advanced to give him a fraternal embrace, but, instead of what I expected, I met a cold, yielding matter, in which I should have sunk, had I not speedily turned about, and caught hold of the leaf, by which I drew myself up again. And now I found this great plain to consist of that fluid which sometimes falls from the sky, and causes us so much trouble, by filling our holes.

" As I stood considering how to proceed on my journey, a gentle breeze arose, which, before I was aware, carried the leaf I was upon away from the solid land into this yielding fluid, which, however, bore it up, and me along with it. At first, I was greatly alarmed, and ran round and round my leaf, in order to find some way of getting back; but, perceiving this to be impracticable, I resigned myself to my fate, and even began to take some pleasure in the easy motion by which I was borne forwards. But what new and wonderful forms of living creatures did I see inhabiting this liquid land! Bodies of prodigious bulk, covered with shining scales of various colours, shot by me with vast rapidity, and sported a thousand ways. They had large heads and staring eyes, tremendous wide mouths, but no legs; and they seemed to be carried on by the action of what appeared like small wings planted on various parts of their body, and especially at the end of the tail, which continually waved about. Other smaller creatures, of a great variety of extraordinary forms, were moving through the clear fluid, or resting upon its surface; and I saw with terror numbers of them continually seized and swallowed by the larger ones before mentioned.

" When I had got near the middle, the smooth surface of this plain was all roughened, and moved up and down, so as to toss about my leaf, and nearly overset it. I trembled to think what would become of me, should I be thrown amidst all these terrible monsters. At last, however, I got safe to the other side, and with joy set my feet on dry land again. I ascended a gentle green slope, which led to a tall plantation like that which I had before passed through. Another green plain, and another stony desert succeeded; which brought me at length to the opposite boundary of our world, enclosed by the same immense mound rising to the heavens, which limits us on this side.

" Here I fell in with another nation of our species, differing little in their way of life from ourselves.

They invited me to their settlement, and entertained
me hospitably, and I accompanied them in several
excursions in the neighbourhood.   There was a charming fruit-tree at no great distance, to which we made
frequent visits.   One day, as I was regaling deliciously
on the heart of a green-gage plum, I felt myself all on
a sudden carried along with great swiftness, till I got
into a dark-place, where a horrid crash threw me upon
a soft moist piece of flesh, whence I was soon driven
forth in a torrent of wind and moisture, and found
myself on the ground all covered with slime.   I disengaged myself with difficulty, and, looking up, descried one of those enormous two-legged animals,
which often shake the ground over our heads, and put
us into terror.

" My new friends now began to hint to me that it
was time to depart, for you know we are not fond of
naturalizing strangers.   And lucky, indeed, it was for
me that I received the hint when I did ; for I had but
just left the place, and was travelling over a neighbouring eminence, when I heard behind me a tremendous noise ; and looking back, I saw the whole of their
settlement blown into the air, with a prodigious explosion of fire and smoke.   Numbers of half-burnt bodies,
together with the ruins of their habitations, were
thrown to a vast distance around ; and such a suffo-
cating vapour arose, that I lay for some time deprived
of sense and motion.   From some of the wretched
fugitives I learned that the disaster was attributed to
subterranean fire bursting its way to the surface ; the
cause of which, however, was supposed to be connected
with the machinations of that malignant two-legged
monster, from whose jaws I had so narrowly escaped,
who had been observed, just before the explosion, to
pour through the holes leading to the great apartment
of the settlement, a number of black shining grains.

" On my return from this remote country, I kept
along the boundary-wall, which I knew by observation must at length bring me back to my own home.

I met with several wandering tribes of our species in my road, and frequently joined their foraging parties in search of food. One day, a company of us, allured by the smell of something sweet, climbed up some lofty pillars, on which was placed a vast round edifice, having only one entrance. At this were continually coming in and going out those winged animals, somewhat like ourselves in form, but many times bigger, and armed with a dreadful sting, which we so often meet with sipping the juices of flowers; but whether they were the architects of this great mansion, or it was built for them by some beneficent being of greater powers, I am unable to decide. It seemed, however, to be the place where they deposited what they so industriously collect; for they were perpetually arriving loaded with a fragrant substance, which they carried in, and then returned empty. We had a great desire to enter with them, but were deterred by their formidable appearance, and a kind of angry hum which continually proceeded from the house. At length, two or three of the boldest of our party, watching a time when the entrance was pretty free, ventured to go in; but we soon saw them driven out in great haste, and trampled down and massacred just at the gate-way. The rest of us made a speedy retreat.

" Two more adventures which happened to me, had very nearly prevented my return to my own country. Having one evening, together with a companion, taken up my quarters in an empty snail-shell, there came on such a shower of rain in the night, that the shell was presently filled. I awoke nearly suffocated; but luckily, having my head turned towards the mouth of the shell, I arose to the top, and made a shift to crawl to a dry place. My companion, who had got further into the shell, never arose again.

" Not long after, as I was travelling under the wall, I descried a curious pit, with a circular orifice, gradually growing narrower to the bottom. On coming close to the brink, in order to survey it, the edge, which was of fine sand, gave way, and I slid down the pit. As soon as I had reached the bottom, a creature with a huge pair of horns and dreadful claws made his appearance from beneath the sand, and attempted to seize me. I flew back, and ran up the side of the pit, when he threw over me such a shower of sand as blinded me, and had like to have brought me down again. However, by exerting all my strength, I got out of his reach, and did not cease running till I was at a considerable distance. I was afterward informed that this was the den of an ant-lion, a terrible foe of our species, which, not equalling us in speed, is obliged to make use of this crafty device to entrap his heedless prey.

"This was the last of my perils. To my great joy, I reached my native place last night, where I mean to stay content for the future. I do not know how far I have benefited from my travels, but one important conclusion I have drawn from them."

"What is that?" said his friend.

"Why, you know it is the current opinion with us, that everything in this world was made for our use. Now, I have seen such vast tracts not at all fit for our residence, and peopled with creatures so much larger and stronger than ourselves, that I cannot help being convinced that the Creator had in view their accommodation as well as ours, in making this world."

"I confess this seems probable enough; but you had better keep your opinion to yourself."

"Why so?"

"You know we ants are a vain race, and make high pretensions to wisdom as well as antiquity. We shall be affronted with any attempts to lessen our importance in our own eyes."

"But there is no wisdom in being deceived."

"Well—do as you think proper. Meantime, farewell, and thanks for the entertainment you have given me."—"Farewell!"

THE COLONISTS.

" Come," said Mr. Barlow to his boys, "I have a new play for you. I will be the founder of a colony; and you shall be people of different trades and professions coming to offer yourselves to go with me. What are you, *A?*"

A. I am a farmer, sir.

Mr. B. Very well! Farming is the chief thing we have to depend upon, so we cannot have too much of it. But you must be a working farmer, not a gentleman farmer. Labourers will be scarce among us, and every man must put his own hand to the plough. There will be woods to clear and marshes to drain, and a great deal of stubborn work to do.

A. I shall be ready to do my part, sir.

Mr. B. Well then, I shall entertain you willingly, and as many more of your profession as you can bring. You shall have land enough, and utensils ; and you may fall to work as soon as you please. Now for the next.

B. I am a miller, sir.

Mr. B. A very useful trade! The corn we grow must be ground, or it will do us little good. But what will you do for a mill, my friend ?

B. I suppose we must make one, sir.

Mr. B. True; but then you must bring with you a millwright for the purpose. As for millstones, we will take them out with us. Who is next ?

C. I am a carpenter, sir.

Mr. B. The most necessary man that could offer! We shall find you work enough, never fear. There will be houses to build, fences to make, and all sorts of wooden furniture to provide. But our timber is all growing. You will have a deal of hard work to do in felling trees, and sawing planks, and shaping posts, and the like. You must be a field carpenter as well as a house carpenter.

C. I will, sir.

Mr. B. Very well; then I engage you; but you had better bring two or three able hands along with you.

D. I am a blacksmith, sir.

Mr. B. An excellent companion for the carpenter! We cannot do without either of you; so you may bring your great bellows and anvil, and we will set up a forge for you as soon as we arrive. But, by the by, we shall want a mason for that purpose.

E. I am one, sir.

Mr. B. That's well. Though we may live in log houses at first, we shall want brick or stone work for chimneys, and hearths, and ovens, so there will be employment for a mason. But if you can make bricks and burn lime too, you will be still more useful.

E. I will try what I can do, sir.

Mr. B. No man can do more. I engage you. Who is next?

F. I am a shoemaker, sir.

Mr. B. And shoes we cannot well do without. But can you make them, like Eumæus in the Odyssey, out of a raw hide? for I fear we shall get no leather.

F. But I can dress hides, too.

Mr. B. Can you? Then you are a clever fellow, and I will have you, though I give you double wages.

G. I am a tailor, sir.

Mr. B. Well—Though it will be some time before we want holiday suits, yet we must not go naked; so there will be work for the tailor. But you are not above mending and patching, I hope, for we must not mind patched clothes while we work in the woods.

G. I am not, sir.

Mr. B. Then I engage you.

H. I am a weaver, sir.

Mr. B. Weaving is a very useful art, but I question if we can find room for it in our colony for the present.

We shall not grow either hemp or flax for some time to come, and it will be cheaper for us to import our cloth than to make it. In a few years, however, we may be very glad of you.

J. I am a silversmith and jeweller, sir.

Mr. B. Then, my friend, you cannot go to a worse place than a new colony to set up your trade in. You will break us, or we shall starve you.

J. But I understand clock and watch making, too.

Mr. B. That is somewhat more to our purpose, for we shall want to know how time goes. But I doubt we cannot give you sufficient encouragement for a long while to come. For the present, you had better stay where you are.

K. I am a barber and hair-dresser, sir.

Mr. B. Alas, what can we do with you? If you will shave our men's rough beards once a week, and crop their hair once a quarter, and be content to help the carpenter, or follow the plough the rest of your time, we shall reward you accordingly. But you will have no ladies and gentlemen to dress for a ball, or wigs to curl and powder for Sundays, I assure you. Your trade will not stand by itself with us for a great while to come.

L. I am a doctor, sir.

Mr. B. Then, sir, you are very welcome. Health is the first of blessings, and if you can give us that, you will be a valuable man, indeed. But I hope you understand surgery as well as physic, for we are likely enough to get cuts and bruises, and broken bones occasionally.

L. I have had experience in that branch too, sir.

Mr. B. And if you understand the nature of plants, and their uses both in medicine and diet, it will be a great addition to your usefulness.

L. Botany has been a favourite study with me, sir; and I have some knowledge of chemistry, and the other parts of natural history, too.

Mr. B. Then you will be a treasure to us, sir, and

I shall be happy to make it worth your while to go with us.

M. I, sir, am a lawyer.

Mr. B. Sir, your most obedient servant. When we are rich enough to go to law, we will let you know.

N. I am a schoolmaster, sir.

Mr. B. That is a profession which I am sure I do not mean to undervalue; and as soon as ever we have young folk in our colony, we shall be glad of your services. Though we are to be hardworking, plain people, we do not intend to be ignorant, and we shall make it a point to have every one taught reading and writing, and the first rules of ciphering, at least. In the mean time, till we have employment enough for you in teaching, you may keep the accounts and records of the colony; and on Sunday you may read prayers to all those that choose to attend upon you.

N. With all my heart, sir.

Mr. B. Then I engage you. Who comes here with so bold an air?

O. I am a soldier, sir; will you have me?

Mr. B. We are peaceable people, and I hope shall have no occasion to fight. We mean honestly to purchase our land from the natives, and to be just and fair in all our dealings with them. William Penn, the founder of Pennsylvania, followed that plan; and, when the Indians were at war with all the other European settlers, a person in a Quaker's habit might pass through all their most ferocious tribes without the least injury. It is my intention, however, to make all my colonists soldiers, so far as to be able to defend themselves if attacked, and that being the case, we shall have no need of *soldiers by trade.*

P. I am a gentleman, sir; and I have a great desire to accompany you, because I hear game is very plentiful in that country.

Mr. B. A gentleman! And what good will you do us, sir?

P. O, sir, that is not at all my object. I only mean to amuse myself.

Mr. B. But do you mean, sir, that we should pay for your amusement?

P. As to maintenance, I expect to be able to kill game enough for my own eating, with a little bread and garden stuff, which you will give me. Then I will be content with a house somewhat better than the common ones; and your barber shall be my valet; so I shall give very little trouble.

Mr. B. And pray, sir, what inducement can we have for doing all this for you?

P. Why, sir, you will have the credit of having *one gentleman* at least in your colony.

Mr. B. Ha, ha, ha! A facetious gentleman, truly! Well, sir, when we are ambitious of such a distinction, we will send for you.

FIFTH EVENING.

THE DOG AND HIS RELATIONS.

KEEPER was a farmer's mastiff, honest, brave, and vigilant. One day as he was ranging at some distance from home, he espied a Wolf and a Fox sitting together at the corner of a wood. Keeper, not much liking their looks, though by no means fearing them, was turning another way, when they called after him, and civilly desired him to stay. "Surely, sir," says Reynard, "you won't disown your relations. My Cousin Ghaunt and I were just talking over family matters, and we both agreed that we had the honour of reckoning you among our kin. You must know that, according to the best accounts, the wolves and dogs were originally one race in the forests of Armenia; but the dogs taking to living with man, have since become inhabitants of towns and villages, while the wolves have retained their ancient mode of life. As to my ancestors, the foxes, they were a branch of the same family, who settled farther northwards, where they became stinted in growth, and adopted the custom of living in holes under-ground. The cold has sharpened our noses, and given us a thicker fur and bushy tails to keep us warm. But we have all a family likeness which it is impossible to mistake; and I am sure it is our interest to be good friends with each other."

The wolf was of the same opinion; and Keeper, looking narrowly at them, could not help acknowledging their relationship. As he had a generous heart, he readily entered into friendship with them. They took a ramble together; but Keeper was rather surprised at observing the suspicious shyness with which some of the weaker sort of animals surveyed them, and wondered at the hasty flight of a flock of sheep as soon as they came within view. However, he gave his cousins a cordial invitation to come and see him at his yard, and then took his leave.

They did not fail to come the next day, about dusk. Keeper received them kindly, and treated them with part of his own supper. They staid with him till after dark, and then marched off with many compliments. The next morning, word was brought to the farm that a goose and three goslings were missing, and that two lambs were found almost devoured in the Home Field. Keeper was too honest himself readily to suspect others, so he never thought of his kinsmen on the occasion. Soon after, they paid him a second evening visit, and next day another loss appeared, of a hen and her chickens, and a fat sheep. Now Keeper could not help mistrusting a little, and blamed himself for admitting strangers without his master's knowledge. However, he still did not love to think ill of his own relations.

They came a third time. Keeper received them rather coldly, and hinted that he should like better to

see them in the daytime; but they excused themselves
for want of leisure. When they took their leave, he
resolved to follow at some distance and watch their
motions. A litter of young pigs happened to be lying
under a haystack, outside of the yard. The wolf
seized one by the back, and ran off with him. The pig
set up a most dismal squeal; and Keeper, running up
at the noise, caught his dear cousin in the fact. He
flew at him and made him relinquish his prey, though
not without much snarling and growling. The fox,
who had been prowling about the hen-roost, now came
up and began to make protestations of his own innocence, with heavy reproaches against the wolf for thus
disgracing the family. "Begone, scoundrels, both!"
cried Keeper, "I know you now too well. You may
be of my blood, but I am sure you are not of my spirit.
Keeper holds no kindred with villains." So saying,
he drove them from the premises.

THE HISTORY AND ADVENTURES OF A CAT.

Some days ago died Grimalkin, the favourite tabby
cat of Mrs. Petlove. Her disorder was a shortness of
breath, proceeding partly from old age, and partly
from fat. As she felt her end approaching, she called
her children to her, and, with a great deal of difficulty,
spoke as follows:—

"Before I depart from this world, my children, I mean,
if my breath will give me leave, to relate to you the
principal events of my life, as the variety of scenes I
have gone through may afford you some useful instruction for avoiding those dangers to which our species
are particularly exposed.

"Without further preface, then, I was born at a
farm-house in a village some miles hence; and almost
as soon as I came into the world, I was very near
leaving it again. My mother brought five of us at a
litter; and as the frugal people of the house kept cats
only to be useful, and were already sufficiently stocked,

we were immediately doomed to be drowned; and accordingly a boy was ordered to take us all and throw us into the horse-pond. This commission he performed with the pleasure boys seem naturally to take in acts of cruelty, and we were presently set a swimming. While we were struggling for life, a little girl, daughter to the farmer, came running to the pond-side, and begged very hard that she might save one of us, and bring it up for her own. After some dispute, her request was granted; and the boy reaching out his arm, took hold of me, who was luckily nearest him, and brought me out when I was just spent. I was laid on the grass, and it was some time before I recovered. The girl then restored me to my mother, who was overjoyed to get again one of her little ones; and, for fear of another mischance, she took me in her mouth to a dark hole, where she kept me till I could see, and was able to run by her side. As soon as I came to light again, my little mistress took possession of me, and tended me very carefully. Her fondness, indeed, was sometimes troublesome, as she pinched my sides with carrying me, and once or twice hurt me a good deal by letting me fall. Soon, however, I became strong and active, and played and gambolled all day long, to the great delight of my mistress and her companions.

"At this time I had another narrow escape. A man brought into the house a strange dog, who had been taught to worry all the cats that came in his way. My mother slunk away at his entrance; but I, thinking, like a little fool, as I was, that I was able to protect myself, staid on the floor, growling and setting up my back by way of defiance. The dog instantly ran at me, and, before I could get my claws ready, seized me with his mouth, and began to gripe and shake me most terribly. I screamed out, and by good luck my mistress was within hearing. She ran to us, but was not able to disengage me; however, a servant, seeing her distress, took a great stick, and gave the dog such a bang on the back, that he was forced to let me go. He had used me so roughly, that I was not able to stand for some time; but by care and a good constitution I recovered.

"I was now running after everybody's heels, by which means I got one day locked up in the dairy. I was not sorry for this accident, thinking to feast upon the cream and other good things. But having climbed up a shelf to get at a bowl of cream, I unluckily fell backwards into a large vessel of butter-milk, where I should probably have been drowned, had not the maid heard the noise and come to see what was the matter. She took me out, scolding bitterly at me, and after making me undergo a severe discipline at the pump, to clean me, she dismissed me with a good whipping. I took care not to follow her into the dairy again.

"After a while, I began to get into the yard, and my mother took me into the barn upon a mousing expedition. I shall never forget the pleasure this gave me. We sat by a hole, and presently out came a mouse with a brood of young ones. My mother darted among them, and first demolished the old one, and then pursued the little ones, who ran about squeaking in dreadful perplexity. I now thought it was time for me to do something, and accordingly ran after a straggler, and soon overtook it. O, how proud was I, as I stood over my trembling captive, and patted him with my paws! My pride, however, soon met with a check; for seeing one day a large rat, I courageously flew at him; but, instead of turning tail, he gave me such a bite on the nose, that I ran away to my mother, mewing piteously, with my face all bloody and swelled. For some time I did not meddle with rats again; but at length growing stronger and more skilful, I feared neither rats nor any other vermin, and acquired the reputation of an excellent hunter.

"I had some other escapes about this time. Once I happened to meet with some poisoned food laid for the rats, and, eating it, I was thrown into a disorder that was very near killing me. At another time, I chanced to set my foot in a rat-trap, and received so many deep wounds from its teeth, that though I was loosened as gently as possible by the people who heard me cry, I was rendered lame for some weeks after.

"Time went on, and I arrived at my full growth; and forming an acquaintance with a he-cat about my own age, we made a match of it. I became a mother in due time, and had the mortification of seeing several broods of my kittens disposed of in the same manner as my brothers and sisters had been. I shall mention two or three more adventures in the order I remember them. I was once prowling for birds along a hedge, at some distance from home, when the squire's greyhounds came that way a-coursing. As soon as they spied me, they set off at full speed, and running much faster than I could do, were just at my tail, when I reached a tree, and saved myself by climbing up it. But a greater danger befel me on meeting with a parcel of boys returning from school. They surrounded me before I was aware, and obliged me to take refuge in a tree; but I soon found that a poor defence against such enemies; for they assembled about it, and threw stones on all sides, so that I could not avoid receiving many hard blows, one of which brought me senseless to the ground. The biggest boy now seized me, and proposed to the rest making what he called rare sport with me. This sport was to tie me to a board, and, launching me on a pond, to set some water-dogs at me, who were to duck and half-drown me, while I was to defend myself by biting their noses, and scratching their eyes. Already was I bound, and just ready to be set a-sailing, when the schoolmaster, taking a walk that way, and seeing the bustle, came up, and obliged the boys to set me at liberty, severely reprimanding them for their cruel intentions.

"The next remarkable incident of my life was the occasion of my removal from the country. My mistress's brother had a tame linnet, of which he was very fond; for it would come and alight on his shoulder when he called it, and feed out of his hand; and it sang well besides. This bird was usually either in its cage or upon a high perch; but one unlucky day, when he and I were alone in the room together, he came down on the table, to pick up crumbs. I spied him, and, not being able to resist the temptation, sprang at him, and, catching him in my claws, soon began to devour him. I had almost finished, when his master came into the room; and seeing me with the remains of the poor linnet in my mouth, he ran to me in the greatest fury, and after chasing me several times round the room, at length caught me. He was proceeding instantly to hang me, when his sister, by many entreaties and tears, persuaded him, after a good whipping, to forgive me, upon the promise that I should be sent away. Accordingly, the next market-day I was despatched in the cart to a relation of theirs in this town, who wanted a good cat, as the house was overrun with mice.

"In the service of this family I continued a good while, performing my duty as a mouser extremely well, so that I was in high esteem. I soon became acquainted with all the particulars of a town life, and distinguished my activity in climbing up walls and houses, and jumping from roof to roof, either in pursuit of prey, or upon gossiping parties with my companions. Once, however, I had like to have suffered for my venturing; for having made a great jump from one house to another, I alighted on a loose tile, which giving way with me, I fell from a vast height into the street, and should certainly have been killed, had I not had the luck to fall into a dung-cart, whence I escaped with no other injury but being half-stifled with filth.

"Notwithstanding the danger I had run from killing the linnet, I am sorry to confess that I was again guilty of a similar offence. I contrived one night to

F

leap down from a roof upon the board of some pigeon-holes, which led to a garret inhabited by pigeons. I entered, and finding them asleep, made sad havoc among all that were within my reach, killing and sucking the blood of nearly a dozen. I was near paying dearly for this, too; for, on attempting to return, I found it was impossible for me to leap up again to the place whence I had descended, so that, after several dangerous trials, I was obliged to wait trembling in the place where I had committed all these murders, till the owner came up in the morning to feed his pigeons. I rushed out between his legs as soon as the door was opened, and had the good fortune to get safe down stairs, and make my escape through a window unknown; but never shall I forget the horrors I felt that night! Let my double danger be a warning to you, my children, to control your savage appetites, and on no acount to do harm to those creatures which, like ourselves, are under the protection of man. We cats all lie under a bad name for treacherous dispositions in this respect, and with shame I must acknowledge, it is but too well merited.

"Well—but my breath begins to fail me, and I must hasten to a conclusion. I still lived in the same family, when our present kind mistress, Mrs. Petlove, having lost a favourite tabby, advertised a very handsome price for another that should as nearly as possible resemble her dead darling. My owners, tempted by the offer, took me for the good lady's inspection, and I had the honour of being preferred to a multitude of rivals. I was immediately settled in the comfortable mansion we now inhabit, and had many favours and indulgences bestowed upon me, such as I had never before experienced. Among these, I reckon one of the principal, that of being allowed to rear all my children, and to see them grow up in peace and plenty. My adventures here have been few; for after the monkey had spitefully bitten off the last joint of my tail (for which I had the satisfaction to see him soundly corrected), I kept beyond the length of his chain; and neither the parrot nor the lapdogs ever dared to molest me. One of the greatest afflictions I have felt here, was the stifling of a whole litter of my kittens by a fat old lady, a friend of my mistress's, who sat down on the chair where they lay, and never perceived the mischief she was doing till she arose, though I pulled her clothes, and used all the means in my power to show my uneasiness. This misfortune my mistress took to heart almost as much as myself, and the lady has never since entered our doors. Indeed, both I and mine have ever been treated here with the utmost kindness—perhaps with too much; for to the pampering me with delicacies, together with Mrs. Abigail's frequent washings, I attribute this asthma, which is now putting an end to my life, rather sooner than its natural period. But I know all was meant well; and with my last breath I charge you all to show your gratitude to our worthy mistress, by every return in your power.

"And now, my dear children, farewell; we shall perhaps meet again in a land where there are no dogs to worry us, or boys to torment us—Adieu!"

Having thus said, Grimalkin became speechless, and presently departed this life, to the great grief of all the family.

CANUTE'S REPROOF TO HIS COURTIERS.

Persons :

CANUTE .... *King of England.*
OSWALD, OFFA .... *Courtiers.*

Scene.—*The Sea-Side, near Southampton—The Tide coming in.*

Canute. Is it true, my friends, what you have so often told me, that I am the greatest of monarchs?

Offa. It is true, my liege; you are the most powerful of all kings.

Oswald. We are all your slaves; we kiss the dust of your feet.

Offa. Not only we, but even the elements, are your slaves. The land obeys you from shore to shore; and the sea obeys you.

Canute. Does the sea, with its loud boisterous waves, obey me? Will that terrible element be still at my bidding?

Offa. Yes, the sea is yours; it was made to bear your ships upon its bosom, and to pour the treasures of the world at your royal feet. It is boisterous to your enemies, but it knows you to be its sovereign.

Canute. Is not the tide coming up?

Oswald. Yes, my liege; you may perceive the swell already.

Canute. Bring me a chair, then; set it here upon the sands.

Offa. Where the tide is coming up, my gracious lord?

Canute. Yes, set it just here.

Oswald (aside). I wonder what he is going to do!

Offa (aside). Surely he is not such a fool as to believe us!

Canute. O, mighty Ocean! thou art my subject; my courtiers tell me so; and it is thy bounden duty to obey me. Thus, then, I stretch my sceptre over thee, and command thee to retire. Roll back thy swelling waves, nor let them presume to wet the feet of me, thy royal master.

Oswald (aside). I believe the sea will pay very little regard to his royal commands.

Offa. See how fast the tide rises!

Oswald. The next wave will come up to the chair. It is a folly to stay; we shall be covered with salt-water.

Canute. Well, does the sea obey my commands? If it be my subject, it is a very rebellious subject. See how it swells, and dashes the angry foam and salt spray over my sacred person. Vile sycophants! did you think I was the dupe of your base lies? that I believed your abject flatteries? Know, there is only one Being whom the sea will obey. He is Sovereign of heaven and earth, King of kings, and Lord of lords. It is only He who can say to the ocean, "Thus far shalt thou go, but no farther, and here shall thy proud waves be stayed." A king is but a man, and a man is but a worm. Shall a worm assume the power of the great God, and think the elements will obey him? Take away this crown, I will never wear it more. May kings learn to be humble from my example, and courtiers learn truth from your disgrace!

DIALOGUE, ON THINGS TO BE LEARNED.
Between Mamma and Kitty.

Kitty. PRAY, mamma, may I leave off working? I am tired.

Mamma. You have done very little, my dear; you know you were to finish all that hem.

K. But I had rather write now, mamma, or read, or get my French grammar.

M. I know very well what that means, Kitty; you had rather do anything than what I set you about.

K. No, mamma; but you know I can work very well already, and I have a great many more things to learn. There's Miss Rich, that cannot sew half so well as I, and she is learning music and drawing already, besides dancing, and I don't know how many other things. She tells me that they hardly work at all in their school.

M. Your tongue runs at a great rate, my dear; but in the first place you cannot sew very well, for if you could, you would not have been so long in doing this little piece. Then I hope you will allow, that mammas know better what is proper for their little girls to learn than they do themselves.

K. To be sure, mamma; but as I suppose I must learn all these things some time or other, I thought

you would like to have me begin them soon, for I
have often heard you say that children cannot be set
too early about what is necessary for them to do.

M. That's very true, but all things are not equally
necessary to every one; for some, that are very fit for
one, are scarcely proper at all for others.

K. Why, mamma?

M. Because, my dear, it is the purpose of all education to fit persons for the station in which they are
hereafter to live; and you know there are very great
differences in that respect, both among men and
women.

K. Are there? I thought all *ladies* lived alike.

M. It is usual to call all well-educated women, who
have no occasion to work for their livelihood, *ladies;*
but if you will think a little, you must see that they
live very differently from each other; for their fathers
and husbands are in very different ranks and situations in the world, you know.

K. Yes, I know that some are lords, and some are
squires, and some are clergymen, and some are merchants, and some are doctors, and some are shop-
keepers.

M. Well; and do you think that the wives and
daughters of these persons have just the same things
to do, and the same duties to perform? You know
how I spend my time. I have to go to market, and
provide for the family, to look after the servants, to
help in taking care of you children, and in teaching
you, to see that your clothes are in proper condition,
and assist in making and mending for myself, and for
you, and your papa. All this is my necessary duty;
and besides this, I must go out a-visiting, to keep up
our acquaintance; this I call partly business, and partly
amusement. Then when I am tired, and have done
all that I think is necessary, I may amuse myself with
reading, or in any other proper way. Now a great
many of these employments do not belong to Lady
Wealthy, or Mrs. Rich, who keep housekeepers and

governesses, and servants of all kinds, to do everything for them. It is very proper, therefore, for them to pay more attention to music, drawing, ornamental work, and any other elegant manner of passing their time, and making themselves agreeable.

K. And shall I have all the same things to do, mamma, that you have?

M. It is impossible, my dear, to foresee what your future station will be; but you have no reason to expect that if you have a family, you will have fewer duties to perform than I have. This is the way of life for which your education should prepare you; and everything will be useful and important for you to learn, in proportion as it will make you fit for this.

K. But when I am grown a young lady, shall I not have to visit, and go to assemblies and plays, as the Misses Wilson and the Misses Johnson do?

M. It is very likely you may enter into some amusement of this sort; but even then you will have several more serious employments, which will take up a much greater part of your time; and if you do not perform those duties properly, you will have no right to partake of the pleasure.

K. What will they be, mamma?

M. Why don't you think it proper that you should assist me in my household affairs a little, as soon as you are able?

K. O, yes, mamma, I should be very glad to do that.

M. Well, consider what talents will be necessary for that purpose; will not a good hand at your needle be one of the very first qualities?

K. I believe it will.

M. Yes, and not only in assisting *me*, but in making things for *yourself*. You know how we admired Miss Smart's ingenuity when she was with us, in contriving and making so many articles of her dress, for which she must otherwise have gone to the milliner's, which would have cost a great deal of money.

K. Yes, she made my pretty bonnet, and she made you a very handsome cap.

M. Very true; she was so clever as not only to furnish herself with these things, but to oblige her friends with some of her work. And I dare say she does a great deal of plain work also for herself and her mother. Well, then, you are convinced of the importance of this business, I hope.

K. Yes, mamma.

M. Reading and writing are such necessary parts of education, that I need not say much to you about them.

K. O no, for I love reading dearly.

M. I know you do, if you can get entertaining stories to read; but there are many books also to be read for instruction, which perhaps may not be so pleasant at first.

K. But what need is there of so many books of this sort?

M. Some are to teach you your duty to your Maker and your fellow-creatures, of which I hope you are sensible you ought not to be ignorant. Then it is very right to be acquainted with geography; for you remember how poor Miss Blunder was laughed at for saying, that if ever she went to France, it should be by land.

K. That was because England is an island, and all surrounded with water, was it not?

M. Yes, Great Britain, which contains both England and Scotland, is an island. Well, it is very useful to know something of the value of plants, and animals, and minerals, because we are always using some or other of them. Something, too, of the heavenly bodies is very proper to be known, both that we may admire the power and wisdom of God in creating them, and that we may not make foolish mistakes when their motions and properties are the subject of conversation. The knowledge of history, too, is very important, especially that of our own country; and, in short, everything that makes part of the discourse of rational and well-educated people ought, in some degree, to be studied by every one who has proper opportunities.

K. Yes, I like some of those things very well. But pray, mamma, what do I learn French for—am I ever to live in France?

M. Probably not, my dear; but there are many books written in French that are very well worth reading; and it may every now and then happen that you may be in company with foreigners who cannot speak English, and as they almost all talk French, you may be able to converse with them in that language.

K. Yes, I remember there was a gentleman here that came from Germany, I think, and he could hardly talk a word of English, but papa and you could talk to him in French; and I wished very much to be able to understand what you were saying, for I believe part of it was about me.

M. It was. Well, then, you see the use of French. But I cannot say this is a *necessary* part of knowledge to young women in general, only it is well worth acquiring if a person have leisure and opportunity. I will tell you, however, what is quite necessary for one in your situation, and that is, to write a good hand, and to cast accounts well.

K. I should like to write well, because then I should send letters to my friends when I pleased, and it would not be such a scrawl as our maid Betty writes, that I dare say her friends can hardly make out.

M. She had not the advantage of learning when young, for you know she taught herself since she came to us, which was a very sensible thing of her, and I suppose she will improve. Well, but accounts are almost as necessary as writing; for how could I cast up all the market bills and tradesmen's accounts, and keep my house-books without it?

K. And what is the use of that, mamma?

M. It is of use to prevent us being overcharged in anything, and to know exactly how much we spend, and whether or no we are exceeding our income, and in what articles we ought to be more saving. Without keeping accounts, the richest man might soon come to be ruined before he knew that his affairs were going wrong.

K. But do women always keep accounts? I thought that was generally the business of the men.

M. It is their business to keep the accounts belonging to their trade, or profession, or estate; but it is the business of their wives to keep all the household accounts; and a woman in almost any rank, unless, perhaps, some of the highest of all, is to blame if she do not take upon her this necessary office. I remember a remarkable instance of the benefit which a young lady derived from an attention to this point. An eminent merchant in London failed for a great sum.

K. What does that mean, mamma?

M. That he owed a great deal more than he could pay. His creditors, that is, those to whom he was indebted, on examining his accounts, found great deficiencies, which they could not make out; for he had kept his books very irregularly, and had omitted to put down many things that he had bought and sold. They suspected, therefore, that great waste had been made in the family expenses; and they were the more suspicious of this, as a daughter, who was a very genteel young lady, was his housekeeper, his wife being dead. She was told of this; upon which, when the creditors all met, she sent them her house-books for their examination. They were all written in a very fair hand, and every single article was entered with the greatest regularity, and the sums were all cast up with perfect exactness. The gentlemen were so highly pleased with the proof of the young lady's ability, that they all agreed to make her a handsome present out of the effects; and one of the richest of them, who was in want of a clever wife, soon after paid his addresses to her, and married her.

K. That was very lucky, for I suppose she took care of her poor father, when she was rich. But I shall have nothing of that sort to do for a long time to come.

M. No; but young women should keep their own account of clothes, and pocket-money, and other expenses, as I intend you shall do when you grow up.

K. Am I not to learn dancing, and music, and drawing too, mamma?

M. Dancing you shall certainly learn pretty soon, because it is not only an agreeable accomplishment in itself, but is useful in forming the body to ease and elegance in all its motions. Music is a highly ornamental accomplishment; but, though a woman of middling station may be admired for its possession, she will never be censured for being without it. The propriety of attempting to acquire a practical acquaintance with music must depend upon natural genius for it, and upon leisure and other accidental circumstances. For some it is too expensive, and many are unable to make such progress in it as will repay the pains of beginning. Drawing, on the other hand, is of far more value than music, even as a mere accomplishment; and, in point of utility as well as of interest, it is infinitely more important. There is hardly a station in life—hardly any mechanical art, howsoever humble—in which drawing may not occasionally be found serviceable. In the making of patterns for all sorts of fancy-work, in the designing of draperies for the decoration of an apartment, and in various other household affairs, it is extremely useful; and, while in the country, or when travelling abroad, to be able to sketch a remarkable building, a rare bird or other animal, or a beautiful landscape, is an elegant and highly intellectual attainment, that, for its intrinsic value, can hardly be appreciated too highly. It is soon enough, however, for us to think about these things, and at any rate, they are not to come in till you have made a proficiency in what is yet more useful and necessary. But I see you have now finished what I set you about, so you shall take a walk with me into the market-place, where there are two or three things I wish to purchase.

K. Shall we not call at the bookseller's, to inquire for those new books that Miss Reader was talking about?

M. Perhaps we may. Now lay up your work neatly, and get on your hat and tippet.

SIXTH EVENING.

ON THE OAK.—A DIALOGUE.

Tutor—George—Harry.

Tut. Come, my boys, let us sit down awhile under yon shady tree. I don't know how your young legs feel, but mine are almost tired.

Geo. I am not tired, but I am very hot.

Har. And I am hot, and very thirsty too.

Tut. When you have cooled yourself, you may drink out of that clear brook. In the mean time, we will read a little out of a book I have in my pocket.

[*They go and sit down at the foot of a tree.*]

Har. What an amazingly large tree! How wide its branches spread! Pray what tree is it?

Geo. I can tell you that. It is an Oak. Don't you see the acorns?

Tut. Yes, it is an Oak—the noblest tree this country produces;—not only grand and beautiful to the sight, but of the greatest importance from its uses.

Har. I should like to know something about it.

Tut. Very well; then instead of reading, we will sit and talk about Oaks. George, you knew the oak by its acorns—should you have known it if there had been none?

Geo. I don't know—I believe not.

Tut. Observe, then, in the first place, that its bark is very rugged. Then see in what manner it grows. Its great arms run out almost horizontally from its trunk, giving the whole tree a sort of round form, and making it spread far on every side. Its branches are also subject to be crooked or kneed. By these marks you might guess at an oak even in winter, when quite bare of leaves. But its leaves afford a surer mark of distinction, since they differ a good deal from those of other English trees, being neither whole and even at the edges, nor yet cut like the teeth of a saw, but rather deeply scolloped, and formed into several rounded divisions. Their colour is a fine deep green. Then the fruit—

Har. Fruit!

Tut. Yes—all kinds of plants have what may properly be called fruit, though we are apt to give that name only to such as are food for man. The fruit of a plant is the seed, with what contains it. This, in the oak, is called an acorn, which is a kind of nut, partly enclosed in a cup.

Geo. Acorn-cups are very pretty things. I have made boats of them, and set them swimming in a basin.

Tut. And if you were no bigger than a fairy, you might use them for drinking-cups, as those imaginary little beings are said to do.

> " Pearly drops of dew we drink
> In acorn-cups, filled to the brink."

Har. Are acorns good to eat?

Geo. No, that they are not. I have tried, and did not like them at all.

Tut. In the early ages of man, before he cultivated the earth, but lived upon such wild products as nature afforded, we are told that acorns made a considerable

part of his food, and at this day I believe they are
eaten in some countries.   But this is in warmer climates, where they probably become sweeter and better-
flavoured than with us.   The chief use we make of
them is to feed hogs.   In those parts of England
where oak woods are common, great herds of swine are
kept, which are driven into the woods in autumn,
when the acorns fall, and provide themselves plentifully for two or three months.   This, however, is a
small part of the praise of the oak.   You will be surprised when I tell you, that to this tree our country
owes its chief glory and security.

Har. Ay, how can that be ?

Tut. I don't know whether, in your reading, you
have ever met with the story, that Athens, a famous
city in Greece, consulting the oracle how it might best
defend itself against its enemies, was advised to trust
to wooden walls.

Har. Wooden walls !—that's odd—I should think
stone walls better, for wooden ones might be set on
fire.

Tut. True ; but the meaning was, that as Athens
was a place of great trade, and its people were skilled
in maritime affairs, they ought to trust to their ships.
Well, this is the case with Great Britain.   As it is an
island, it has no need of walls and fortifications, while
it possesses ships to keep all enemies at a distance.
Now, we have the greatest and finest navy in the
world, by which we both defend ourselves, and attack
other nations when they insult us ; and this is nearly
all built of oak.

Geo. Would no other wood do to build ships ?

Tut. With the exception of teak, an East Indian
wood, none nearly so well, especially for men-of-war ;
for it is the stoutest and strongest wood we have ; and
therefore best fitted, both to keep sound under water,
and to bear the blows and shocks of the waves, and the
terrible strokes of cannon-balls.   It is a peculiar excellence for this last purpose, that oak is not so liable

to splinter or shiver as other woods, so that a ball can pass through it without making a large hole. Did you never hear the old song,—

> " Hearts of Oak are our Ships,
> Hearts of Oak are our men," &c.?

Geo. No.

Tut. It was made at a time when England was more successful in war than had ever before been known, and our success was properly attributed chiefly to our fleet, the great support of which is the British oak; so I hope you will henceforth look upon oaks with due respect.

Har. Yes; the oak shall always be my favourite tree.

Tut. Had not Pope reason, when he said, in his *Windsor Forest,*

> " Let India boast her plants, nor envy we
> The weeping amber or the balmy tree,
> While by our Oaks the precious loads are borne,
> And realms commanded, which those trees adorn!"

These lines refer to its use as well for merchant-ships as for men-of-war; and in fact nearly all our ships are built of either native or foreign oak.

Har. But are not some ships made of iron?

Tut. Yes; of late years, since steam has been brought into operation for the propulsion of vessels on the water, as well as for a thousand other purposes, numbers of ships (called steam-ships, or steamers), and many of them very large, and capable of proceeding against wind and tide, have been constructed of iron.

Geo. Are the masts of ships made of oak?

Tut. No—it would be too heavy. Besides, it would not be easy to find trunks of oak long and straight enough for that purpose. They are made of various sorts of fir and pine, which grow very tall and taper.

Geo. Is oak wood used for anything besides ship-building?

Tut. O yes!—It is one of the principal woods of the carpenter, being employed wherever great strength and durability are required. It is used for door and window frames, and the beams that are laid in walls, to strengthen them. Floors and staircases are sometimes made with it; and in old houses in the country, which were built when oak was more plentiful than at present, almost all the timber about them was oak. It is also occasionally used for furniture, as tables, chairs, drawers, and bedsteads; though mahogany has now much taken its place for the better sort of goods, and the lighter and softer woods for the cheaper; for the hardness of oak renders it difficult and expensive to work. It is still, however, the chief material used in mill-work, in bridge and water-works, for waggon and cart bodies, for large casks and tubs, and for the last piece of furniture a man has occasion for. What is that, do you think, George?

Geo. I don't know.

Har. A coffin.

Tut. So it is.

Har. But why should that be made of such strong wood?

Tut. There can be no other reason than the weak attachment that we are apt to have for our bodies when we have done with them, which has made men in various countries desirous of keeping them as long as possible from decay. But I have not yet done with the oak. Were either of you ever in a tanner's yard?

Geo. We often go by one at the end of the town; but we durst not go in for fear of the great dog.

Tut. But he is always chained in the daytime.

Har. Yes—but he barks so loud, and looks so fierce, that we were afraid he would break his chain.

Tut. I doubt you are a couple of cowards. However, I suppose you came near enough to observe great stacks of bark in the yard.

Geo. O yes;—there are several.

Tut. Those are oak bark, and it is used in tanning the hides.

Har. What does it do to them?

Tut. I'll tell you. Every part of the oak abounds in a quality called *astringency*, or a binding power. The effect of this is to make more close and compact, or to shrivel up, all soft things, and thereby make them firmer and less liable to decay. The hide, then, when taken from the animal, after being steeped in lime and water, to get off the hair and grease, is put to soak in a liquor made by boiling oak bark in water. This liquor is strongly astringent, and by stiffening the soft hide, turns it into what we call leather. Other things are also tanned for the purpose of preserving them, as fishing-nets and boat-sails. This use of the bark of the oak makes it a very valuable commodity; and you may see people in the woods carefully stripping the oaks, when cut down, and piling up the bark in heaps.

Geo. I have seen such heaps of bark, but I thought they were only to burn.

Tut. No—they are much too valuable for that. But I have another use of the oak to mention, and that is in dyeing.

Har. Dyeing! I wonder what colour it can dye?

Tut. Oak sawdust is a principal ingredient in dyeing a sort of cloth called fustian. By various mixtures and management, it is made to give fustians all the different shades of drab and brown. Then, all the parts of the oak, like all other astringent vegetables, produce a dark blue, or black, by the addition of any preparation of iron. The bark is sometimes used in this way for dyeing black. And did you ever see what boys call the oak-apple?

Geo. Yes—I have gathered oak-apples myself.

Tut. Do you know what they are?

Geo. I thought they were the fruit of the oak.

Tut. No—I have told you that the acorns are the fruit. These are excrescences formed by an insect.

G

Geo. An insect!—how can insects make such a thing?

Tut. It is a sort of a fly, that has a power of piercing the outer skin of the oak boughs, under which it lays its eggs. The part then swells into a sort of ball, and the young insects, when hatched, eat their way out. Well; this ball, or apple, is a pretty strong astringent, and is sometimes used in dying black. But in the warm countries, there is a species of oak which bears round excrescences of the same kind, called galls, which become hard, and are the strongest astringents known. They are the principal ingredient in the black dyes, and common ink is made with them, together with a substance called green vitriol, or copperas, which contains iron.

I have now told you the chief uses that I can recollect of the oak; and these are so important, that whoever drops an acorn into the ground, and takes proper care of it when it comes up, may be said to be a benefactor to his country. Besides, no sight can be more beautiful and majestic than a fine oak wood. It is an ornament fit for the habitation of the first nobleman in the land.

Har. I wonder, then, that all rich gentlemen, who have ground enough, do not cover it with oaks.

Tut. Many of them, especially of late years, have made great plantations of these trees. But all soils do not suit them: and then there is another circumstance which prevents many from being at this trouble and expense, which is, the long time an oak takes in growing, so that no person can reasonably expect to profit by those of his own planting. An oak of fifty years is greatly short of its full growth, and they are scarcely arrived at perfection under a century. Some say, not under five centuries. However, it is our duty to think of posterity as well as ourselves; and they who receive oaks from their ancestors, ought certainly to furnish others to their successors.

Har. Then I think that every one who cuts down an oak should be obliged to plant another.

Tut. Very right—but he should plant two or three for one, for fear of accidents in their growing.

I will now repeat to you some verses, describing the oak in its state of full growth, or rather of the commencement of decay, with the various animals living upon it—and then we will walk.

" See where yon Oak its awful structure rears,
The massive growth of twice a hundred years;
Survey his rugged trunk, with moss o'ergrown,
His lusty arms in rude disorder thrown,
His forking branches wide at distance spread,
And, dark'ning half the sky, his lofty head;
A mighty castle, built by nature's hands,
Peopled by various living tribes, he stands.
His airy top the clamorous rooks invest,
And crowd the waving boughs with many a nest.
Midway the nimble squirrel builds his bower;
And sharp-bill'd pies the insect tribes devour,
That gnaw beneath the bark their secret ways,
While unperceived the stately pile decays."

ALFRED.—A DRAMA.

Persons of the Drama :

ALFRED.......... *King of England.*
GUBBA .... *a Farmer.*
GANDELIN........ *his Wife.*
ELLA .... *an Officer of Alfred.*

Scene—*The Isle of Athelney.*

Alfred. How retired and quiet is everything in this little spot! The river winds its silent waters round this retreat; and the tangled bushes of the thicket fence it from the attack of an enemy. The bloody Danes have not yet pierced into this wild solitude. I believe I am safe from their pursuit. But I hope I shall find some inhabitants here, otherwise I shall die of hunger.—Ha! here is a narrow path through the wood; and I think I see the smoke of a cottage rising between the trees. I will bend my steps thither.

Scene—*Before the Cottage.*

G<small>UBBA</small> *coming forward.* G<small>ANDELIN</small> *within.*

Alfred. Good even to you, good man. Are you disposed to show hospitality to a poor traveller?

Gubba. Why truly there are so many poor travellers now-a-days, that if we entertain them all, we shall have nothing left for ourselves. However, come along to my wife, and we will see what can be done for you. Wife, I am very weary; I have been chopping wood all day.

Gandelin. You are always ready for your supper, but it is not ready for you, I assure you; the cakes will take an hour to bake, and the sun is yet high; it has not yet dipped behind the old barn. But who have you with you, I trow?

Alfred. Good mother, I am a stranger; and entreat you to afford me food and shelter.

Gandelin. Good mother, quotha! Good wife, if you please, and welcome. But I do not love strangers; and the land has no reason to love them. It has never been a merry day for Old England, since strangers came into it.

Alfred. I am not a stranger in England, though I am a stranger here. I am a true-born Englishman.

Gubba. And do you hate those wicked Danes, that eat us up, and burn our houses, and drive away our cattle?

Alfred. I do hate them.

Gandelin. Heartily! he does not speak heartily, husband.

Alfred. Heartily I hate them;—most heartily.

Gubba. Give me thy hand, then; thou art an honest fellow.

Alfred. I was with King Alfred in the last battle he fought.

Gandelin. With King Alfred? Heaven bless him!

Gubba. What is become of our good King?

Alfred. Did you love him, then?

Gubba. Yes, as much as a poor man may love a king; and knelt down and prayed for him every night, that he might conquer those Danish wolves; but it was not to be so.

Alfred. You could not love Alfred better than I did.

Gubba. But what is become of him?

Alfred. He is thought to be dead.

Gubba. Well, these are sad times; Heaven help us! Come, you shall be welcome to share the brown loaf with us; I suppose you are too sharp-set to be nice.

Gandelin. Ay, come with us; you shall be as welcome as a prince! But hark ye, husband; though I am very willing to be charitable to this stranger (it would be a sin to be otherwise), yet there is no reason he should not do something to maintain himself; he looks strong and capable.

Gubba. Why, that's true. What can you do, friend?

Alfred. I am very willing to help you in anything you choose to set me about. It will please me best to earn my bread before I eat it.

Gubba. Let me see. Can you tie up faggots neatly?

Alfred. I have not been used to it. I am afraid I should be awkward.

Gubba. Can you thatch? There is a piece blown off the cow-house.

Alfred. Alas! I cannot thatch.

Gandelin. Ask him if he can weave rushes; we want some new baskets.

Alfred. I have never learned.

Gubba. Can you stack hay?

Alfred. No.

Gubba. Why, here's a fellow! and yet he hath as many pair of hands as his neighbours. Dame, can you employ him in the house? He might lay wood on the fire, and rub the tables.

Gandelin. Let him watch these cakes, then ; I must go and milk the kine.

Gubba. And I'll go and stack the wood, since supper is not ready.

Gandelin. But pray, observe, friend! do not let the cakes burn ; turn them often on the hearth.

Alfred. I shall observe your directions.

ALFRED, *alone.*

Alfred. For myself, I could bear it ; but England, my bleeding country, for thee my heart is wrung with bitter anguish!—From the Humber to the Thames the rivers are stained with blood——My brave soldiers cut to pieces!—My poor people—some massacred, others driven from their warm homes, stripped, abused, insulted ;—and I, whom Heaven appointed their shepherd, unable to rescue my defenceless flock from the ravenous jaws of these devourers!—Gracious Heaven, if I am not worthy to save this land from the Danish sword, raise up some other hero to fight with more success than I have done, and let me spend my life in this obscure cottage, in these servile offices! I shall be content, if England be happy.

O! here come my blunt host and hostess.

Enter GUBBA *and* GANDELIN.

Gandelin. Help me down with the pail, husband. This new milk, with the cakes, will make an excellent supper ; but, mercy on us, how they are burnt! black as my shoe! they have not once been turned ; you oaf, you lubber, you lazy loon—

Alfred. Indeed, dame, I am sorry for it ; but my mind was full of sad thoughts.

Gubba. Come, wife, you must forgive him ; perhaps he is in love. I remember when I was in love with thee—

Gandelin. You remember!

Gubba. Yes, dame, I do remember it, though it is many a long year since : my mother was making a kettle of furmety—

Gandelin. Pr'ythee, hold thy tongue, and let us eat our suppers.

Alfred. How refreshing is this sweet new milk, and this wholesome bread!

Gubba. Eat heartily, friend. Where shall we lodge him, Gandelin?

Gandelin. We have but one bed, you know; but there is fresh straw in the barn.

Alfred (aside). If I shall not lodge like a king, at least I shall lodge like a soldier. Alas! how many of my poor soldiers are stretched on the bare ground.

Gandelin. What noise do I hear? It is the trampling of horses. Good husband, go and see what is the matter.

Alfred. Heaven forbid my misfortunes should bring destruction on this simple family! I had rather have perished in the wood.

GUBBA *returns, followed by* ELLA *with his sword drawn.*

Gandelin. Mercy defend us, a sword!

Gubba. The Danes! the Danes! O, do not kill us!

Ella (kneeling). My liege, my lord, my sovereign! have I found you?

Alfred (embracing him). My brave Ella!

Ella. I bring you good news, my sovereign! Your troops that were shut up in Kinwith Castle made a desperate sally—the Danes were slaughtered. The fierce Hubba lies gasping on the plain.

Alfred. Is it possible! Am I yet a king?

Ella. Their famous standard, the Danish raven, is taken; their troops are panic-struck; the English soldiers call aloud for Alfred. Here is a letter which will inform you of more particulars. (*Gives a letter.*)

Gubba (aside). What will become of us? Ah! dame, that tongue of thine has undone us!

Gandelin. O, my poor dear husband! we shall all be hanged, that's certain. But who could have thought it was the king?

Gubba. Why, Gandelin, do you see, we might have guessed he was born to be a King, or some such great man, because, you know, he was fit for nothing else.

Alfred (coming forward). God be praised for these tidings! Hope has sprung up out of the depths of despair. O, my friend! shall I again shine in arms, —again fight at the head of my brave Englishmen,— lead them on to victory! Our friends shall now lift up their heads again.

Ella. Yes, you have many friends, who have long been obliged, like their master, to skulk in deserts and caves, and wander from cottage to cottage. When they hear you are alive, and in arms again, they will leave their fastnesses, and flock to your standard.

Alfred. I am impatient to meet them: my people shall be revenged.

Gubba and Gandelin (throwing themselves at the feet of ALFRED). O my lord——

Gandelin. We hope your majesty will put us to a merciful death. Indeed, we did not know your majesty's grace.

Gubba. If your majesty could but pardon my wife's tongue; she means no harm, poor woman.

Alfred. Pardon you, good people! I not only pardon you, but thank you. You have afforded me protection in my distress; and if ever I am seated again on the throne of England, my first care shall be to reward your hospitality. I am now going to protect you. Come, my faithful Ella, to arms! to arms! My bosom burns to face once more the haughty Dane; and here I vow to Heaven, that I will never sheath the sword against these robbers, till either I lose my life in this just cause, or

> Till dove-like Peace return to England's shore,
> And war and slaughter vex the land no more.

SEVENTH EVENING.

ON THE PINE AND FIR TRIBE.
A Dialogue.
Tutor—George—Harry.

Tut. Let us sit down awhile on this bench, and look about us. What a charming prospect!

Har. I admire those pleasure-grounds. What beautiful clumps of trees there are in that lawn!

Geo. But what a dark, gloomy wood that is at the back of the house!

Tut. It is a fir plantation; and those trees always look dismal in the summer, when there are so many finer greens to compare them with. But the winter is their time for show, when other trees are stripped of their verdure.

Geo. Then they are evergreens!

Tut. Yes; most of the fir tribe are evergreens; and as they are generally natives of cold, mountainous countries, they contribute greatly to cheer the wintry landscape.

Geo. You were so good, when we walked out last, to tell us a great deal about oaks. I thought it one of the prettiest lessons I ever heard. I should be glad if you would give us such another about firs.

Har. So should I too, I am sure.

Tut. With all my heart, and I am pleased that you ask me. Nothing is so great an encouragement to a tutor as to find his pupils of their own accord seeking after useful knowledge.

Geo. And I think it is very useful to know such things as these.

Tut. Certainly it is. Well then — You may know the Pine or Fir tribe in general at first sight, as most of them are of a bluish-green colour, and all have leaves consisting of a strong, narrow, pointed blade, which gives them somewhat of a stiff appearance. Then all of them bear a hard, scaly fruit, of a longish or conical form.

Har. Are they what we call fir-apples?

Tut. Yes; that is one of the names boys give them.

Har. We often pick them up under trees, and throw them at one another.

Geo. I have sometimes brought home my pocket full, to burn. They make a fine clear flame.

Tut. Well—do you know where the seed lies in them?

Geo. No—have they any?

Tut. Yes; at the bottom of every scale lie two winged seeds; but when the scales open, the seeds fall out; so that you can seldom find any in those you pick up.

Har. Are the seeds good for anything?

Tut. There is a kind of pine in the south of Europe, called the *Stone Pine*, the kernels of which are eaten, and said to be as sweet as an almond. And birds pick out the seeds of other sorts, though they are so well defended by the woody scales.

Har. They must have good strong bills, then.

Tut. Of this tribe of trees a variety of species are found in different countries and are cultivated in this. But the only kind native here, is the *Wild Pine*, or *Scotch Fir.* Of this there are large natural forests in the highlands of Scotland; and the principal planta- tions consist of it. It is a hardy sort, fit for barren and mountainous soils, but grows slowly.

Geo. Pray what are those very tall trees, that grow in two rows before the old hall in our village?

Tut. They are the *Common* or *Spruce Fir*, a native of Norway, and other northern countries, and one of the loftiest of the tribe. But observe those trees that grow singly in the grounds opposite to us, with wide- spread branches pointing downwards, and trailing on the ground, thence gradually lessening, till the top of the tree ends almost in a point.

Har. What beautiful trees!

Tut. They are the pines called *Larches,* natives of the Alps and Apennines, and now frequently planted to decorate our gardens. These are not properly evergreens, as they shed their leaves in winter, but quickly recover them again. Then we have, besides, the *Weymouth Pine,* which is the tallest species in America— the *Silver Fir,* so called from the silvery hue of its foliage—the *Pinaster*—and a tree of ancient fame, the *Cedar of Lebanon.*

Geo. I suppose that is a very great tree.

Tut. It grows to a large size, but is very slow in coming to its full growth.

Geo. Are Pines and Firs very useful trees?

Tut. Perhaps the most so of any. By much the greatest part of the wood used among us comes from them.

Har. What—more than from the oak?

Tut. Yes, much more. Almost all the timber used in building houses, for floors, beams, rafters, and roofs, is fir.

Geo. Does it all grow in this country?

Tut. Scarcely any of it. Norway, Sweden, and Russia, are the countries whence we chiefly draw our timber, and a vast trade there is in it. You have seen timber-yards?

Geo. O yes—several.

Tut. In them you would observe some very long, thick beams, called *balks.* These are whole trees, only stripped of the bark and squared. You would also see great piles of planks, and boards, of different lengths and thickness. Those are called *deal,* and are brought over, ready sawn, from the countries where they grow. They are of different colours. The white are chiefly from the fir-tree; the yellow and red from the pine.

Har. I suppose there must be great forests of them in those countries, or else they could not send us so much.

Tut. Yes. The mountains of Norway are overrun with them, enough for the supply of all Europe; but on account of their ruggedness, and the want of roads, it is found impossible to get the trees, when felled, down to the sea-coast, unless they grow near some river.

Geo. How do they manage them?

Tut. They take the opportunity when the rivers are swelled with rains, or melted snow, and tumble the trees into them, when they are carried down to the mouth of the rivers, where they are stopped by a sort of pens.

Har. I should like to see them swimming down the stream.

Tut. Yes—it would be curious enough; for in some places these torrents roll over rocks, making steep waterfalls, down which the trees are carried headlong, and often do not rise again till they have got to a considerable distance; and many of them are broken and torn to pieces in the passage.

Geo. Are these woods used for anything besides building?

Tut. For a variety of purposes; such as boxes, trunks, packing-cases, pales, wainscots, and the like. Deal is a very soft wood, easily worked, light, and cheap, which makes it preferred for so many uses, though it is not very durable, and is very liable to split.

Har. Yes—I know; my box is made of deal, and the lid is split all to pieces, with driving nails into it.

Geo. Are ships ever built with fir?

Tut. It was one of the first woods made use of for naval purposes; and in the poets you will find the words *Pine* and *Fir* frequently employed to signify *ship.* But as navigation has improved, the stronger and more durable woods have generally taken its place. However, in the countries where fir is very plentiful, large ships are still built with it; for though they last only a short time, they cost so little in proportion, that the profit of a few voyages is sufficient to repay the expense. Then, from the great lightness of the wood, they swim higher in the water, and consequently will bear more loading. Most of the large ships that bring timber from Archangel, in Russia, are built of fir. As for the masts of ships, they, as I have already told you, are all made of fir or pine, on account of their straightness and lightness.

Geo. Are there not some lines in Milton's *Paradise Lost* about that?

Tut. Yes: the spear of Satan is magnified by a comparison with a lofty pine.

> " His spear, to equal which the tallest Pine
> Hewn on Norwegian hills, to be the mast
> Of some great ammiral, were but a wand."

Har. I remember, too, that the walking staff of the giant Polypheme was a pine.

Tut. Ay—so Homer and Ovid tell us ; and he must have been a giant, indeed, to use such a stick. Well, so much for the wood of these trees. But I have more to say about their uses.

Har. I am glad of it.

Tut. All of the tribe contain a juice of a bitterish taste and strong fragrant smell. This, in some, is so abundant as to flow out from incisions ; when it is called *Turpentine.* The larch, in particular, yields a large quantity. Turpentine is one of the substances called *resinous ;* it is sticky, transparent, very inflammable, and will not mix with water, but will dissolve in spirits of wine.

Geo. What is it used for ?

Tut. It is used medicinally, and surgically, particularly in the composition of plasters and ointments. It also is an ingredient in varnishes, cements, and the like. An oil, distilled from turpentine, is employed in medicine, and is much used by painters, for mixing up their colours. What remains, after getting this oil, is common *resin.* All these substances take fire very

easily, and burn with a great flame; and the wood of
the pine has so much of this quality, when dry, that
it has been used in many countries for torches.

Har. I know deal shavings burn very briskly.

Geo. Yes; and matches are made of thin slips of
deal, pointed, and dipped in brimstone.

Tut. True;—and when it was the custom to burn
the bodies of the dead, as you read in Homer, and
other old authors, the pines and pitch-trees composed
great part of the funeral pile.

Har. But what are pitch-trees? Does pitch grow
upon trees?

Tut. I was going on to tell you about that. *Tar* is
a product of the trees of this kind, especially of one
species, called the pitch-pine. The wood is burned in
a sort of oven, made in the earth, and the resinous
juice sweats out, and acquires a peculiar taste, and a
black colour, from the fire. This is *tar*. Tar, when
boiled down to dryness, become *pitch*.

Geo. Tar and pitch are chiefly used about ships;
are they not?

Tut. They resist moisture, and therefore are of
great service in preventing things from decaying that
are exposed to wet. For this reason, the cables and
other ropes of ships are well soaked with tar; and the
sides of ships are covered with pitch, mixed with other
ingredients. Their seams, too, or the places where
the planks join, are filled with tow, dipped in a composition of resin, tallow, and pitch, to keep out the
water. Wood, for paling, for piles, for coverings of
roofs, and other purposes of the like nature, is often
tarred over. Cisterns and casks are pitched, to prevent leaking.

Har. But what are sheep tarred for, after they are
sheared?

Tut. To cure wounds and sores in their skin.
For the like purposes, an ointment made with tar is
often rubbed upon children's heads. Several parts of
the pine are medicinal. The tops and green cones of

the spruce fir are fermented with treacle, and the liquor, called spruce beer, is much drunk in America, particularly for the scurvy?

Geo. Is it pleasant?

Tut. Not to those who are unaccustomed to it. Well, I have now finished my lesson, so let us walk.

Har. Shall we go through the grounds?

Tut. Yes; and then we will view some of the different kinds of fir and pine more closely, and I will show you the difference of their leaves and cones, by which they are distinguished.

A DIALOGUE ON DIFFERENT STATIONS IN LIFE.

LITTLE Sally Meanwell had one day been to pay an afternoon's visit to Miss Harriet, the daughter of Sir Thomas Pemberton. The evening proving rainy, she was sent home in Sir Thomas's coach; and, on her return, the following conversation passed between her and her mother:—

Mrs. Meanwell. Well, my dear, I hope you have had a pleasant visit.

Sally. O yes, mamma, very pleasant; you cannot think what a great many fine things I have seen. And then it is so charming to ride in a coach!

Mrs. M. I suppose Miss Harriet showed you all her playthings?

Sally. O yes, such fine large dolls, so smartly dressed, as I never saw in my life before. Then she has a baby-house, and all sorts of furniture in it; and a grotto all made of shells and shining stones. And then she showed me all her fine clothes for the next ball; there's a white slip all full of spangles and pink ribands; you can't think how beautiful it looks.

Mrs. M. And what did you admire most of all these fine things?

Sally. I don't know—I admired them all; and I think I liked riding in the coach better than all the rest. Why don't we keep a coach, mamma? and why have not I such fine clothes and playthings as Miss Harriet?

Mrs. M. Because we cannot afford it, my dear. Your papa is not so rich, by a great deal, as Sir Thomas; and if we were to lay out our money upon such things, we should not be able to procure food, and raiment, and other necessaries for you all.

Sally. But why is not papa as rich as Sir Thomas?

Mrs. M. Sir Thomas had a large estate left him by his father; but your papa has little but what he gains by his own industry.

Sally. But why should not papa be as rich as anybody else? I am sure he deserves it as well.

Mrs. M. Do you not think that there are a great many people poorer than he that are also very deserving?

Sally. Are there?

Mrs. M. Yes, to be sure. Don't you know what a number of poor people there are all around us, who have very few of the comforts we enjoy? What do you think of Plowman, the labourer? I believe you never saw him idle in your life.

Sally. No; he is gone to work long before I am up, and he does not return till almost bedtime, unless it be for his dinner.

Mrs. M. Well! how do you think his wife and children live? should you like that we should change places with them?

Sally. O no! they are so dirty and ragged.

Mrs. M. They are, indeed, poor creatures; but I am afraid they suffer worse evils than that.

Sally. What, mamma?

Mrs. M. Why, I am afraid they often do not get as much food as they could eat. And then in winter they must be half-starved, for want of fire and warm clothing. How do you think you could bear all this?

Sally. Indeed, I don't know. But I have seen Plowman's wife carry great brown loaves into the house;

and I remember once eating some brown bread and milk, and I thought it very good.

Mrs. M. I believe you would not much like it constantly: besides, they can hardly get enough of that. But you seem to know almost as little of the poor as the young French princess did.

Sally. What was that, mamma?

Mrs. M. Why, there had been one year so bad a harvest in France, that numbers of the poor were famished to death. This calamity was so much talked of, that it reached the court, and was mentioned before the young princesses. "Dear me!" said one of them, "how silly that was! Why, rather than be famished, I would eat bread and cheese." Her governess was then obliged to acquaint her that the greater part of her father's subjects scarcely ever ate anything better than black bread all their lives; and that vast numbers would now think themselves very happy to get only half their usual pittance of that. Such wretchedness as this, was what the princess had not the least idea of; and the account shocked her so much, that she was glad to sacrifice all her finery to afford some relief to the sufferings of the poor.

Sally. But I hope there is nobody famished in our country.

Mrs. M. I hope not, for we have laws by which every person is entitled to relief from the parish, if unable to gain a subsistence; and, were there no laws about it, I am sure it would be our duty to part with every superfluity, rather than let a fellow-creature perish for want of necessaries.

Sally. Then do you think it was wrong for Miss Pemberton to have all those fine things?

Mrs. M. No, my dear, if they are suitable to her fortune, and do not consume the money which ought to be employed in more useful things for herself and others.

Sally. But why might she not be contented with such things as I have; and give the money that the rest cost to the poor?

Mrs. M. Because she can afford both to be charitable to the poor, and also to indulge herself in these pleasures. But do you recollect that **the** children of Mr. White, the baker, and Mr. Shape, the tailor, might justly ask the same questions about you?

Sally. How so?

Mrs. M. Are not you much better dressed, and as much more plentifully supplied with playthings than they are, as Miss Pemberton is than you?

Sally. Why, I believe I am; for I remember Polly White was very glad of one of my old dolls; and Nancy Shape cried for such a sash as mine, but her mother would not let her have one.

Mrs. M. Then you see, my dear, that there are many who have fewer things to be thankful for than you have; and you may also learn what ought to be the true measure of the expectations of children and the indulgences of parents.

Sally. I don't quite understand you, mamma.

Mrs. M. Everything ought to be suited to the station in which we live, or are likely to live, and the wants and duties of that station. Your papa and I do not grudge laying out part of our money to promote the innocent pleasure of our children; but it would be very wrong in us to lay out so much on this account as would oblige us to spare in more necessary articles, as in their education, and the common household expenses required in our way of living. Besides, it would be so far from making you happier, that it would be doing you the greatest injury.

Sally. How could that be, mamma?

Mrs. M. If you were now to be dressed like Miss Pemberton, don't you think you would be greatly mortified at being worse dressed when you came to be a young woman?

Sally. I believe I should, mamma; for then perhaps I might go to assemblies; and, to be sure, I should like to be as well dressed then as others.

Mrs. M. Well, but it would be still more improper

for us to dress you now beyond our circumstances, because your necessary clothes will then cost more, you know. Then, if we were now to hire a coach or chair for you to go a-visiting in, should you like to leave it off ever afterwards? But you have no reason to expect that you will be able to have those indulgences when you are a woman. And so it is in everything else. The more fine things, and the more gratifications you have now, the more you will require hereafter; for custom makes things so familiar to us, that while we enjoy them less, we wish for them more.

Sally. How is that, mamma?

Mrs. M. Why, don't you think you have enjoyed your ride in the coach this evening more than Miss Harriet would have done?

Sally. I suppose I have; because if Miss Harriet liked it so well, she would be always riding, for I know she might have the coach whenever she pleased.

Mrs. M. But if you were both told that you were never to ride in a coach again, which would think it the greater hardship? You could walk, you know, as you have always done before; but she would rather stay at home, I believe, than expose herself to the cold wind, and trudge through the wet and dirt in clogs.

Sally. I believe so too; and now, mamma, I see that all you have told me is very right.

Mrs. M. Well, my dear, let it dwell upon your mind, so as to make you cheerful and contented in your station, which you see is so much happier than that of many and many other children. So now we will talk no more on this subject.

EIGHTH EVENING.

THE ROOKERY.

There the hoarse-voiced, hungry Rook,
Near her stick-built nest doth croak,
Waving on the topmost bough.

THESE lines Mr. Stangrove repeated, pointing up to
a rookery, as he was walking in an avenue of tall trees,
with his son Francis.

Francis. Is that a rookery, papa?

Mr. St. It is. Do you hear what a cawing the
birds make?

Fr. Yes—and I see them hopping about among the
boughs. Pray are not rooks the same as crows?

Mr. St. They are a species of crow; but they differ
from the carrion crow and raven in not living upon
dead flesh, but upon corn and other seeds, and grass.
They indeed pick up beetles and other insects, and
worms. See what a number of them have alighted on
yonder ploughed field, almost blackening it over.

Fr. What are they doing?

Mr. St. Searching for grubs and worms. You see
the men in the field do not molest them, for they do a
great deal of service, by destroying grubs, which, if
they were suffered to grow to winged insects, would do
much mischief to the trees and plants.

Fr. But do they not hurt the corn?

Mr. St. Yes—they are said to tear up a good deal
of green corn, if they are not driven away. But upon
the whole, rooks are considered the farmers' friends;
and they do not choose to have them destroyed.

Fr. Do all rooks live in rookeries?

Mr. St. It is the general nature of them to associate together, and build in numbers on the same or
adjoining trees. But this is often in the midst of

woods or natural groves. However, they have no objection to the neighbourhood of man, but readily take to a plantation of tall trees, though it be close to a house; and this is commonly called a rookery. They will even fix their habitations on trees in the midst of towns; and I have seen a rookery in a churchyard in one of the closest parts of London.

Fr. I think a rookery is a sort of town itself.

Mr. St. It is :—a village in the air, peopled with numerous inhabitants; and nothing can be more amusing than to view them all in motion, flying to and fro, and busied in their several occupations. The spring is their busiest time. Early in the year they begin to repair their nests, or build new ones.

Fr. Do they all work together, or every one for itself?

Mr. St. Each pair, after they have coupled, build their own nest; and, instead of helping, they are very apt to steal the materials from one another. If both birds go out at once in search of sticks, they often find, at their return, the work all destroyed, and the materials carried off; so that one of them generally stays at home to keep watch. However, I have met with a story which shows that they are not without some sense of the criminality of thieving. There was in a rookery a lazy pair of rooks, who never went out to get sticks for themselves, but made a practice of watching when their neighbours were abroad, and helped themselves from their nests. They had served most of the community in this manner, and by these means had just finished their own nest; when all the other rooks in a rage fell upon them at once, pulled their nest in pieces, beat them soundly, and drove them from their society.

Fr. That was very right—I should have liked to have seen it. But why do they live together if they do not help one another?

Mr. St. They probably receive pleasure from the company of their own kind, as men, and various other creatures do. Then, though they do not assist one another in building, they are mutually serviceable in many ways. Should a large bird of prey hover about a rookery, for the purpose of carrying off any of the young ones, they all unite to drive him away. When they are feeding in a flock, several are placed as sentinels upon the trees all around, who give an alarm if any danger approach. They often go a long way from home to feed; but every evening the whole flock returns, making a loud cawing as they fly, as though to direct and call in the stragglers. The older rooks take the lead; you may distinguish them by the whiteness of their bills, occasioned by their frequent digging in the ground, by which the black feathers at the root of the bill are worn off.

Fr. Do rooks always keep to the same trees?

Mr. St. Yes—they are much attached to them; and when the trees happen to be cut down, they seem greatly distressed, and keep hovering about them as they are falling, and will scarcely desert them when they lie on the ground.

Fr. Poor things! I suppose they feel as we should, if our town were burned down or overthrown by an earthquake.

Mr. St. No doubt! Societies of brute animals greatly resemble those of men; and that of rooks is like those of men in a savage state, such as the communities of the North-American Indians. It is a sort of league for mutual aid and defence, but in which every one is left to do as he pleases, without any obligation to employ himself for the whole body. Others unite in a manner resembling more civilized societies of men. This is the case with the beavers. They perform great public works by the united efforts of the whole community; such as damming up streams, and constructing mounds for their habitations. As these are works of great art and labour, some of them must probably act under the direction of others, and be compelled to work, whether they will or not. Many curious stories are told to this purpose by those who have observed them in their remotest haunts, where they exercise their full sagacity.

Fr. But are they all true?

Mr. St. That is more than I can answer for; yet what we certainly know of the economy of bees may justify us in believing extraordinary things of the sagacity of animals. The society of bees goes farther than that of beavers, and, in some respects, beyond most among men themselves. They not only inhabit a common dwelling, and perform great works in common, but they lay up a store of provision, which is the property of the whole community, and is not used except at certain seasons and under certain regulations. A bee-hive is a true image of a commonwealth, where no member acts for himself alone, but for the whole body.

Fr. But there are drones among them, who do not work at all.

Mr. St. Yes—and at the approach of winter they are driven out of the hive, and left to perish with cold and hunger. But I have not leisure at present to tell you more about bees. You shall one day see them at work in a glass hive. In the mean time, remember one thing, which applies to all the societies of brute animals; and I wish it did as well to all those of men likewise.

Fr. What is that?

Mr. St. The principle upon which they all associate, is to obtain some benefit for the *whole body*, not to give particular advantages to a few.

** The researches and observations of entomologists, however, tend to show that the government and modes of action of bees, beautiful and interesting as they are, and displaying the wisdom and goodness of the Creator in an eminent degree, are the results of *instinct* rather than of any *reasoning* or intellectual power. The labours of the beaver, on the contrary, and also the conduct of some of the monkey tribes,

may be regarded as flowing from an *intellectually con-trolling power*: in other words, that those creatures, with the elephant and some others, possess the attri-bute of *reason*, in a *degree*. Ants, also, in their forms of government—in their method of leading, under regularly-appointed officers, their squadrons in hostile array to battle—in their taking of prisoners in the hour of victory—and in their making slaves of those prisoners, which they condemn to the performance of menial offices, though they treat them kindly—all indicate the possession of a loftier intellect than that of bees.—EDITOR.

THE SHIP.

CHARLES OSBORN, when at home in the holidays, had a visit from a schoolfellow who was just entered as a midshipman on board of a man-of-war. Tom Hardy (that was his name) was a free-hearted, spirited lad, and a favourite among his companions; but he never liked his book, and had left school ignorant of almost everything he went there to learn. What was worse, he had imbibed a contempt for learning of all kinds, and was fond of showing that contempt. " What does your father mean," said he to Charles, " by keep-ing you moping and studying over things of no use in the world but to plague folk?—Why can't you go into his majesty's service like me, and be made a gentleman of? You are old enough, and I know you are a lad of spirit." This sort of talk made some impression upon young Osborn. He became less attentive to the lessons his father set him, and less willing to enter into instructive conversation. This change gave his father much concern; but, as he knew the cause, he thought it best, instead of employing direct authority, to attempt to make a new impression on his son's mind, which might counteract the effects of his com-panion's suggestions.

Being acquainted with an East-India captain, who

was on the point of sailing, he went with his son to pay him a farewell visit on board his ship. They were shown all about the vessel, and viewed all the preparations for so long a voyage. They saw her weigh anchor and unfurl her sails; and they took leave of their friend amidst the shouts of the seamen and all the bustle of departure.

Charles was highly delighted with this scene; and as they were returning, could think and talk of nothing else. It was easy, therefore, for his father to lead him into the following train of discourse.

After Charles had been warmly expressing his admiration of the grand sight of a large ship completely fitted out and getting under sail; " I do not wonder," said his father, " that you are so much struck with it:—it is, in reality, one of the finest spectacles created by human skill, and the noblest triumph of art over untaught nature. Nearly two thousand years ago, when Julius Cæsar came over to this island, he found the natives in possession of no other sort of vessel than a sort of canoe, called a coracle, formed of wicker-work covered with hides, and no bigger than a man might carry. But the largest ship in Cæsar's fleet was not more superior to the coracle of the Britons, than the Indiaman you have been seeing is to what that ship was. Our savage ancestors ventured only to paddle along the rivers and coasts, or cross small arms of the sea in calm weather; and Cæsar himself would probably have been alarmed to be a few days out of sight of land. But the ship we have just left is going by itself to the opposite side of the globe, prepared to encounter the tempestuous winds and mountainous waves of the vast Southern Ocean, and to find its way to its destined port, though many weeks must pass with nothing in view but sea and sky. Now what do you think can be the cause of this prodigious difference in the powers of man at one period and another?"

Charles was silent.

" Is it not," said his father, " that there is a great deal more knowledge in one than in the other ? "

" To be sure it is," said Charles.

Father. Would it not, think you, be as impossible for any number of men, untaught, by their utmost efforts, to build and navigate such a ship as we have seen, as to fly through the air ?

Charles. I suppose it would.

Fa. That we may be the more sensible of this, let us consider how many arts and professions are necessary for this purpose. Come—you shall begin to name them, and if you forget any, I will put you in mind. What is the first ?

Ch. The ship-carpenter, I think.

Fa. True—what does he do ?

Ch. He builds the ship.

Fa. How is that done ?

Ch. By fastening the planks and beams together.

Fa. But do you suppose he can do this as a common carpenter or joiner makes a box or set of shelves ?

Ch. I do not know.

Fa. Do you not think that such a vast bulk requires a great deal of contrivance to bring it into shape, and fit it for all its purposes ?

Ch. Yes.

Fa. Some ships, you have heard, sail quicker than others—some bear storms better—some carry more lading—some draw less water—and so on. You do not suppose all these things are left to chance ?

Ch. No.

Fa. In order with certainty to produce these effects, it is necessary to study proportions very exactly, and to lay down an accurate scale, by mathematical lines and figures, after which to build the ship. Much has been written upon this subject, and nice calculations have been made of the resistance a ship meets with in making way through the water, and the best means of overcoming it ; also of the action of the wind on the sails, and their action in pushing on the ship by means of the masts. All these must be understood by a perfect master of ship-building.

Ch. But I think I know ship-builders who have never had an education to fit them for understanding these things.

Fa. Very likely; but they have followed by rote the rules laid down by others; and as they work merely by imitation, they cannot alter or improve as occasion may require. Then, though common merchant ships are intrusted to such builders, yet in constructing men-of-war and Indiamen, persons of science are always employed. The French, however, attend to this matter more than we do, and, in consequence, their ships generally sail better than ours.

Ch. But need a captain of a ship know all these things?

Fa. It may not be absolutely necessary; yet occasions may frequently arise in which it would be of great advantage for him to be able to judge and give directions in these matters. But suppose the ship built—what comes next?

Ch. I think she must be rigged.

Fa. Well—who are employed for this purpose?

Ch. Mast-makers, rope-makers, sail-makers, and I know not how many other people.

Fa. These are all mechanical trades; and though in carrying them on much ingenuity has been applied, in the invention of machines and tools, yet we will not stop to consider them. Suppose her, then, rigged—what next?

Ch. She must take in her guns and powder.

Fa. Stop there, and reflect how many arts you have now set to work. Gunpowder is one of the greatest inventions of modern times, and that which has given such a superiority to civilized nations over the barbarous. An English frigate, surrounded by the canoes of all the savages in the world, would easily beat them off by means of her guns; and if Cæsar were to come again to England with his fleet, a battery of cannon would sink all his ships, and set his legions a-swim-ming in the sea. But the making of gunpowder, and the casting of cannon, are arts that require an exact knowledge of the science of *chemistry*.

Ch. What is that?

Fa. It comprehends the knowledge of all the pro-perties of metals and minerals, salts, sulphur, oils, and gums, and of the action of fire, and water, and air upon all substances, and the effects of mixing different things together. Gunpowder is a mixture of three things only—saltpetre or nitre, sulphur or brimstone, and charcoal. But who could have thought such a wonderful effect would have been produced by it?

Ch. Was it not first discovered by accident?

Fa. Yes—but it was by one who was making che-mical experiments, and many more experiments have been employed to bring it to perfection.

Ch. But need a captain know how to make gun-powder and cannon?

Fa. It is not necessary, though it may often be useful to him. However, it is quite necessary that he should know how to employ them. Now the sciences of gunnery and fortification depend entirely upon mathematical principles; for by these are calculated the direction of a ball through the air, the distance it will reach to, and the force with which it will strike anything. All engineers, therefore, must be good mathematicians.

Ch. But I think I have heard of gunners being little better than the common men.

Fa. True—there is a way of doing that business, as well as many others, by mere practice; and an uneducated man may acquire skill in pointing a can-non, as well as in shooting with a common gun. But this is only in ordinary cases, and an abler head is required to direct. Well—now suppose your ship completely fitted out for sea, and the wind blowing fair; how will you navigate her?

Ch. I would spread the sails, and steer by the rudder.

Fa. Very well—but how would you find your way to the port you were bound for ?

Ch. That I cannot tell.

Fa. Nor, perhaps, can I make you exactly comprehend it ; but I can show you enough to convince you that it is an affair that requires much knowledge and early study. In former times, when a vessel left the sight of land, it was steered by observation of the sun by day, and the moon and stars by night. The sun, you know, rises in the east, and sets in the west ; and at noon, in these parts of the world, it is exactly south of us. These points, therefore, may be found out when the sun shines. The moon and stars vary; however, their places in the sky may be known by exact observation. Then, there is one star that always points to the north pole, and is therefore called the pole-star. This was of great use in navigation, and the word pole-star is often used by the poets to signify a sure guide. Do you recollect the description in Homer's Odyssey, when Ulysses sails away by himself from the island of Calypso,—how he steers by the stars ?

Ch. I think I remember the lines in Pope's translation.

Fa. Repeat them, then.

> *Ch.* Placed at the helm, he sat and marked the skies,
> Nor closed in sleep his ever-watchful eyes.
> There viewed the Pleiads, and the northern team,
> And great Orion's more refulgent beam,
> To which, around the axle of the sky,
> The Bear revolving, points his golden eye :
> Who shines exalted on th' ethereal plain,
> Nor bathes his blazing forehead in the main.

Fa. Very well—they are fine lines, indeed ! You see, then, how long ago sailors thought it necessary to study astronomy. But as it frequently happens, especially in stormy weather, that the stars are not to be seen, this method was subject to great uncertainty, which rendered it dangerous to undertake distant voyages. At length, nearly five hundred years ago, a property was discovered in a mineral, called the magnet, or loadstone, which removed the difficulty. This was, its *polarity*, or quality of always pointing to the poles of the earth, that is, due north and south. This it can communicate to any piece of iron, so that a needle well rubbed in a particular manner by a loadstone, and then balanced upon its centre, so as to turn round freely, will always point to the north. With an instrument called a mariner's compass, made of one of these needles, and a card marked with all the points, North, South, East, West, and the divisions between these, a ship may be steered to any part of the globe.

Ch. It is a very easy matter, then.

Fa. Not quite so easy, neither. In a long voyage, cross or contrary winds blow a ship out of her direct course, so that, without nice calculations, both of the straight track she has gone, and all the deviations from it, the sailors would not know where they were, nor to what point to steer. It is also frequently necessary to take observations, as they call it; that is, to observe with an instrument where the sun's place in the sky is at noon, by which they can determine the *latitude* they are in. Other observations are necessary to determine their *longitude*. What these mean, I can show you upon the globe. It is enough now to say that, by means of both together, they can tell the exact spot they are on at any time; and then, by consulting their map, and setting their compass, they can steer right to the place they want. But all this requires a very exact knowledge of astronomy, the use of the globes, mathematics, and arithmetic, which you may suppose is not to be acquired without much study. A great number of curious instruments have been invented to assist in these operations; so that there is scarcely any matter in which so much art and science have been employed as in navigation; and none but a very learned and civilized nation can excel in it.

Ch. But how is Tom Hardy to do; for I am

pretty sure he does not understand any of these things ?

Fa. He must learn them, if he mean to come to anything in his profession. He may, indeed, head a press-gang, or command a boat's crew, without them ; but he will never be fit to take charge of a man-of-war, or even a merchant ship.

Ch. However, he need not learn Latin and Greek.

Fa. I cannot say, indeed, that a sailor has occasion for those languages ; but a knowledge of Latin makes it much easier to acquire all modern languages ; and I hope you do not think them unnecessary to him.

Ch. I did not know they were of much importance.

Fa. No ! Do you think that one who may probably visit most countries in Europe, and their foreign settlements, should be able to converse in no other language than his own ? If the knowledge of languages be not useful to *him*, I know not to whom it is so. He can hardly do at all, without knowing some ; and the more, the better.

Ch. Poor Tom ! then I doubt he has not chosen so well as he thinks.

Fa. I doubt so, too.

Here ended the conversation. They soon after reached home, and Charles did not forget to desire his father to show him on the globe what longitude and latitude meant.

THINGS BY THEIR RIGHT NAMES.

Charles. PAPA, you grow very lazy. Last winter you used to tell us stories, and now you never tell us any ; and we are all got round the fire, quite ready to hear you. Pray, dear papa, let us have a very pretty one.

Father. With all my heart—What shall it be ?

C. A bloody murder, papa !

F. A bloody murder ! Well, then—Once upon a time, some men, dressed all alike—

C. With black crapes over their faces.

F. No ; they had steel caps on :—having crossed a dark heath, wound cautiously along the skirts of a deep forest—

C. They were ill-looking fellows, I dare say.

F. I cannot say so ; on the contrary, they were as tall, personable men as most one shall see ;—leaving on their right hand an old ruined tower on the hill—

C. At midnight, just as the clock struck twelve; was it not, papa ?

F. No, really; it was on a fine balmy summer's morning ;—they moved forward, one behind another—

C. As still as death, creeping along under the hedges.

F. On the contrary—they walked remarkably upright ; and, so far from endeavouring to be hushed and still, they made a loud noise as they came along, with several sorts of instruments.

C. But, papa, they would be found out immediately.

F. They did not seem to wish to conceal themselves : on the contrary, they gloried in what they were about.—They moved forward, I say, to a large plain, where stood a neat pretty village, which they set on fire—

C. Set a village on fire, wicked wretches !

F. And while it was burning, they murdered—twenty thousand men !

C. O fie ! papa ! You don't intend I should believe this ; I thought all along you were making up a tale, as you often do ; but you shall not catch me this time. What ! they lay still, I suppose, and let these fellows cut their throats !

F. No, truly, they resisted as long as they could.

C. How should these men kill twenty thousand people, pray ?

F. Why not ? the *murderers* were thirty thousand.

C. O, now I have found you out ! you mean a battle.

F. Indeed, I do. I do not know any *murders* half so bloody.

Indur espied a large venomous serpent advancing to make the poor defenceless creature his prey. He immediately descended from his post, and taking the little monkey in his arms, ran with it to the tree.

P. 113.

NINTH EVENING.

THE TRANSMIGRATIONS OF INDUR.

AT the time when Fairies and Genii possessed the powers which they have now lost, there lived in the country of the Brachmans a man named Indur, who was distinguished, not only for that gentleness of disposition and humanity towards all living creatures, which are so much cultivated among those people, but for an insatiable curiosity respecting the nature and way of life of all animals. In pursuit of knowledge of this kind, he would frequently spend the night among lonely rocks, or in the midst of thick forests; and there, under shelter of a hanging cliff, or mounted upon a high tree, he would watch the motions and actions of all the animals that seek their prey in the night; and, remaining in the same spot till the break of day, he would observe this tribe of creatures retiring to their dens, and all others coming forth to enjoy the beams of the rising sun. On these occasions, if he saw any opportunity of exercising his benevolence towards animals in distress, he never failed to make use of it; and many times rescued the small bird from the pitiless hawk, and the lamb or kid from the gripe of the wolf and lynx. One day, as he was sitting on a tree in the forest, a little frolicksome monkey, in taking a great leap from one bough to another, chanced to miss its hold, and fell from a great height to the ground. As it lay there, unable to move, Indur espied a large venomous serpent advancing to make the poor defenceless creature his prey. He immediately descended from his post, and taking the little monkey in his arms, ran with it to the tree, and gently placed it upon a bough. In the mean time, the enraged serpent pursuing him, overtook him before he could mount the

I

tree, and bit him in the leg. Presently the limb began to swell, and the effects of the venom became visible over Indur's whole frame. He grew faint, sick, and pale; and, sinking on the ground, was sensible that his last moments were fast approaching. As thus he lay, he was surprised to hear a human voice from the tree; and looking up, he beheld on the bough where he had placed the monkey, a beautiful woman, who thus addressed him: "Indur, I am truly grieved, that thy kindness to me should have been the cause of thy destruction. Know, that in the form of the poor monkey, it was the potent fairy Perezinda, to whom thou gavest succour. Obliged to pass a certain number of days every year under the shape of an animal, I had chosen this form; and though not mortal, I should have suffered extreme agonies from the bite of the serpent, hadst thou not so humanely assisted me. It is not in my power to prevent the fatal effect of the poison; but I am able to grant thee any wish thou shalt form respecting the future state of existence to which thou art now hastening. Speak, then, before it be too late, and let me show my gratitude."—"Great Perezinda!" replied Indur, "since you deign so bounteously to return my service, this is the request that I make: In all my transmigrations may I retain a rational soul, with the memory of the adventures I have gone through; and when death sets me free from one body, may I instantly animate another in the prime of its powers and faculties, without passing through the helpless state of infancy."—"It is granted," answered the Fairy; and immediately breaking a small branch from the tree, and breathing on it, she threw it down to Indur, and bade him hold it fast in his hand. He did so, and presently expired.

Instantly he found himself in a green valley, by the side of a clear stream, grazing amidst a herd of antelopes. He admired his elegant shape, sleek, spotted skin, and polished spiral horns; and drank with delight of the cool rivulet, cropped the juicy herb, and sported

with his companions. Soon an alarm was given of the
approach of an enemy; and they all set off with the
swiftness of the wind to the neighbouring immense
plains, where they were presently out of the reach of
injury. Indur was highly delighted with the case and
rapidity of his motions; and snuffing the keen air of
the desert, bounded away, scarcely deigning to touch
the ground with his feet. This way of life went on
very pleasantly for some time, till at length the herd
was one morning alarmed with noises of trumpets,
drums, and loud shouts, on every side. They started,
and ran first to the right, then to the left, but were
continually driven back by the surrounding crowd,
which now appeared to be a whole army of hunters,
with the king of the country and all his nobles, assembled on a solemn chase, after the manner of the
eastern people. And now the circle began to close,
and numbers of affrighted animals of various kinds
thronged together in the centre, keeping as far as possible from the dangers that approached them from all
quarters. The huntsmen had now come near enough
to reach their game with their arrows; and the prince
and his lords shot at them as they passed and repassed,
killing and wounding great numbers. Indur and his
surviving companions, seeing no other means of escape,
resolved to make a bold push towards that part of the
ring which was the most weakly guarded; and though
many perished in the attempt, yet a few, leaping over
the heads of the people, got clear away, and Indur
was among the number. But whilst he was scouring
over the plain, rejoicing in his good fortune and conduct, an enemy swifter than himself overtook him.
This was a falcon, who, let loose by one of the huntsmen, dashed like lightning after the fugitives; and
alighting upon the head of Indur, began to tear his
eyes with his beak, and flap his wings over his face.
Indur, terrified and blinded, knew not which way he
went; and, instead of proceeding straight forwards,
turned round, and came again towards the hunters.

One of these, riding full speed, with a javelin in his
hand, came up to him, and ran the weapon into his
side. He fell down, and with repeated wounds was
soon despatched.

When the struggle of death was over, Indur was
equally surprised and pleased on finding himself soaring high in the air, as one of a flight of Wild Geese,
in their annual migration to breed in the arctic regions.
With vast delight he sprang forward, on easy wing,
through the immense fields of air, and surveyed beneath him extensive tracts of earth perpetually varying with plains, mountains, rivers, lakes, and woods.
At the approach of night, the flock alighted on the
ground, and fed on the green corn or grass, and at
daybreak they were again on the wing, arranged in a
regular wedge-like body, with an experienced leader at
their head. Thus, for many days, they continued their
journey, passing over countries inhabited by various
nations, till at length they arrived in the remotest part
of Lapland, and settled in a wide, marshy lake, filled
with numerous reedy islands, and surrounded on all
sides with dark forests of pine and birch. Here, in
perfect security from man and all hurtful animals, they
followed the great business of breeding, and providing
for their young, living plentifully upon the insects and
aquatic reptiles that abounded in this sheltered spot.
Indur with great pleasure exercised his various powers
of swimming, diving, and flying; sailing around the
islands, penetrating into every creek and bay, and
visiting the deepest recesses of the woods. He surveyed with astonishment the sun, instead of rising and
setting, making a complete circle in the heavens, and
cheering the earth with a perpetual day. Here he
met with innumerable tribes of kindred birds, varying
in size, plumage, and voice, but all passing their time
in a similar manner, and furnished with the same
powers for providing food and a safe retreat for themselves and their young. The whole lake was covered
with parties fishing or sporting, and resounded with

their loud cries; while the islands were filled with their nests, and new broods of young were continually coming forth and launching upon the surface of the waters. One day, Indur's curiosity having led him, at a distance from his companions, to the woody border of the lake, he was near paying dearly for his heedlessness; for a fox, that lay in wait among the bushes, sprang upon him, and it was with the utmost difficulty that by a strong exertion he broke from his hold, not without the loss of some feathers.

Summer now drawing to an end, the vast congregation of waterfowl began to break up; and large bodies of them daily took their way southwards, to pass the winter in climates where the waters are never so frozen as to become uninhabitable by the feathered race. The wild geese, to whom Indur belonged, proceeded with their young ones, by long daily journeys, across Sweden, the Baltic Sea, Poland, and Turkey, to Lesser Asia, and finished their journey at the celebrated plains on the banks of the Cayster, a noted resort for their species ever since the age of Homer, who, in some very beautiful verses, has described the manners and actions of the various tribes of aquatic birds in that favourite spot.* Here they soon recruited from the fatigue of their march, and enjoyed themselves in the delicious climate till winter. This season, though here extremely mild, yet causing the means of sustenance to be somewhat scarce, they were obliged to make foraging excursions to the cultivated lands in the neighbourhood. Having committed great depredations upon a fine field of young wheat, the owner spread a net on the ground, in which Indur, with several of his

---

* Not less their number than th' embodied cranes
Or milk-white swans on Asia's wat'ry plains,
That o'er the windings of the Cayster's springs
Stretch their long necks, and clap their rustling wings,
Now tow'r aloft, and course in airy rounds;
Now light with noise: with noise the field resounds.
Pope's Homer.

companions, had the misfortune to be caught. No mercy was shown them, but as they were taken out one by one, their necks were all broken.

Indur was not immediately sensible of the next change he underwent, which was into a Dormouse, fast asleep in a hole at the foot of a bush. As it was in a country where the winter was rather severe, he did not awake for some weeks; when a thaw having taken place, and the sun beginning to warm the earth, he unrolled himself one day, stretched, opened his eyes, and not being able to make out where he was, he aroused a female companion whom he found by his side. When she was sufficiently awakened, and they both began to feel hungry, she led the way to a magazine of nuts and acorns, where they made a comfortable meal, and soon fell asleep again. This nap having lasted a few days, they awoke a second time, and having eaten, they ventured to crawl to the mouth of their hole, where, pulling away some withered grass and leaves, they peeped out into the open air. After taking a turn or two in the sun, they grew chill, and went down again, stopping up the entrance after them. The cold weather returning, they took another long nap, till at length spring having fairly set in, they aroused in earnest, and began to make daily excursions abroad. Their winter stock of provisions being now exhausted, they were for some time reduced to great straits, and obliged to dig for roots and pig-nuts. Their fare was mended as the season advanced, and they made a nest near the bottom of a tree, where they brought up a young family. They never ranged far from home, nor ascended the higher branches of the tree, and passed great part of their time in sleep, even during the midst of summer. When autumn came, they were busily employed in collecting the nuts, acorns, and other dry fruits that fell from the trees, and laying them up in their storehouses under-ground. One day, as Indur was closely engaged in this occupation, at some distance from his dwelling, he was seized

by a wild cat, who, after tormenting him for a time,
gave him a gripe, and put him out of his pain.

From one of the smallest and most defenceless of
animals, Indur found himself instantly changed into
a majestic Elephant, in a lofty forest in the isle of
Ceylon. Elated with this wonderful advancement in
the scale of creation, he stalked along with conscious
dignity, and surveyed with pleasing wonder his own
form and the forms of his companions, together with
the rich scenery of the ever-verdant woods, which perfumed the air with their spicy odour, and lifted their
tall heads to the clouds. Here, fearing no injury, and
not desirous to do any, the gigantic herd roamed at
large, feeding on the green branches, which they tore
down with their trunks, bathing in deep rivers during
the heat of the day, and reposing in the depths of the
forests, reclined against the massy trunks of trees by
night. It was long before Indur met with any adventure that could lead him to doubt his security. But,
one day, having penetrated into a close, entangled
thicket, he espied, lurking under the thick covert, a
grim tiger, whose eyes flashed rage and fury. Though
the tiger was one of the largest of his species, yet his
bulk was trifling compared to that of an elephant, a
single foot of which seemed sufficient to crush him;
yet the fierceness and cruelty of his looks, his angry
growl, and grinning teeth, struck some terror into
Indur. There was little time, however, for reflection;
for when Indur had advanced a single step, the tiger,
setting up a roar, sprang to meet him, attempting to
seize his lifted trunk. Indur was dexterous enough to
receive him upon one of his tusks, and exerting all his
strength, threw the tiger to a great distance. He was
somewhat stunned by the fall, but recovering, renewed
the assault with redoubled fury. Indur again, and a
third time, threw him off; after which the tiger, turning about, bounded away into the midst of the thicket.
Indur drew back, and rejoined his companions, with
some abatement in the confidence he had placed in his

size and strength, which had not prevented him from
undergoing so dangerous an attack.

Soon after, he joined the rest of the herd in an expedition beyond the bounds of the forest, to make depredations on some fields of maize.   They committed
great havoc, devouring part, but tearing up and trampling down much more ; when the inhabitants, taking
the alarm, assembled in great numbers, and with fierce
shouts and flaming brands drove them back to the
woods.   Not contented with this, they were resolved
to make them pay for the mischief they had done, by
taking some prisoners.   For this purpose they enclosed
a large space among the trees, with strong posts and
stakes, bringing it to a narrower and narrower compass, and ending at last in a passage capable of admitting only one elephant at a time.   This was divided by
strong cross-bars, which would lift up and down, into
several apartments.   They then sent out some tame
female elephants bred to the business, who approaching the herd of wild ones, inveigled the males to follow
them towards the enclosures.   Indur was among the
first who were decoyed by their artifices ; and with
some others following heedlessly, he got into the nar-
rowest part of the enclosure, opposite to the passage.
Here they stood awhile, doubting whether they should
go further.   But the females leading the way, and
uttering their cry of invitation, they ventured at
length to follow.   When a sufficient number was in
the passage, the bars were let down by men placed for
that purpose, and the elephants were fairly caught in
a trap.   As soon as they were sensible of their situation, they fell into a fit of rage, and with all their
efforts endeavoured to break through.   But the hunters
throwing nooses over them, bound them fast with
strong ropes and chains to the posts on each side, and
thus kept them without food or sleep for three days ;
when, being exhausted with hunger and fatigue, they
gave signs of sufficient tameness.   They were now let
out one by one, and were bound each of them to two

large tame elephants, with riders on their backs, and
thus without resistance were led away close prisoners.
They were then put into separate stables, and, by
proper discipline, were presently rendered quite tame
and gentle.

Not long after, Indur, with five more, was sent over
from Ceylon to the continent of India, and sold to one
of the princes of the country. He was now trained to
all the services elephants are there employed in, which
were to carry persons on his back in a sort of sedan or
litter, to draw cannon, ships, and other great weights,
to kneel and rise at command, make obeisance to his
lord, and perform all the motions and attitudes he was
ordered. Thus he lived a long time, well fed and
caressed, clothed in costly trappings on days of ceremony, and contributing to the pomp of eastern royalty.
At length a war broke out, and Indur came to be
employed in a different scene. After proper training,
he was marched, with a number of his fellows, into the
field, bearing on his back a small wooden tower, in
which were placed some soldiers with a small field-
piece. They soon came in sight of the enemy, and
both sides were drawn up for battle. Indur and the
rest were urged forward by their leaders, wondering
at the same time at the scene in which they were
engaged, so contrary to their nature and manners.
Presently all was involved in smoke and fire. The elephants advancing, soon put to flight those who were
drawn up before them; but their career was stopped
by a battery of cannon, which played furiously against
them. Their vast bodies offered a fair mark to the
ball, which presently struck down some, and wounded
others. Indur received a shot on one of his tusks,
which broke it, and put him to such pain and affright,
that turning about, he ran with all speed over the
plain; and falling in with a body of their own infantry,
he burst through, trampling down whole ranks, and
filling them with terror and confusion. His leader
having now lost all command over him, and finding

him hurtful only to his own party, applied the sharp
instrument he carried to the nape of his neck, and
driving it in with all his force, pierced his spinal mar-
row, so that he fell lifeless to the ground.

In the next stage of his existence, Indur, to his
great surprise, found even the vast bulk of the elephant prodigiously exceeded; for he was now a Whale
of the largest species, rolling in the midst of the arctic
seas. As he darted along, the lash of his tail made
whirlpools in the mighty deep. When he opened his
immense jaws, he drew in a flood of brine, which, on
rising to the surface, he spouted out again in a rushing fountain, that rose high in the air with the noise
of a mighty cataract. All the other inhabitants of
the ocean seemed as nothing to him. He swallowed,
almost without knowing it, whole shoals of the smaller
kinds; and the larger swiftly turned aside at his
approach. "Now," he cried to himself, "whatever
other evils may await me, I am certainly secure from
the molestations of other animals; for what is the
creature that can dare to cope with me, or measure
his strength with mine?" Having said this, he saw
swimming near him a fish not a quarter of his length,
armed with a dreadful row of teeth. This was a
grampus, which, directly flying upon Indur, fastened
on him, and made his great teeth meet in his flesh.
Indur roared with pain, and lashed the sea, till it was
all in a foam; but could neither reach nor shake off
his cruel foe. He rolled over and over, rose and
sank, and exerted all his boasted strength; but to no
purpose. At length the grampus quitted his hold,
and left him not a little mortified with the adventure.
This was however forgotten, and Indur received pleasure from his new situation, as he roamed through the
boundless fields of ocean, now diving to its very bottom, now shooting swiftly to its surface, and sporting
with his companions in unwieldy gambols. Having
chosen a mate, he took his course with her southwards, and in due time brought up two young ones, of

A man presently, planting a ladder, ascended with a beehive, and swept them in.   P. 123.

whom he was extremely fond. The summer season having arrived, he more frequently than usual rose to the surface, and basking in the sunbeams, floated unmoved with a large part of his huge body above the waves. As he was thus one day enjoying a profound sleep, he was awakened by a sharp instrument penetrating deep into his back. Instantly he sprang away with the swiftness of lightning, and, feeling the weapon still sticking, he dived into the recesses of the deep, and stayed there till want of air obliged him to ascend to the surface. Here another harpoon was plunged into him, the smart of which again made him fly from his unseen foes; but, after a shorter course, he was again compelled to rise, much weakened by the loss of blood, which, gushing in a torrent, tinged the waters as he passed. Another wound was inflicted, which soon brought him almost lifeless to the surface; and the line fastened to the first harpoon being now pulled in, this enormous creature was brought, an unresisting prey, to the side of a ship, where he was soon quite despatched, and then cut to pieces.

The soul of this huge carcass had next a much narrower lodging, for Indur was changed into a Bee, which, with a great multitude of its young companions, was on flight in search of a new settlement, their parents having driven them out of the hive, which was unable to contain them all. After a rambling excursion, the queen, by whom all their motions were directed, settled on the branch of a lofty tree. They all immediately clustered around her, and soon formed a large black bunch, depending from the bough. A man presently planted a ladder, ascended with a beehive, and swept them in. After they were quietly settled in their new habitation, they were placed on a stand in the garden along with some other colonies, and left to begin their labours. Every fine morning, as soon as the sun was up, the greater part of them sallied forth, and roamed over the garden and the neighbouring fields in search of fresh and fragrant flowers. They first collected a quantity of gluey matter, with which they lined all the inside of their house. Then they brought wax, and began to make their cells, building them with the utmost regularity, though it was their first attempt, and they had no teacher. As fast as they were built, some were filled with liquid honey gathered from the nectaries of flowers; and, as they filled the cells, they sealed them up with a thin covering of wax. In other cells, the queen bee deposited her eggs, which were to supply a new progeny for the ensuing year. Nothing could be a more pleasing sight, than to behold on a sunshiny day the insects continually going forth to their labour, while others were as constantly arriving at the mouth of the hole, either with yellow balls of wax under their thighs, or full of the honey which they had drawn in with their trunks, for the purpose of spouting it out into the cells of the honeycomb. Indur felt much delight in this useful and active way of life, and was always one of the first abroad at the dawn, and latest home in the evening. On rainy and foggy days they stayed at home, and employed themselves in finishing their cells, and all the necessary work within doors; and Indur, though endued with human reason, could not but admire the readiness with which he and the rest formed the most regular plans of work, all corresponding in design and execution, guided by instinct alone.

The end of autumn now approaching, the bees had filled their combs with honey; and nothing more being to be got abroad, they stayed within doors, passing most of their time in sleep. They ate a little of their store, but with great frugality; and all their meals were made in public, none daring to make free with the common stock by himself. The owner of the hives now came and took them one by one into his hands, that he might judge by the weight whether they were full of honey. That in which Indur was, proved to be one of the heaviest; and it was, therefore, resolved to take the contents. For this purpose, one cold night, when the bees were all fast asleep, the hive was placed over a hole in the ground, in which had been put brimstone matches set on fire. The fumes arose into the hive, and soon suffocated great part of the bees, and stupified the rest, so that they all fell from the combs. Indur was amongst the dead.

He soon revived, in the form of a young Rabbit, in a spacious warren. This was like a populous town; being everywhere hollowed by burrows running deep under-ground, and each inhabited by one or more families. In the evening, the warren was covered with a vast number of rabbits, old and young, some feeding, others frisking about, and pursuing one another in wanton sport. At the least alarm, they all hurried into the holes nearest them, and were in an instant safe from enemies, who either could not follow them at all, or, if they did, were foiled in the chase by the numerous ways and turnings in the earth, communicating with each other, so as to afford easy means of escape. Indur delighted much in this secure and social life; and, taking a mate, was soon the father of a numerous offspring. Several of the little ones, however, not being sufficiently careful, fell a prey either to hawks and crows continually hovering over the warren, or to cats, foxes, and other wild quadrupeds, who employed every art to catch them at a distance from their holes. Indur himself ran several hazards. He was once very near being caught by a little dog, trained for the purpose, who kept playing around for a considerable time, not seeming to attend to the rabbits, till, having got near, he all at once darted into the midst of them. Another time he received some shot from a sportsman who lay on the watch behind a hedge adjoining the warren.

The number of rabbits here was so great, that a hard winter coming on, which killed most of the vegetables, or buried them deep under the snow, they were reduced to great straits, and many were famished to death. Some turnips and hay, however, which were laid for them, preserved the greater part. The approach of spring renewed their sport and pleasure; and Indur was made the father of another family. One night, however, was fatal to them all. As they were sleeping, they were alarmed by the attack of a ferret; and running with great speed to the mouth of their burrow to escape it, they were all caught in nets placed over their holes. Indur, with the rest, was despatched by a blow on the back of the neck, and his body was sent to the nearest market-town.

His next change was into a young Mastiff, brought up in a farm-yard. Having nearly acquired his full size, he was sent as a present to a gentleman in the neighbourhood, who wanted a faithful guard for his house and grounds. Indur presently attached himself to his master and all his family, and showed every mark of a noble and generous nature. Though fierce as a lion, whenever he thought the persons or properties of his friends invaded, he was gentle as a lamb at other times, and would patiently suffer any sort of freedoms from those he loved. He permitted the children of the house to lug him about, ride on his back, and use him as roughly as their little hands were capable of; never, even when hurt, showing any displeasure, further than by a low growl. He was extremely indulgent to all the other animals of his species in the yard; and when abroad, would treat the impertinent barking of little dogs with silent contempt. Once, indeed, being provoked beyond bearing, not only by the noise, but by the snaps of a malicious whelp, he suddenly seized him in his open mouth; but when the bystanders thought that the poor cur was going instantly to be devoured, they were equally diverted and pleased at seeing Indur go to the side of a muddy ditch, and drop his antagonist unhurt into the middle of it.

He seized one of the villains by the throat, brought him to the
ground, and presently disabled him.   P. 127.

Frequently, however, he had more serious conflicts to sustain. He was accustomed to attend the servant on market-days to the neighbouring town, when it was his office to guard the provision-cart, while the man was making his purchases in the shops. On these occasions, the boldest dogs in the street would sometimes make an onset in a body; and, while some of them were engaging Indur, others would be mounting the cart, and pulling down the meat-baskets. Indur had much ado to defend himself and the baggage too; however, he never failed to make some of the assailants pay dearly for their impudence; and by his loud barking, he summoned his human fellow-servant to his assistance, in time to prevent their depredations.

At length his courage was exerted on the most important service to which it could be applied. His master returning home late one evening, was attacked near his own house by three armed ruffians. Indur heard his voice calling for help, and instantly flew to his relief. He seized one of the villains by the throat, brought him to the ground, and presently disabled him. The master, in the mean time, was keeping off the other two with a large stick, but had received several wounds with a cutlass; and one of the men had presented a pistol, and was just on the point of firing. At this moment Indur, leaving his vanquished foe on the ground, rushed forward, and, seizing the man's arm, made him drop the pistol. The master took it up, on which the other robber fled. He now advanced to him with whom Indur was engaged, and fired the pistol at him. The ball broke the man's arm, and thence entered the body of Indur, and mortally wounded him. He fell, but had the satisfaction of seeing his master remain lord of the field; and the servants now coming up, made prisoners of the two wounded robbers. The master threw himself by the side of Indur, and expressed the warmest concern at the accident which had made him the cause of the death of

the faithful animal that had preserved his life.   Indur
died, licking his hand.

So generous a nature was now no longer to be connected with a brute form.   Indur, awaking as it were
from a trance, found himself again in the happy region
he had formerly inhabited, and recommenced the innocent life of a Brachman.   He cherished the memory
of his transmigrations, and handed them down to posterity, in a relation from which the present account
has been extracted, for the amusement of my young
readers.

TENTH EVENING.

THE SWALLOW AND THE TORTOISE.

A TORTOISE in a garden's bound,
An ancient inmate of the place,
Had left his winter-quarters, under-ground,
And, with a sober pace,
Was crawling o'er a sunny bed,
And thrusting from his shell his pretty, toad-like
    head.
    Just come from sea, a Swallow,
As to and fro he nimbly flew,
Beat our old racer hollow:
At length he stopp'd, direct in view,
And said, "Acquaintance, brisk and gay,
How have you fared this many a day?"
    "Thank you!" replied the close housekeeper,
"Since you and I last autumn parted,
I've been a precious sleeper,
And never stirr'd nor started,
But in my hole I lay as snug
As fleas within a rug;
Nor did I put my head abroad
Till all the snow and ice were thawed."

" But I," rejoined the bird,
" Who love cold weather just as well as you,
Soon as the warning blasts I heard,
Away I flew,
And, mounting in the wind,
Left gloomy winter far behind.
Directed by the mid-day sun,
O'er sea and land my vent'rous course I steer'd;
Nor was my distant journey done
Till Afric's verdant coast appear'd.
There, all the season long,
I chased gay butterflies and gnats,
And gave my negro friends a morning song,
And housed at night among the bats.
Then, at the call of spring,
I northward turn'd my wing,
And here, again, her joyous message bring."
   " Lord, what a deal of needless ranging,"
Return'd the reptile grave;
" For ever hurrying, bustling, changing,
As though it were your life to save !
Why need you visit foreign nations ?
Rather, like me, and some of your relations,
Take out a pleasant, half-year's nap,
Secure from trouble and mishap."
   " A pleasant nap, indeed!" replied the Swallow;
" When I can neither see nor fly,
The bright example I may follow;
Till then, in truth, not I !
I measure time by its employment,
And only value life for life's enjoyment.
As well be buried all at once,
As doze out half one's days, like your, you stupid
    dunce !"

THE GRASS TRIBE.
Tutor— George—Harry.

Harry. PRAY what is that growing on the other side of the hedge ?

George. Why it is corn—don't you see it is in ear ?

H. Yes—but it seems too short for corn; and the corn we just now passed is not in ear by a great deal.

G. Then I don't know what it is. Pray, sir, will you tell us ?

Tutor. I don't wonder you were puzzled about it, It is a sort of grass sown for hay, and is called *rye-grass.*

H. But how happens it that it is so very like corn ?

T. There is no great wonder in that, for all corn is really a kind of grass ; and, on the other hand, if you were a Lilliputian, every species of grass would appear to you amazingly large corn.

G. Then there is no difference between corn and grass, but the size ?

T. None at all.

H. But we eat corn, and grass is not good to eat.

T. It is only the seeds of corn that we eat. We leave the stalks and leaves for cows and horses. Now we might eat the seeds of grass, if they were big enough to be worth gathering ; and some particular kinds are in fact eaten in certain countries.

H. But are wheat and barley really grass ?

T. Yes—they are a species of that great family of plants, which botanists call *grasses ;* and I will take this opportunity of telling you something about them. Go, George, and pull us up a root of that rye-grass. Harry and I will sit down on this stile till you come to us.

H. Here is grass enough all around us.

T. Well, then— pull up a few roots that you see in ear.

G. Here is my grass.

H. And here is mine.

T. Well, spread them all in a handkerchief before us. Now look at the roots of them all. What do you call them?

G. I think they are what you have told us are *fibrous* roots.

T. Right—they consist of a bundle of strings. Then look at their stalks; you will find them jointed and hollow, like the straw of corn.

H. So they are.

T. The leaves, you see, of all the kinds are very long and narrow, tapering to a point at their ends. Those of corn, you know, are the same.

H. Yes; they are so like grass at first, that I can never tell the difference.

T. Next observe the ears, or heads. Some of these, you see, are thick and close, exactly like those of wheat or barley; others are more loose and open, like oats. The first are generally called *spikes;* the second, *panicles.* If you examine them closely, you will find that they all consist of a number of distinct husky bodies, which are properly the flowers; each of which is succeeded by a single seed. I dare say you have picked ears of wheat.

H. O yes—I am very fond of them.

T. Well, then; you found that the grains all lay single, contained in a scaly husk, making a part of the ear, or head. Before the seed was formed, there was a flower in its place. I do not mean a gay, fine-coloured flower, but a few scales with threads coming out among them, each crowned with a white tip. And soon after the ears of corn appear, you will find their flowers open, and these white tips coming out of them. This is the structure of the flowers and flowering heads of every one of the grass tribe.

G. But what are the *beards* of corn?

T. The beards are bristles, or points, running out from the ends of the husks. They are properly called *awns.* Most of the grass tribe have something of these, but they are much longer in some kinds than in others. In barley, you know, they are very long, and give the whole field a sort of downy or silky appearance, especially when waved by the wind.

H. Are there the same kinds of corn and grass in all countries?

T. No. With respect to corn, that is in all countries the product of cultivation; and different sorts are found best to suit different climates. Thus in the northern parts of the temperate zone, oats and rye are chiefly grown. In the middle and southern, barley and wheat. Wheat is universally the species preferred for bread-corn; but there are various kinds of it, differing from each other in size of grain, firmness, colour, and other qualities.

H. Does not the best wheat of all grow in England?

T. By no means. Wheat is better suited to the warmer climates; and it is only by great attention, and upon particular soils, that it is made to succeed well here. On the other hand, the torrid zone is too hot for wheat and our other grains; and they chiefly cultivate rice there and Indian corn, or maize.

G. I have seen heads of Indian corn, as thick as my wrist, but they do not look at all like our corn.

T. Yes—the seeds all grow single, in a sort of chaffy head; and the stalk and leaves resemble those of the grass tribe, but of a gigantic size. But there are other plants of this family, which perhaps you have not thought of.

G. What are they?

T. Canes and reeds—from the sugar-canes and bamboo of the tropics, to the common reed of our ditches and marshes, of which you make arrows. All these have the general character of the grasses.

H. I know that reeds have very fine, feathery heads, like the tops of the grass.

T. They have so. And the stalks are composed of

many joints; as are also those of the sugar-cane, and the bamboo, of which fishing-rods and walking-sticks are often made. Some of these are very tall plants; but the seeds of them are small in proportion, and not useful for food. But there is yet another kind of grass-like plants common among us.

G. What is that?

T. Have you not observed in the marshes, and on the sides of ditches, a coarse, broader-leaved sort of grass, with large dark-coloured spikes? This is *sedge*, in Latin *carex;* and there are many sorts of it.

H. What is that good for?

T. It is eaten by cattle, both fresh and dry; but is inferior in quality to good grass.

G. What is it that makes one kind of grass better than another?

T. There are various properties which give value to grasses. Some spread more than others, resist frost and drought better; yield a greater crop of leaves, and are therefore better for pasturage and hay. The juices of some are more nourishing and sweet than those of others. In general, however, different grasses are suited to different soils; and by improving soils, the quality of the grass is improved.

G. Does grass grow in all countries?

T. Yes—the green turf, which naturally covers fertile soils of all countries, is composed chiefly of grasses of various kinds. They form, therefore, the verdant carpet extended over the earth; and, humble as they are, they contribute more to beauty and utility, than any other part of the vegetable creation.

H. What—more than trees?

T. Yes, certainly. A land entirely covered with trees would be gloomy, unwholesome, and scarcely inhabitable; whereas the meadow, the down, and the corn-field, afford the most agreeable prospects to the eye, and furnish every necessary, and many of the luxuries of life. Give us corn and grass, and what shall we want for food?

H. Let me see—what should we have? There are bread, and flour for puddings.

G. Ay, and milk; for you know cows live on grass and hay—so there are cheese and butter, and all things that are made of milk.

T. And are there not all kinds of meat too, and poultry? And then for drink, there are beer and ale, which are made from barley. For all these we are chiefly indebted to the grasses.

G. Then I am sure we are very much obliged to the grasses.

T. Well—let us now walk homewards. Some time hence, you shall make a collection of all the kinds of grasses, and learn to know them from each other.

A TEA LECTURE.
Tutor—Pupil.

Tut. COME—the tea is ready. Lay by your book, and let us talk a little—You have assisted in tea-making a great many times, and yet I dare say you never considered what sort of an operation it was.

Pup. An operation of cookery—is it not?

Tut. You may call it so; but it is properly an operation of *chemistry.*

Pup. Of chemistry! I thought that had been a very deep sort of a business.

Tut. O—there are many things in common life that belong to the deepest of sciences. Making tea is the chemical operation called *infusion,* which is, when a hot liquor is poured upon a substance, in order to extract something from it. The water, you see, extracts from the tea-leaves their colour, taste, and flavour.

Pup. Would not cold water do the same?

Tut. It would, but more slowly. Heat assists almost all liquors in their power of extracting the virtues of herbs and other substances. Thus good house-wives formerly used to boil their tea, in order to get all the goodness from it as completely as possible. The greater heat and agitation of boiling make it act more powerfully. The liquor in which a substance has been boiled is called a *decoction* of that substance.

Pup. Then we had a decoction of mutton at dinner to-day ?

Tut. We had;—broth is a decoction, and so are gruel and barley-water. But when anything is put to steep in a cold liquor, it is called *maceration*. The ingredients of which ink is made are macerated. In all these cases, you see, the whole substance does not mix with the liquor, but only part of it. The reason is, that part of it is *soluble* in the liquor, and part not.

Pup. What is the meaning of that ?

Tut. *Solution* is when a solid put into a fluid entirely disappears in it, leaving the liquor clear. Thus, when I throw this lump of sugar into my tea, you see it gradually wastes away till it is all gone, and then I can taste it in every single drop of my tea ; but the tea is as clear as before.

Pup. Salt would do the same.

Tut. It would. But if I were to throw in a lump of chalk, it would lie undissolved at the bottom.

Pup. But it would make the water white.

Tut. True, while it was stirred ; and then it would be a *diffusion*. But while the chalk was thus mixed with the liquor, the latter would lose its transparency, and not recover it again, till, by standing, the chalk had all subsided, and left the liquor as it was before.

Pup. How is the cream mixed with the tea ?

Tut. Why, that is only *diffused*, for it takes away the transparency of the tea. But the particles of cream being finer and lighter than those of chalk, it remains longer united with the liquor. However, in time, the cream would separate too, and rise to the top, leaving the tea clear. Now, suppose you had a mixture of sugar, salt, chalk, and tea-leaves, and were to throw it into water, either hot or cold ;—what would be the effect ?

Pup. The sugar and salt would be dissolved and disappear. The tea-leaves would yield their colour and taste. The chalk—I do not know what would become of that.

Tut. Why, if the mixture were stirred, the chalk would be diffused through it, and make it *turbid*, or muddy; but, on standing, it would leave it unchanged.

Pup. Then there would remain at bottom the chalk and tea-leaves.

Tut. Yes. The clear liquor would contain in *solution* salt, sugar, and those particles of the tea, in which its colour and taste consisted: the remainder of the tea and the chalk would lie undissolved.

Pup. Then I suppose tea-leaves, after the tea is made, are lighter than at first.

Tut. Undoubtedly. If taken out and dried, they would be found to have lost part of their weight, and the water would have gained it. Sometimes, however, it is an extremely small portion of a substance which is soluble, but it is that in which its most remarkable qualities reside. Thus, a small piece of spice will communicate a strong flavour to a large quantity of liquid, with very little loss of weight.

Pup. Will all liquors dissolve the same things?

Tut. By no means. Many dissolve in water, that will not in spirit of wine; and the contrary. And upon this difference many curious matters in the arts are founded. Thus spirit varnish is made of a solution of various gums or resins in spirits that will not dissolve in water. Therefore, when it has been laid over any surface with a brush, and has become dry, the rain or moisture of the air will not affect it. This is the case with the beautiful varnish laid upon coaches. On the other hand, the varnish left by gum-water could not be washed off by spirits.

Pup. I remember when I made gum-water, upon setting the cup in a warm place, it all dried away, and left the gum just as it was before. Would the same happen if I had sugar or salt dissolved in water?

Tut. Yes—upon exposing the solution to warmth, it would dry away, and you would get back your salt and sugar in a solid state, as before.

Pup. But if I were to do so with a cup of tea, what should I get?

Tut. Not tea-leaves, certainly! But your question requires a little previous explanation. It is the property of heat to make most things fly off in vapour, which is called *evaporation,* or *exhalation.* But this it does in very different degrees to different substances. Some are very easily made to evaporate; others very difficultly; and others not at all, by the most violent fire we can raise. Fluids in general are easily evaporable; but not equally so. Spirit of wine flies off in vapour much sooner than water; so that if you had a mixture of the two, by applying a gentle heat, you might drive off all the spirit, and leave the water pure. Water, again, is more evaporable than oil. Some solid substances are much disposed to evaporate. Thus, smelling-salts, by a little heat, may entirely be driven away in the air. But, in general, solids are more *fixed* than fluids; and therefore, when a solid is dissolved in a fluid, it may commonly be recovered again by evaporation. By this operation, common salt is got from sea-water and salt springs, both artificially, and in hot countries, by the natural heat of the sun. When the water is no more than is just sufficient to dissolve the salt, it is called a *saturated solution;* and on evaporating the water further, the salt begins to separate, forming little regular masses, called *crystals.* Sugar may be made in like manner to form crystals; and then it is sugar-candy.

Pup. But what is a syrup?

Tut. That is, when so much sugar is dissolved as sensibly to thicken the liquor, but not to separate from it. Well—now to your question about tea. On exposing it to considerable heat, those fine particles in which its flavour consists, being as *volatile* or evaporable as the water, would fly off along with it; and,

when the liquor came to dryness, there would only be
left those particles in which its roughness and colour
consist. This would make what is called an *extract*
of a plant.

Pup. What becomes of the water that evaporates?

Tut. It ascends into the air, and unites with it.
But if in its way it be stopped by any cold body, it is
condensed, that is, it returns to the state of water
again. Lift up the lid of the tea-pot, and you will see
water collected on the inside of it, which is condensed
steam from the hot tea beneath. Hold a spoon or
knife in the way of the steam, which bursts out from
the spout of the tea-kettle, and you will find it immediately covered with drops. This operation of turning
a fluid into vapour, and then condensing it, is called
distillation. For this purpose, the vessel in which the
liquor is heated is closely covered with another, called
the head, into which the steam rises, and is condensed.
It is then drawn off by means of a pipe into another
vessel called the receiver. In this way, all sweet-
scented and aromatic liquors are drawn from fragrant
vegetables, by means of water or spirits. The fragrant
part, being very volatile, rises along with the steam
of the water or spirit, and remains united with it after
it is condensed. Rose-water and spirit of lavender are
liquors of this kind.

Pup. Then the water collected on the inside of
the tea-pot lid should have the fragrance of the
tea.

Tut. It should—but unless the tea were fine, you
could scarcely perceive it.

Pup. I think I have heard of making salt-water
fresh by distilling.

Tut. Yes. That is an old discovery, revived within
these few years. The salt in sea-water, being of a
fixed nature, does not rise with the steam; and therefore, on condensing the steam, the water is found to
be fresh. And this, indeed, is the method nature employs in raising water by exhalation from the ocean,

which, collecting into clouds, is condensed in the cold regions of the air, and falls down in rain.

But our tea is done; so we will now put an end to our chemical lecture.

Pup. But is this real chemistry?

Tut. Yes, it is.

Pup. Why, I understand it all, without any difficulty.

Tut. I intended you should.

THE KIDNAPPERS.

MR. B. was accustomed to read in the evening to his young folk some select story, and then ask them in turn what they thought of it. From the reflections they made on these occasions, he was enabled to form a judgment of their dispositions, and was led to throw in remarks of his own, by which their hearts and understandings might be improved. One night, he read the following narrative from "Churchill's Voyages."

"In some voyages of discovery made from Denmark to Greenland, the sailors were instructed to seize some of the natives by force or stratagem, and bring them away. In consequence of these orders, several Greenlanders were kidnapped and brought to Denmark. Though they were treated there with kindness, the poor wretches were always melancholy, and were observed frequently to turn their faces towards the north, and sigh bitterly. They made several attempts to escape, by putting out to sea in their little canoes which had been brought with them. One of them had got as far as thirty leagues from land before he was overtaken. It was remarked, that this poor man, whenever he met a woman with a child in her arms, used to utter a deep sigh; whence it was conjectured that he had left a wife and child behind him. They all pined away, one after another, and died miserably."

" Now, *Edward*," said he, " what is your opinion of this story ?"

Edward. Poor creatures ! I think it was very barbarous to take them from home.

Mr. B. It was, indeed !

Ed. Have civilized nations any *right* to behave so to savages ?

Mr. B. I think you may readily answer that question yourself. Suppose you were a savage—what would be your opinion ?

Ed. I dare say I should think it very wrong. But can savages think about right and wrong as we do ?

Mr. B. Why not ? are they not *men ?*

Ed. Yes—but not like civilized men, surely !

Mr. B. I know no important difference between ourselves and those people we are pleased to call savage, but in the degree of knowledge and virtue possessed by each. And I believe many individuals among the Greenlanders, as well as other unpolished people, exceed in these respects many among us. In the present case, I am sure the Danish sailors showed themselves the greater savages.

Ed. But what did they take away the Greenlanders for ?

Mr. B. The pretence was, that they might be brought to be instructed in a Christian country, and then sent back to civilize their countrymen.

Ed. And was not that a good thing ?

Mr. B. Certainly—if it had been done by proper means ; but to attempt it by an act of violence and injustice could not be right ; for they could teach them nothing so good as their example was bad ; and the poor people were not likely to learn willingly from those who had begun with injuring them so cruelly.

Ed. I remember Captain Cook brought over somebody from Otaheite ; and poor Le Boo was brought here from the Pelew Islands. But I believe they both came of their own accord.

Mr. B. They did. And it is a great proof of the

better way of thinking of modern voyagers than of former ones, that they do not consider it as justifiable to use violence, even for the supposed benefit of the people they visit.

Ed. I have read of taking possession of a newly-discovered country by setting up the king's standard, or some such ceremony, though it was full of inhabitants.

Mr. B. Such was formerly the custom; and a more impudent mockery of all right and justice cannot be conceived. Yet this, I am sorry to say, is the title by which European nations claim the greatest part of their foreign settlements.

Ed. And might not the natives drive them out again, if they were able?

Mr. B. I am sure I do not know why they might not; *for force can never give right.*

Now, *Harry*, tell me what *you* think of the story.

Harry. I think it very strange that people should want to go back to such a cold, dismal place as Greenland.

Mr. B. Why, what country do you love best in all the world?

H. England, to be sure.

Mr. B. But England is by no means the warmest and finest country. Here are no grapes growing in the fields, nor oranges in the woods and hedges, as there are in more southern climates.

H. I should like them very well, to be sure—but then England is my own native country, where you, and mamma, and all my friends live. Besides, it is a very pleasant country, too.

Mr. B. As to your first reason, you must be sensible that the Greenlander can say just the same; and the poor fellow, who left a wife and children behind, must have had the strongest of all ties to make him wish to return. Do you think I should be easy to be separated from all of you?

H. No—and I am sure we should not be easy neither.

Mr B. Home, my dear, wherever it is, is the spot towards which a good heart is the most strongly drawn. Then, as for the pleasantness of a place, that all depends upon habit. The Greenlander, being accustomed to the way of living, and all the objects of his own country, could not fancy any other so well. He loved whale-fat and seal as well as you can do pudding and beef. He thought rowing his little boat amidst the boisterous waves, pleasanter employment than driving a plough or a cart. He fenced himself against the winter's cold by warm clothing; and the long night of many weeks, which you would think so gloomy, was to him a season of ease and festivity in his habitation under-ground. It is a very kind and wise dispensation of Providence, that every part of the world is rendered the most agreeable to those who live in it.

Now, little Mary, what have you to say?

Mary. I have only to say, that if they were to offer to carry me away from home, I would scratch their eyes out.

Mr. B. Well said, my girl! stand up for yourself. Let nobody run away with you—*against your will.*

Mary. That I won't.

ELEVENTH EVENING.

ON MANUFACTURES.

Father—Henry.

Hen. My dear father, you observed the other day that we had a great many *manufactures* in England. Pray, what is a manufacture?

Fa. A manufacture is something made by the hand of man. It is derived from two Latin words,—*manus* the hand, and *facere*, to make. Manufactures are, therefore, opposed to *productions*, which latter are what the bounty of nature spontaneously affords us; as fruits, corn, marble.

Hen. But there is a great deal of trouble with corn; you have often made me take notice how much pains it costs the farmer to plough his ground, and put the seed in the earth, and keep it clean from weeds.

Fa. Very true; but the farmer does not make the corn; he only prepares for it a proper soil and situation, and removes every hindrance arising from the hardness of the ground, or the neighbourhood of other plants, which might obstruct the secret and wonderful process of vegetation; but with the vegetation itself he has nothing to do. It is not *his* hand that draws out the slender fibres of the root, pushes up the green stalk, and, by degrees, the spiky ear; swells the grain, and embrowns it with that rich tinge of tawny russet, which informs the husbandman it is time to put in his sickle: all this operation is performed without his care or even knowledge.

Hen. Now, then, I understand; corn is a *production*, and bread a *manufacture*.

Fa. Bread is certainly, in strictness of speech, a manufacture; but we do not in general apply the term to anything in which the original material is so little changed. If we wanted to speak of bread philosophically, we should say, it is a *preparation* of corn.

Hen. Is sugar a manufacture?

Fa. No, for the same reason. Besides which, I do not recollect the term being applied to any article of food; I suppose from an idea that food is of too perishable a nature, and generally obtained by a process too simple to deserve the name. We say, therefore, sugar-works, oil-mills, chocolate-works; we do not say a beer-manufactory, but a brewery; but this is only a nicety of language; for, properly, all those are manufactories, if there be much of art and curiosity in the process.

Hen. Do we say a manufactory of *pictures?*

Fa. No; but for a different reason. A picture, especially if it belong to any of the higher classes of painting, is an effort of genius. A picture cannot be produced by any given combinations of canvas and colour. It is the hand, indeed, that executes, but the head that works. Sir Joshua Reynolds could not have gone, when he was engaged to paint a picture, and hired workmen, the one to draw the eyes, another the nose, a third the mouth; the whole must be the painter's own, that particular painter's, and no other; and no one, who has not his ideas, can do his work. His work is therefore nobler,—of a higher order.

Hen. Pray give me an instance of a manufacture.

Fa. The making of watches is a manufacture; the silver, iron, gold, or whatever else is used in it, are productions,—the materials of the work; but it is by the wonderful art of man that they are wrought into the numberless wheels and springs of which the complicated machine, termed a watch, is composed.

Hen. Then, is there not as much art in making a watch as a picture? Does not the head work?

Fa. Certainly, in the original invention of watches, as much, or more, than in painting; but, when once invented, the art of watch-making is capable of being reduced to a mere mechanical labour, which may be exercised by any man of common capacity, according to certain precise rules, when made familiar to him by practice. This, painting is not.

Hen. But, my dear father, making books surely requires a great deal of thinking and study; and yet I remember, the other day at dinner, a gentleman said that Mr. Pica had *manufactured* a large volume in less than a fortnight.

Fa. It was meant to convey a satirical remark on his book, because it was compiled from other authors, from whom he had taken a page in one place, and a page in another; so that it was not produced by the labour of his brain, but of his hands. Thus, you heard your mother complain that the London cream was *manufactured;* which was a pointed and concise way of saying that the cream was not what it ought to be, or what it pretended to be; for cream, when genuine, is a pure production; but when mixed up and adulterated with flour and isinglass, and I know not what, it becomes a manufacture. It was as much as to say, art has been here where it has no business; where it is not beneficial, but hurtful. A great deal of the delicacy of language depends upon an accurate knowledge of the specific meaning of single terms, and a nice attention to their relative propriety.

Hen. Have all nations manufactures?

Fa. All that are in any degree cultivated; but it very often happens that countries naturally the poorest have manufactures of the greatest extent and variety.

Hen. Why so?

Fa. For the same reason, 1 apprehend, that individuals, who are rich without any labour of their own, are seldom so industrious and active as those who depend upon their own exertions : thus the Spaniards, who possess the richest gold and silver mines in the world, excepting those recently discovered in California, are in want of many conveniences of life which are enjoyed in London and Amsterdam.

Hen. I can comprehend that; I believe if my uncle Ledger were to find a gold-mine under his warehouse, he would soon shut up shop.

Fa. I believe so. It is not, however, easy to establish manufactures in a *very poor* nation; they require science and genius for their invention, art and contrivance for their execution; order, peace, and union, for their flourishing; they require, too, a number of men to combine together in an undertaking, and to prosecute it with the most patient industry; they require, therefore, laws and government for their protection. If you see extensive manufactures in any nation, you may be sure it is a civilized nation; you may be

sure property is accurately ascertained and protected.
They require great expenses for their first establish-
ment, costly machines for shortening manual labour,
and money and credit for purchasing materials from
distant countries. There is not a single manufacture
of Great Britain which does not require, in some part
or other of its process, productions from the different
parts of the globe,—oils, drugs, varnish, quicksilver, and
the like; it requires, therefore, ships and a friendly
intercourse with foreign nations, to transport commodities, and exchange productions. We could not be a
manufacturing, unless we were also a commercial
nation. Manufactures require time to take root in
any place, and their excellence often depends upon
some nice and delicate circumstance; a peculiar quality, for instance, in the air or water, or some other
local circumstance not easily ascertained. Thus, I
have heard, that the Irish women spin better than the
English, because the moister temperature of their climate makes their skin more soft and their fingers
more flexible; thus, again, we cannot dye so beautiful
a scarlet as the French can, though with the same
drugs, perhaps on account of the superior purity of their
air. But though so much is necessary for the perfection of the more curious and complicated manufactures,
all nations possess those which are subservient to the
common conveniences of life—the loom and the forge,
particularly, are of the highest antiquity.

Hen. Yes: I remember Hector bids Andromache
return to her apartment, and employ herself in weaving with her maids; and I remember the shield of
Achilles.

Fa. True; and you also remember, in an earlier
period, the fine linen of Egypt; and, to go still higher,
the working of iron and brass is recorded of Tubal
Cain before the flood.

Hen. Which is the more important, manufactures
or agriculture?

Fa. Agriculture is the more *necessary*, because it is

first of all necessary that man should live; but almost all the enjoyments and comforts of life are produced by manufactures.

Hen. Why are we obliged to take so much pains to make ourselves comfortable?

Fa. To exercise our industry. Nature provides the materials for man. She pours out at his feet a profusion of gems, metals, dyes, plants, ores, barks, stones, gums, wax, marbles, woods, roots, skins, earths, and minerals of all kinds! She has also given him tools.

Hen. I did not know that Nature gave us tools.

Fa. No! what are those two instruments you carry always about with you, so strong and yet so flexible, so nicely jointed, and branched out into five long, taper, unequal divisions, any of which may be contracted or stretched out at pleasure; the extremities of which have a feeling so wonderfully delicate, and which are strengthened and defended by horn?

Hen. The hands.

Fa. Yes. Man is as much superior to the brutes in his outward form, by means of the hand, as he is in his mind by the gifts of reason. The trunk of the elephant comes, perhaps, the nearest to it in its exquisite feeling and flexibility (it is, indeed, called his hand in Latin), and accordingly that animal has always been reckoned the wisest of brutes. When Nature gave man the hand, she said to him, "Exercise your ingenuity, and work." As soon as ever man rises above the state of a savage, he begins to contrive, and to make things, in order to improve his forlorn condition: thus you may remember Thomson represents Industry coming to the poor shivering wretch, and teaching him the arts of life:—

> " Taught him to chip the wood and hew the stone,
> Till, by degrees, the finish'd fabric rose ;
> Tore from his limbs the blood-polluted fur,
> And wrapt them in the woolly vestment warm,
> Or dight in glossy silk and flowing lawn."

Hen. It must require a great deal of knowledge, I

suppose, for so many curious works; what sort of knowledge is most necessary?

Fa. There is not any which may not be occasionally employed; but the two sciences which most assist the manufacturer are *mechanics* and *chemistry*. The one for building mills, working of mines, and in general for constructing wheels, wedges, pulleys, &c., either to shorten the labour of man, by performing it in less time, or to perform what the strength of man alone could not accomplish:—the other in fusing and working ores, in dyeing and bleaching, and extracting the virtues of various substances for particular uses; making of soap, for instance, is a chemical operation; and, by chemistry, an ingenious gentleman, some time ago, found out a way of bleaching a piece of cloth in eight-and-forty hours, which by the common process would have taken up a great many weeks.—You have heard of Sir Richard Arkwright, who died some years since?

Hen. Yes, I have heard he was at first only a barber, and shaved people for a penny apiece.

Fa. He did so; but having a strong turn for mechanics, he invented, or at least perfected, a machine, by which one pair of hands might do the work of twenty or thirty; and, as in this country every one is free to rise by merit, he acquired the largest fortune in the county, had a great many hundreds of workmen under his orders, and had leave given him by the king to put *Sir* before his name.

Hen. Did that do him any good?

Fa. It pleased him, I suppose, or he would not have accepted of it; and you will allow, I imagine, that if titles are used, it does honour to those who bestow them, when they are given to such as have made themselves noticed for something useful.—Arkwright used to say, that if he had time to perfect his inventions, he would put a fleece of wool into a box, and it should come out broad-cloth.

Hen. What did he mean by that? was there any fairy in the box to turn it into broad-cloth with her wand?

Fa. He was assisted by the only fairies that ever had the power of transformation,—Art, and Industry; he meant that he would contrive so many machines, wheel within wheel, that the combing, carding, and other various operations, should be performed by mechanism, almost without the hand of man.

Hen. I think, if I had not been told, I should never have been able to guess that my coat came off the back of the sheep.

Fa. You hardly would; but there are manufactures in which the material is much more changed than in woollen cloth. What can be meaner in appearance than sand and ashes? Would you imagine anything beautiful could be made out of such a mixture? Yet the furnace transforms this into that transparent crystal we call *glass*, than which nothing is more sparkling, more brilliant, more full of lustre. It throws about the rays of light as though it had life and motion.

Hen. There is a glass-shop in London, which alway? puts me in mind of Aladdin's palace.

Fa. It is certain, that if a person, ignorant of the manufacture, were to see one of our capital shops, he would think all the treasures of Golconda were centred there, and that every drop of cut glass was worth a prince's ransom. Again, who would suppose, on seeing the green stalks of a plant, that it could be formed into a texture so smooth, so snowy white, so firm, and yet so flexible, as to wrap around the limbs and adapt itself to every movement of the body? Who would guess this fibrous stalk could be made to float in such light, undulating folds as in our lawns and cambrics; not less fine, we presume, than that transparent drapery which the Romans called *ventus textilis*,—woven wind.

Hen. I wonder how anybody can spin such fine thread.

Fa. Their fingers must have the touch of a spider, that, as Pope says,

"Feels at each thread, and lives along the line;"

and, indeed, you recollect that Arachne *was* a spinster. Lace is a still finer production from flax, and is one of those in which the original material is most improved. How many times the price of a pound of flax do you think that flax will be worth, when made into lace?

Hen. A great many times, I suppose.

Fa. Flax, at the first hand, is bought at fourteen-pence a pound. They make lace at Valenciennes, in French Flanders, of ten guineas a yard; I believe, indeed, higher, but we will say ten guineas : this yard of lace will weigh probably not more than half an ounce. What is the value of half an ounce of flax?

Hen. It comes to one farthing and three quarters of a farthing.

Fa. Right; now tell me how many times the original value the lace is worth.

Hen. Prodigious! it is worth 5,760 times as much as the flax it is made of.

Fa. Yet there is another material that is still more improvable than flax.

Hen. What can that be?

Fa. Iron. Suppose the price of pig-iron to be ten shillings a hundredweight; this is not quite one farthing for two ounces; now you have seen some of the beautiful cut steel, that looks like diamonds?

Hen. Yes; I have seen buckles, and pins, and watch-chains.

Fa. Then you can form an idea of it; but you have seen only the most common sorts. There was a chain made at Woodstock, in Oxfordshire, and sent to France, which weighed only two ounces, and cost 170*l*. Calculate how many times *that* had increased its value.

Hen. Amazing! It was worth 163,600 times the value of the iron it was made of.

Fa. That is what manufacturers can do; here man is a kind of a creator, and, like the great Creator, he may please himself with his work, and say, it is good. In the last-mentioned manufacture, too, that of steel, the English have the honour of excelling all the world.

Hen. What are the chief manufactures of England?

Fa. We have, at present, a greater variety than I can pretend to enumerate; but our staple manufacture is woollen cloth. England abounds in fine pastures and extensive downs, which feed great numbers of sheep: hence our wool has always been a valuable article of trade; but we did not always know how to work it. We used to sell it to the Flemish or Lombards, who wrought it into cloth; till, in the year 1326, Edward the Third invited some Flemish weavers over, to teach us the art. But there was not much cloth made in England till the reign of Henry the Seventh. Manchester and Birmingham are towns which have arisen to great consequence from small beginnings, almost within the memory of old men now living; the first for cotton and muslin goods, the second for cutlery and hardware, in which we at this moment excel all Europe. Of late years, too, carpets, beautiful as fine tapestry, have been fabricated in this country. Our clocks and watches are greatly esteemed. The earthenware plates and dishes, which we all use in common, and the elegant set for the tea-table, ornamented with musical instruments, which we admired in our visit yesterday, belong to a very extensive manufactory, the seat of which is at Burslem, in Staffordshire. The principal potteries there belong to one person, an excellent chemist, and a man of great taste; he, in conjunction with another man of taste, who is since dead, has made our clay more valuable than the finest porcelain of China. He has moulded it into all the forms of grace and beauty that are to be met with in the precious remains of the Greek and Etruscan artists. In the more common articles, he has pencilled it with the most elegant designs, shaped it into shells and leaves, twisted it into wicker-work, and trailed the ductile foliage around the light basket. He has filled our cabinets and chimney-pieces with urns, lamps, and vases, on which are lightly traced, with the purest simplicity, the fine forms and floating draperies of Herculaneum. In short, he has given to our houses a classic air, and has made every saloon and every dining-room schools of taste. I should add, that there is a great demand abroad for this elegant manufacture. The Empress Catherine of Russia had some magnificent services of it; and subsequently a service was sent to the King of Spain, intended as a present from him to the Archbishop of Toledo, which cost a thousand pounds. Some morning you shall go through the rooms in the London warehouses.

Hen. I should like very much to see manufactures, now you have told me such curious things about them.

Fa. You will do well. There is much more entertainment to a cultivated mind in seeing a pin made, than in many a fashionable diversion which young people half ruin themselves to attend. In the mean time I will give you some account of one of the most elegant of them, which is *paper*.

Hen. Pray do, my dear father.

Fa. It shall be left for another evening, however for it is now late. Good night.

TWELFTH EVENING.

A LESSON IN THE ART OF DISTINGUISHING.

F. COME hither, Charles. What is it that you see grazing in the meadow before you?

C. It is a horse.

F. Whose horse is it?

C. I do not know; I never saw it before.

F. How do you know it is a horse, if you never saw it before?

C. Because it is like other horses.

F. Are all horses alike, then?

C. Yes.

F. If they are alike, how do you know one horse from another?

C. They are not quite alike.

F. But they are so much alike, that you can easily distinguish a horse from a cow?

C. Yes, indeed.

F. Or from a cabbage?

C. A horse from a cabbage! yes, surely I can.

F. Very well; then let me see if you can tell how a horse differs from a cabbage.

C. Very easily; a horse is alive.

F. True; and how is everything called which is alive?

C. I believe all things that are alive are called *animals.*

F. Right; but can you tell me what a horse and a cabbage are alike in?

C. Nothing, I believe.

F. Yes, there is one thing in which the slenderest moss that grows upon the wall is like the greatest man or the highest angel.

C. Because God made them.

F. Yes; and how do you call everything that is made by the hand of God?

C. A creature.

F. A horse, then, is a creature, but also a living creature; that is to say, an animal.

C. And a cabbage is a dead creature, that is the difference?

F. Not so, neither; nothing is dead that has never been alive.

C. What must I call it, then, if it be neither dead nor alive?

F. An inanimate creature; there is the animate and the inanimate creation. Plants, stones, metals, are of the latter class; horses belong to the former.

C. But the gardener told me some of my cabbages were *dead*, and some were *alive*.

F. Very true. Plants have a *vegetable* life, a principle of growth and decay; this is common to them with all organized bodies; but they have not sensation; at least we do not know that they have; they have not life, therefore, in the sense in which animals enjoy it.

C. A horse is called an animal, then.

F. Yes; but a salmon is an animal, and so is a sparrow; how will you distinguish a horse from these?

C. A salmon lives in the water, and swims; a sparrow flies, and lives in the air.

F. I think a salmon could not walk upon the ground, even if it could live out of the water.

C. No, indeed; it has no legs.

F. And a bird could not gallop like a horse.

C. No; it would hop away upon its two slender legs.

F. How many legs has a horse?

C. Four.

F. And an ox?

C. Four, also.

F. And a camel?

C. Four, still.

F. Do you know any animals, which live upon the earth, that have not four legs?

C. I think not; they have all four legs; except worms, and insects, and such things.

F. You remember, I suppose, what an animal is called that has four legs; you have it in your little books?

C. A quadruped.

F. A horse, then, is a *quadruped*: by this we distinguish him from birds, fishes, and insects.

C. And from men.

F. True; but, if you had been talking about birds, you would not have found it so easy to distinguish them.

C. How so ? a man is not at all like a bird.

F. Yet an ancient philosopher could find no way to distinguish them, but by calling man *a two-legged animal without feathers.*

C. I think he was very silly; they are not at all alike, though they have each two legs.

F. Another ancient philosopher, called Diogenes, was of your opinion. He stripped a cock of his feathers, and turned him into the school where Plato —that was his name—was teaching, and said, "Here is Plato's man for you."

C. I wish I had been there ; I should have laughed very much.

F. Probably. Before we laugh at others, however, let us see what we can do ourselves. We have not yet found anything that will distinguish a horse from an elephant, or from a Norway rat.

C. O, that is easy enough. An elephant is very large, and a rat is very small ; a horse is neither large nor small.

F. Before we go any farther, look what is settled on the skirt of your coat.

C. It is a butterfly ; what a prodigiously large one ! I never saw such a one before.

F. Is it larger than a rat, think you ?

C. No ; that it is not.

F. Yet you called the butterfly large, and you called the rat small.

C. It is very large for a butterfly.

F. It is so. You see, therefore, that large and small are *relative terms.*

C. I do not well understand that phrase.

F. It means, that they have no precise and determinate signification in themselves, but are applied differently, according to the other ideas which you join with them, and the different positions in which you view them. This butterfly, therefore, is *large*, compared with those of its own species, and *small* compared with many other species of animals. Besides, there is no circumstance which varies more than the size of individuals. If you were to give an idea of a horse from its size, you would certainly say it was much bigger than a dog; yet if you take the smallest Shetland horse, and the largest Irish greyhound, you will find them very much upon a par : size, therefore, is not a circumstance by which you can accurately distinguish one animal from another; nor yet is colour.

C. No, there are black horses, and bay, and white, and pied.

F. But you have not seen that variety of colours in a hare, for instance.

C. No, a hare is always brown.

F. Yet, if you were to depend upon that circumstance, you would not convey the idea of a hare to a mountaineer, or an inhabitant of Siberia, for he sees them white as snow. We must, therefore, find out some circumstances that do not change like size and colour, and I may add shape, though they are not so obvious, nor perhaps so striking.—Look at the feet of quadrupeds; are they not alike?

C. No; some have long taper claws, and some have thick clumsy feet, without claws.

F. The thick feet are horny; are they not?

C. Yes; I recollect they are called hoofs.

F. And the feet that are not covered with horn, and are divided into claws, are called *digitated;* from *digitus*, a finger; because they are parted like fingers. Here, then, we have one grand division of quadrupeds into *hoofed* and *digitated.* Of which division is the horse?

C. He is hoofed.

F. There are a great many different kinds of horses; did you ever know one that was not hoofed?

C. No, never.

F. Do you think we run any hazard of a stranger telling us, Sir, horses are hoofed indeed in your country, but in mine, which is in a different climate, and where we feed them differently, they have claws?

C. No, I dare say not.

F. Then we have got something to our purpose ; a circumstance, easily marked, which always belongs to the animal, under every variation of situation or treatment. But an ox is hoofed, and so is a sheep ; we must distinguish still farther. You have often stood by, I suppose, while the smith was shoeing a horse. What kind of a hoof has he ?

C. It is round, and all in one piece.

F. And is that of an ox so ?

C. No ; it is divided.

F. A horse, then, is not only hoofed, but *whole-hoofed*. Now, how many quadrupeds do you think there are in the world that are whole-hoofed ?

C. Indeed, I do not know.

F. There are, among all animals that we are acquainted with, either in this country or in any other, only the horse, the ass, and the zebra, which is a species of wild ass. Now, therefore, you see we have nearly accomplished our purpose ; we have only to distinguish him from the ass.

C. That is easily done, I believe ; I should be sorry if anybody could mistake my little horse for an ass.

F. It is not so easy, however, as you imagine ; the eye readily distinguishes them by the air and general appearance, but naturalists have been rather puzzled to fix upon any specific difference, which may serve the purpose of a definition. Some have, therefore, fixed upon the ears, others on the mane and tail. What kind of ears has an ass ?

C. O, very long, clumsy ears. Asses' ears are always laughed at.

F. And the horse ?

C. The horse has small ears, nicely turned, and upright.

F. And the mane, is there no difference there ?

C. The horse has a fine, long, flowing mane ; the ass has hardly any.

F. And the tail; is it not fuller of hair in the horse than in the ass?

C. Yes; the ass has only a few long hairs at the end of the tail; but the horse has a long, bushy tail, when it is not cut.

F. Which, by the way, it is pity it ever should. Now, then, observe what particulars we have got. *A horse is an animal of the quadruped kind, whole-hoofed, with short, erect ears, a flowing mane, and a tail covered in every part with long hairs.* Now, is there any other animal, think you, in the world, that answers these particulars?

C. I do not know; this does not tell us a great deal about him.

F. And yet it tells us enough to distinguish him from all the different tribes of the creation which we are acquainted with in any part of the earth. Do you know now what we have been making?

C. What?

F. A DEFINITION. It is the business of a definition to distinguish precisely the thing defined from any other thing, and to do it in as few terms as possible. Its object is to separate the subject of definition, first, from those with which it has only a general resemblance; then, from those which agree with it in a greater variety of particulars; and so on, till by constantly throwing out all which have not the qualities we have taken notice of, we come at length to the individual or the species we wish to ascertain. It is a sort of chase, and resembles the manner of hunting in some countries, where they first enclose a large circle with their dogs, nets, and horses, and then, by degrees, draw their toils closer and closer, driving their game before them, till it is at length brought into so narrow a compass, that the sportsmen have nothing to do but to knock down their prey.

C. Just as we have been hunting this horse, till at last we held him fast by his ears and his tail.

F. I should observe to you, that in the definition

naturalists give of a horse, it is generally mentioned
that he has six cutting teeth in each jaw; because this
circumstance of the teeth has been found a very convenient one for characterizing large classes : but as it
is not absolutely necessary here, I have omitted it; a
definition being the more perfect the fewer particulars
you make use of, provided you can say with certainty
from those particulars,—The object so characterized
must be this, and no other whatever.

C. But, papa, if I had never seen a horse, I should
not know what kind of animal it was by this definition.

F. Let us hear, then, how you would give me an
idea of a horse.

C. I should say it was a fine, large, prancing creature,
with slender legs and an arched neck, and a sleek,
smooth skin, and a tail that sweeps the ground, and
that he snorts and neighs very loud, and tosses his
head, and runs as swift as the wind.

F. I think you learned some verses upon the horse
in your last lesson ? repeat them—

> *C.* " The wanton courser thus, with reins unbound,
> Breaks from his stall, and beats the trembling ground ;
> Pamper'd and proud, he seeks the wonted tides,
> And laves, in height of blood, his shining sides ;
> His head, now freed, he tosses to the skies ;
> His mane, dishevell'd, o'er his shoulders flies ;
> He snuffs the females in the distant plain,
> And springs, exulting, to his fields again."—*Pope's Homer.*

F. You have said very well ; but this is not a *Definition*, it is a *Description*.

C. What is the difference ?

F. A description is intended to give you a lively
picture of an object, as though you saw it ; it ought to
be very full. A definition gives no picture to those
who have not seen it, it rather tells you what its subject
is not, than what it is, by giving you such clear, specific
marks, that it shall not be possible to confound it with
anything else ; and hence it is of the greatest use in
throwing things into classes. We have a great many

beautiful descriptions from ancient authors, so loosely worded, that we cannot certainly tell what animals are meant by them; whereas, if they had given us definitions, three lines would have ascertained their meaning.

C. I like a description best, papa.

F. Perhaps so; I believe I should have done the same at your age. Remember, however, that nothing is more useful, than to learn to form ideas with precision, and to express them with accuracy; I have not given you a definition to teach you what a horse is, but to teach you to *think*.

THE PHŒNIX AND THE DOVE.

A PHŒNIX, who had long inhabited the solitary deserts of Arabia, once flew so near the habitations of men, as to meet with a tame dove, who was sitting on her nest, with wings expanded, and fondly brooding over her young ones, while she expected her mate, who was foraging abroad, to procure them food. The Phœnix, with a sort of insulting compassion, said to her, "Poor bird, how much I pity thee! confined to a single spot, and sunk in domestic cares, thou art continually employed either in laying eggs or providing for thy brood; and thou exhaustest thy life and strength in perpetuating a feeble and defenceless race. As to myself, I live exempt from toil, care, and misfortune. I feed upon nothing less precious than rich gums and spices; I fly through the trackless regions of the air, and, when I am seen by men, am gazed at with curiosity and astonishment. I have no one to control my range, no one to provide for; and, when I have fulfilled my five centuries of life, and seen the revolution of ages, I rather vanish than die, and a successor, without my care, springs up from my ashes. I am an image of the great sun whom I adore; and glory in being, like him, single and alone, and having no likeness."

The Dove replied, "O Phœnix, I pity thee much more than thou affectest to pity me! What pleasure

canst thou enjoy, who livest forlorn and solitary in a
trackless and unpeopled desert? who hast no mate to
caress thee; no young ones to excite thy tenderness
and reward thy cares; no kindred, no society amongst
thy fellows? Not long life only, but immortality itself,
would be a curse, if it were to be bestowed on such
uncomfortable terms. For my part, I know that my
life will be short, and therefore I employ it in raising
a numerous posterity, and in opening my heart to all
the sweets of domestic happiness. I am beloved by
my partner; I am dear to man; and shall leave marks
behind me that I have lived. As to the sun, to whom
thou hast presumed to compare thyself, that glorious
being is so totally different from, and so infinitely
superior to, all the creatures upon earth, that it does
not become us to liken ourselves to him, or to determine upon the manner of his existence. One obvious
difference, however, thou mayest remark; that the sun,
though alone, by his prolific heat produces all things;
and though he shines so high above our heads, gives
us reason every moment to bless his beams; whereas
thou, swelling with imaginary greatness, dreamest
away a long period of existence, equally void of comfort and usefulness."

THE MANUFACTURE OF PAPER.

F. I WILL now, as I promised, give you an account
of the elegant and useful manufacture of *Paper*, the
basis of which is itself a manufacture. This delicate
and beautiful substance is made from the meanest and
most disgusting materials,—from old rags, which have
passed from one poor person to another, and have,
perhaps, at length dropped in tatters from the child of
the beggar. These are carefully picked up from dung-
hills, or bought from servants by Jews, who make it
their business to go about and collect them. They
sell them to the rag-merchant, who gives from twopence to fourpence a pound, according to their quality;

M

and he, when he has got a sufficient quantity, disposes
of them to the owner of the paper-mill. He gives
them first to women to sort and pick, agreeably to
their different degrees of fineness; they, also, with a
knife, cut out carefully all the seams, which they throw
into a basket for other purposes; they then put them
into the dusting-engine, a large circular wire sieve,
where they receive some degree of cleansing. The
rags are then conveyed to the mill. Here they were
formerly beaten to pieces with vast hammers, which
rose and fell continually with a tremendous noise, that
was heard at a great distance. But now they put the
rags into a large trough, or cistern, into which a pipe
of clear spring water is constantly flowing. In this
cistern is placed a cylinder, about two feet long, set
thick round with rows of iron spikes, standing as near
as they can to one another without touching. At the
bottom of the trough, there are corresponding rows of
spikes. The cylinder is made to whirl round with
inconceivable rapidity, and, with these iron teeth, rends
and tears the cloth in every possible direction; till, by
the assistance of the water, which continually flows
through the cistern, it is thoroughly masticated, and
reduced to a fine pulp; and, by the same process, all
its impurities are cleansed away, and it is restored to
its original whiteness. This process takes about six
hours. This fine pulp is next put into a copper of
warm water. It is the substance of paper, but the
form must now be given it: for this purpose they use
a mould. It is made of wire, strong one way, and
crossed with finer. This mould they just dip horizontally into the copper, and take it out again. It has
a little wooden frame on the edge, by means of which
it retains as much of the pulp as is wanted for the
thickness of the sheet, and the superfluity runs off
through the interstices of the wires. Another man
instantly receives it, opens the frame, and turns out
the thin sheet, which has now shape, but not consistence, upon soft felt, which is placed on the ground
to receive it. On that is placed another piece of felt.

and then another sheet of paper, and so on, till they have made a pile of forty or fifty. They are then pressed with a large screw-press, moved by a long lever, which forcibly squeezes the water out of them, and gives them immediate consistence. There is still, however, a great deal to be done. The felts are taken off, and thrown on one side, and the paper on the other, whence it is dexterously taken up with an instrument in the form of a T, three sheets at a time, and hung on lines to dry. There it hangs for a week or ten days, which likewise further whitens it; and any knots and roughnesses it may have, are picked off carefully by the women. It is then sized. Size is a sort of glue; and without this preparation, the paper would not bear ink; it would run and blot, as you see it does on grey paper. The sheets are just dipped into the size and taken out again. The exact degree of sizing is a matter of nicety, which can only be known by experience. They are then hung up again to dry, and, when dry, taken to the finishing-room, where they are examined anew, pressed in the dry-presses, which gives them their last gloss and smoothness; counted up into quires, made up into reams, and sent to the stationer's, from whom we have it, after he has folded it again and cut the edges; some, too, he makes to shine like satin, by glossing it with hot plates. The whole process of paper-making takes about three weeks.

H. It is a very curious process, indeed. I shall almost scruple for the future to blacken a sheet of paper with a careless scrawl, now I know how much pains it costs to make it so white and beautiful.

F. It is true, that there is hardly anything we use with so much waste and profusion as this manufacture; we should think ourselves confined in the use of it, if we might not tear, disperse, and destroy it in a thousand ways; so that it is really astonishing whence linen enough can be procured to answer so vast a demand. As to the coarse brown papers, of which an immense quantity is used by every shopkeeper in packages, &c.,

these are made chiefly of oakum, that is, old hempen ropes. A fine paper is made in China of silk.

H. I have heard of woven paper; pray what is that? they cannot weave paper, surely!

F. Your question is very natural. In order to answer it, I must desire you to take a sheet of common paper, and hold it up against the light. Do not you see marks in it?

H. I see a great many white lines running along lengthways, like ribs, and smaller, that cross them. I see, too, letters, and the figure of a crown.

F. These are all the marks of the wires; the thickness of the wire prevents so much of the pulp lying upon the sheet in those places, consequently, wherever the wires are, the paper is thinner, and you see the light through more readily, which gives that appearance of white lines. The letters, too, are worked in the wire, and are the maker's name. Now to prevent these lines, which take off from the beauty of the paper, particularly of drawing-paper, there are now used moulds of brass wire, exceedingly fine, of equal thickness, and woven or latticed one within another; the marks, therefore, of these are easily pressed out, so as to be hardly visible; if you look at this sheet you will see it is quite smooth.

H. It is so.

F. I should mention to you, that a discovery was made some time since, by which they can make paper equal to any in whiteness of the coarsest brown rags, and even of dyed cottons, which formerly they were obliged to throw by for inferior purposes. This is by means of manganese, a sort of metal, or rather a metallic oxide, and oil of vitriol; a mixture of which they just pass through the pulp, while it is in water, for otherwise it would burn it, and in an instant it discharges the colours of the dyed cloths, and bleaches the brown to a beautiful whiteness.

H. That is like what you told me before, of bleaching cloth in a few hours.

F. It is, indeed, founded upon the same discovery

The paper made of these brown rags is, also, more valuable, from being very tough and strong, almost like parchment.

H. But is not paper sometimes made from other substances besides those which you have named?

F. Yes; paper has been made from straw, the nettle, hops, moss, reeds, couch-grass, even wood shavings, and from a variety of other substances.

H. And have there not been many improvements in the manufacture of paper effected of late years, by means of machinery?

F. Yes; but it would be somewhat difficult to make you comprehend them without the aid of drawings, or of actual inspection. The processes which I have been describing, relate chiefly to what is termed hand-made paper, and which has been, to a great extent, superseded by the employment of complicated and costly machinery. The largest sheet of hand-made paper known to have been manufactured, was four feet seven inches in length, by two feet seven inches and a half in width; but, by machinery, paper may be made five feet in width, and of an unlimited length, like cloth. Some of the machines are equal to the production of twenty-five superficial feet of paper in a minute. Other machinery is employed for cutting the paper into sheets of different required sizes. Another improvement, of incalculable value, consists in the addition of drying-rollers. These, as I find mentioned in BRANDE'S *Dictionary of Science, Literature, and Art*, " are three cylinders of polished metal, which effect in a few moments the perfect drying of the paper: while yet moist, it passes over the first moderately warm; again over the second, of larger diameter, of greater warmth; and again over the third with an augmented heat. The paper is now perfectly dry, and any casual inequalities are removed from its surface. The final action of the machine is to wind the paper round a last roller or reel, which, when full, is exchanged for another; and so on successively."

H. Then, I suppose, with all these surprising improvements, the progress of the manufacture is much more expeditious than it was formerly?

F. Yes; according to the old method, three months were occupied from the time of receiving the rags into the mill until the completion of the paper; now, the rags may be received one day, and the paper manufactured from them be delivered on the day following.

H. When was the making of paper found out?

F. It is a disputed point; but probably in the fourteenth century. The invention has been of almost equal consequence to literature, with that of printing itself; and shows how the arts and sciences, like children of the same family, mutually assist and bring forward each other.

THE TWO ROBBERS.

Scene.—*Alexander the Great in his tent.   Guards.   A Man with a fierce countenance, chained and fettered, brought before him.*

Alex. WHAT, art thou the Thracian Robber, of whose exploits I have heard so much?

Rob. I am a Thracian and a soldier.

A. A soldier!—a thief, a plunderer, an assassin! the pest of the country! I could honour thy courage, but I must detest and punish thy crimes.

R. What have *I* done of which *you* can complain?

A. Hast thou not set at defiance my authority? violated the public peace, and passed thy life in injuring the persons and properties of thy fellow-subjects?

R. Alexander! I am your captive—I must hear what you please to say, and endure what you please to inflict. But my soul is unconquered; and if I reply at all to your reproaches, I will reply like a free man.

A. Speak freely. Far be it from me to take the advantage of my power to silence those with whom I deign to converse!

R. I must then answer your question by another: How have *you* passed your life?

A. Like a hero. Ask Fame, and she will tell you. Among the brave, I have been the bravest: among sovereigns, the noblest: among conquerors, the mightiest.

R. And does not Fame speak of me too? Was there ever a bolder captain of a more valiant band? Was there ever—but I scorn to boast. You yourself know that I have not been easily subdued.

A. Still, what are you but a *robber*—a base, dishonest *robber?*

R. And what is a *conqueror?* Have not you, too, gone about the earth, like an evil genius, blasting the fair fruits of peace and industry;—plundering, ravaging, killing, without law, without justice, merely to gratify an insatiable lust for dominion? All that I have done to a single district with a hundred followers, you have done to whole nations with a hundred thousand. If I have stripped individuals, you have ruined kings and princes. If I have burned a few hamlets, you have desolated the most flourishing kingdoms and cities of the earth. What is, then, the difference, but that, as you were born a king, and I a private man, you have been able to become a mightier *robber* than I?

A. But, if I have taken like a king, I have given like a king. If I have subverted empires, I have founded greater. I have cherished arts, commerce, and philosophy.

R. I, too, have freely given to the poor, what I took from the rich. I have established order and discipline among the most ferocious of mankind; and have stretched out my protecting arm over the oppressed. I know, indeed, little of the philosophy you talk of; but I believe neither you nor I shall ever repay to the world the mischiefs we have done it.

A. Leave me—take off his chains, and use him well. (*Exit robber.*)—Are we, then, so much alike?— Alexander, too, a robber?—Let me reflect.

THIRTEENTH EVENING.

THE COUNCIL OF QUADRUPEDS.

IN the interior of the Cape of Good Hope, the beasts of the forest had for ages lived in comparative peace; but when the Europeans spread themselves along the coast, and forced their way into the woods, the wounded and terrified animals felt that the security they had so long enjoyed was gone. They perceived that a different race of men, armed with new and more formidable weapons, had usurped the place of the Hottentot and Bushman.

As the new settlers increased in number, the wild beasts sensibly diminished. In this state of things, a party of hunters one day entered the forest, and, with the assistance of their dogs, raised and gave chase to many different species of animals with which that part of Africa abounds. Several were killed, but others escaped by swimming across the White River, among whom were the lion and the elephant. The dogs had the temerity to follow them; and the boldest, attempting to seize the lion, received a blow from his paw that laid him dead at his feet; another made a spring at the elephant, but that sagacious animal caught him with his trunk, and threw him senseless into the stream. The rest were terrified, and returned to their masters.

After congratulating each other on their escape, the thoughts of the elephant and lion naturally turned on the means of revenge. Various plans were suggested and dismissed, but at last they resolved to call a general council of the quadrupeds, wherein the subject might receive the maturest deliberation, and their decision be carried into prompt and vigorous execution.

The jackal, who happened to be at a short distance, was instantly despatched on this important business. He was instructed to invite all, without exception, to repair to the Antelope's Fountain, near the banks or the river, by sunrise on the following morning; the lion pledging his royal word for the safety of the weak or the timid, who might otherwise scruple to attend an assembly, where their bitterest foes would predominate.

The messenger soon found the huge rhinoceros ruminating in a shady grove. He approached without fear, and delivered his message, which gained a ready assent. The buffalo and the wild boar seemed careless and indifferent, yet promised to attend: the tiger and the wolf rejoiced at the summons, as it promised to gratify their thirst for blood ; but many of the smaller and timid animals either fled at the jackal's approach, or heard his message with incredulity and contempt. He unexpectedly met with the camelopard (or giraffe), who, not only concurred in the measure, but also promised to bring with him to the assembly his friends, the antelope and zebra, who received the invitation with less distrust from him than they would have done from one whose enmity they had often experienced.

The place of meeting was a valley near the northern bank of the White River: at the farther extremity, a small stream issued from the rock, forming, in its progress, a circular pool of the clearest water, which was surrounded on all sides by beautiful trees. Here, beneath the shade of a spreading mangrove, the lion took his seat, and the other animals stationed themselves in silence around him.

After a pause of a few moments, the Lion arose, and spoke in the following manner:—" It is well known to the present assembly, that our native woods have lately been exposed to the destructive incursions of a new race of men. They are easily distinguished from the ancient inhabitants by the whiteness of their

skins; and their dwellings are more closely united
together, and defended on all sides from our ravages.
They have acquired and maintain the superiority over
a great number of different animals; and, above all,
they seem to carry about with them the power of producing thunder and lightning at pleasure, which they
employ against us with the most fatal effect. Their
numbers seem to increase, while we daily diminish.
They penetrate the inmost recesses of the forest, and
circumscribe our range on every side; they appear
to be bent upon our total extermination. Shall we
tamely submit to the slaughter?—No. Let us lay
aside our mutual animosities, and unite against him,
as though animated by one spirit. By the wisdom and
courage of the present respectable assembly, I hope
a plan will be devised and executed, which shall at
once revenge our past wrongs, and prevent future
aggression."

Here the impatient Tiger exclaimed, "Let us advance against our enemy boldly, and he will flee from
us. Man takes courage from our remissness. I am
confident that the thunder and lightning, which he
appears to wield, are often directed against us in vain.
Let us make an attack on him this very night. I long
to dip my paws in the blood of these murderous inter-
lopers."

"No one," replied the Wolf, "has greater reason, or
is more inclined to join in an attack upon these new
settlers than myself, but I would by no means advise
the assault to be made by night. While the rest
sleep, one or more are continually on the watch, accompanied by dogs, who give an alarm on the slightest
appearance of danger; as I have learned to my cost,
having narrowly escaped from them several times,
while attempting, under cover of night, to carry off
the tame animals which are under their protection.
Besides, it would be almost impossible to surmount
the obstacles we should find in our way, their dwellings
are fenced round with such security."

"Let us make the onset in the broad daylight," grunted the Boar: "if once I get to close quarters with man, the sharpness of my tusks will soon put an end to the combat."

The Rhinoceros was also of opinion that night was an improper time for the attack. "We then," he observed, "cannot see our foes; and the sudden blazes of fire which man in that season so often produces, in all probability would throw us into confusion. But as for his thunder and lightning, I regard them not. Often his balls have struck me, and as often rebounded from my sides.—We shall be able to drive them from the forest; and if they take refuge in their enclosures, howsoever strong they may be, I am confident that we should soon trample them under our feet."

Here he was interrupted by the Buffalo, who cried, "As the Rhinoceros is so confident of success, and his skin is so impenetrable, he can have no objection to lead the van, and receive the first fire of the enemy."

"Whatever I do," replied the Rhinoceros, "rather than fight for your liberty, I believe you would tamely submit to be a slave to man, as many of your relations are at this moment."

"I am not responsible for the faults or the misfortunes of my relations," rejoined the Buffalo; "as well may you upbraid the Zebra with the patient spirit of the Ass, because he happens to resemble him in shape. In the day of battle, it will be seen whether I am more fearful than they who boast a thicker skin: a huge carcass is not always endued with the greatest portion of courage."

The anger of the Rhinoceros was aroused by this insinuation, and, regardless of the respect due to the august assembly, he would have pinned him to the earth with his horn, had not the Tiger (who was delighted by the last observation of the Buffalo) rushed to his assistance. The Rhinoceros paused in his career, when he beheld the new and more formidable antagonist whose glaring eyeballs were fixed upon him.

The Lion now interposed, and commanded silence in a tone of authority, which was instantly obeyed. After reprimanding the delinquents for interrupting the harmony of the meeting, he observed: "I am by no means convinced of the advantages to be derived from an attack in the daylight—for myself I should prefer the dusk of the evening. True courage never hesitates because of danger—he presses boldly forward, and meets with victory. But we have not yet been favoured with the opinion of the Elephant; from his acknowledged sagacity, we may hope for the plan of a successful attack."

The Elephant now slowly arose, elevated his trunk, and spoke in the following manner:—"I am by no means certain that my opinion will meet the approbation of this august assembly, yet I hope the reasons which have induced me to adopt it will be heard with patience. I have long and attentively watched the motions of this new race of men, and am fully persuaded that they intend to drive us from our native woods, or to accomplish our utter destruction:—and whether by our union we can prevent it, seems to me a very doubtful matter. That they are more powerful than the ancient tribes, arises principally from the weapons they possess, and the mutual assistance they afford to each other in times of danger. Individually, they are not so bold. The black man has often approached within the length of my trunk before he has struck his assagay into my side. He has provoked the Lion in his den; or induced him to spring over a precipice or a high enclosure, which he had rendered attractive by the bleating of a sheep. How many have been miserably strangled in the woods, or have perished in pits which he has dug by the river's side, and covered over, so as to resemble the solid ground? And those awful blazes of fire, which man alone can produce, the ancient inhabitants lighted every night for their protection and our annoyance. These methods of defence or attack seem to be despised by the new settlers, who trust almost solely to the sudden explosions which they can direct against us at their pleasure with such deadly effect. The possession of this power more than counterbalances their deficiencies of courage or of skill, and in its application they are often prompted by the most wanton cruelty; for not only we, but their own species also, whose only offence appears to be a darker skin, are shot for their amusement. When their passions are excited by a real or supposed injury, their barbarity knows no bounds: of this I shall relate an instance, from which the assembly may perceive the perfidiousness as well as power of the beings whose destruction forms the subject of our debate:—

" Soon after the settlement of the whites in our neighbourhood, the natives had great cause for complaint: they were deprived, on various pretexts, of their most fertile grounds, they were driven farther into the interior, and many of them were put to death: at last, being goaded to desperation, they took their weapons, and, attacking the nearest settlements, killed several of the whites, and put the rest to flight. Having collected the sheep and oxen (who have always been slaves to man), they returned in triumph, thinking their enemies would never dare to approach them again. But they were deceived. Before the expiration of two moons, a great number of the whites were collected, and marched against them. They spread death and desolation throughout the country, and pursued the natives from one place to another, until they reached the river, near which we are now assembled. There they halted; and messengers of peace appeared among the whites, offering restitution, and craving forgiveness. A day was appointed when the terms of reconciliation were to be agreed upon, and on that day, from a neighbouring grove, I witnessed the proceedings. Many hundreds of the natives were assembled on the sloping bank of the river. The cattle were given up, and the boundaries of their future possessions were marked out. The whites appeared to be highly gratified, and in token of friendship, at the conclusion of the interview, threw a number of small trinkets among the natives, and then retired. Suddenly, my attention was arrested by a flash of fire, followed by a tremendous explosion, which proceeded from the bushes immediately above the spot where the natives were busily employed picking up the gifts of their friends. When the smoke cleared away, I saw the margin of the river covered with dead bodies—the stream was dyed with their blood. Of the hundreds who had there assembled, only one escaped to tell the children how their fathers fell by the treachery of the whites. Such, I am afraid, would be our fate were we to brave their power. We might, perhaps, be successful at the first onset, but they would soon collect in such numbers as to destroy every hope of resistance or escape. My advice therefore is, to retire from their settlements—in a few days we should be far beyond their reach, and roam in our wonted security."

"That is my intention," cried the Zebra: "I am free, and never will submit to the yoke of man; but, as I am unfit to contend with him, I shall flee to the distant mountains."

The Tiger, who, during the speech of the Elephant, had exhibited evident symptoms of impatience, could scarcely restrain his rage, on hearing such sentiments.

The Camelopard now raised his tall and graceful head above the rest of the beasts, and said, "I neither intend to fight nor to flee, but shall remain here, to crop the leaves of the forest. I have no greater reason to complain of the white than of the black inhabitants of this region—and less of them than of some of the present assembly. Have not my friend the Antelope and myself been the constant prey of the Lion, the Tiger, and the Wolf?"

Here the Tiger, lashing his sides with his tail, while his eyes flashed fire, made a sudden spring on the Camelopard, and fixed his claws in his back. It was in vain that the poor animal bounded from the centre of the group, and scoured through the forest—he soon fell dead beneath his foe.

The Antelope, who was admiring his elegant shape and polished horns, reflected in the pool, instead of attending to the debate, started in terror at the noise, and fled with the utmost speed. He was closely pursued by the Wolf and Jackal, who had for some time beheld him with longing eyes.

The thundering roar of the Lion, which was intended to enforce order, only increased the confusion—all fled from him in the greatest disorder, except the Elephant; and he, disliking the angry growl of his companion, soon marched in solemn dignity to his wonted haunts —wondering more at the folly of attempting to subdue their common foe while they were at variance with each other, than at the abrupt termination of the *Council of Quadrupeds.*

TIT FOR TAT.

A Tale.

A LAW there is, of ancient fame,
By nature's self in every land implanted,
   Lex Talionis is its Latin name;
But if an English term be wanted,
   Give your next neighbour but a pat,
He'll give you back as good, and tell you—*tit for tat.*

This *tit for tat*, it seems, not men alone,
But Elephants, for legal justice own;
In proof of this, a story I shall tell ye,
Imported from the famous town of Delhi.

A mighty Elephant, that swell'd the state
   Of Aurungzebe the Great,
   One day was taken by his driver
   To drink and cool him in the river;

The driver on his neck was seated,
    And, as he rode along,
  By some acquaintance in the throng,
With a ripe cocoa-nut was treated.

A cocoa-nut's a pretty fruit enough,
But guarded by a shell both hard and tough:
  The fellow tried, and tried, and tried,
    Working and sweating,
    Pishing and fretting,
  To find out its inside,
And pick the kernel for his eating.

At length, quite out of patience grown,
" Who'll reach me up," he cries, " a stone,
  To break this plaguy shell ?
  But stay, I've here a solid bone,
    May do, perhaps, as well."
  So, half in earnest, half in jest,
He bang'd it on the forehead of his beast.

An Elephant, they say, has human feeling,
  And full as well as we he knows
  The diff'rence between words and blows,
Between horse-play and civil dealing.
  Use him but well, he'll do his best,
And serve you faithfully and truly:
  But insults unprovoked he can't digest,—
He studies o'er them, and repays them duly.

" To make my head an anvil," thought the creature,
" Was never, certainly, the will of Nature;
  So, master mine, you may repent:"
Then, shaking his broad ears, away he went:
  The driver took him to the water,
  And thought no more about the matter;
But Elephant within his mem'ry hid it;
He *felt* the wrong—the other only *did* it.

  A week or two elapsed, one market-day
  Again the beast and driver took their way:

Through rows of shops and booths they pass'd,
With eatables and trinkets stored;
Till to a gard'ner's stall they came at last,
Where cocoa-nuts lay piled upon the board.

"Ha!" thought the Elephant, "'tis now my turn
To show this method of nut-breaking;
My friend above will like to learn,
Though at the cost of a head-aching."

Then, in his curling trunk, he took a heap,
And waved it o'er his neck with sudden sweep,
  And, on the hapless driver's sconce,
    He laid a blow so hard and full,
  That crack'd the nuts at once,
    But with them crack'd his skull.

Young folk, whene'er you feel inclined
To rompish sports and freedoms rough,
  Bear *tit for tat* in mind,
Nor give an elephant a cuff,
  To be repaid in kind.

ON WINE AND SPIRITS.

GEORGE and Harry, accompanied by their Tutor, went one day to pay a visit to a neighbouring gentleman, their father's friend. They were very kindly received, and shown all about the gardens and pleasure-grounds; but nothing took their fancy so much as an extensive grapery, hung round with bunches of various kinds fully ripe, and almost too large for the vines to support. They were liberally treated with the fruit, and allowed to carry away some fine specimens, to eat as they walked. During their return, as they were picking their grapes, George said to the Tutor, "A thought is just come into my head, sir. Wine, you know, is called the juice of the grape; but wine is hot, and intoxicates people that drink much of it. Now we have had a good deal of grape-juice this morning, and yet I do not feel heated, nor does it seem at all to have got into our heads. What is the reason of this?"

Tut. The reason is, that grape-juice is not wine, though wine is made from it.

G. Pray how is it made, then?

T. I will tell you; for it is a matter worth knowing. The juice pressed from grapes, called *must*, is at first a sweet, watery liquor, with a little tartness, but with no strength or spirit. After it has stood awhile, it begins to grow thick and muddy; it moves up and down, and throws scum and bubbles of air to the surface. This is called *working* or *fermenting*. It continues in this state for some time, more or less, according to the quantity of the juice and the temperature of the weather, and then gradually settles again, becoming clearer than at first. It has now lost its sweet, flat taste, and acquired a briskness and pungency, with a heating and intoxicating property; that is, it has become *wine*. This natural process is called the *vinous fermentation*, and many liquors besides grape-juice are capable of undergoing it.

G. I have heard of the working of beer and ale. Is that of the same kind?

T. It is; and beer and ale may properly be called barley-wine; for you know they are clear, brisk, and intoxicating. In the same manner, cider is apple-wine, and mead is honey-wine; and you have heard of raisin and currant-wine, and a great many others.

Har. Yes; there is elder-wine, and cowslip-wine, and orange-wine.

G. Will everything of that sort make wine?

T. All vegetable juices that are sweet are capable of being fermented, and of producing a liquor of a vinous nature; but if they have little sweetness, the liquor is proportionably weak and poor, and is apt to become sour or vapid.

H. But barley is not sweet.

T. Barley, as it comes from the ear, is not; but

before it is used for brewing, it is made into *malt*, and then it is sensibly sweet. You know what malt is?

H. I have seen heaps of it in the malt-house, but I do not know how it is made.

T. Barley is converted into malt by putting it in heaps and wetting it, when it becomes hot, and swells, and would sprout out just as though it had been sown, unless it were then dried in a kiln. By this operation it acquires a sweet taste. You have drunk sweet-wort?

H. Yes.

T. Well, this is made by steeping malt in hot water. The water extracts and dissolves all the sweet, or sugary, part of the malt. It then becomes like a naturally sweet juice.

G. Would not sugar and water, then, make wine?

T. It would; and the wines made in England of our common fruits and flowers have all a good deal of sugar in them. Cowslip flowers, for example, give little more than the flavour to the wine named from them, and it is the sugar added to them which properly makes the wine.

G. But none of these wines are so good as grape-wine.

T. No. The grape, from the richness and abundance of its juice, is the fruit universally preferred for making wine, where it comes to perfection, which it seldom does in our climate, except by means of artificial heat.

H. I suppose, then, grapes are finest in the hottest countries.

T. Not so, neither; they are properly a fruit of the temperate zone, and do not grow well between the tropics. And in very hot countries it is scarcely possible to make wines of any kind to keep, for they ferment so strongly as to turn sour almost immediately.

G. I think I have read of palm-wine on the coast of Guinea.

T. Yes. A sweet juice flows abundantly from incisions in certain species of the palm, which ferments immediately, and makes a very pleasant sort of weak wine. But it must be drunk the same day it is made, for, on the next, it is as sour as vinegar.

G. What is vinegar—is it not sour wine ?

T. Everything that makes wine will make vinegar also ; and the stronger the wine, the stronger the vinegar. The vinous fermentation must be first brought on, but it need not produce perfect wine ; for when the intention is to make vinegar, the liquor is kept still warm, and it goes on, without stopping, to another kind of fermentation, called the *acetous*, the product of which is vinegar.

G. I have heard of alegar. I suppose that is vinegar made of ale.

T. It is—but as ale is not so strong as wine, the vinegar made from it is not so sharp or perfect. But housewives make good vinegar with sugar and water.

H. Will vinegar make people drunk, if they take too much of it ?

T. No ; the wine loses its intoxicating quality, as well as its taste, on turning to vinegar.

G. What are spirituous liquors—have they not something to do with wine ?

T. Yes. They consist of the spirituous or intoxicating part of wine separated from the rest. You may remember, that on talking of distillation, I told you, that it was the raising of a liquor in steam or vapour, and condensing it again ; and that some liquors were more easily turned to vapour than others, and were therefore called more volatile or evaporable. Now wine is a mixed or compound liquor, of which the greater part is water, but what heats and intoxicates is *vinous spirit*. This spirit being much more volatile than water, on the application of a gentle heat, flies off in vapour, and may be collected by itself in distilling vessels ; and thus are made spirituous liquors.

G. Will everything that you call wine yield spirits?

T. Yes; everything that has undergone the vinous fermentation. Thus, in England, a great deal of malt-spirit is made from a kind of wort brought into fermentation, and then set directly to distil, without first making ale or beer of it. Gin is a spirituous liquor also obtained from corn, and flavoured with juniper-berries. Even potatoes, carrots, and turnips, may be made to afford spirits, by first fermenting their juices. In the West Indies, rum is distilled from the dregs of the sugar-canes, washed out by water and fermented. But brandy is distilled from the fermented juice of the grape, and is made in the wine countries.

G. Is spirit of wine different from spirituous liquors?

T. It is the strongst part of them, got by distilling over again; for all these still contain a good deal of water, along with a pure spirit, which may be separated by a gentler heat than was used at first. But, in order to procure this as strong and pure as possible, it must be distilled several times over, always leaving some of the watery part behind. When perfectly pure, it is the same, whatever spirituous liquor it is got from.

H. My mamma has little bottles of lavender-water; what is that?

T. It is the spirit of wine flavoured with lavender flowers; and it may in like manner be flavoured with many other fragrant things, since their odoriferous part is volatile, and will rise in vapour along with the spirit.

H. Will not spirit of wine burn violently?

G. That it will, I can tell you; and so will rum and brandy, for you know it was set on fire when we made snap-dragon.

T. All spirituous liquors are highly inflammable, and the more so the purer they are. One way of trying the purity of spirit is to see if it will burn all away, without leaving any moisture behind. Then, it is much lighter than water, and that affords another way of judging of its strength. A hollow ivory ball is set to swim in it; and the deeper it sinks down, the lighter, and therefore the more spirituous, is the liquor.

G. I have heard much of the mischief done by spirituous liquors—pray what good do they do?

T. The use and abuse of wine and spirits, is a very copious subject; and there is scarcely any gift of human art, the general effects of which are more dubious. You know what wine is said to be given for in the Bible?

G. To make glad the heart of man.

T. Right. And nothing has such an immediate effect in inspiring vigour of body and mind as wine. It banishes sorrow and care, recruits from fatigue, enlivens the fancy, inflames the courage, and performs a hundred fine things, of which I could bring you abundant proof from the poets. The physicians, too, speak almost as much in its favour, both in diet and medicine. But its really good effects are only when used in moderation; and it unfortunately is one of those things which man can hardly be brought to use moderately. Excess in wine brings on effects the very contrary to its benefits. It stupifies and enfeebles the mind, and fills the body with incurable diseases. And this it does even when used without intoxication. But a drunken man loses for the time every distinction of a reasonable creature, and becomes worse than a brute beast. On this account, Mahomet entirely forbade its use to his followers, and to this day it is not publicly drunk in any of the countries that receive the Mahometan religion.

H. Was not that right?

T. I think not. If we were entirely to renounce everything that may be misused, we should have scarcely any enjoyments left; and it is a proper exercise of our strength of mind, to use good things with moderation, when we have it in our power to do otherwise.

G. But spirituous liquors are not good at all; are they?

T. They have so little good, and so much bad in them, that, I confess, I wish their common use could be abolished altogether. They are generally taken—gin especially—by the lowest class of people, for the express purpose of intoxication; and they are much sooner prejudicial to the health than wine, and, indeed, when drunk unmixed, are no better than slow poison. Still, at certain seasons, and under certain circumstances, they may be taken with advantage, medicinally, when diluted with water, and in small quantities.

G. Spirit of wine is useful, though, for several things—is it not?

T. Yes; and I would have all spirits kept in the hands of chemists and artists, who know how to employ them usefully. Spirit of wine will dissolve many things that water will not. Apothecaries use it in drawing tinctures, and artists in preparing colours and making varnishes. They are also very powerful preservatives from corruption. You may have seen serpents and insects brought from abroad in phials full of spirits.

G. I have.

H. And I know of another use of spirits.

T. What is that?

H. To burn in lamps. My grandmamma has a tea-kettle with a lamp under it, to keep the water hot, and she burns spirits in it.

T. So she does. Well—so much for the uses of these liquors.

G. But you have said nothing about ale and beer. Are they wholesome?

T. Yes, in moderation. But they are sadly abused, too, and rob many men of their health, as well as their money and senses.

G. Small beer does no harm, however.

T. No—and we will indulge in a good draught of it when we get home; that is, should we be thirsty.

H. I like water better.

T. Then drink it, by all means. He that is satisfied with water, has one want the less, and may defy thirst, in this country, at least.

FOURTEENTH EVENING.

THE BOY WITHOUT A GENIUS.

Mr. Wiseman, the schoolmaster, at the end of the summer vacation, received a new scholar with the following letter :—

" Sir,—This will be delivered to you by my son Samuel, whom I beg leave to commit to your care, hoping that, by your well-known skill and attention, you will be able to make something of him, which, I am sorry to say, none of his masters have hitherto done. He is now eleven, and yet can do nothing but read his mother tongue, and that but indifferently. We sent him at seven to a grammar-school in our neighbourhood; but his master soon found that his genius was not turned to the learning of languages. He was then put to writing, but he set about it so awkwardly, that he made nothing of it. He was tried at accounts, but it appeared that he had no genius for them either. He could do nothing in geography, for want of memory. In short, if he has any genius at all, it does not yet show itself. But I trust to your experience in cases of this nature, to discover what he is fit for, and to instruct him accordingly. I beg to be favoured shortly with your opinion about him, and remain,   " Sir

" Your most obedient servant,

" Humphrey Acres."

When Mr. Wiseman had read this letter, he shook his head, and said to his assistant, " A pretty subject they have sent us here ! a lad that has a great genius for nothing at all. But perhaps my friend, Mr. Acres, expects that a boy should show a genius for a thing before he knows anything about it—no uncommon error ! Let us see, however, what the youth looks like. I suppose he is a human creature, at least."

Master Samuel Acres was now called in. He came hanging down his head, and looking as though he was going to be flogged.

" Come hither, my dear !" said Mr. Wiseman—" Stand by me, and do not be afraid. Nobody will hurt you. How old are you ?

Eleven, last May, sir.

A well-grown boy of your age, indeed. You love play, I dare say.

Yes, sir.

What, are you a good hand at marbles ?

Pretty good, sir.

And can spin a top, and drive a hoop, I suppose ?

Yes, sir.

Then you have the full use of your hands and fingers ?

Yes, sir.

Can you write, Samuel ?

I learned a little, sir, but I left it off again.

And why so ?

Because I could not make the letters.

No ! Why, how do you think other boys do ?—have they more fingers than you ?

No, sir.

Are you not able to hold a pen as well as a marble ?

Samuel was silent.

Let me look at your hand.

Samuel held out both his paws like a dancing bear.

I see nothing here to hinder you from writing as well as any boy in the school. You can read, I sup pose?

Yes, sir.

Tell me, then, what is written over the school-room door.

Samuel, with some hesitation, read—

WHATEVER MAN HAS DONE, MAN MAY DO.

Pray, how did you learn to read?—Was it not by taking pains?

Yes, sir.

Well—taking more pains, will enable you to read better. Do you know anything of the Latin grammar?

No, sir.

Have you never learned it?

I tried, sir, but I could not get it by heart.

Why, you can say some things by heart. I dare say you can tell me the names of the days of the week in their order?

Yes, sir, I know them.

And the months in the year, perhaps?

Yes, sir.

And you could probably repeat the names of your brothers and sisters, and all your father's servants, and half the people in the village, besides?

I believe I could, sir.

Well—and is *hic, hæc, hoc,* more difficult to remember than these?

Samuel was silent.

Have you learned anything of accounts?

I went into addition, sir; but I did not go on with it.

Why so?

I could not do it, sir.

How many marbles can you buy for a penny?

Twelve new ones, sir.

And how many for a halfpenny?

Six.

And how many for twopence?

Twenty-four.

If you were to have a penny a day, what would that make in a week?

Sevenpence.

But if you paid twopence out of that, what would you have left?

Samuel studied awhile, and then said, fivepence.

Right. Why here you have been practising the four great rules of arithmetic,—addition, subtraction, multiplication, and division. Learning accounts is no more than this. Well, Samuel, I see what you are fit for. I shall set you about nothing but what you are able to do; but observe, you *must* do it. We have no *I can't* here. Now go among your schoolfellows.

Samuel went away, glad that his examination was over, and with more confidence in his powers than he had felt before.

The next day he began business. A boy less than himself was called out to set him a copy of letters, and another was appointed to hear him grammar. He read a few sentences in English that he could perfectly understand, to the master himself. Thus, by going on steadily and slowly, he made a sensible progress. He had already joined his letters, got all the declensions perfectly, and half the multiplication table, when Mr. Wiseman thought it time to answer his father's letter, which he did as follows:—

" Sir,—I now think it right to give you some information concerning your son. You perhaps expected it sooner, but I always wish to avoid hasty judgments. You mentioned in your letter that it had not yet been discovered which way his genius pointed. If by *genius* you meant such a decided bent of mind to any one pursuit, as will lead to excel with little or no labour or instruction, I must say that I have not met with such a quality in more than three or four boys in my life, and your son is certainly not among the number. But if you mean only the *ability* to do some of those things which the greater part of mankind can do, when properly taught, I can affirm that I find in him no peculiar deficiency. And whether you choose to bring him up

to trade, or to some practical profession, I see no reason
to doubt that he may in time become sufficiently qualified for it.   It is my favourite maxim, sir, that everything most valuable in this life may generally be
acquired by taking pains for it.   Your son has already
lost much time in the fruitless expectation of finding
out what he would take up of his own accord.   Believe
me, sir, few boys will take up anything of their own
accord, but a top or a marble.   I will take care, while
he is with me, that he loses no more time this way,
but is employed about things that are fit for him, not
doubting that we shall find him fit for them.

" I am, Sir, yours, &c.

" SOLON WISEMAN."

Though the doctrine of this letter did not perfectly
agree with Mr. Acres's notions, yet, being convinced
that Mr. Wiseman was more likely to make something
of his son than any of his former preceptors, he continued him at this school for some years, and had the
satisfaction to find him going on in a steady course of
gradual improvement.   In due time, a profession was
chosen for him, which seemed to suit his temper and
talents, but for which he had no *particular turn,*
having never thought at all about it.   He made a
respectable figure in it, and went through the world
with credit and usefulness, though *without a genius.*

HALF A CROWN'S WORTH.

VALENTINE was in his thirteenth year, and a scholar
in one of our great schools.   He was a well-disposed
boy, but could not help envying a little some of his
companions, who had a larger allowance of money than
himself.   He ventured, in a letter, to sound his father
on the subject, not directly asking for a particular
sum, but mentioning, that many of the boys in his class
had half a crown a week for pocket-money.

His father, who, for various reasons, did not choose
to comply with his wishes, nor yet to refuse him in a

mortifying manner, wrote an answer, the chief purpose of which was to make him sensible what sort of a sum half a crown a week was, and to how many more important uses it might be put, than to provide a schoolboy with things absolutely superfluous.

"It is calculated," said he, "that a grown man may be kept in health, and fit for labour, upon a pound and a half of good bread a day. Suppose the value of this to be twopence halfpenny, and add a penny for a quart of milk, which will greatly improve his diet, half a crown will keep him eight or nine days in this manner.

"A common labourer's wages in our country are seven shillings per week, and if you add somewhat extraordinary for harvest work, this will not make it amount to three half-crowns on an average the year round. Suppose his wife and children to earn another half-crown. For this ten shillings per week, he will maintain himself, his wife, and half a dozen children, in food, lodging, clothes, and fuel. A half-crown, then, may be reckoned the full weekly maintenance of two human creatures in everything necessary.

"Where potatoes are much cultivated, two bushels, weighing eighty pounds apiece, may be purchased for half a crown. Here are one hundred and sixty pounds of solid food, of which, allowing for the waste in dressing, you may reckon two pounds and a half sufficient for the sole daily nourishment of one person. At this rate, nine people might be fed a week for half a crown; poorly, indeed, but so as many thousands are fed, with the addition of a little salt or buttermilk.

"If the father of a numerous family were out of work, or the mother lying-in, a parish would think half a crown a week a very ample assistance to them.

"Many of the cottagers around us would receive with great thankfulness a sixpenny loaf per week, and reckon it a very material addition to their children's bread. For half a crown, therefore, you might purchase—the weekly blessings of five poor families.

" Porter is a sort of luxury to a poor man, but not a useless one, since it will stand in the place of some solid food, and enable him to work with better heart. You could treat a hard-working man with a pint a day of this liquor for a fortnight, with half a crown.

" Many a cottage in the country, inhabited by a large family, is let for forty shillings a year. Half a crown a week would pay the full rent of three such cottages, and allow somewhat over, for repairs.

" The usual price for schooling at a dame-school in a village is twopence a week. You might, therefore, get fifteen children instructed in reading, and the girls in sewing, for half a crown weekly. But even in a town you might get them taught reading, writing, and accounts, and so fitted for any common trade, for five shillings a quarter; and, therefore, half a crown a week would keep six children at such a school, and provide them with books besides.

" All these are ways in which half a crown a week might be made to do a great deal of good to *others*. I shall now just mention one or two ways of laying it out with advantage to yourself.

" I know you are very fond of coloured plates of plants, and other objects of natural history. There are now several works of this sort publishing, in monthly numbers; as the Botanical Magazine, the English Botany, the Flora Rustica, and the Naturalist's Magazine. Now, half a crown a week would reach the purchase of the best of these.

" The same sum laid out in the old book-shops in London, would buy you more classics, and pretty editions too, in one year, than you could read in five.

" Now I do not grudge laying out half a crown a week upon you; but when so many good things for yourself and others may be done with it, I am unwilling you should squander it away, like your schoolfellows, in tarts and trinkets."

TRIAL

OF A COMPLAINT MADE AGAINST SUNDRY PERSONS FOR BREAKING THE WINDOW OF DOROTHY CAREFUL, WIDOW, AND DEALER IN GINGERBREAD.*

THE Court being seated, there appeared in person the Widow Dorothy Careful, to make a complaint against Henry Luckless, and some other person or persons unknown, for breaking three panes of glass, value ninepence, in the house of the said widow. Being directed to state her case to the Court, she made a curtsey, and began as follows:—

" Please your lordship, I was sitting at work by my fireside, between the hours of six and seven in the evening, just as it was growing dusk, and little Jack was spinning beside me, when, all at once, crack went the window, and down fell a little basket of cakes that was set up against it. I started up, and cried to Jack, ' Bless me, what's the matter?' So says Jack, ' Somebody has thrown a stone, and broken the window, and I dare say it is some of the schoolboys.' With that, I ran out of the house, and saw some boys making off as fast as they could go. So I ran after them as quick as my old legs would carry me; but I should never have come near them, if one had not happened to fall down. Him I caught, and brought back to my house; when Jack knew him at once to be Master Harry Luckless. So I told him I would complain of him the next day; and I hope your worship will make him pay the damage; and I think he deserves a good whipping into the bargain, for injuring a poor widow woman.''

* This was meant as a sequel of that very pleasing and ingenious little work, entitled *Juvenile Trials*, in which a Court of Justice is supposed to be instituted in a boarding-school, composed of the scholars themselves, for the purpose of trying offences committed at school.

The Judge, having heard Mrs. Careful's story, desired her to sit down; and then, calling up Master Luckless, asked him what he had to say for himself. Luckless appeared with his face a good deal scratched, and looking very ruefully. After making his bow, and sobbing two or three times, he said:—

"My lord, I am as innocent of this matter as any boy in the school, and I am sure I have suffered enough about it already. My lord, Billy Thompson and I were playing in the lane near Mrs. Careful's house, when we heard the window crash; and directly after she came running out towards us. Upon this, Billy ran away, and I ran too, thinking I might bear the blame. But, after running a little way, I stumbled over something that lay in the road, and before I could get up again, she overtook me, and caught me by the hair, and began lugging and cuffing me. I told her it was not I that broke her window, but it did not signify; so she dragged me to the light, lugging and scratching me all the while, and then said she would inform against me; and that is all I know of the matter."

Judge. I find, good woman, you were willing to revenge yourself, without waiting for the justice of this court.

Widow Careful. My lord, I confess I was put into a passion, and did not properly consider what I was doing.

Judge. Well, where is Billy Thompson?

Billy. Here, my lord.

Judge. You have heard what Harry Luckless says. Declare, upon your honour, whether he has spoken the truth.

Billy. My lord, I am sure neither he, nor I, had any concern in breaking the window. We were standing together at the time; and I ran, on hearing the door open, for fear of being charged with it, and he followed. But what became of him I did not stay to see.

Judge. So, you let your friend shift for himself, and only thought of saving yourself. But did you see any other person about the house or in the lane?

Billy. My lord, I thought I heard somebody on the other side of the hedge, creeping along, a little before the window was broken, but I saw nobody.

Judge. You hear, good woman, what is alleged in behalf of the person you have accused. Have you any other evidence against him?

Widow Careful. One might be sure that they would deny it, and tell lies for one another; but I hope I am not to be put off in that manner.

Judge. I must tell you, mistress, that you give too much liberty to your tongue, and are guilty of as much injustice as that of which you complain. I should be sorry, indeed, if the young gentlemen of this school deserved the general character of liars. You will find among us, I hope, as just a sense of what is right and honourable as among those who are older; and our worthy master certainly would not permit us to try offences in this manner, if he thought us capable of bearing false witness in each other's favour.

Widow Careful. I ask your lordship's pardon, I did not mean to offend; but it is a heavy loss for a poor woman, and though I did not catch the boy in the fact, he was the nearest when it was done.

Judge. As that is no more than a suspicion, and he has the positive evidence of his schoolfellow in his favour, it will be impossible to convict him, consistently with the rules of justice. Have you discovered any other circumstance that may point out the offender?

Widow Careful. My lord, next morning Jack found on the floor this top, which I suppose the window was broken with.

Judge. Hand it up—Here, gentlemen of the jury, please to examine it, and see if you can discover anything of its owner.

Juryman. Here is P. R. cut upon it

o

Another. Yes, and I am sure I recollect Peter Riot's having just such a one.

Another. So do I.

Judge. Master Riot, is this your top?

Riot. I don't know, my lord; perhaps it may be mine; I have had a great many tops, and when I have done with them I throw them away, and anybody may pick them up that pleases. You see it has lost its peg.

Judge. Very well, sir. Mrs. Careful, you may retire.

Widow Careful. And must I have no amends, my lord?

Judge. Have patience. Leave everything to the Court. We shall do you all the justice in our power.

As soon as the widow was gone, the Judge arose from his seat, and with much solemnity thus addressed the assembly:—

" Gentlemen,—This business, I confess, gives me much dissatisfaction. A poor woman has been insulted and injured in her property, apparently without provocation; and though she has not been able to convict the offender, it cannot be doubted that she, as well as the world in general, will impute the crime to some of our society. Though I am in my own mind convinced that, in her passion, she charged an innocent person, yet the circumstance of the top is a strong suspicion, indeed almost a proof, that the perpetrator of this unmanly mischief was one of our body. The owner of the top has justly observed, that its having been his property is no certain proof against him. Since, therefore, in the present defect of evidence, the whole school must remain burdened with the discredit of this action, and share in the guilt of it, I think fit, in the first place, to decree, that restitution shall be made to the sufferer out of the public chest; and next, that a court of inquiry be instituted, for the express purpose of searching thoroughly into this affair, with power to examine all persons upon honour, who are thought likely to be able to throw light upon it. I hope, gentlemen, these measures meet with your concurrence!''

The whole Court bowed to the Judge, and expressed their entire satisfaction with his determination.

It was then ordered that the public treasurer should go to Widow Careful's house, and pay her the sum of one shilling, making at the same time a handsome apology in the name of the school. And six persons were taken by lot out of the jury to compose the Court of Inquiry, which was to sit in the evening.

The Court then adjourned.

On the meeting of the Court of Inquiry, the first thing proposed by the President was, that the persons who usually played with Master Riot should be sent for. Accordingly Tom Frisk and Bob Loiter were summoned, when the President asked them upon their honour if they knew the top to have been Riot's. They said they did. They were then asked whether they remembered when Riot had it in his possession?

Frisk. He had it the day before yesterday, and split a top of mine with it.

Loiter. Yes; and then, as he was making a stroke at mine, the peg flew out.

Presid. What did he then do with it?

Frisk. He put it into his pocket, and said, as it was a strong top, he would have it mended.

Presid. Then he did not throw it away, or give it to anybody?

Loiter. No; he pocketed it up, and we saw no more of it.

Presid. Do you know of any quarrel he had with Widow Careful?

Frisk. Yes; a day or two before, he went to her shop for some gingerbread; but, as he already owed her sixpence, she would not let him have any till he paid his debts.

Presid. How did he take the disappointment?

Frisk. He said he would be revenged on her.

Presid. Are you sure he used such words ?

Frisk. Yes; Loiter heard him as well as myself.

Loiter. I did, sir.

Presid. Do either of you know any more of this affair ?

Both. No, sir.

Presid. You may go.

The President now observed, that these witnesses had done a great deal in establishing proofs against Riot; for it was now pretty certain that no one but he could have been in possession of the top at the time the crime was committed; and also it appeared, that he had declared a malicious intention against the woman, which it was highly probable he would put into execution.—As the Court were debating about the next step to be taken, they were acquainted that Jack, the widow's son, was waiting at the school door for admission; and a person being sent out for him, Riot was found threatening the boy, and bidding him go home about his business. The boy, however, was conveyed safely into the room, where he thus addressed himself to the President :—

Jack. Sir, and please your worship, as I was looking about this morning for sticks in the hedge over against our house, I found this buckle. So I thought to myself, sure this must belong to the rascal that broke our window. So I have brought it, to see if anybody in the school would own it.

Presid. On which side of the hedge did you find it ?

Jack. On the other side from our house, in the close.

Presid. Let us see it.   Gentlemen, this is so smart a buckle, that I am sure I remember it at once; and so I dare say you all do.

All. It is Riot's.

Presid. Has anybody observed Riot's shoes to-day ?

One Boy. Yes, he has got them tied with strings.

Presid. Very well, Gentlemen; we have nothing more

to do than to draw up an account of all the evidence we have heard, and lay it before his lordship. Jack, you may go home.

Jack. Pray, sir, let somebody go with me, for I am afraid of Riot, who has just been threatening me at the door.

Presid. Master Bold will please to go along with the boy.

The minutes of the court were then drawn up, and the President took them to the Judge's chamber. After the Judge had perused them, he ordered an indictment to be drawn up against Peter Riot, "for that he meanly, clandestinely, and with malice aforethought, had broken three panes in the window of Widow Careful, with a certain instrument called a top, whereby he had committed an atrocious injury on an innocent person, and had brought a disgrace upon the society to which he belonged." At the same time he sent an officer to inform Master Riot that his trial would come on the next morning.

Riot, who was with some of his gay companions, affected to treat the matter with great indifference, and even to make a jest of it. However, in the morning he thought it best to endeavour to make it up; and accordingly, when the Court were assembled, he sent one of his friends with a shilling, saying that he would not trouble them with any further inquiries, but would pay the sum that had been issued out of the public stock. On the receipt of this message, the Judge rose, with much severity in his countenance, and observed, that by such a contemptuous behaviour towards the Court the criminal had greatly added to his offence; he ordered two officers with their staves immediately to go and bring in Riot, and to use force if he should resist them. The culprit, thinking it best to submit, was presently led in between the two officers; when, being placed at the bar, the Judge thus addressed him :—

" I am sorry, sir, that any member of this society

can be so little sensible of the nature of a crime, and
so little acquainted with the principles of a court of
justice, as you have shown yourself to be, by the proposal you took the improper liberty of sending to us.
If you meant it as a confession of your guilt, you certainly ought to have waited to receive from us the
penalty we thought proper to inflict, and not to have
imagined that an offer of the mere payment of damages
would satisfy the claims of justice against you. If you
had broken the window only by accident, and, of your
own accord, offered restitution, nothing less than the
full damages could have been accepted.   But you now
stand charged with having done this mischief, meanly,
secretly, and maliciously, and thereby have added a
great deal of criminal intention to the act.   Can you,
then, think that a court like this, designed to watch
over the morals, as well as protect the properties of
our community, can so slightly pass over such aggravated offences ?   You can claim no merit from confessing the crime, now that you know so much evidence
will appear against you.   And if you choose still to
plead not guilty, you are at liberty to do it, and we
will proceed immediately to the trial, without taking
any advantage of the confession implied by your offer
of payment."

Riot stood silent for some time, and then begged to
be allowed to consult with his friends, what was best
for him to do.   This was agreed to, and he was permitted to retire, though under guard of an officer.
After a short absence, he returned with more humility
in his looks, and said that he pleaded guilty, and threw
himself on the mercy of the Court.   The Judge then
made a speech of some length, for the purpose of con-
vincing the prisoner, as well as the by-standers, of the
enormity of the crime.   He then pronounced the following sentence :—

"You, Peter Riot, are hereby sentenced to pay the
sum of half a crown to the public treasury, as a satisfaction for the mischief you have done, and your at-

tempt to conceal it. You are to repair to the house of Widow Careful, accompanied by such witnesses as we shall appoint, and there having first paid her the sum you owe her, you shall ask her pardon for the insult you offered her. You shall likewise, to-morrow, after school, stand up in your place, and before all the scholars ask pardon for the disgrace you have been the means of bringing upon the society; and, in particular, you shall apologize to Master Luckless, for the disagreeable circumstance you were the means of bringing him into. Till all this is complied with, you shall not presume to come into the playground, or join in any of the diversions of the school; and all persons are hereby admonished not to keep your company till this is done."

Riot was then dismissed to his room; and in the afternoon he was taken to the widow's, who was pleased to receive his submission graciously, and at the same time to apologize for her own improper treatment of Master Luckless, to whom she sent a present of a nice ball, by way of amends.

Thus ended this important business.

FIFTEENTH EVENING.

THE LEGUMINOUS PLANTS.
Tutor—George—Harry.

G. WHAT a delightful scent!

H. Charming! It is sweeter than Mr. Essence's shop.

T. Do you know whence it comes?

G. O—it is from the bean-field on the other side of the hedge, I suppose.

T. It is. This is the month in which beans are in blossom. See—the stalks are full of their black and white flowers.

H. I see peas in blossom, too, on the other side of the field.

G. You told us some time ago of grass and corn flowers; but they make a poor figure compared to these.

T. They do. The glory of a corn-field is when it is ripe; but peas and beans look very shabbily at that time. But suppose we take a closer view of these blossoms. Go you, George, and bring me a bean-plant; and you, Harry, a pea.

[They· go and bring them.

T. Now let us sit down and compare them. Do you think these flowers much alike?

H. O no—very little.

G. Yes—a good deal.

T. A little and a good deal! How can that be? Come, let us see. In the first place, they do not much resemble each other in size or colour.

G. No—but I think they do in shape.

T. True. They are both irregular flowers, and have the same distribution of parts. They are of the kind called *papilionaceous;* from *papilio,* the Latin word for a butterfly, which insect they are thought to resemble.

G. The pea does a little, but not much.

T. Some do much more than these. Well—you see first a broad leaf standing upright, but somewhat bent back; this is named the *standard.* On each side are two narrower, called the *wings.* The under-side of the flower is formed of a hollow part resembling a boat; this is called a *keel.*

G. It is very like a boat, indeed!

T. In some kinds, however, it is divided in the middle, and so is like a boat split in two. All these parts have claws, which unite to form a tube, set in a *calyx* or flower-cup. This tube, you observe, is longer in the bean than in the pea, and the proportions of the other parts are somewhat different; but the parts themselves are found in both.

H. So they are. I think them alike now.

T. That is the consequence of examining closely. Now, let us strip off all the leaves of this bean-flower but the keel. What do you think this boat contains?

G. It must be those little things you told us are in all flowers.

H. The chives and pistil.

T. Right. I will draw down the keel gently, and you shall see them.

H. How curious!

T. Here are a number of chives joining in their bodies so as to make a round tube, or cylinder, through which comes out a crooked thread, which is the pistil. I will now, with a pin, slit this cylinder. What do you see within it?

G. Somewhat like a little pod.

T. True—and, to show you that it is a pod, I will open it, and you shall see the seeds within it.

H. What tiny things! Is this, then, what makes the bean-pod afterwards?

T. It is. When the blossom drops, this seed-vessel grows bigger and bigger, and at length hardens as the seeds grow ripe, becomes black and shrivelled, and would burst and shed the seeds, if they were not gathered.

G. I have seen several burst pods of our sweet-peas under the wall, with nothing left in them.

T. And it is common for the field-peas and beans to lose a great part of the seeds while they are getting in.

H. At the bottom of this pea-stalk there are some pods set already.

T. Open one. You see that the pod is composed of two shells, and that all the seeds are fastened to one side of the pod, but alternately to each shell.

G. Is it the same in beans?

T. Yes, and in all other pods of the papilionaceous flowers. Well, this is the general structure of a very numerous and useful class of plants, called the *leguminous* or *podded*. Of these, in this country, tho greater part are herbaceous, with some shrubs. In the warm climates, there are also tall trees. Many of the leguminous plants afford excellent nourishment for man and beast; and their pods have the name of *pulse*.

G. I have read of persons living on pulse, but I did not know what it meant before.

T. It is frequently mentioned as part of the diet of abstemious persons. Of this kind, we eat peas, beans, and kidney, or French beans, of all which there are a variety of sorts cultivated. Other nations eat lentils and lupins, which are of this class; with several others.

H. I remember our lupins in the garden have flowers of this kind, with pods growing in clusters. But we cultivate them only for the colour and smell.

T. But other nations eat them. Then, all the kinds of clover, or trefoil, which are so useful in feeding cattle, belong to this tribe; as do also vetches, sainfoin, and lucerne, which are used for the same purpose. These principally compose what are usually, though improperly, called in agriculture, *artificial grasses*.

G. Clover-flowers are as sweet as beans; but do they bear pods?

T. Yes, very short ones, with one or two seeds in each. But there is a kind called *nonsuch*, with a very small, yellow flower, that has a curious, twisted pod, like a snail-shell. Many of the leguminous plants are weak, and cannot support themselves; hence they are furnished with tendrils, by means of which they clasp neighbouring plants, and run up them. You know the garden peas do so to the sticks which are set in the rows with them. Some kind of vetches run in this manner up the hedges, which they decorate with their long bunches of blue or purple flowers. Tares, which are some of the slenderest of the family, do much mischief among corn by twining around it, and choking it.

H. What are they good for, then?

T. They are weeds, or noxious plants, with respect to us; but doubtless they have their uses in the creation. There is a kind of tares, however, which, when grown by themselves, are excellent food for cattle. Some of our papilionaceous plants are able enough to shift for themselves; for gorse or furze is of the number.

G. What, that prickly bush all covered over with yellow flowers, that overruns our common?

T. Yes. Then there is broom, a plant as big, but without thorns, and with larger flowers. This is as frequent as furze in some places.

H. I know it grows in abundance in the Broom-field.

T. It does; but the naming of fields and places from it is a proof that it is not so common as the other.

G. We have some bushes of white broom in the shrubbery, and some trees of Spanish broom.

T. True. You have also a small tree which flowers early, and bears a great many pendent branches of yellow blossoms, that look peculiarly beautiful when intermixed with the purple lilacs.

H. I know it—laburnum.

T. Right. That is one of our class of plants, too. Then there is a large tree, with delicate little leaves, protected by long thorns, and bearing bunches of white papilionaceous flowers.

G. I know which you mean, but I cannot tell the name.

T. It is the bastard acacia, or locust-tree, a native of America. Thus, you see, we have traced this class of plants through all sizes, from the trefoil that covers the turf, to a large tree. I should not, however, forget two others,—the liquorice, and the tamarind. The liquorice, with the sweet root of which you are well acquainted, grows in the warmer countries, especially Spain, but is cultivated in England. The tamarind is a larger spreading tree, growing in the West

Indies, and valued for its shade, as well as for the cooling acid pulp of its pods, which are preserved with sugar, and sent over to us.

H. I know them very well.

T. Well—do you think, now, you shall both be able to discover a papilionaceous flower when you meet with it again?

G. I believe I shall, if they are all like these we have been examining.

T. They have all the same parts, though variously proportioned. What are these?

G. There is the standard, and there are the two wings.

H. And the keel.

T. Right—the keel, sometimes cleft into two, and then it is an irregular, five-leaved flower. The chives are generally ten, of which one stands apart from the rest. The pistil single, and ending in a pod. Another circumstance, common to most of this tribe, is, that their leaves are *winged* or *pinnated;* that is, having leaflets set opposite each other upon a middle rib. You see this structure in these bean-leaves. But in the clovers there are only two opposite leaflets, and one terminating; whence their name of trefoil, or three-leaf. What we call a club on cards is properly a clover-leaf, and the French call it *trèfle*, which means the same.

G. I think this tribe of plants almost as useful as the grasses.

T. They, perhaps, come the next in utility; but their seeds, such as beans and peas, are not quite such good nourishment as corn; and bread cannot be made of them.

G. But clover is better than grass for cattle.

T. It is more fattening, and makes cows yield plenty of fine milk. Well—let us march.

ON MAN.

Charles. You gave me the definition of a horse some time ago. Pray, sir, how is a man defined?

Father. That is worth inquiring. Let us consider, then. He must either stand by himself, or be ranked among the quadrupeds; for there are no other two-legged animals but birds, which he certainly does not resemble.

C. But how can he be made a quadruped?

F. By setting him to crawl on the ground, in which case, he will as much resemble a baboon, as a baboon set on his hind legs resembles a man. In reality, there is little difference between the arms of a man and the fore legs of a quadruped; and, in all other circumstances of internal and external structure, they are evidently formed upon the same model.

C. I suppose that we must call him a digitated quadruped, that generally goes upon its hind legs.

F. A naturalist could not reckon him otherwise; and, accordingly, Linnæus has placed him in the same division with apes, macocos, and bats.

C. Apes, macocos, and bats!

F. Yes—they have all four cutting teeth in the upper jaw, and teats on the breast. How do you like your relations?

C. Not at all!

F. Then we will get rid of them by applying to the other part of human nature—the *mind.* Man is an animal possessed of *reason,* and the only one; at least in an equal degree, or anything like a near approach to it. This, therefore, is sufficient to define him.

C. I have often heard, that man is a rational creature, and I have a notion what that means; but I should like to have an exact definition of reason.

F. Reason is the faculty by which we compare ideas, and draw conclusions. A man walking in the woods of an unknown country finds a bow. He compares it in his mind with other bows, and forms the conclusion that it must have been made by man, and that, therefore, the country is probably inhabited. He discovers a hut ; sees in it half-burnt wood, and finds that the ashes are not quite cold. He concludes, therefore, with certainty, not only that there are inhabitants, but that they cannot be far distant. No other animal could do this.

C. But would not a dog, who had been used to live with men, run into such a hut, and expect to find people in it ?

F. He probably would—and this, I acknowledge, is very like reason, for he may be supposed to compare in his mind, the hut he has lived in with that which he sees, and to conclude, that as there were men in the former, there are men in the latter. But how little does this aid him. He finds no men there, and he is unable, by any marks, to form a judgment how long they have been absent, or what sort of people they were ; still less does he form any plan of conduct in consequence of his discovery.

C. Then, is not the difference only, that man has much reason, and brutes little ?

F. If we adhere to the mere words of the definition of reason, I believe this must be admitted ; but in the exercise of it, the superiority of the human faculties is so great, that man is in many points absolutely distinguished from brutes. In the first place, he has the *use of speech*, which no other animal has attained.

C. Cannot many animals make themselves understood by one another by their cries ?

F. They can make known their common wants and desires, but they cannot *discourse*, or, it is presumed, communicate ideas stored up in the memory. It is this faculty, which makes man an *improvable* being, the wisdom and experience acquired by one individual, being thus transmitted to others, and so on in an endless series of progression.—There is no reason to suppose that the dogs of the present day are more knowing than those which lived a thousand years ago; but the men of this age are much better acquainted with numberless arts and sciences, than their remote ancestors; since by the use of speech, and of writing (which is speech addressed to the eye), every age adds its own discoveries to all former ones. This knowledge of the past also gives a man a great insight into the future. Shakspeare excellently defines man, by saying, that he is a creature " made with large discourse, looking before and after."

C. Brute animals must surely know something of the future, when they lay up a store of provision for the winter?

F. No—it is pretty certain that this is not the case, for they will do it as much the first year of their lives as any other. Young bees turned out of their hive, as soon as they have swarmed, and got a habitation, begin laying up honey, though they cannot possibly foresee the use they shall have for it. There are a vast number of actions of this sort in brute animals, which are directed to a useful end, but an end of which the animal knows nothing. And this is what we call *instinct*, and properly distinguished from reason. Man has less of it than almost any other animal, because he requires it less. Another point of essential difference is, that man is the only animal that makes use of *instruments* in any of his actions. He is a *toolmaking* and *machine-making* animal. By means of this faculty alone, he is everywhere Lord of the creation, and has equally triumphed over the subtlety of the cunning, the swiftness of the fleet, and the force of the strong. He is the only animal that has found out the use of *fire*, a most important acquisition.

C. I have read of some large apes, that will come and sit round a fire in the woods, when men have left it, but have not the sense to keep it in, by throwing on sticks.

F. Still less, then, could they light a fire. In conse-

quence of this discovery, man cooks his food, which no
other animal does.   He alone fences against the cold
by clothing as well as by fire.   He alone cultivates the
earth, and keeps living animals for future uses.

C. But have not there been wild men bred in the
woods that could do none of these things ?

F. Some instances of this nature are recorded, and
they are not to be wondered at ; for man was meant
to be a *gregarious* animal, or one living in society, in
which alone his faculties have full scope, and especially
his power of improving by the use of speech.   These
poor solitary creatures, brought up with the brutes,
were in a state entirely unnatural to them.   Unless
from instinct, a solitary bee, ant, or beaver, would have
none of the skill and sagacity of those animals in their
proper social condition.   Thus it would appear that,
in some instances, and under some circumstances,
reason and instinct are separated by a very narrow
line of demarcation.   Society sharpens all the faculties, and gives ideas and views which never could have
been entertained by an individual.

C. But some men that live in society seem to be
little above the brutes, at least, when compared to other
men.   What is a Hottentot or a Bushman in comparison to one of us ?

F. The difference, indeed, is great ; but we agree in
the most essential characters of *man*, and perhaps the
advantage is not all on our side.   The Hottentot cultivates the earth, and rears cattle.   He not only herds
with his fellows, but he has instituted some sort of
government for the protection of the weak against the
strong.   He has a notion of right and wrong, and is
sensible of the necessity of controlling present appetites and passions for the sake of a future good.   He
has, therefore, *morals.*   He is possessed of weapons,
tools, clothing, and furniture, of his own making.   In
agility of body, and the knowledge of various circumstances relative to the nature of animals, he surpasses
us.   His inferiority lies in those things in which many

of the lower classes among us are almost equally inferior to the instructed.

C. But Hottentots are said to have no notion of a
God, or of a future state.

F. I am not certain how far that may be fact; but,
alas! how many among us have no knowledge at all on
these subjects, or only some vague notions, full of
absurdity and superstition! People far advanced in
civilization have entertained the grossest errors on
these subjects, which are to be corrected only by the
serious application of reason, or by a direct revelation
from Heaven.

C. You said man was an *improvable* creature—but
have not many nations been a long time in a savage
state without improvement?

F. Man is always *capable of improvement;* but he
may exist a long time, in society, without *actually
improving* beyond a certain point. There is little
improvement among nations who have not the *art of
writing;* for tradition is not capable of preserving very
accurate or extensive knowledge; and many arts and
sciences, after flourishing greatly, have been entirely
lost, in countries which have been overrun by barbarous
and illiterate nations. Then there is a principle which
I might have mentioned as one of the principles which
distinguish man from brutes, but it as much distinguishes some men from others. This is *curiosity,* or
the love of knowledge for its own sake. Most savages
have little or nothing of this; but, without it, we
should want one of the chief inducements to exert our
faculties. It is curiosity that impels us to search into
the properties of every part of nature, to try all sorts
of experiments, to visit distant regions, and even to
examine the appearances and motions of the heavenly
bodies. Every fact thus discovered, leads to other
facts; and there is no limit to be set to this progress.
The time may come, when what we now know may
seem as much ignorance to future ages, as the knowledge of early times seems to us.

C. What nations know the most at present ?

F. The Europeans have long been distinguished for superior ardour after knowledge, and they possess, beyond all comparison, the greatest share of it, whereby they have been enabled to command the rest of the world. The countries in which the arts and sciences most flourish at present, are the northern and middle parts of Europe, and also North America, which, you know, is inhabited by descendants of Europeans. In these countries man may be said to be *most man ;* and they may apply to themselves the poet's boast—

"*Man* is the nobler growth these realms supply,
And *souls* are ripen'd in our northern sky."

WALKING THE STREETS.
A Parable.

HAVE you ever walked through the crowded streets of a great city ?

What shoals of people pouring in from opposite quarters, like torrents meeting in a narrow valley! You would imagine it impossible for them to get through ; yet all pass on their way, without stop or molestation.

Were each man to proceed exactly in the line in which he set out, he could not move many paces without encountering another full in his track. They would strike against each other, fall back, push forward again, block up the way for themselves, and those after them, and throw the whole street into confusion.

All this is avoided by every man's *yielding a little.*

Instead of advancing square, stiff, with arms stuck out, every one who knows how to walk the streets, glides along, his arms close, his body oblique and flexible, his track gently winding, leaving now a few inches on this side, now on that, so as to pass and be passed, without touching, in the smallest possible space.

He pushes no one into the kennel, nor goes into it

himself. By *mutual accommodation*, the path, though narrow, admits them all.

He goes neither much faster nor much slower than others who go in the same direction. In the first case, he would elbow; in the second, he would be elbowed.

If any accidental stop arise, from a carriage crossing, a cask rolled, a pickpocket detected, or the like, he does not increase the bustle by rushing into the midst of it, but checks his pace, and patiently awaits its removal.

Like this is the *march of life.*

In our progress through the world, a thousand things continually stand in our way. Some people meet us full in the face with opposite opinions and inclinations; some stand before us in our pursuit of pleasure or interest, and others follow close upon our heels. Now, we ought in the first place to consider, that *the road is as free for one as for another;* and therefore we have no right to expect that persons should go out of their way to let us pass, any more than we out of ours to let them pass. Then, if we do not mutually yield and accommodate a little, it is clear that we must all stand still, or be thrown into a perpetual confusion of squeezing and justling. If we are all in a hurry to get on as fast as possible to some point of pleasure or interest in our view, and do not occasionally hold back, when the crowd gathers, and angry contentions arise, we shall only augment the tumult, without advancing our own progress. On the whole, it is our business to move onwards, steadily, but quietly, obstructing others as little as possible, yielding a little to this man's prejudices and that man's desires, and doing everything in our power to make the *journey of life* easy to all our fellow-travellers as well as to ourselves.

SIXTEENTH EVENING.

THE COMPOUND-FLOWERED PLANTS.

Tutor—George—Harry.

George. HARRY, can you blow off all these dandelion feathers at a blast?

Harry. I will try.

G. See, you have left almost half of them.

H. Can you do better?

G. Yes; look here.

H. There are still several left.

Tutor. A pretty child's play you have got there. Bring me one of the dandelion heads, and let us see if we can make no other use of it.

H. Here is a very full one.

T. Do you know what these feathers, as you call them, are?

G. I believe they belong to the seeds.

T. They do, and they are worth examining. Look at this single one through my magnifying-glass: you observe the seed at the bottom, like the point of a dart. From it springs a slender hairy shaft, crowned by a most elegant, spreading plume. You see, it is a complete arrow of nature's manufacture.

G. How exact!

H. What a beautiful thing!

T. I am sure you see the use of it at once.

G. It is to set the seeds flying with the wind.

H. And, I suppose, they sow themselves where they alight.

T. They do. This is one of nature's contrivances for *dissemination,* or that scattering of the seeds of plants which makes them reach all the places proper for their growth. I dare say you have observed other plants furnished with the same winged, or feathered, seeds.

H. O yes; there are groundsel, and ragwort, and thistles.

C. In a windy day, I have seen the air all full of thistle-down.

T. Very likely; and for that reason you never saw a new-made bank of earth, or a heap of dung in the fields, but it was presently covered with thistles. These, and the other plants that have been named, belong to a very extensive class, which it is worth while to be acquainted with. They are called the *compound-flowered plants.*

G. Will you be so good as to give us a lecture about them?

T. With all my heart. Get me a dandelion in flower, a thistle-head, and a daisy. If you cannot find a common daisy, one of the great ox-eye daisies in the corn will do as well.

G. and H. Here they are.

T. Very well. All these are *compound flowers;* for, if you will examine them narrowly, you will perceive that they consist of a number of little flowers, or *florets,* enclosed in a common cup, which cup is made of a number of scales lying upon each other like the tiles of a house.

G. I see it.

T. The florets are not all alike in shape. In the dandelion, you will observe that they consist of a tube, from which, at its upper end, proceeds a sort of strap-shaped tongue, or fillet : in the thistle, they are tubular, or funnel-shaped, throughout: in the daisy, the centre ones which form the *disk,* as it is called, are tubular, while those in the circumference have a broad strap on one side, which altogether compose the *rays* of the flowers; whence this sort are called *radiated.* Now take the glass and examine the florets singly. Can you discern their chives and pointals ?

G. I can.

T. You may remark that there are five chives to each, the tips of which unite into a tube, through which the pointal passes, having its summit double, and curled back.

H. I can just make it out with the glass, but hardly with the naked eye.

T. It is from this circumstance of the tips of the chives growing together, that Linnæus has taken his distinction of the whole class, and he has named it *Syngenesia*, from two Greek words having that signification. You will farther observe, that all these florets stand upon a stool, or receptacle, at the bottom of the flower, which is the cushion left on the dandelion stalk after the seeds are blown away. Into this the seeds are slightly stuck, which are one apiece to every perfect or fertile floret. This is the general structure of the compound flowers.

H. Are all their seeds feathered ?

T. Not all. These of the daisy are not. But in a great many species they are.

H. I should have thought these were a very useful class of plants, by the pains nature has taken to spread them, if you had not told us that thistles, and ragwort, and groundsel were some of them.

T. And if you do not confine your idea of usefulness to what is serviceable to man, but extend it to the whole creation, you may safely conclude, from their abundance, that they must be highly useful in the general economy of nature. It fact, no plants feed a greater number of insects, and none are more important to the small birds, to whom they furnish food by their seeds, and a fine warm down for lining their nests. On the approach of winter, you may see whole flocks of linnets and goldfinches pecking among the thistles ; and you know that groundsel is a favourite treat to birds in a cage. To man, however, they are, for the most part, troublesome and unsightly weeds. Burdock, thistles, and yarrow, overrun his hedge-banks ; dandelion and hawk-weed, which much resemble them, fill his meadows; the tall and branching ragwort, and blue succory, cumber his pastures; and wild chamomile, ox-eye, and corn marigold, choke up his corn-fields. These plants, in general, have a bitter, nauseous taste, so that no cattle will touch them. Daisies, I believe, are the chief exception.

G. But some of them, I suppose, are useful to man?

T. Yes, several, and in various ways. Some that have milky, bitter juices are employed in medicine, for purifying the blood and removing obstructions. Of these are dandelion, succory, and sowthistle. Many other sare bitter, and strongly aromatic; as chamomile, wormwood, southernwood, feverfew, and tansy; these are good for strengthening the stomach, and expelling worms. That capital ingredient in salad, lettuce, is of this class, and so is endive. Artichoke forms a very singular article of diet, for the part chiefly eaten, called the bottom, is the receptacle of the flower, upon which the choke, or seeds with their feathers, is placed. It is said that some of the larger species of thistles may be dressed and eaten the same way. Then there is Jerusalem artichoke, which is the root of a species of sunflower, and, when boiled, much resembles in taste an artichoke bottom. On the whole, however, a very small proportion of this class of plants is used in food.

G. Are there no garden flowers belonging to them?

T. Several, especially of the autumnal ones. There are sunflowers of various kinds, which are the largest flowers the garden produces, though not the most sightly; marigolds, both the common, and the French and African; asters, china-asters, golden-rod, and chrysanthemums. Very few flowers of this class have an agreeable scent, and their shape is not the most pleasing; but they have often gay colours, and make a figure in the garden when other things are over. Well—this is most that I recollect worth noticing of the compound-flowered plants. They are a difficult class to make out botanically, though pretty easily known from each other by sight. I will take care to point out to you the principal of them that we meet with in our walks, and you must get acquainted with them.

ON PRESENCE OF MIND.

MRS. F. one day, having occasion to be bled, sent for the surgeon. As soon as he entered the room, her young daughter, Eliza, started up, and was hastily going away, when her mother called her back·

Mrs. F. Eliza, do not go; I want you to stay by me.

Eliza. Dear mamma! I can never bear to see you bled.

Mrs. F. Why not? what harm will it do you?

E. O dear! I cannot look at blood. Besides, I cannot bear to see you hurt, mamma!

Mrs. F. O, if I can bear to feel it, surely you may to see it. But, come—you *must* stay, and we will talk about it afterwards.

Eliza, then, pale and trembling, stood by her mother, and saw the whole operation. She could not help, however, turning her head away when the incision was made, and the first flow of blood made her start and shudder. When all was over, and the surgeon gone, Mrs. F. began:—

Well, Eliza, what do you think of this mighty matter now? Would it not have been very foolish to have run away from it?

E. O mamma! how frightened I was when he took out his lancet! Did it not hurt you a great deal?

Mrs. F. No, very little. And, if it had, it was to do me good, you know.

E. But why should I stay to see it? I could do you no good?

Mrs. F. Perhaps not; but it will do you good to be accustomed to such sights.

E. Why, mamma?

Mrs. F. Because instances are every day happening

in which it is our duty to assist fellow-creatures in circumstances of pain and distress; and, if we were to indulge a reluctance to come near to them on those occasions, we should never acquire either the knowledge or the presence of mind necessary for the purpose.

E. But if I had been told how to help people in such cases, could not I do it without being used to see them?

Mrs. F. No. We have all naturally a horror at everything which is the cause of pain and danger to ourselves or others; and nothing but habit can give most of us the presence of mind necessary to enable us, in such occurrences, to employ our knowledge to the best advantage.

E. What is *presence of mind*, mamma?

Mrs. F. It is that steady possession of ourselves in cases of alarm, that prevents us from being flurried and frightened. You have heard the expression of *having all our wits about us*. That is the effect of presence of mind, and a most inestimable quality it is; for, without it, we are quite as likely to run into danger as to avoid it. Do you not remember hearing of your cousin Mary's cap taking fire from the candle?

E. O yes—very well.

Mrs. F. Well—the maid, as soon as she saw it, set up a great scream, and ran out of the room; and Mary might have been burnt to death for any assistance she could give her.

E. How foolish that was!

Mrs. F. Yes—the girl had not the least presence of mind; and the consequence was, depriving her of all recollection, and making her entirely useless. But as soon as your aunt came up, she took the right method for preventing the mischief. The cap was too much on fire to be pulled off; so she whipped a quilt from the bed, and flung it round Mary's head, and thus stifled the flame.

E. Mary was a good deal scorched, though.

Mrs. F. Yes—but it was very well that it was not worse. If the maid, however, had acted with any sense at first, no harm at all would have been done, except burning the cap. I remember a much more fatal example of the want of presence of mind. The mistress of a family was awakened by flames bursting through the wainscot into her chamber. She flew to the staircase; and, in her confusion, instead of going up stairs to call her children, who slept together in the nursery overhead, and who might have all escaped by the top of the house, she ran down, and with much danger, made way through the fire into the street. When she had got thither, the thought of her poor children rushed into her mind, but it was too late. The stairs had caught fire, so that nobody could get near them, and they were burned in their beds.

E. What a sad thing!

Mrs. F. Sad, indeed! Now, I will tell you of a different conduct. A lady was awakened by the crackling of fire, and saw it shining under her chamber door. Her husband would immediately have opened the door, but she prevented him, since the smoke and flame would then have burst in upon them. The children, with a maid, slept in a room opening out of theirs. She went and awakened them; and, tying together the sheets and blankets, she sent down the maid from the window first, and then let down the children one by one to her. Last of all she descended herself. A few minutes after, the floor fell in, and all the house was in flames.

E. What a happy escape!

Mrs. F. Yes—and with what cool recollection of mind it was managed! For mothers to love their children, and be willing to run any hazards for them, is common; but, in weak minds, that very love is apt to prevent exertions in the time of danger. I knew a lady who had a fine little boy sitting in her lap. He put a whole plum into his mouth, which slipped into his throat, and choked him. The poor fellow turned black, and struggled violently; and the mother was so frightened, that, instead of putting her finger into his throat and pulling out the plum, which might easily have been done, she laid him on the floor, and ran to call for assistance. But the maids who came up were as much flurried as she; and the child died before anything effectual was done to relieve him.

E. How unhappy she must have been about it!

Mrs. F. Yes. It threw her into an illness, which had like to have cost her her life.

Another lady, seeing her little boy climb up a high ladder, set up a violent scream, that frightened the child, so that he fell down and was much hurt; whereas if she had possessed command enough over herself to speak to him gently, he might have got down safely.

E. Dear mamma! what is that running down your arm? O, it is blood!

Mrs. F. Yes; my arm bleeds again. I have stirred it too soon.

E. Dear! what shall I do?

Mrs. F. Don't frighten yourself. I shall stop the blood by pressing on the orifice with my finger. In the mean time, do you ring the bell.

[*Eliza rings—a servant comes.*

Mrs. F. Betty, my arm bleeds. Can you tie it up again?

Betty. I believe I can, madam.

[*She takes off the bandage and puts on another.*

E. I hope it is stopped now.

Mrs. F. It is. Betty has done it very well. You see she went about it with composure. This accident puts me in mind of another story which is very well worth hearing. A man once reaping in a field cut his arm dreadfully with his sickle, and divided an artery.

E. What is that, mamma?

Mrs. F. It is one of the canals, or pipes, through which the blood from the heart runs like water in a pipe brought from a reservoir. When one of these is cut, it bleeds very violently, and the only way to stop it is to make a pressure between the wounded place and the heart, in order to intercept the course of the blood towards it. Well, this poor man bled profusely, and the people about him, both men and women, were so stupified with fright, that some ran one way, some another, and some stood stock still. In short, he would have soon bled to death, had not a brisk, stout-hearted wench, who came up, slipped off her garter, and bound it tight above the wound, by which means the bleeding was stopped till proper help could be procured.

E. What a clever girl! But how did she know what to do?

Mrs. F. She had, perhaps, heard it, as you have now; and so probably had some of the others, but they had not presence of mind enough to put it into practice. It is a much greater trial of courage, however, when the danger presses upon ourselves as well as others. Suppose a furious bull were to come upon you in the midst of a field. You could not possibly escape him by running, and attempting it would destroy your only chance of safety.

E. What would that be?

Mrs. F. I have a story for that, too. The mother of that Mr. Day who wrote *Sandford and Merton*, was distinguished, as he also was, for courage and presence of mind. When a young woman, she was one day walking in the fields with a companion, when they perceived a bull coming to them, roaring, and tossing about his horns in the most tremendous manner.

E. O, how I should have screamed!

Mrs. F. I dare say you would; and so did her companion. But she bade her walk away behind her, as gently as she could, whilst she herself stopped short, and faced the bull, eyeing him with a determined countenance. The bull, when he had come near, stopped also, pawing the ground and roaring. Few animals will attack a man who steadily waits for them. In a while, she drew back some steps, still facing the bull. The bull followed. She stopped, and then he stopped. In this manner, she made good her retreat to the stile, over which her companion had already got. She then turned and sprang over it, and got clear out of danger.

E. That was bravely done, indeed! But I think very few women could have done so much.

Mrs. F. Such a degree of cool resolution, to be sure, is not common. But I have read of a lady in the East Indies who showed at least as much. She was sitting out of doors with a party of pleasure, when they became aware of a huge tiger, that had crept through a hedge near them, and was just ready to make his fatal spring. They were struck with the utmost consternation; but she, with an umbrella in her hand, turned to the tiger, and suddenly spread it full in his face. This unusual assault so terrified the beast, that, taking a prodigious leap, he sprang over the fence, and plunged out of sight into the neighbouring thicket.

E. Well, that was the boldest thing I ever heard of. But is it possible, mamma, to make one's self courageous?

Mrs. F. Courage, my dear, is of two kinds; one the gift of nature, the other of reason and habit. Men have naturally more courage than women; that is, they are less affected by danger: it makes a less impression upon them, and does not flutter their spirits so much. This is owing to the difference of their bodily constitution; and, from the same cause, some men and some women are more courageous than others. But the other kind of courage may, in some measure, be acquired by every one. Reason teaches us to face smaller dangers in order to avoid greater, and even to undergo the greatest when our duty requires it. Habit makes us less affected by particular dangers which have often come in our way. A sailor does not feel the danger of a storm so much as a landsman; but if he were mounted upon a spirited horse in a fox-chase, he would probably be the most timorous man in company. The courage of women is tried chiefly in domestic dangers. They are attendants on the sick and dying, and they must qualify themselves to go through many scenes of terror in these situations, which would alarm the stoutest-hearted man who was not accustomed to them.

E. I have heard that women generally bear pain and illness better than men.

Mrs. F. They do so, because they are more used to them, both in themselves and others.

E. I think I should not be afraid again to see anybody bled.

Mrs. F. I hope not. It was for that purpose I made you stand by me. And I would have you always force yourself to look on and give assistance in cases of this kind, however painful it may at first be to you, that you may as soon as possible gain that presence of mind which arises from habit.

E. But would that make me like to be bled myself?

Mrs. F. Not to *like* it, but to lose all foolish fears about it, and submit calmly to it when good for you. But I hope you have sense enough to do that already.

SEVENTEENTH EVENING.

PHAETON JUNIOR;

OR, THE GIG DEMOLISHED.

Ye heroes of the upper form,
  Who long for whip and reins,
Come listen to a dismal tale,
  Set forth in dismal strains.

Young Jehu was a lad of fame,
  As all the school could tell;
At cricket, taw, and prison-bars,
  He bore away the bell.

Now welcome Whitsuntide was come,
　And boys, with merry hearts,
Were gone to visit dear mamma,
　And eat her pies and tarts.

As soon as Jehu saw his sire,
　" A boon ! a boon !" he cried ;
" O, if I am your darling boy,
　Let me not be denied."

" My darling boy, indeed thou art,"
　The father wise replied ;
" So name the boon ; I promise thee
　It shall not be denied."

" Then give me, sir, your long-lash'd whip,
　And give your gig and pair,
To drive along to yonder town,
　And flourish through the fair."

The father shook his head ; " My son,
　You know not what you ask,
To drive a gig in crowded streets
　Is no such easy task.

" The horses full of rest and corn,
　Scarce I myself can guide ;
And much I fear, if you attempt,
　Some mischief will betide.

" Then think, dear boy, of something else
　That's better worth your wishing ;
A bow and quiver, bats and balls,
　A rod and lines, for fishing."

But nothing could young Jehu please,
　Except a touch at driving ;
'Twas all in vain, his father found,
　To spend his breath in striving.

" At least attend, rash boy !" he cried,
　And follow good advice,

Or in a ditch, both gig and you
　　Will tumble in a trice.

" Spare, spare the whip, hold hard the reins,
　　The steeds go fast enough ;
Keep in the middle, beaten track,
　　Nor cross the ruts so rough :

" And when within the town you come,
　　Be sure, with special care,
Drive clear of signposts, booths, and stalls,
　　And monsters of the fair."

The youth scarce heard his father out,
　　But roar'd, " Bring out the whisky !"
With joy he view'd the rolling wheels,
　　And prancing ponies frisky.

He seized the reins, and up he sprang,
　　And waved the whistling lash ;
" Take care ! take care !" his father cried ;
　　But off he went, slap-dash.

" Who's this light spark ?" the horses thought,
　　" We'll try your strength, young master ;"
So, o'er the rugged turnpike-road,
　　Still faster ran, and faster.

Young Jehu, tott'ring in his seat,
　　Now wish'd to pull them in ;
But pulling, from so young a hand,
　　They valued not a pin.

A drove of grunting pigs, before,
　　Fill'd up the narrow way ;
Dash through the midst the horses drove,
　　And made a rueful day :

For some were trampled under foot,
　　Some crush'd beneath the wheel ;
Lord ! how the drivers cursed and swore,
　　And how the pigs did squeal !

A farmer's wife, on old, blind Ball,
    Went slowly on the road,
With butter, eggs, and cheese, and cream,
    In two large panniers stow'd.

Ere Ball could stride the rut, amain
    The gig came thund'ring on;
Crash went the panniers, and the dame
    And Ball lay overthrown.

Now, through the town the mettled pair
    Ran, rattling o'er the stones;
They drove the crowd from side to side,
    And shook poor Jehu's bones.

When, lo! directly in their course,
    A monstrous form appear'd;
A shaggy bear, that stalk'd and roar'd,
    On hinder legs uprear'd.

Sideways they started, at the sight,
    And whisk'd the gig half round,
Then, cross the crowded market-place,
    They flew with furious bound.

First, o'er a heap of crock'ry-ware,
    The rapid car they whirl'd;
And jugs, and mugs, and pots, and pans,
    In fragments, wide were hurl'd.

A booth stood near, with tempting cakes,
    And grocery richly fraught;
All Birmingham, on t'other side,
    The dazzled optics caught.

With active spring, the nimble steeds
    Rush'd through the pass between,
And scarcely touch'd;—the car behind
    Got through not quite so clean:

For, while one wheel one stall engaged,
    Its fellow took the other;

Dire was the clash; down fell the booths,
    And made a dreadful pother.

Nuts, oranges, and gingerbread,
    And figs here roll'd around;
And scissors, knives, and thimbles there,
    Bestrew'd the glitt'ring ground.

The fall of boards, the shouts and cries,
    Urged on the horses faster;
And, as they flew, at ev'ry step,
    They caused some new disaster.

Here lay, o'erturned, in woful plight,
    A pedlar and his pack;
There, in a showman's broken box,
    All London went to wreck.

But now the fates decreed to stop
    The ruin of the day,
And make the gig, and driver too,
    A heavy reck'ning pay.

A ditch there lay, both broad and deep,
    Where streams, as black as Styx,
From every quarter of the town,
    Their muddy currents mix.

Down to its brink, in heedless haste,
    The frantic horses flew,
And in the midst, with sudden jerk,
    Their burden overthrew.

The prostrate gig, with desp'rate force,
    They soon pull'd out again,
And, at their heels, in ruin dire,
    Dragg'd, lumb'ring, o'er the plain.

Here lay a wheel, the axle there,
    The body there remain'd,
Till, sever'd limb from limb, the car,
    Nor name nor shape retain'd.

Sir Isaac Newton was led to make some of his great discoveries by seeing an apple fall from a tree. P. 227.

But Jehu must not be forgot,
   Left flound'ring in the flood,
With clothes all drench'd, and mouth and eyes
   Beplaster'd o'er with mud.

In piteous case he waded through,
   And gain'd the slipp'ry side,
Where grinning crowds were gather'd round,
   To mock his fallen pride.

They led him to a neighbouring pump,
   To clear his dismal face,
Whence, cold and heartless, home he slunk,
   Involved in sore disgrace.

And many a bill, for damage done,
   His father had to pay.
Take warning, youthful drivers all!
   From Jehu's first essay.

WHY AN APPLE FALLS.

" Papa," said Lucy, " I have been reading to-day, that Sir Isaac Newton was led to make some of his great discoveries by seeing an apple fall from a tree. What was there extraordinary in that ?"

P. There was nothing extraordinary; but it happened to catch his attention, and set him a-thinking.

L. And what did he think about ?

P. He thought, by what means the apple was brought to the ground.

L. Why, I could have told him that—because the stalk gave way, and there was nothing left to support it.

P. And what then ?

L. Why then—it must fall, you know.

P. But why must it fall ? that is the point.

L. Because it could not help it.

P. But why could it not help it ?

L. I don't know—that is an odd question. Because there was nothing to keep it up.

P. Suppose there was not—does it follow that it must come to the ground?

L. Yes, surely!

P. Is an apple animate or inanimate?

L. Inanimate, to be sure!

P. And can inanimate things move of themselves?

L. No—I think not—but the apple falls because it is forced to fall.

P. Right! some force out of itself acts upon it, otherwise it would remain for ever where it was, notwithstanding it were loosened from the tree.

L. Would it?

P. Undoubtedly! for there are only two ways in which it could be moved; by its own power of motion, or the power of somewhat else moving it. Now the first you acknowledge it has not; the cause of its motion must therefore be the second. And what that is, was the subject of the philosopher's inquiry.

L. But everything falls to the ground, as well as an apple, when there is nothing to keep it up.

P. True—there must therefore be a universal cause of this tendency to fall.

L. And what is it?

P. Why, if things out of the earth cannot move themselves to it, there can be no other cause of their coming together, than that the earth pulls them.

L. But the earth is no more animate than they are; so how can it pull?

P. Well objected! This will bring us to the point. Sir Isaac Newton, after deep meditation, discovered that there was a law in nature called *attraction*, by virtue of which every particle of matter, that is, everything of which the world is composed, draws towards it every other particle of matter, with a force proportioned to its size and distance. Lay two marbles on the table. They have a tendency to come together, and, if there were nothing else in the world, they would come together; but they are also attracted by the table, by the ground, and by everything besides in the room ; and these different attractions pull against each other. Now, the globe of the earth is a prodigious mass of matter, to which nothing near it can bear any comparison. It draws, therefore, with mighty force, everything within its reach; which is the cause that everything falls, or has a tendency to fall ; and this is called the *gravitation* of bodies, or what gives them *weight*. When I lift up anything, I act contrary to this force ; for which reason it seems *heavy* to me, and the heavier the more matter it contains; since that increases the attraction of the earth for it. Do you understand this ?

L. I think I do. It is like a loadstone drawing a needle.

P. Yes—that is an attraction, but of a particular kind, taking place only between the magnet and iron. But gravitation, or the attraction of the earth, acts upon everything alike.

L. Then it is pulling you and me at this moment.

P. It is.

L. But why do not we stick to the ground, then ?

P. Because, as we are alive, we have a power of self-motion, which can, to a certain degree, overcome the attraction of the earth. But the reason you cannot jump a mile high as well as a foot, is this attraction, which brings you down again after the force of your jump is spent.

L. I think, then, I begin to understand what I have heard of people living on the other side of the world. I believe they are called *Antipodes*, who have their feet turned towards ours, and their heads in the air. I used to wonder how it could be that they did not fall off; but I suppose the earth pulls them to it.

P. Very true. And whither should they fall ? What have they over their heads ?

L. I don't know—sky, I suppose.

P. They have. This earth is a vast ball, hung in

the air, and continually spinning round, and that is the cause why the sun and stars seem to rise and set. At noon we have the sun over our heads, when the antipodes have the stars over theirs; and at midnight the stars are over our heads, and the sun over theirs. So whither should they fall to more than we?—to the stars or the sun.

L. But we are up, and they are down.

P. What is up, but *from* the earth and *towards* the sky? Their feet touch the earth and their heads point to the sky, as well as ours; and we are under their feet, as much as they are under ours. If a hole were dug quite through the earth, what would you see through it?

L. Sky, with the sun or the stars; and now I see the whole matter plainly. But pray what supports the earth in the air?

P. Why, whither should it go?

L. I don't know—I suppose towards the point where there might be most to draw it. I have heard that the sun is a great many times bigger than the earth. Would it not go to that?

P. You have thought very justly on the matter, I perceive. But I shall take another opportunity of showing you how this is, and why the earth does not fall into the sun, of which, I confess, there seems to be some danger. Meanwhile, think how far the falling of an apple has carried us.

L. To the antipodes, and I know not whither.

P. You may see thence what use may be made of the commonest fact by a thinking mind.

NATURE AND EDUCATION,
A Fable.

NATURE and Education were one day walking together through a nursery of trees. "See," says Nature, "how straight and fine those firs grow—that is my doing! But, as to those oaks, they are all crooked and stunted: that, my good sister, is your fault. You have planted them too close, and not pruned them properly." "Nay, sister," said Education, "I am sure I have taken all possible pains about them; but you gave me bad acorns, so how should they ever make fine trees?"

The dispute grew warm; and, at length, instead of blaming one another for negligence, they began to boast of their own powers, and to challenge each other to a contest for the superiority. It was agreed that each should adopt a favourite, and rear it up in spite of the ill offices of her opponent. Nature fixed upon a vigorous young Weymouth Pine, the parent of which had grown to be the main-mast of a man-of-war. "Do what you will to this plant," said she to her sister, "I am resolved to push it up as straight as an arrow." Education took under her care a crab-tree. "This," said she, "I will rear to be at least as valuable as your pine."

Both went to work. While Nature was feeding her pine with plenty of wholesome juices, Education passed a strong rope round its top, and, pulling it downwards with all her force, fastened it to the trunk of a neighbouring oak. The pine laboured to ascend, but not being able to surmount the obstacle, it pushed out to one side, and presently became bent like a bow. Still, such was its vigour, that its top, after descending as low as its branches, made a new shoot upwards; but its beauty and usefulness were quite destroyed.

The crab-tree cost Education a world of pains. She pruned and pruned, and endeavoured to bring it into shape, but in vain. Nature thrust out a bow this way, and a knot that way, and would not push a single leading shoot upwards. The trunk was, indeed, kept tolerably straight by constant efforts; but the head grew awry and ill-fashioned, and made a scrubby figure. At length, Education, despairing of making a sightly plant of it, ingrafted the stock with an apple, and brought it to bear tolerable fruit.

At the end of the experiment, the sisters met, to compare their respective success. "Ah, sister!" said Nature, " I see it is in your power to spoil the best of my works." "Ah, sister!" said Education, " it is a hard matter to contend against you; however, something may be done by taking pains enough."

AVERSION SUBDUED.

A Drama.

Scene.—*A Road in the Country—Arbury, Belford, walking.*

Belford. PRAY, who is the present possessor of the Brookby estate?

Arbury. A man of the name of Goodwin.

B. Is he a good neighbour to you?

A. Far from it; and I wish he had settled a hundred miles off, rather than come here to spoil our neighbourhood.

B. I am sorry to hear that; but what is your objection to him?

A. O, there is nothing in which we agree. In the first place, he is quite of the other side in politics; and that, you know, is enough to prevent all intimacy.

B. I am not entirely of that opinion; but what else?

A. He is no sportsman, and refuses to join in our association for protecting the game. Neither does he choose to be a member of any of our clubs.

B. Has he been asked?

A. I don't know that he has directly; but he might easily propose himself, if he liked it. But he is of a close, unsociable temper, and, I believe, very niggardly.

B. How has he shown it?

A. His style of living is not equal to his fortune; and I have heard of several instances of his attention to petty economy.

B. Perhaps he spends his money in charity.

A. Not he, I dare say. It was but last week that a

poor fellow, who had lost his all by a fire, went to him with a subscription-paper, in which were the names of all the gentlemen in the neighbourhood; and all the answer he got was, that he would consider of it.

B. And did he consider?

A. I don't know; but I suppose it was only an excuse. Then his predecessor had a park well stocked with deer, and used to make liberal presents of venison to all his neighbours. But this frugal gentleman has sold them all off, and got a flock of sheep instead.

B. I don't see much harm in that, now mutton is so dear.

A. To be sure, he has a right to do as he pleases with his park; but that is not the way to be beloved, you know. As to myself, I have reason to think he bears me particular ill-will.

B. Then he is much in the wrong, for I believe you are as free from ill-will to others as any man living. But how has he shown it, pray?

A. In twenty instances. He had a horse upon sale the other day, to which I took a liking, and bade money for it. As soon as he found I was about it, he sent it off to a fair, on the other side of the country. My wife, you know, is passionately fond of cultivating flowers. Riding lately by his grounds, she observed something new, and took a great longing for a root or cutting of it. My gardener mentioned her wish to his (contrary, I own, to my inclination), and he told his master; but instead of obliging her, he charged the gardener on no account to touch the plant. A little while ago, I turned off a man for saucy behaviour; but as he had lived many years with me, and was a very useful servant, I meant to take him again, upon his submission, which, I did not doubt, would soon happen. Instead of that, he goes and offers himself to my civil neighbour, who, without deigning to apply to me even for a character, entertains him immediately. In short, he has not the least of a gentleman about him; and I would give anything to be well rid of him.

B. Nothing, to be sure, can be more unpleasant in the country than a bad neighbour, and I am concerned it is your lot to have one. But there is a man who seems as though he wanted to speak with you.

[*A countryman approaches.*

A. Ah! it is the poor fellow that was burnt out. Well, Richard, how go you on?—what has the subscription produced you?

Richard. Thank your honour, my losses are nearly all made up.

A. I am very glad of that; but when I saw the paper last, it did not reach half way.

R. It did not, sir; but you may remember asking me, what Mr. Goodwin had done for me, and I told you he took time to consider of it. Well, sir—I found that the very next day he had been at our town, and had made very particular inquiry about me and my losses, among my neighbours. When I called upon him in a few days after, he told me he was very glad to find that I bore such a good character, and that the gentlemen around had so kindly taken up my case; and he would prevent the necessity of my going any further for relief. Upon which he gave me, God bless him! a draught upon his banker for fifty pounds.

A. Fifty pounds!

R. Yes, sir—it has made me quite my own man again; and I am now going to purchase a new cart and team of horses.

A. A noble gift, indeed; I could never have thought it. Well, Richard, I rejoice at your good fortune. I am sure you are much obliged to Mr. Goodwin.

R. Indeed I am, sir, and to all my good friends. God bless you!   [*Goes on.*

B. Niggardliness, at least, is not this man's foible.

A. No—I was mistaken in that point. I wronged him, and I am sorry for it. But what a pity it is that men of real generosity should not be amiable in their manners, and as ready to oblige in trifles as in matters of consequence.

B. True—'tis a pity, when that is really the case.

A. How much less an exertion it would have been, to have shown some civility about a horse or a flower-root!

B. A-propos of flowers!—there's your gardener carrying a large one in a pot.

Enter Gardener.

A. Now, James, what have you got there?

Gard. A flower, sir, for Madam, from Mr. Good·win's.

A. How did you come by it?

G. His gardener, sir, sent me word to come for it. We should have had it before, but Mr. Goodwin thought it would not move safely.

A. I hope he has got more of them.

G. He has only a seedling plant or two, sir; but hearing that Madam took a liking to it, he was resolved to send it her; and a choice thing it is! I have a note for Madam in my pocket.

A. Well, go on.   [*Exit Gardener.*

B. Methinks this does not look like deficiency in civility.

A. No—it is a very polite action—I can't deny it, and I am obliged to him for it. Perhaps, indeed, he may feel he owes me a little amends.

B. Possibly—It shows he *can* feel, however.

A. It does. Ha! there's Yorkshire Tom coming with a string of horses from the fair. I'll step up and speak to him. Now, Tom! how have horses gone at Market-hill?

Tom. Dear enough, your honour!

A. How much more did you get for Mr. Goodwin's mare than I offered him?

T. Ah! sir, that was not a thing for your riding, and that Mr. Goodwin well knew. You never saw such a vicious toad. She had like to have killed the groom two or three times. So I was ordered to offer her to the mail-coach people, and get what I could from them. I might have sold her better, if Mr. Goodwin would have let me, for she was a fine creature to look at as need be, and quite sound.

A. And was that the true reason, Tom, why the mare was not sold to me?

T. It was, indeed, sir.

A. Then I am highly obliged to Mr. Goodwin. (*Tom rides on.*) This was handsome behaviour, indeed!

B. Yes, I think it was somewhat more than politeness—it was real goodness of heart.

A. It was. I find I must alter my opinion of him, and I do it with pleasure. But, after all, his conduct with respect to my servant is somewhat unaccountable.

B. I see reason to think so well of him in the main, that I am inclined to hope he will be acquitted in this matter too.

A. There the fellow is, I wonder he has my old livery on yet.

[*Ned approaches, pulling off his hat.*

N. Sir, I was coming to your honour.

A. What can you have to say to me now, Ned?

N. To ask pardon, sir, for my misbehaviour, and beg you to take me again.

A. What—have you so soon parted with your new master?

N. Mr. Goodwin never was my master, sir. He only kept me in his house till I could make it up with you again; for he said he was sure you were too honourable a gentleman to turn off an old servant without good reason, and he hoped you would admit my excuses, after your anger was over.

A. Did he say all that?

N. Yes, sir; and he advised me not to delay any longer to ask your pardon.

A. Well—go to my house, and I will talk with you on my return.

B. Now, my friend, what think you of this?

A. I think more than I can well express. It will

be a lesson to me never to make nasty judgments again.

B. Why, indeed, to have concluded that such a man had nothing of the gentleman about him must have been rather hasty.

A. I acknowledge it. But it is the misfortune of these reserved characters, that they are so long in making themselves known; though, when they are known, they often prove the most truly estimable. I am afraid, even now, that I must be content with esteeming him at a distance.

B. Why so?

A. You know I am of an open, sociable disposition.

B. Perhaps he is so too.

A. If he were, surely we should have been better acquainted before this time.

B. It may have been prejudice, rather than temper, that has kept you asunder.

A. Possibly so. That vile spirit of party has such a sway in the country, that men of the most liberal dispositions can hardly free themselves from its influence. It poisons all the kindness of society; and yonder comes an instance of its pernicious effects.

B. Who is he?

A. A poor schoolmaster with a large family in the next market-town, who has lost all his scholars by his activity on our side in the last election. I heartily wish it were in my power to do something for him; for he is a very honest man, though perhaps rather too warm.   [*The schoolmaster comes up.*

Now, Mr. Penman, how go things with you?

P. I thank you, sir, they have gone poorly enough; but I hope they are in a way to mend.

A. I am glad to hear it—but how?

P. Why, sir, the free-school of Stoke is vacant, and, I believe, I am likely to get it.

A. Ay!—I wonder at that. I thought it was in the hands of the other party.

P. It is, sir; but Mr. Goodwin has been so kind as

to give me a recommendation, and his interest is sufficient to carry it.

A. Mr. Goodwin!—you surprise me.

P. I was much surprised, too, sir. He sent for me
of his own accord (for I should never have thought of
asking *him* a favour), and told me he was sorry a man
should be injured in his profession on account of party,
and, as I could not live comfortably where I was, he
would try to settle me in a better place. So he mentioned the vacancy of Stoke, and offered me letters to
the trustees. I was never so affected in my life, sir;
I could hardly speak to return him thanks. He kept
me to dinner, and treated me with the greatest respect.
Indeed, I believe there is not a kinder man breathing,
than Mr. Goodwin.

A. You have the best reason in the world to say so,
Mr. Penman. What—did he converse familiarly with
you?

P. Quite so, sir. We talked a great deal about
party affairs in this neighbourhood, and he lamented
much that differences of this kind should keep worthy
men at a distance from each other. I took the liberty,
sir, of mentioning your name. He said he had not the
honour of being acquainted with you, but he had a
sincere esteem for your character, and should be glad
of any occasion to cultivate a friendship with you.
For my part, I confess to my shame, I did not think
there could have been such a man on that side.

A. Well—good morning!

P. Your most obedient, sir.   [*He goes.*

A. (*After some silence.*) Come, my friend, let us
go.

B. Whither?

A. Can you doubt it?—to Mr. Goodwin's, to be
sure! After all I have heard, can I exist a moment,
without acknowledging the injustice I have done him,
and soliciting his friendship?

B. I shall be happy, I am sure, to accompany you
on that errand. But who is to introduce us?

A. O, what are form and ceremony in a case like this! Come—come.

B. Most willingly. [*Exeunt.*

EIGHTEENTH EVENING.

THE LITTLE PHILOSOPHER.

Mr. L. was one morning riding by himself, when, dismounting to gather a plant in the hedge, his horse got loose and galloped away before him. He followed, calling the horse by his name, which stopped, but, on his approach, set off again. At length, a little boy, in a neighbouring field, seeing the affair, ran across where the road made a turn, and, getting before the horse, took him by the bridle, and held him till his owner came up. Mr. L. looked at the boy, and admired his ruddy, cheerful countenance. "Thank you, my good lad!" said he, "you have caught my horse very cleverly. What shall I give you for your trouble?" (putting his hand into his pocket).

"I want nothing, sir," said the boy.

Mr. L. Don't you? So much the better for you. Few men can say as much. But, pray what were you doing in the field?

B. I was rooting up weeds, and tending the sheep that are feeding on turnips.

Mr. L. And do you like this employment?

B. Yes, very well, this fine weather.

Mr. L. But had you not rather play?

B. This is not hard work; it is almost as good as play.

Mr. L. Who set you to work?

B. My daddy, sir.

Mr. L. Where does he live?

B. Just by, among the trees there.

Mr. L. What is his name?

B. Thomas Hurdle.

Mr. L. And what is yours?

B. Peter, sir.

Mr. L. How old are you?

B. I shall be eight, at Michaelmas.

Mr. L. How long have you been out in this field?

B. Ever since six in the morning.

Mr. L. And are you not hungry?

B. Yes; I shall go to my dinner soon.

Mr. L. If you had sixpence now, what would you do with it?

B. I don't know; I never had so much in my life.

Mr. L. Have you no playthings?

B. Playthings? what are those?

Mr. L. Such as balls, ninepins, marbles, tops, and wooden horses.

B. No, sir; but our Tom makes footballs, to kick in the cold weather, and we set traps for birds; and then I have a jumping-pole, and a pair of stilts, to walk through the dirt with; and I had a hoop, but it is broken.

Mr. L. And, do you want nothing else?

B. No. I have hardly time for those; for I always ride the horses to field, and bring up the cows, and run to the town of errands, and that is as good as play, you know.

Mr. L. Well; but you could buy apples or gingerbread at the town, I suppose, if you had money?

B. O! I can get apples at home; and, as for gingerbread, I don't mind it much, for my mammy gives me a pie now and then, and that is as good.

Mr. L. Would you not like a knife, to cut sticks?

B. I have one—here it is—brother Tom gave it me.

Mr. L. Your shoes are full of holes—don't you want a better pair?

B. I have a better pair for Sundays.

Mr. L. But these let in water.

B. O, I don't care for that.

Mr. L. Your hat is all torn, too.

B. I have a better at home; but I had as lief have none at all, for it hurts my head.

Mr. L. What do you do when it rains?

B. If it rains very hard, I get under the hedge till it is over.

Mr. L. What do you do when you are hungry, before it is time to go home?

B. I sometimes eat a raw turnip.

Mr. L. But if there are none?

B. Then I do as well as I can: I work on, and never think of it.

Mr. L. Are you not thirsty sometimes this hot weather?

B. Yes; but there is water enough.

Mr. L. Why, my little fellow, you are quite a philosopher.

B. Sir?

Mr. L. I say, you are a philosopher; but I am sure you do not know what that means.

B. No, sir—no harm, I hope.

Mr. L. No, No! (*laughing*). Well, my boy, you seem to want nothing at all, so I shall not give you money to make you want anything. But were you ever at school?

B. No, sir; but daddy says I shall go after harvest.

Mr. L. You will want books then?

B. Yes; the boys have all a spelling-book and a Testament.

Mr. L. Well, then, I will give you them—tell your daddy so, and that it is because I thought you a very good, contented little boy. So now go to your sheep again.

B. I will, sir. Thank you.

Mr. L. Good bye, Peter.

B. Good bye, sir.

R

WHAT DIFFERENT KINDS OF LIVING CREATURES ARE MADE FOR.

" PRAY, papa," said Sophia, after she had been a long while teased with the flies, that buzzed about her ears, and settled on her nose and forehead, as she sat at work—" Pray what were flies made for ?"

" For some good, I dare say," replied her Papa.

S. But I think they do a great deal more harm than good, for I am sure they plague me sadly ; and in the kitchen they are so troublesome, that the maids can hardly do their work for them.

P. Flies eat up many things, that would otherwise corrupt and become loathsome; and they serve for food to birds, spiders, and many other creatures.

S. But we could clean away everything that was offensive, without their help ; and as to their serving for food, I have seen whole heaps of them lying dead in a window, without seeming to have done good to anything.

P. Well, then : suppose a fly capable of thinking ; would he not be equally puzzled to find out what men were good for ? " This great, two-legged monster," he might say, " instead of helping us to live, devours more food at a meal than would serve a whole legion of flies. Then he kills us by hundreds, when we come within his reach ; and I see him destroy and torment all other animals, too. And when he dies, he is nailed up in a box, and put a great way under ground, as though he grudged doing any more good after his death than when alive." Now, what would you answer to such a reasoning fly ?

S. I would tell him he was very impertinent for talking so of his betters; for that he and all other creatures were made for the use of man, and not man for theirs.

P. But would that be telling him the truth ? You have just been saying that you could not find out of what use flies were to us : whereas, when they suck our blood, there is no doubt that we are of use to them.

S. It is that which puzzles me.

P. There are many other living creatures which we call *noxious*, and which are so far from being useful to us, that we take all possible pains to get rid of them. More than that, there are vast tracts of the earth where few or no men inhabit, which are yet full of beasts, birds, insects, and all living things. These certainly do not exist for his use alone. On the contrary, they often keep man away.

S. Then what are they made for ?

P. They are made to be happy. It is a manifest purpose of the Creator to give being to as much life as possible, for life is enjoyment to all creatures in health and in possession of their faculties. Man surpasses other animals in his powers of enjoyment, and he has prospects in a future state which they do not share with him. But the Creator equally desires the happiness of all his creatures, and looks down with as much benignity upon these flies that are sporting around us, as upon ourselves.

S. Then we ought not to kill them, if they are ever so troublesome.

P. I do not say that. We have a right to make a reasonable use of all creatures for our advantage, and also to free ourselves from such as are hurtful to us. So far, our superiority over them may fairly extend. But we should never abuse them for our mere amusement, nor take away their lives wantonly. Nay, a good-natured man will rather undergo a *little* inconvenience, than take away from a creature all that it possesses. An infant may destroy life, but all the kings upon earth cannot restore it. I remember reading of a good-tempered old gentleman, that, having been a long time plagued with a great fly, that buzzed about his face all dinner-time, at length, after many efforts, caught it. Instead of crushing it to

death, he held it carefully in his hand, and opening
the window, "Go," said he; "get thee gone, poor
creature; I won't hurt a hair of thy head; surely
the world is wide enough for thee and me."

S. I should have loved that man.

P. One of our poets has written some very pretty
lines to a fly, that came to partake with him of his
wine. They begin,—

> " Busy, curious, thirsty fly,
> Drink with me, and drink as I;
> Welcome freely to my cup,
> Couldst thou sip and sip it up."

S. How pretty! I think they will almost make me
love flies. But pray, papa, do not various animals
destroy one another?

P. They do, indeed. The greatest part of them
live only by the destruction of life. There is a perpetual warfare going on, in which the stronger prey
upon the weaker, and, in their turns, are the prey of
those which are a degree stronger than themselves.
Even the innocent sheep, with every mouthful of grass,
destroys hundreds of small insects. In the air we
breathe, and the water we drink, we give death to
thousands of invisible creatures.

S. But is not that very strange? If they were
created to live and be happy, why should they be
destroyed so fast?

P. They are destroyed no faster than others are
produced; and if they enjoyed life while it lasted,
they have had a good bargain. By making animals
the food of animals, Providence has filled up every
chink, as it were, of existence. You see these swarms
of flies. During all the hot weather, they are continually coming forth from the state of eggs and
maggots, and, as soon as they get the use of wings,
they roam about, and fill every place in search of food.
Meantime, they are giving sustenance to the whole
race of spiders; they maintain all the swallow tribe,
and contribute greatly to the support of many other

small birds; and even afford many a delicate morsel to the fishes. Their own numbers, however, seem scarcely diminished, and vast multitudes live on till the cold weather comes and puts an end to them. Were nothing to touch them, they would probably become so numerous as to starve each other. As it is, they are full of enjoyment themselves, and afford life and enjoyment to other creatures, which, in their turn, supply the wants of others.

S. It is no charity, then, to tear a spider's web in pieces, in order to set a fly at liberty.

P. None at all—no more than it would be to demolish the traps of a poor Indian hunter, who depended upon them for his dinner. They both act as nature directs them. Shall I tell you a story?

S. O yes—pray do.

P. A venerable Bramin, who had never in his days eaten anything but rice and milk, and held it the greatest of crimes to shed the blood of anything that had life, was one day meditating on the banks of the Ganges. He saw a little bird on the ground picking up ants as fast as he could swallow. "Murderous wretch," cried he, "what scores of lives are sacrificed to one gluttonous meal of thine!" Presently a sparrow-hawk, pouncing down, seized him in his claws, and flew off with him. The Bramin was at first inclined to triumph over the little bird; but, on hearing his cries, he could not help pitying him. "Poor thing," said he, "thou art fallen into the clutches of thy tyrant!" A stronger tyrant, however, took up the matter; for a falcon, in mid-air, darting on the sparrow-hawk, struck him to the ground, with the bird lifeless in his talons. "Tyrant against tyrant," thought the Bramin, "is well enough." The falcon had not finished tearing his prey, when a lynx, stealing from behind a rock on which he was perched, sprang on him, and, having strangled him, bore him to the hedge of a neighbouring thicket, and began to suck his blood. The Bramin was atten-

tively viewing this new display of retributive justice,
when a sudden roar shook the air, and a huge tiger,
rushing from the thicket, came like thunder on the
lynx. The Bramin was near enough to hear the
crashing bones, and was making off in great terror,
when he met an English soldier, armed with his
musket. He pointed eagerly to the place where the
tiger was making his bloody repast. The soldier
levelled his gun, and laid the tiger dead. "Brave
fellow!" exclaimed the Bramin. "I am very hungry,"
said the soldier, "can you give me a beef-steak? I see
you have plenty of cows here." "Horrible!" cried
the Bramin; "what! I kill the sacred cows of Brama!"
"Then kill the next tiger yourself," said the soldier.

TRUE HEROISM.

You have read, my Edmund, the stories of Achilles,
and Alexander, and Charles of Sweden, and have, I
doubt not, admired the high courage, which seemed
to set them above all sensations of fear, and rendered
them capable of the most extraordinary actions.
The world calls these men *heroes;* but, before we give
them that noble appellation, let us consider what were
the motives which animated them to act and suffer as
they did.

The first was a ferocious savage, governed by the
passions of anger and revenge, in gratifying which he
disregarded all impulses of duty and humanity. The
second was intoxicated with the love of glory—swollen
with absurd pride—and enslaved by dissolute pleasures, and, in pursuit of these objects, he reckoned
the blood of millions as of no account. The third
was unfeeling, obstinate, and tyrannical, and preferred
ruining his country, and sacrificing all his faithful followers, to the humiliation of giving up any of his mad
projects. *Self,* you see, was the spring of all their
conduct; and a selfish man can never be a hero.
I will give you two examples of genuine heroism, one

shown in acting, the other in suffering; and these shall be *true stories*, which is, perhaps, more than can be said of half that is recorded of Achilles and Alexander.

You have probably heard something of Mr. Howard, the reformer of prisons, to whom a monument may be seen in St. Paul's church. His whole life, almost, was heroism; for he confronted all sorts of dangers, with the sole view of relieving the miseries of his fellow-creatures. When he began to examine the state of prisons, scarcely any in this country was free from a very fatal and infectious distemper, called the gaol-fever. Wherever he heard of it, he made a point of seeing the poor sufferers, and often went down into their dungeons, when the keepers themselves would not accompany him. He travelled several times over almost the whole of Europe, and even into Asia, in order to gain knowledge of the state of prisons and hospitals, and point out means for lessening the calamities that prevail in them. He even went into countries where the plague was, that he might learn the best methods of treating that terrible contagious disease; and he voluntarily exposed himself to perform a strict quarantine, as one suspected of having the infection of the plague, only that he might be thoroughly acquainted with the methods used for prevention. He at length died of a fever, caught in attending on the sick on the borders of Crim Tartary, honoured and admired by all Europe, after having greatly contributed to enlighten his own and many other countries, with respect to some of the most important objects of humanity. Such was Howard the Good; as great a hero in preserving mankind, as some of the false heroes above mentioned were in destroying them.

My second hero is a much humbler, but not less genuine one.

There was a journeyman bricklayer, in this town, an able workman, but a very drunken, idle fellow, who spent at the alehouse almost all he earned, and left his wife and children to shift for themselves as they could.

This is, unfortunately, a common case; and of all the tyranny and cruelty exercised in the world, I believe that of bad husbands and fathers is by much the most frequent and the worst.

The family might have starved, but for his eldest son, whom from a child the father brought up to help him in his work, and who was so industrious and attentive, that being now at the age of thirteen or fourteen, he was able to earn pretty good wages, every farthing of which, that he could keep out of his father's hands, he brought to his mother. And when his brute of a father came home drunk, cursing and swearing, and in such an ill humour that his mother and the rest of the children durst not come near him, for fear of a beating, this good lad (Tom was his name) kept near him, to pacify him, and get him quietly to bed. His mother, therefore, justly looked upon Tom as the support of the family, and loved him dearly.

It chanced that one day, Tom, in climbing up a high ladder with a load of mortar in his hod, missed his hold, and fell down to the bottom, on a heap of bricks and rubbish. The bystanders ran up to him and found him all bloody, and with his thigh broken, and bent quite under him. They raised him up, and sprinkled water in his face, to recover him from a swoon into which he had fallen. As soon as he could speak, looking around, with a lamentable tone he cried, " O, what will become of my poor mother !"

He was carried home. I was present while the surgeon set his thigh. His mother was hanging over him half distracted. " Don't cry, mother," said he, " I shall get well again in time." Not a word more, or a groan, escaped him while the operation lasted.

Tom was a ragged boy, that could not read or write; yet Tom has always stood on my list of heroes.

NINETEENTH EVENING.

ON METALS.—PART I.

GEORGE and Harry, with their Tutor, one day in their walk were driven by the rain to take shelter in a blacksmith's shed. The shower lasting some time, the boys, in order to amuse themselves, began to examine the things around them. The great bellows first attracted their notice, and they admired the roaring it made, and the expedition with which it raised the fire to a heat too intense for them to look at. They were surprised at the dexterity with which the smith fashioned a bar of iron into a horse-shoe ; first heating it, then hammering it well on the anvil, cutting off a proper length, bending it round, turning up the ends, and, lastly, punching the nail-holes. They watched the whole process of fitting it to the horse's foot, and fastening it on ; and it had become fair some minutes before they showed a desire to leave the shop and proceed on their walk.

"I could never have thought," said George, beginning the conversation, "that such a hard thing as iron could have been so easily managed."

"Nor I, neither," said Harry.

Tut. It was managed, you saw, by the help of fire. The fire made it soft and flexible, so that the smith could easily hammer it, and cut it, and bend it to the shape he wanted ; and then dipping it in water, made it hard again.

G. Are all other metals managed in the same manner ?

T. They are all worked by the help of fire in some way or other, either in melting them, or making them soft.

G. There are many sorts of metals, are there not ?

T. Yes, several; and, if you have a mind, I will tell you about some of them, and their uses.

G. Pray do, sir.

H. Yes; I should like to hear it, of all things.

T. Well, then; first, let us consider what a metal is. Do you think you should know one from a stone?

G. A stone! Yes, I could not mistake a piece of lead or iron for a stone.

T. How would you distinguish it?

G. A metal is bright and shining.

T. True; brilliancy is one of the qualities of metals. But glass and crystal are very bright, too.

H. But one may see through glass, and not through a piece of metal.

T. Right. Metals are brilliant, but opaque, or not transparent. The thinnest plate of metal that can be made, will keep out the light as effectually as a stone wall.

G. Metals are very heavy, too.

T. True. They are the heaviest bodies in nature; for the lightest metal is nearly twice as heavy as the heaviest stone. Well, what else?

G. Why, they will bear beating with a hammer, which a stone would not, without flying in pieces.

T. Yes; that property of extending, or spreading, under the hammer is called *malleability ;* and another, like it, is that of bearing to be drawn out into a wire, which is called *ductility.* Metals have both these, and much of their use depends upon them.

G. Metals will melt, too.

H. What! will iron melt?

T. Yes; all metals will melt, though some require greater heat than others. The property of melting is called *fusibility.* Do you know anything more about them?

G. No; except that they come out of the ground, I believe.

T. That is properly added; for it is this circumstance which makes them rank among *fossils,* or minerals.

To sum up their character, then, a metal is a brilliant, opaque, heavy, malleable, ductile, and fusible mineral.

G. I think I can hardly remember all that.

T. The *names* may slip your memory, but you cannot see metals at all used, without being sensible of the *things.*

G. But what are *ores?* I remember seeing a heap of iron ore, which men were breaking with hammers, and it looked only like stones.

T. The *ore* of a metal is the state in which it is generally met with in the earth, when it is so mixed with stony and other matters, as not to show its proper qualities as a metal.

H. How do people know it, then?

T. By experience. It was probably accident that, in the early ages, discovered that certain fossils, by the force of fire, might be made to yield a metal. The experiment was repeated on other fossils; so that, in length of time, all the different metals were found out, and all the different forms in which they lie concealed in the ground. The knowledge of this is called *Mineralogy,* and a very important science it is.

G. Yes, I suppose so; for metals are very valuable things. Our next neighbour, Mr. Sterling, I have heard, gets a great deal of money every year from his mines in Wales.

T. He does. The mineral riches of some countries are much superior to that of their products above ground, and the revenues of many kings are in great part derived from their mines.

H. I suppose they must be gold and silver mines.

T. Those, to be sure, are the most valuable, if the metals are found in tolerable abundance. But do you know why they are so?

H Because money is made of gold and silver.

T. That is a principal reason, no doubt. But these metals have intrinsic properties, that make them highly valuable, else, probably, they would not have been chosen in so many countries to make money of. In the first place, gold and silver are both *perfect metals*, that is, indestructible in the fire. Other metals, if kept a considerable time in the fire, change by degrees into a powdery or scaly matter, called a calx. You have melted lead, I dare say?

G. Yes, often.

T. Have you not, then, perceived a drossy film collect upon its surface, after it had been kept melting a while?

G. Yes.

T. That is a calx ; and, in time, the whole lead would change to such a substance. You may see, too, when you have heated the poker red hot, some scales separate from it, which are brittle.

H. Yes—the kitchen poker is almost burnt away, by putting it into the fire.

T. Well—all metals undergo these changes, except gold and silver ; but these, if kept ever so long in the hottest fire, sustain no loss or change. They are, therefore, called *perfect metals*. Gold has several other remarkable properties. It is the heaviest of all metals.

H. What, is it heavier than lead?

T. Yes—about half as heavy again. It is between nineteen and twenty times as heavy as an equal bulk of water. This great weight is a ready means of discovering counterfeit gold coin from genuine ; for as gold must be adulterated with something much lighter than itself, a false coin, if of the same weight with the true, will be sensibly larger. Gold, too, is the most ductile of all metals. You have seen leaf-gold?

G. Yes ; I bought a book of it once.

T. Leaf-gold is made by beating a plate of gold, placed between pieces of skin, with heavy hammers, till it is spread out to the utmost degree of thinness. And, so great is its capacity for being extended, that a single grain of the metal, which would be scarcely larger than a large pin's head, is beaten out to a surface of fifty square inches.

G. That is wonderful, indeed! but I know leaf-gold must be very thin, for it will almost float upon the air.

T. By drawing gold out to a wire, it may be still farther extended. Gold wire, as it is called, is made with silver, overlaid with a small proportion of gold, and they are drawn out together. In the wire commonly used for laces, and embroidery, and the like, a grain of gold is made completely to cover a length of three hundred and fifty-two feet; and when it is stretched still farther, by flatting, it will reach four hundred and one feet.

G. Prodigious! What a vast way a guinea might be drawn out, then!

T. Yes; the gold of a guinea, at that rate, would reach above nine miles and a half; that of a sovereign of course not quite so much. This property in gold, of being capable of extension to so extraordinary a degree, is owing to its great tenacity or cohesion of particles, which is such, that you can hardly break a piece of gold wire by twisting it; and a wire of gold will sustain a greater weight than one of any other metal, equally thick.

H. Then it would make very good wire for hanging bells.

T. It would; but such bell-hanging would come rather too dear. Another valuable quality of gold is its fine colour. You know, scarcely anything makes a more splendid appearance than gilding. And a peculiar advantage of it is, that gold is not liable to rust or tarnish, as other metals are. It will keep its colour fresh for a great many years in a pure and clear air.

H. I remember the vane of the church steeple was newly gilt two years ago, and it looks as well as at first.

T. This property of not rusting, would render gold very useful for a variety of purposes, if it were more common. It would make excellent cooking utensils, water-pipes, mathematical instruments, clock-work, and the like.

G. But is not gold soft ?   I have seen pieces of gold bent double.

T. Yes ; it is next in softness to lead, and therefore, when it is made into coin, or used for any common purposes, it is mixed with a small proportion of some other metal, in order to harden it.   This is called its *alloy.*   Our gold coin has one-twelfth part of alloy, which is a mixture of silver and copper.

G. How beautiful new gold coin is !

T. Yes—there is no metal takes a stamp or impression better ; and it is capable of a very fine polish.

G. What countries yield the most gold ?

T. South America, the East Indies, and the coast of Africa.   California, in North America, is at this time wonderfully productive, and likely to continue so. Europe affords but little ; yet a moderate quantity is got every year from Hungary.

G. I have read of rivers rolling sands of gold.   Is there any truth in that ?

T. The poets, as usual, have greatly exaggerated the matter ; however, there are various streams in different parts of the world, the sands of which contain particles of gold, and some of them in such quantity, as to be worth the search ; those of California, especially.

H. How does the gold come there ?

T. It is washed down, along with the soil, from mountains by the torrents, which are the sources of rivers.

H. What a fine thing it would be to find a gold-mine on one's estate !

T. Perhaps not so fine as you may imagine, for many a one does not pay the cost of working.   A coal-pit would probably be a better thing.   Who do you think are the greatest gold-finders in Europe ?

H. I don't know.

T. The gipsies in Hungary.   A number of half-starved, half-naked wretches of that community employ themselves in washing and picking the sands of some mountain-streams in that country, which contain gold, from which they obtain just profit enough to keep body and soul together! whereas, had they employed themselves in agriculture or manufactures, they might have got a comfortable subsistence. Gold, almost all the world over, is first got by slaves, and it too often makes slaves of those who possess much of it.

G. For my part, I should be content with a silver-mine.

H. But we have no silver-mines in England, have we?

T. None, properly so called; but silver is procured in some of our lead-mines. There are, however, pretty rich silver-mines in various parts of Europe; but the richest of all are in Peru, in South America.

G. Are not the famous mines of Potosi there?

T. They are. Shall I now tell you some of the properties of silver?

G. By all means.

T. It is the other *perfect* metal. It is also as little liable to rust as gold, though, indeed, it readily gets tarnished.

H. Yes; I know our footman is often obliged to clean our plate before it is used.

T. Plate, however, is not made of pure silver, any more than silver coin, and silver utensils of all sorts. An alloy is mixed with it, as with gold, to harden it; and that makes it more liable to tarnish.

G. Bright silver, I think, is almost as beautiful as gold.

T. It is the most beautiful of the white metals, and is capable of a very fine polish; and this, together with its rarity, makes it used for a great variety of ornamental purposes. Then it is nearly as ductile and malleable as gold.

G. I have had silver-leaf, and it seemed as thin as gold-leaf.

T. It is nearly so. That is used for silvering, as gold-leaf is for gilding. It is common, too, to cover metals with a thin coating of silver, which is called plating.

H. The child's saucepan is silvered over on the inside. What is that for?

T. To prevent the food from getting any taint from the metal of the saucepan; for silver is not capable of being corroded or dissolved by any of the acids or other liquids used in food, as iron and copper are.

H. And that is the reason, I suppose, that fruit-knives are made of silver?

T. It is; but the softness of the metal makes them bear a very poor edge.

G. Does silver melt easily?

T. Silver and gold both melt more difficultly than lead; nor till they are above a common red heat. As to the weight of silver, it is nearly one-half less than that of gold, being only eleven times as heavy as water.

H. Is quicksilver a kind of silver?

T. It takes its name from silver, being very like it in colour; but in reality it is a very different thing, and one of the most singular of the metal kind.

G. It is not *malleable*, I am sure.

T. No; not when it is quick or fluid, as it always is in our climate. But a very great degree of cold makes it solid, and then it is malleable, like other metals.

G. I have heard of *killing* quicksilver; pray what does that mean?

T. It means destroying its property of running about, by mixing it with something else. Thus, if quicksilver be well rubbed with fat, or oil, or gum, it unites with them, losing all its metallic appearance, or fluidity. It also unites readily with gold and silver, and several other metals, into the form of a sort of shining paste, which is called an *amalgam*. This is one of the ways of gilding or silvering a thing. Your buttons are gilt by means of an amalgam.

G. How is that done?

T. The shells of the buttons, which are made of copper, are shaken in a hat with a lump of amalgam of gold and quicksilver, till they are all covered over with it. They are then put into a sort of frying-pan, and held over the fire. The quicksilver, being very volatile in its nature, flies off in the form of smoke, or vapour, when it is heated, leaving the gold behind it spread over the surface of the buttons. Thus, many dozen are gilt at once, with the greatest ease.

H. What a clever way! I should like vastly to see it done.

T. You may see it any day at Birmingham, if you happen to be there; as well as a great many other curious operations on metals.

G. What a weight quicksilver is; I remember taking up a bottle full of it, and I had like to have dropped it again, it was so much heavier than I expected.

T. Yes; it is one of the heaviest of the metals— about fifteen times as heavy as water.

G. Is not *mercury* a name for quicksilver? I have heard them talk of the mercury rising and falling in the thermometer and barometer, or weather-glasses.

T. It is. You, perhaps, may have heard too of *mercurial medicines,* which are those made of quicksilver prepared in one manner or another.

G. What are they good for?

T. For a great variety of complaints. Your brother took some lately, for the worms; and they are often given for breakings out on the skin, for sores and swellings, and for affections of the liver. But they have one remarkable effect, when taken in a considerable quantity, which is, to loosen the teeth, and cause great expectoration. This state is called salivation.

H. I used to think quicksilver was poison.

T. When in its common state of running quicksilver, it generally does neither good nor harm; but it may be prepared, so as to be a most violent medicine, or even a poison.

G. Is it useful for anything else?

T. Yes—for a variety of purposes in the arts, which I cannot now very well explain to you. But you will perhaps be surprised to hear that one of the finest red paints is made from quicksilver.

G. A red paint!—which is that?

T. Vermilion, or cinnabar, which is a particular mixture of sulphur with quicksilver.

H. Is quicksilver found in this country?

T. No. The greatest quantity comes from Spain. Istria, and South America. It is a considerable object of commerce, and bears a high value, though much inferior to silver. Well—so much for metals at present. We will talk of the rest on some future opportunity.

FLYING AND SWIMMING.

" How I wish I could fly!" cried Robert, as he was gazing after his pigeons, that were exercising themselves in a morning's flight. "How fine it must be to soar to such a height, and to dash through the air with so swift a motion!"

"I doubt not," said his father, "that the pigeons have great pleasure in it; but we have our pleasures, too; and it is idle to indulge longings for things quite beyond our power."

R. But do you think it impossible for men to learn to fly?

F. I do—for I see they are not furnished by nature with organs requisite for the purpose.

R. Might not artificial wings be contrived, such as Dædalus is said to have used?

F. Possibly they might; but the difficulty would be, to put them in motion.

R. Why could not a man move them, if they were fastened to his shoulders, as well as a bird?

F. Because he has got arms to move, which the bird has not. The same organs which in quadrupeds are employed to move the fore legs, and in man the arms, are used by birds in the motion of the wings. Nay, the muscles, or bundles of flesh, that move the wings, are proportionally much larger and stronger than those bestowed upon our arms; so that it is impossible, formed as we are, that we should use wings, were they made and fastened on with ever so much art.

R. But angels, and cupids, and such things, are painted with wings; and I think they look very natural.

F. To you they may appear so; but an anatomist sees them at once to be monsters, which could not really exist.

R. God might have created winged men, however, if he had pleased.

F. No doubt; but they could not have had the same shape that men have now. They would have been different creatures, such as it was not in his plan to create. But you, that long to fly—consider if you have made use of all the faculties already given you! You want to subdue the element of air—what can you do with that of water? Can you swim?

R. No, not yet.

F. Your companion, Johnson, I think, can swim very well.

R. Yes.

F. Reflect, then, on the difference between him and you. A boat oversets with you both, in a deep stream. You plump at once to the bottom, and almost inevitably lose your life. He rises like a cork, darts away with the greatest ease, and reaches the shore in perfect safety. Both of you, pursued by a bull, come to the side of a river. He jumps in, and crosses it. You are drowned if you attempt it, and tossed by the bull if you do not. What an advantage he has over you! Yet you are furnished with exactly the same bodily powers that he is. How is this?

R. Because he has been taught, and I have not.

F. True—but it is an easy thing to learn, and requires no other instruction than boys can give one another, when they bathe together; so that I wonder anybody should neglect to acquire an art at once so agreeable and useful. The Romans used to say, by

way of proverb, of a blockhead, " He can neither read
nor swim." You may remember how Cæsar was saved
at Alexandria, by throwing himself into the sea, and
swimming with one hand, while he held up his Com-
mentaries with the other.

R. I should like very well to swim, and I have often
tried, but I always pop under water, and that daunts
me.

F. And it is that fear which prevents you from succeeding.

R. But is it as natural for man to swim as for
other creatures ? I have heard that the young of all
other animals swim the first time they are thrown into
the water.

F. They do—they are without fear. In our climate,
the water is generally cold, and is early made an object
of terror. But in hot countries, where bathing is
one of the greatest of pleasures, young children swim
so early and well, that I should suppose they take to
it almost naturally.

R. I am resolved to learn, and I will ask Johnson
to take me with him to the river.

F. Do; but let him find you a safe place to begin at.
I don't want you, however, to proceed so cautiously as
Sir Nicholas Gimcrack did.

R. How was that ?

F. He spread himself out on a large table, and,
placing before him a basin of water with a frog in it,
he struck with his arms and legs, as he observed the
animal do.

R. And did that teach him ?

F. Yes—to swim on dry land ; but he never ventured himself in the water.

R. Shall I get corks or bladders ?

F. No ; learn to depend on your own powers. It is
a good lesson in other things, as well as in swimming.
But corks or bladders, if accidentally allowed to get
out of their proper position, are very dangerous, and
have occasioned the loss of many lives.

THE FEMALE CHOICE.
A Tale.

A YOUNG girl, having fatigued herself one hot day with running about the garden, sat herself down in a pleasant arbour, where she presently fell asleep. During her slumber, two female figures presented themselves before her. One was loosely habited in a thin robe of pink, with light green trimmings. Her sash of silver gauze flowed to the ground. Her fair hair fell in ringlets down her neck, and her head-dress consisted of artificial flowers, interwoven with feathers. She held in one hand a ball-ticket, and in the other a fancy dress all covered with spangles and knots of gay ribbon. She advanced smiling to the girl, and with a familiar air thus addressed her:—

"My dearest Melissa, I am a kind genius, who have watched you from your birth, and have joyfully beheld all your beauties expand, till at length they have rendered you a companion worthy of me. See what I have brought you. This dress and this ticket will give you free access to all the ravishing delights of my palace. With me you will pass your days in a perpetual round of ever-varying amusements. Like the gay butterfly, you will have no other business than to flutter from flower to flower, and spread your charms before admiring spectators. No restraints, no toils, no dull tasks are to be found within my happy domains. All is pleasure, life, and good humour. Come, then, my dear! Let me put you on this dress, which will make you quite enchanting; and away, away, with me!"

Melissa felt a strong inclination to comply with the call of this inviting nymph; but first she thought it would be prudent, at least, to ask her name.

"My name," said she, "is Dissipation."

The other female then advanced. She was clothed

in a close habit of brown stuff, simply relieved with white.   She wore her smooth hair under a plain cap. Her whole person was perfectly neat and clean.   Her look was serious, but satisfied; and her air was staid and composed.   She held in one hand a distaff; on the opposite arm hung a work-basket; and the girdle round her waist was garnished with scissors, knitting-needles, reels, and other implements of female labour. A bunch of keys hung at her side.   She thus accosted the sleeping girl:—

"Melissa, I am the genius who have ever been the friend and companion of your mother; and I now offer my protection to you.   I have no allurements to tempt you with, like those of my gay rival.   Instead of spending all your time in amusements, if you enter yourself of my train, you must rise early, and pass the long day in a variety of employments, some of them difficult, some laborious, and all requiring some exertion of body or mind.   You must dress plainly, live mostly at home, and aim mostly at being useful, rather than shining. But, in return, I will insure you content, even spirits, self-approbation, and the esteem of all who thoroughly know you.   If these offers appear to your young mind less inviting than those of my rival, be assured, however, that they are more real.   She has promised much more than she can ever make good.   Perpetual pleasures are no more in the power of Dissipation, than of Vice or Folly, to bestow.   Her delights quickly pall, and are inevitably succeeded by languor and disgust. She appears to you under a disguise, and what you see is not her real face.   For myself, I shall never seem to you less amiable than I now do, but, on the contrary, you will like me better and better.   If I look grave to you now, you will hear me sing at my work; and, when work is over, I can dance too.   But I have said enough.   It is time for you to choose whom you will follow, and upon that choice all your happiness depends.   If you would know my name, it is House-wifery."

Melissa heard her with more attention than delight;

and though overawed by her manner, she could not help turning again to take another look at the first speaker. She beheld her still offering her presents with so bewitching an air, that she felt it scarcely possible to resist; when, by a lucky accident, the mask, with which Dissipation's face was so artfully covered, fell off. As soon as Melissa beheld, instead of the smiling features of youth and cheerfulness, a countenance wan and ghastly with sickness, and soured by fretfulness, she turned away with horror, and gave her hand un-reluctantly to her sober and sincere companion.

TWENTIETH EVENING.

ON METALS.—PART II.

Tutor—George—Harry.

T. WELL—have you forgotten what I told you about metals the other day?

G. O no!

H. I am sure I have not.

T. What metals were they that we talked about?

G. Gold, silver, and quicksilver.

T. Suppose, then, we go on to some of the others?

G. Pray do.

H. Yes, by all means.

T. Very well. You know *copper,* I don't doubt.

G. O yes!

T. What colour do you call it?

G. I think it is a sort of reddish brown.

T. True. Sometimes, however, it is of a bright red, like sealing-wax. It is not a very heavy metal, being not quite nine times the weight of water. It is very ductile, bearing to be rolled or hammered out to a very thin plate, and also to be drawn out to a fine wire.

H. I remember seeing a halfpenny that had been rolled out to a long ribbon.

G. Yes; and I have seen half a dozen men at a

time, with great hammers, beating out a piece of copper at the brazier's.

T. Copper requires a very considerable heat to melt it; and by long exposure to the fire, it may be burned, or calcined; for it, like all we are now to speak of, is an *imperfect* metal.

H. And it rusts very easily, does it not?

T. It does; for all acids dissolve or corrode it, so do salts of every kind; whence even air and common water in a short time act upon it, for they are never free from somewhat of a saline nature.

G. Is not verdigris the rust of copper?

T. It is;—a rust produced by the acid of grapes. But every rust of copper is of a blue or green colour, as well as verdigris.

H. And are they all poison, too?

T. They are all so, in some degree, producing violent sickness and pain in the bowels. They are all, too, extremely nauseous to the taste; and the metal itself, when heated, tastes and smells very disagreeably.

G. Why is it used, then, so much in cooking, brewing, and the like.

T. Because it is a very convenient metal for making vessels, especially large ones, as it is easily worked, and is sufficiently strong, though hammered thin, and bears the fire well. And if vessels of it are kept quite clean, and the liquor not suffered to stand long in them when cold, there is no danger in their use. But copper vessels for cooking are generally lined on the inside with tin.

G. What else is copper used for?

T. A variety of things. Sheets of copper are sometimes used to cover buildings; and a great quantity is consumed in sheathing ships, that is, in covering all the part under water; the purpose of which is to protect the timber from the worms, and also to make the ship sail faster, by means of the greater smoothness and force with which the copper makes way through the water.

H. Money is made of copper, too.

T. It is; for it takes an impression in coining very well, and its value is a proper proportion below silver for a price for the cheapest commodities. In some poor countries, they have little other than copper coin. Another great use of copper is as an ingredient in mixed metals; such as bell-metal, cannon-metal, and particularly brass.

H. But brass is yellow.

T. True; it is converted to that colour by means of another metallic substance, named *zinc,* or *spelter,* the natural colour of which is white. Zinc, as much cheaper than copper, and less liable to corrode, has been extensively brought into use of late years, for a variety of purposes. A kind of brown stone called *calamine,* is an ore of zinc. By filling a pot with layers of powdered calamine and charcoal, placed alternately with copper, and applying a pretty strong heat, the zinc is driven in vapour out of the calamine, and penetrates the copper, changing it into brass.

G. What is the use of turning copper into brass?

T. It gains a fine, gold-like colour, and becomes harder, more easy to melt, and less liable to rust. Hence it is preferred for a variety of utensils, ornamental and useful. Brass does not bear hammering well, but is generally cast in the shape wanted, and then turned in a lathe and polished. Well—these are the principal things I have to say about copper.

H. But where does it come from?

T. Copper is found in many countries. Our island yields abundance, especially in Wales and Cornwall. In Anglesey is a whole hill, called Paris-mountain, consisting of copper ore, from which immense quantities are dug every year. Now for *iron.*

H. Ay! That is the most useful of all the metals.

T. I think it is; and it is also the most common, for there are few countries in the world possessing hills and rocks, where it is not met with, more or less. Iron is the hardest of metals, the most elastic or springy, the most tenacious or difficult to break, next to gold, the most difficultly fusible, and one of the lightest, being only seven or eight times as heavy as water.

G. You say it is difficult to break; but I snapped the blade of a penknife the other day, by only bending it a little; and my mother is continually breaking her needles.

T. Properly objected! But the qualities of iron differ extremely, according to the method of preparing it. There are forged iron, cast iron, and steel, which are very different from each other. Iron, when first melted from its ore, has little malleability, and the vessels and other implements that are made of it in that state, by casting into moulds, are easily broken. It acquires toughness and malleability by *forging*, which is done by beating it, when red hot, with heavy hammers, till it becomes ductile and flexible. Steel, again, is made by heating small bars of iron with wood-ashes, charcoal, bone and horn shavings, or other inflammable matters, by which it acquires a finer grain and more compact texture, and becomes harder and more elastic. Steel may be rendered either very flexible, or brittle, by different manners of *tempering*, which is performed by heating and then quenching it in water. Steel is iron in a higher state of excellence.

G. All cutting instruments are made of steel, are they not?

T. Yes; and the very fine-edged ones are generally tempered brittle, as razors, penknives, and surgeons' instruments; but sword-blades are made flexible, and the best of them will bend double, without breaking or becoming crooked. The steel of which springs are made has the highest possible degree of elasticity given it. A watch-spring is one of the finest examples of this kind. Steel, for ornaments, is made extremely hard and close-grained, so as to bear an exquisite polish. Common, hammered iron is chiefly used for works of strength, as horse-shoes, bars, bolts, and the like. It will bend, but not straighten itself again, as you may see in the kitchen poker. Cast iron is used for pots and caldrons, cannon, cannon-balls, grates, pillars, and many other purposes in which hardness, without flexibility, is wanted.

G. What a vast variety of uses this metal is put to !

T. Yes; I know not when I should have done, if I were to tell you of all.

H. Then I think it is really more valuable than gold, though it is so much cheaper.

T. That was the opinion of the wise Solon, when he observed to the rich king Crœsus, who was showing him his treasures, " he who possesses more iron, will soon be master of all this gold."

H. I suppose he meant weapons and armour.

T. He did; but there are many nobler uses for these metals; and few circumstances denote the progress of the arts in a country more than having attained the full use of iron, without which scarcely any manufacture or machinery can be brought to perfection. From the difficulty of melting it out of the ore, many nations have been longer in discovering it than some of the other metals. The Greeks, in Homer's time, seem to have employed copper or brass for their weapons much more than iron; and the ancient Egyptians, as well as the Greeks, are said to have possessed the art, since lost, of hardening their copper or brass, so that it would take an edge similar to that of fine steel. The Mexicans and Peruvians, who possessed gold and silver, were unacquainted with iron when the Spaniards invaded them.

G. Iron is very subject to rust, however.

T. It is so, and that is one of its worst properties. Every liquor, and even a moist air, corrodes it. But the rust of iron is not pernicious; on the contrary, it is a very useful medicine. Of late years, a mode has been invented, by the application of galvanic action, to prevent iron from rusting.

G. I have heard of steel drops and steel-filings given for medicines.

T. Yes; iron is given in a variety of forms; and the property of them all is to strengthen the constitution. Many springs are made medicinal by the iron that they dissolve in the bowels of the earth. These are called *chalybeate* waters, and they may be known by their inky taste, and the rust-coloured sediment they leave in their course.

H. May we drink such water, if we meet with it?

T. Yes; unless long continued, it will do you no harm; and, in some cases, may be beneficial. There is one other property of iron well worth knowing, and that is, that it is the only thing attracted by the magnet or loadstone.

G. I had a magnet once that would take up needles and keys; but it seemed a bar of iron itself.

T. True. The real loadstone, which is a particular ore of iron, can communicate its virtue to a piece of iron, by rubbing it; nay, a bar of iron itself, in length of time, by being placed in a particular position, will acquire the same property.

G. Is all the iron used in England produced here?

T. By no means. Our extensive manufactures require a great importation of iron. Much is brought from Norway, Russia, and Sweden; and the Swedish is reckoned particularly excellent.

Well, now to another metal. I dare say you can tell me a good deal about *lead?*

H. I know several things about it. It is very heavy and soft, and easily melted.

T. True; these are some of its distinguishing properties. Its weight is between eleven and twelve times that of water. Its colour is a dull, bluish white; and from this livid hue, as well as its being totally void of spring or elasticity, it has acquired a sort of character of dulness and sluggishness. Thus we say of a stupid man, that he has a *leaden* disposition.

G. Lead is very malleable, I think.

T. Yes; it may be beaten out into a pretty thin leaf, but it will not bear drawing into fine wire. It is not only very fusible, but very readily calcined by heat, changing into a powder, or a scaly matter, which may be made to take all colours by the fire, from yellow to deep red. You have seen red lead?

G. Yes.

T. That is calcined lead, exposed for a considerable time to a strong flame. Lead may even be changed into glass, by a moderate heat; and there is a good deal of it in our finest glass.

G. What is white lead, or ceruse?

T. It is lead corroded by the steam of vinegar. Lead, in various forms, is much used by painters. Its calces dissolve in oil, and are employed for the purpose of thickening paint and making it dry. All lead-paints, however, are unwholesome as long as they continue to smell, and the fumes of lead, when melted, are also pernicious. This is the cause why painters and plumbers are so subject to various diseases, particularly violent colics and palsies. The white-lead manufacture is so hurtful to the health, that the workmen, in a very short time, are apt to lose the use of their limbs, and be otherwise severely indisposed.

G. I wonder, then, that anybody will work in it.

T. Ignorance and high wages are sufficient to induce them. But it is to be lamented that in a great many manufactures the health and lives of individuals are sacrificed to the convenience and profit of the community. Lead, too, when dissolved, as it may be in all sour liquors, is a slow poison, and the more dangerous, as it imparts no disagreeable taste. A salt of lead, made with vinegar, is so sweet as to be called the sugar of lead. It has been too common to put this, or some other preparation of lead, into sour wines, in order to cure them; and much mischief has been done by this practice.

G. If lead be poisonous, is it not wrong to make water-pipes and cisterns of it?

T. This has been objected to; but it does not appear that water can, of itself, dissolve any of the lead.

Nor does it readily rust in the air; and hence it is much used to cover buildings with, as well as to line spouts and watercourses. For these purposes, the lead is cast into sheets, which are easily cut and hammered into any shape.

H. Bullets and shot, too, are made of lead?

T. Some of them are; and in this way it is ten times more destructive than as a poison.

G. I think lead seems to be more used than any metal, except iron.

T. It is; and the plenty of it in our country is a great benefit to us, both for domestic use, and as an article that brings in much profit by exportation.

G. Where are our principal lead-mines?

T. They are much scattered about our island. The west of England produces a great deal, in Cornwall, Devonshire, and Somersetshire. Wales affords a large quantity. Derbyshire has long been noted for its lead-mines, and so have Northumberland and Durham. And there are considerable ones in the southern part of Scotland.

Now, do you recollect another metal to be spoken about?

G. Tin.

T. True. Tin resembles lead in colour, but has a more silvery whiteness. It is soft and flexible, like lead, but is distinguished by the crackling noise it makes on being bent. It melts as easily as lead, and also is readily calcined, by keeping it in the fire. It is the lightest of all metals, being only seven times heavier than water. It may be beaten into a thin leaf, but not drawn out to wire.

G. Is tin of much use?

T. It is not often used by itself, but very frequently in conjunction with other metals. As tin is little liable to rust, or to be corroded by common liquors, it is employed for a lining or coating of vessels made of copper or iron. The saucepans and kettles in the kitchen, you know, are all tinned.

G. Yes. How is it done?

T. By melting the tin, and spreading it upon the surface of the copper, which is first lightly pitched over, in order to make the tin adhere.

H. But what are the vessels made at the tinman's? Are they not called tin?

T. No. *Tinned*-ware (as it is properly called) is made of thin iron plates, coated over with tin, by dipping them into a vessel full of melted tin. These plates are afterwards cut and bent to proper shapes, and the joinings are soldered together with a mixture of tin and other metals. Another similar use of tin is in what is called the silvering of pins.

G. What—is not that real silvering?

T. No. The pins, which are made of brass wire, after being pointed and headed, are boiled in water, in which grain-tin is put along with tartar, which is a crust that collects on the inside of wine-casks. The tartar dissolves some of the tin, and makes it adhere to the surface of the pins; and thus thousands are covered in an instant.

H. That is as clever as what you told us of the gilding of buttons.

T. It is. Another purpose for which great quantities of tin used to be employed, was the making of pewter. The best pewter consists chiefly of tin, with a small mixture of other metals to harden it; and the London pewter was brought to such a degree of excellence, as to look almost as well as silver.

G. I can just remember a long row of pewter plates at my grandmother's.

T. You may. In her time, all the plates and dishes for the table were made of pewter; and a handsome range of pewter shelves was thought a capital ornament for a kitchen. At present, this trade is almost come to nothing, through the use of earthenware and china; and pewter is employed for little, but the worms of stills, and barber's basins, and porterpots. But a good deal is still exported. Tin is also

an ingredient in other mixed metals for various purposes, but, on the whole, less of it is used than of the
other common metals.

G. Is not England more famous for tin than any
other country? I have read of the Phœnicians trading
here for it in very early times.

T. They did; and tin is still a very valuable article
of export from England. Much of it is sent as far as
China. The tin-mines here are chiefly in Cornwall,
and, I believe, they are the most productive of any in
Europe. Very fine tin is also got in the peninsula
of Malacca, in the East Indies. Well—we have now
gone through the principal metals.

G. But you have said something about a kind of
metal called zinc.

T. That is one of another class of mineral substances, called *semi-metals*. These resemble metals in
every quality but ductility, of which they are almost
wholly destitute, and, for want of it, they can seldom
be used in the arts, except when joined with metals.

G. Are there many of them?

T. Yes, several; but we will not talk of them till I
have taken some opportunity of showing them to you,
for, probably, you may never have seen any of them.
Now try to repeat the names of all the metals to me
in the order of their weight.

H. There is first *gold.*

G. Then *quicksilver, lead, silver.*

H. *Copper, iron, tin.*

T. Very right. Now I must tell you of an odd
fancy that chemists have had of christening these metals
by the names of the heavenly bodies. They have called
gold *Sol,* or the sun.

G. That is suitable enough to its colour and brightness.

H. Then silver should be the moon, for I have heard
moonlight called of a silvery hue.

T. True; and they have named it so. It is *Luna.*
Quicksilver is *Mercury,* so named, probably, from its

great propensity to dance and jump about, for *Mercury*, you know, was very nimble.

G. Yes; he had wings to his heels.

T. Copper is *Venus.*

G. Venus! surely it is scarcely beautiful enough for that.

T. But they had disposed of the most beautiful ones before. Iron is *Mars.*

H. That is right enough, because swords are made of iron.

T. True. Then tin is *Jupiter*, and lead *Saturn.* The dulness of lead might be thought to agree with that planet which is most remote from the sun. These names, childish as they may seem, are worth remembering, since chemists and physicians still apply them to many preparations of the various metals. You will probably often hear of *martial, lunar, mercurial,* and *saturnine;* and you may now know what they mean.

G. I think the knowledge of metals seems more useful than all you have told us about plants.

T. I don't know that. Many nations make no use at all of metals, but there are none which do not owe a great part of their subsistence to vegetables. However, without inquiring what parts of natural knowledge are *most* useful, you may be assured of this, that all are useful in some degree or other; and there are few things that give one man greater superiority over another, than the extent and accuracy of his knowledge in these particulars. One person passes all his life upon the earth, a stranger to it; while another finds himself at home everywhere. To what I have already said respecting metals, may be added, that, of metals and metallic substances, there are, in the aggregate, upwards of fifty. Amongst them may be mentioned antimony, bismuth, arsenic, cobalt, platinum, nickel, manganese, rhodium, potassium, sodium, magnesium, vanadium, &c. Of these, many are extensively used in medicines and in the arts.

T

EYES, AND NO EYES;
OR, THE ART OF SEEING.

" WELL, Robert, whither have you been walking this afternoon?" said Mr. Andrews to one of his pupils at the close of a holiday

R. I have been, sir, to Broom-heath, and so round by the windmill upon Camp-mount, and home, through the meadows, by the river side.

Mr. A. Well, that's a pleasant round.

R. I thought it very dull, sir; I scarcely met with a single person. I had rather by half have gone along the turnpike-road.

Mr. A. Why, if seeing men and horses were your object, you would, indeed, have been better entertained on the high-road. But did you see William?

R. We set out together, but he lagged behind in the lane, so I walked on and left him.

Mr. A. That was a pity. He would have been company for you.

R. O, he is so tedious, always stopping to look at this thing and that! I had rather walk alone. I dare say he has not got home yet.

Mr. A. Here he comes. Well, William, where have you been?

W. O, sir, the pleasantest walk! I went all over Broom-heath, and so up to the mill at the top of the hill, and then down among the green meadows, by the side of the river.

Mr. A. Why, that is just the round Robert has been taking, and he complains of its dulness, and prefers the high-road.

W. I wonder at that. I am sure I hardly took a step that did not delight me, and I have brought home my handkerchief full of curiosities.

Mr. A. Suppose, then, you give us some account of what amused you so much. I fancy it will be as new to Robert as to me.

W. I will, sir. The lane leading to the heath, you know, is close and sandy; so I did not mind it much, but made the best of my way. However, I spied a curious thing enough in the hedge. It was an old crab-tree, out of which grew a great bunch of something green, quite different from the tree itself. Here is a branch of it.

Mr. A. Ah! this is mistletoe, a plant of great fame for the use made of it by the Druids of old in their religious rites and incantations. It bears a very slimy, white berry, of which birdlime may be made, whence its Latin name of *Viscus.* It is one of those plants which do not grow in the ground by a root of their own, but fix themselves upon other plants; whence they have been humorously styled *parasitical*, as being hangers-on, or dependants. It was the mistletoe of the oak that the Druids particularly honoured.

W. A little further on, I saw a green woodpecker fly to a tree, and run up the trunk like a cat.

Mr. A. That was to seek for insects in the bark, on which they live. They bore holes with their strong bills for that purpose, and do much damage to the trees by it.

W. What beautiful birds they are!

Mr. A. Yes; the woodpecker has been called, from its colour and size, the English parrot.

W. When I got upon the open heath, how charming it was! The air seemed so fresh, and the prospect on every side so free and unbounded! Then it was all covered with gay flowers, many of which I had never observed before. There were, at least, three kinds of heath (I have got them in my handkerchief here), and gorse, and broom, and bell-flower, and many others of all colours, that I will beg you presently to tell me the names of.

Mr. A. That I will, readily.

W. I saw, too, several birds that were new to me. There was a pretty, greyish one, of the size of a lark, that was hopping about some great stones; and when he flew, he showed a great deal of white about his tail.

Mr. A. That was a wheat-ear. They are reckoned very delicious birds to eat, and frequent the open downs in Sussex, and some other counties, in great numbers.

W. There was a flock of lapwings upon a marshy part of the heath, that amused me much. As I came near them, some of them kept flying round and round, just over my head, and crying *pewet*, so distinctly, one might almost fancy they spoke. I thought I should have caught one of them, for he flew as though one of his wings was broken, and often tumbled close to the ground; but as I came near, he always made a shift to get away.

Mr. A. Ha, ha! you were finely taken in then! This was all an artifice of the bird's, to entice you away from its nest; for they build upon the bare ground, and their nests would easily be observed, did they not draw off the attention of intruders by their loud cries and counterfeit lameness.

W. I wish I had known that, for he led me a long chase, often over-shoes in water. However, it was the cause of my falling in with an old man and a boy, who were cutting and piling up turf for fuel, and I had a good deal of talk with them, about the manner of preparing the turf, and the price it sells at. They gave me, too, a creature I never saw before—a young viper, which they had just killed, together with its dam. I have seen several common snakes, but this is thicker in proportion, and of a darker colour than they are.

Mr. A. True. Vipers frequent those turfy, boggy grounds pretty much; and I have known several turf-cutters bitten by them.

W. They are very venomous, are they not?

Mr. A. Enough so to make their wounds painful and dangerous, though they seldom prove fatal.

W. Well—I then took my course up to the wind-mill, on the mount. I climbed up the steps of the

mill, in order to get a better view of the country around.
What an extensive prospect! I counted fifteen church-
steeples; and I saw several gentlemen's houses peeping
out from the midst of green woods and plantations;
and I could trace the windings of the river all along
the low grounds, till it was lost behind a ridge of hills.
But I'll tell you what I mean to do, sir, if you will
give me leave.

Mr. A. What is that?

W. I will go again, and take with me the county
map, by which I shall probably be able to make out
most of the places.

Mr. A. You shall have it, and I will go with you,
and take my pocket spying-glass.

W. I shall be very glad of that. Well—a thought
struck me, that as the hill is called Camp-mount,
there might probably be some remains of ditches and
mounds, with which I have read that camps were surrounded. And I really believe I discovered something
of that sort running round one side of the mound.

Mr. A. Very likely you might. I know antiquaries
have described such remains as existing there, which
some suppose to be Roman, others Danish. We will
examine them further, when we go.

W. From the hill, I went straight down to the
meadows below, and walked on the side of a brook
that runs into the river. It was all bordered with
reeds and flags, and tall flowering plants, quite different
from those I had seen on the heath. As I was getting
down the bank, to reach one of them, I heard something plunge into the water near me. It was a large
water-rat, and I saw it swim over to the other side,
and go into its hole. There were a great many large
dragon-flies all about the stream. I caught one of the
finest, and have got him here in a leaf. But how I
longed to catch a bird that I saw hovering over the
water, and that every now and then darted down into it!
It was all over a mixture of the most beautiful green
and blue, with some orange-colour. It was somewhat

less than a thrush, and had a large head and bill, and a short tail.

Mr. A. I can tell you what that bird was—a kingfisher, the celebrated halcyon of the ancients, about which so many tales are told. It lives on fish, which it catches in the manner you saw. It builds in holes in the banks, and is a shy, retired bird, never to be seen far from the stream where it inhabits.

W. I must try to get another sight of him, for I never saw a bird that pleased me so much. Well— I followed this little brook till it entered the river, and then took the path that runs along the bank. On the opposite side, I observed several little birds running along the shore, and making a piping noise. They were brown and white, and about as big as a snipe.

Mr. A. I suppose they were sand-pipers, one of the numerous family of birds that get their living by wading among the shallows, and picking up worms and insects.

W. There were a great many swallows, too, sporting upon the surface of the water, that entertained me with their motions. Sometimes they dashed into the stream; sometimes they pursued one another so quickly, that the eye could scarcely follow them. In one place, where a high, steep sand-bank rose directly above the river, I observed many of them go in and out of holes, with which the bank was bored full.

Mr. A. Those were sand-martins, the smallest of our species of swallows. They are of a mouse-colour above, and white beneath. They make their nests, and bring up their young in these holes, which run a great depth, and by their situation are secure from all plunderers.

W. A little further, I saw a man in a boat, who was catching eels in an odd way. He had a long pole, with broad iron prongs at the end, just like Neptune's trident, only there were five, instead of three. This he pushed straight down among the mud, in the deepest parts of the river, and fetched up the eels sticking between the prongs.

Mr. A. I have seen this method. It is called spearing of eels.

W. While I was looking at him, a heron came flying over my head, with his large, flagging wings. He alighted at the next turn of the river, and I crept softly behind the bank to watch his motions. He had waded into the water as far as his long legs would carry him, and was standing with his neck drawn in, looking intently on the stream. Presently, he darted his long bill, as quick as lightning, into the water, and drew out a fish, which he swallowed. I saw him catch another in the same manner. He then took alarm at some noise I made, and flew away slowly to a wood at some distance, where he settled.

Mr. A. Probably his nest was there, for herons build upon the loftiest trees they can find, and sometimes in society together, like rooks. Formerly, when these birds were valued for the amusement of hawking, many gentlemen had their *heronries*, and a few are still remaining.

W. I think they are the largest wild birds we have.

Mr. A. They are of great length and spread of wing, but their bodies are comparatively small.

W. I then turned homeward, across the meadows, where I stopped awhile to look at a large flock of starlings, which kept flying about at no great distance. I could not tell at first what to make of them; for they arose altogether from the ground as thick as a swarm of bees, and formed themselves into a sort of black cloud, hovering over the field. After taking a short round, they settled again, and presently arose again in the same manner. I dare say there were hundreds of them.

Mr. A. Perhaps so; for in the fenny countries their flocks are so numerous as to break down whole acres of reeds by settling on them. This disposition

of starlings to fly in close swarms was remarked even
by Homer, who compares the foe flying from one of
his heroes, to a *cloud* of *stares* retiring dismayed at
the approach of the hawk.

W. After I had left the meadows, I crossed the
corn-fields in the way to our house, and passed close
by a deep marl-pit. Looking into it, I saw in one of
the sides a cluster of what I took to be shells; and,
upon going down, I picked up a clod of marl, which
was quite full of them; but how sea-shells could get
there, I cannot imagine.

Mr. A. I do not wonder at your surprise, since
many philosophers have been much perplexed to account for the same appearance. It is not uncommon
to find great quantities of shells and relics of marine
animals even in the bowels of high mountains, very
remote from the sea. They are certainly proofs that
the earth was once in a very different state from what
it is at present; but in what manner, and how long
ago these changes took place, can only be guessed at.

W. I got to the high field next our house just as
the sun was setting, and I stood looking at it till it
was quite lost. What a glorious sight! The clouds
were tinged purple and crimson, and yellow of all
shades and hues, and the clear sky varied from blue to
a fine green at the horizon. But how large the sun
appears just as it sets! I think it seems twice as big
as when it is overhead.

Mr. A. It does so; and you may probably have
observed the same apparent enlargement of the moon
at its rising?

W. I have; but, pray, what is the reason of this?

Mr. A. It is an optical deception, depending upon
principles which I cannot well explain to you till you
know more of that branch of science. But what a
number of new ideas this afternoon's walk has
afforded you! I do not wonder that you found it
amusing; it has been very instructive, too. Did *you*
see nothing of all these sights, Robert?

R. I saw some of them, but I did not take particular notice of them.

Mr. A. Why not?

R. I don't know. I did not care about them, and I made the best of my way home.

Mr. A. That would have been right if you had been sent with a message; but as you walked only for amusement, it would have been wiser to have sought out as many sources of it as possible. But so it is—one man walks through the world with his eyes open, and another with them shut; and upon this difference depends all the superiority of knowledge the one acquires above the other. I have known sailors, who had been in all the quarters of the world, and could tell you nothing but the signs of the tippling-houses they frequented in different ports, and the price and quality of the liquor. On the other hand, a Franklin could not cross the Channel without making some observations useful to mankind. While many a vacant, thoughtless youth is whirled throughout Europe without gaining a single idea worth crossing a street for, the observing eye and inquiring mind find matter of improvement and delight in every ramble in town or country. Do *you*, then, William, continue to make use of your eyes; and *you*, Robert, learn that eyes were given you to use.

TWENTY-FIRST EVENING.

WHY THE EARTH MOVES ROUND THE SUN.

Papa—Lucy.

P. You remember, Lucy, that I explained to you, some time ago, what was the cause that things fell to the ground.

L. O yes—it was because the ground drew them to it.

P. True. That is a consequence of the universal law in nature, that bodies attract each other in proportion to their bulk. So a very small thing in the neighbourhood of a very large one always tends to go to it, if not prevented by some other power. Well— you know I told you that the sun was a ball, a vast many times bigger than the ball we inhabit, called the earth; upon which you properly asked, how, then, it happened that the earth did not fall into the sun.

L. And why does it not?

P. That I am going to explain to you. You have seen your brother whirl round an ivory ball, tied to the end of a string which he held in his hand.

L. Yes; and I have done it myself, too.

P. Well, then—you felt that the ball was continually pulling, as though it tried to make its escape.

L. Yes; and one my brother was swinging *did* make its escape, and flew through the sash.

P. It did so. That was a lesson in the *centrifugal* motion, or that power by which a body thus whirled continually endeavours to fly off from the centre round which it moves. This is owing to the force or impulse you give it at setting out, as though you were going to throw it away from you. The string by which you hold it, on the contrary, is the power which keeps the ball towards the centre, called the *centripetal* power. Thus, you see, there are two powers acting upon the ball at the same time; one to make it fly off, the other to hold it in; and the consequence is, that it moves directly according to neither, but between both; that is, round and round. This it continues to do while you swing it properly; but should the string break or slip off, away flies the ball; on the other hand, if you cease to give it the whirling force, it falls towards your hand.

L. I understand all this.

P. I will give you another instance of this double force acting at the same time. Do not you remember seeing some curious feats of horsemanship?

L. Yes.

P. One of them was, that a man standing with one leg upon the saddle and riding full speed, threw up balls into the air and catched them as they fell.

L. I remember it very well.

P. Perhaps you would have expected these balls to have fallen behind him, as he was going at such a rate.

L. So I did.

P. But you saw that they fell into his hand as directly as if he had been standing quite still. That was because at the instant he threw them up, they received the motion of the horse straight forward, as well as the upright motion that he gave them, so that they made a slanting line through the air, and came down in the same place they would have reached if he had held them in his hand all the while.

L. That is very curious, indeed!

P. In the same manner, you may have observed, in riding in a carriage, that if you throw anything out of the window, it falls directly opposite, just as though the carriage were standing still, and is not left behind you.

L. I will try that, the next time I ride in one.

P. You are then to imagine the sun to be a mighty mass of matter, many thousand times larger than our earth, placed in the centre, quiet and unmoved. You are to conceive our earth, as soon as created, launched with vast force in a straight line, as though it were a bowl on a green. It would have flown off in this line for ever, through the boundless regions of space, had it not, at the same instant, received a pull from the sun, by its attraction. By the wonderful skill of the Creator, these two forces were made exactly to counterbalance each other; so that just as much as the earth, from the original motion given it, tends to fly forwards, just so much the sun draws it to the centre; and the consequence is, that it takes a course between the two, which is a circle round and round the sun.

L. But if the earth were set a-rolling, like a bowl

upon a green, I should think it would stop of itself, as the bowl does.

P. The bowl stops because it is continually rubbing against the ground, which checks its motion; but the ball of the earth moves in empty space, where there is nothing to stop it.

L. But if I throw a ball through the air, it will not go on for ever, but it will come down to the ground.

P. That is because the force with which you can throw it is much less than the force by which it is drawn to the earth. But there is another reason, too, which is the resistance of the air. This space all around us and over us is not empty space; it is quite full of a thin, transparent liquid, called air.

L. Is it?

P. Yes. If you move your hand quickly through it, you will find something resisting you, though in a slight degree. And the wind, you well know, is capable of pressing against anything with almost irresistible force; and yet wind is nothing but a quantity of air put into violent motion. Everything, then, that moves through the air is continually obliged to push some of this fluid out of the way, by which means, it is constantly losing part of its motion.

L. Then the earth would do the same.

P. No; for it moves in *empty* space.

L. What! does not it move through the air?

P. The earth does not move *through* the air, but carries the air along with it. All the air is contained in what is called the *atmosphere*, which you may compare to a sort of mist or fog clinging all around to the ball of the earth, and reaching a certain distance above it, which has been calculated at about forty-five or fifty miles.

L. That is above the clouds, then.

P. Yes; all the clouds are within the atmosphere, for they are supported by the air. Well—this atmosphere rolls about along with the earth, as though it were a part of it, and moves with it through the sky, which is a vast field of empty space. In this immense space are all the stars and planets, which have also their several motions. There is nothing to stop them, but they continually go on, by means of the force that the Creator has originally impressed upon them.

L. Do not some of the stars move round the sun, as well as our earth?

P. Yes; those that are called *planets*. These are all subject to the same laws of motion with our earth. They are attracted by the sun as their centre, and form, along with the earth, that assemblage of worlds, which is called the *solar system*.

L. Is the moon one of them?

P. The moon is called a *secondary* planet, because its immediate connexion is with our earth, around which it rolls, as we do around the sun. It, however, accompanies our earth in its journey round the sun. But I will tell you more about its motion, and about the other planets and stars, another time. It is enough at present, if you thoroughly understand what I have been describing.

L. I think I do.

THE UMBELLIFEROUS PLANTS.

Tutor—George—Harry.

H. WHAT plant is that man gathering under the hedge?

G. I don't know; but the boys call the stalks kexes, and blow through them.

H. I have seen them; but I want to know the plant.

G. Will you please to tell us sir, what it is?

T. It is hemlock.

G. Hemlock is poison, is it not?

T. Yes, in some degree; and it is also a medicine. That man is gathering it for the apothecaries.

H. I should like to know it.

T. Well, then, go and bring one. [Harry *fetches it.*

G. I think I have seen a great many of this sort.

T. Perhaps you may; but there are many other kinds of plants extremely like it. It is one of a large family called the *umbelliferous*, which contains both food, physic, and poison. It will be worth while for you to know something about them, so let us examine this hemlock closely. You see this tall, hollow stalk, which divides into several branches, from each of which spring spokes, or *rundles*, as they are called, of flower-stalks. You see they are like rays from a circle, or the spokes of a wheel.

H. Or like the sticks of an umbrella.

T. True; and they are called *umbels*, which has the same derivation. If you pursue one of these rundles, or umbels, you will find that each stick, or spoke, terminates in another set of smaller stalks, each of which bears a single small flower.

G. They are small ones, indeed.

T. But, if you look sharply, I dare say your eyes are good enough to distinguish that they are divided into five leaves, and furnished with five chives and two pistils in the middle.

H. I can see them.

G. And so can I.

T. The pistils are succeeded by a sort of fruit, which is a twin seed, joined in the middle, as you may see in this rundle that is past flowering. Here I divide one of them into two.

G. Would each of these grow?

T. Yes. Well, this is the structure of the flowering part of the umbelliferous tribe. Now for the leaf. Pluck one.

H. Is this one leaf, or many?

T. It is properly one, but it is cut and divided into many portions. From this mid-rib spring smaller leaves, set opposite each other; and from the rib of each of these, proceed others, which themselves are also divided. These are called doubly or trebly pinnated leaves; and most of the umbelliferous plants, but not all, have leaves of this kind.

H. It is like a parsley-leaf.

T. True ; and parsley is one of the same tribe ; and hemlock and others are sometimes mistaken for it.

G. How curiously the stalk of this hemlock is spotted!

T. Yes. That is one of the marks by which it is known. It is also distinguished by its peculiar smell, and by other circumstances, which you can only understand when you have compared a number of the tribe. I will now tell you about some others, the names of which you are probably acquainted with. In the first place, there are carrots and parsnips.

H. Carrots and parsnips !—they are not poisons, I am sure.

G. I remember, now, that carrots have such a leaf as this.

T. They have. It is the *roots* of these, you know, that are eaten. But we eat the *leaves* of parsley and fennel, which are of the same class. Celery is another, the stalks of which are chiefly used, made white by trenching up the earth about them. The stalks of angelica are used differently.

H. I know how—candied.

T. Yes. Then there are many, of which the *seeds* are used. There is caraway.

H. What, the seeds that are put into cakes and comfits ?

T. Yes. They are warm and pungent to the taste ; and so are the seeds of many others of the umbelliferous plants; as coriander, fennel, wild carrot, angelica, anise, cummin, and dill. All these are employed in food or medicine, and are good in warming or strengthening the stomach.

G. Those are pleasant medicines enough.

T. They are; but you will not say the same of some others of the class, which are noted medicines, too ; such as the plant yielding asafœtida, and several more, from which what are called the fetid gums are produced.

G. Asafœtida! that's nasty stuff, I know; does it grow here?

T. No; and most of the sweet seeds I before mentioned, come from abroad, too. Now, I will tell you of some of the poisons.

H. Hemlock is one that we know already.

T. Yes. Then there is another kind, that grows in water, and is more poisonous, called Water-Hemlock. Another is a large plant, growing in ditches, with leaves extremely like celery, called Hemlock-Dropwort. Another, common in drier situations, and distinguished by leaves less divided than most of the class, is cow-parsnip, or madnep. Of some of these, the leaves, of others the roots, are most poisonous. Their effects are, to make the head giddy, bring on stupidity, or delirium, and cause violent sickness. The Athenians used to put criminals to death by making them drink the juice of a kind of hemlock growing in that country, as you may read in the life of that excellent philosopher Socrates, who was killed in that manner.

H. What was he killed for?

T. Because he was wiser and better than his fellow-citizens. Among us it is only by accident that mischief is done by these plants. I remember a melancholy instance of a poor boy, who, in rambling about the fields with his little brothers and sisters, chanced to meet with a root of hemlock-dropwort. It looked so white and nice, that he was tempted to eat a good deal of it. The other children also ate some, but not so much. When they got home, they were all taken very ill. The eldest boy, who had eaten most, died in great agony. The others recovered, after much suffering.

G. Is there any way of preventing their bad effects?

T. The best way is, to clear the stomach, as soon as possible, by a strong emetic, and large draughts of warm water. After that, vinegar is useful in removing the disorder of the head.

H. But are the roots sweet and pleasant, that people should be tempted to eat them?

T. Several of them are. There is a small plant of the tribe, the root of which is much sought after by boys, who dig for it with their knives. It is round, and called earth-nut, or pig-nut.

G. But that is not poison, I suppose?

T. No; but it is not very wholesome. I believe, however, that the roots of the most poisonous become innocent by boiling. I have heard that boiled hemlock roots are as good as carrots.

H. I think I should not like to eat them, however. But, pray, why should there be any poisons at all?

T. What we call poisons are hurtful only to particular animals. They are the proper food of others, and, no doubt, do more good than harm in the creation. Most of the things that are poisonous to us in large quantities, are useful medicines in small ones; and we have reason bestowed upon *us*, to guard us against mischief. Other animals, in general, refuse by instinct what would prove hurtful to them. You see beneath yonder hedge, a great crop of tall, flourishing plants, with white flowers; they are of the umbelliferous family, and are called wild cicely, or cow-weed. The latter name is given them, because the cows will not touch them, though the pasture be ever so bare.

H. Would they poison them?

T. Perhaps they would; at least, they are not proper food for them. We will go and examine them, and I will show you how they differ from hemlock, for which they are sometimes mistaken.

G. I should like to get some of these plants, and dry them.

T. You shall, and write down the names of them all, and learn to know the innocent from the hurtful.

G. That will be very useful.

T. It will. Remember, now, the general character of the umbelliferous class. The flower-stalks are divided into spokes, or umbels, which are again divided into others, each of them terminated by a small five-leaved flower, having five chives and two pistils,

U

succeeded by a twin seed. Their leaves are generally finely divided. You will soon know them, after having examined two or three of the tribe. Remember, too, that they are a *suspicious race,* and not to be made free with till you are well acquainted with them.

HUMBLE LIFE; OR, THE COTTAGERS.
Mr. Everard—Charles (walking in the fields).

Mr. E. WELL, Charles, you seem to be in deep meditation. Pray what are you thinking about?

Ch. I was thinking, sir, how happy it is for us, that we are not in the place of that poor weaver, whose cottage we just passed by.

Mr. E. It is very right to be sensible of all the advantages that Providence has bestowed on us in this world, and I commend you for reflecting on them with gratitude. But what particular circumstance of comparison, between our condition and his, struck you most just now.

Ch. O, almost everything! I could not bear to live in such a poor house, with a cold, clay floor, and half the windows stopped with paper. Then how poorly he and his children are dressed! and, I dare say, they must live as poorly too.

Mr. E. These things would be grievous enough to you, I do not doubt, because you have been accustomed to a very different way of living. But, if they are healthy and contented, I don't know that we have much more to boast of. I believe the man is able to procure wholesome food for his family, and clothes and firing enough to keep them from suffering from the cold; and nature wants little more.

Ch. But what a ragged, barefooted fellow the boy at the door was!

Mr. E. He was; but did you observe his ruddy cheeks, and his stout legs, and the smiling grin upon his countenance? It is my opinion, he would beat you in running, though he is half the head less; and,

I dare say, he never cried because he did not know what to do with himself, in his life.

Ch. But, sir, you have often told me that the mind is the noblest part of man; and these poor creatures, I am sure, can have no opportunity to improve their minds. They must be almost as ignorant as the brutes.

Mr. E. Why so? Do you think there is no knowledge to be got but from books? or that a weaver cannot teach his children right from wrong?

Ch. Not if he have never learned himself.

Mr. E. True—but I hope the country we live in is not so unfriendly to a poor man, as to afford him no opportunity of learning his duty to God and his neighbour. And as to other points of knowledge, necessity and common observation will teach him a good deal. But come—let us go and pay them a visit; for I suppose you hardly think them human creatures.— *They enter the cottage*—Jacob, *the weaver, at his loom. His wife spinning. Children of different ages.*

Mr E. Good morning to you, friend! Don't let us disturb you all, pray. We have just stepped in to look at your work.

Jacob. I have very little to show you, gentlemen; but you are welcome to look on. Perhaps the young gentleman never saw weaving before.

Ch. I never did, near.

Jac. Look here, then, master. These long threads are the warp. They are divided, you see, into two sets, and I pass my shuttle between them, which carries with it the cross-threads, and that makes the weft or woof. [*Explains the whole to him.*

Ch. Dear! how curious! And is all cloth made this way, papa?

Mr. E. Yes; only there are somewhat different contrivances for different sorts of work. Well—how soon do you think you could learn to weave like this honest man?

Ch. O—not for a great while.

Mr. E. But I suppose you could easily turn the wheel, and draw out threads, like that good woman.

Ch. Not without some practice, I fancy. But what is that boy doing?

Jac. He is cutting pegs for the shoemakers, master.

Ch. How quick he does them!

Jac. It is but poor employment, but better than being idle. The first lesson I teach my children is, that their hands were made to get their bread with.

Mr. E. And a very good lesson, too.

Ch. What is this heap of twigs for?

Jac. Why, master, my biggest boy and girl have learned a little how to make basket-work, so I have got them a few osiers, to employ them at leisure hours. That bird-cage is their making; and the back of that chair, in which their grandmother sits.

Ch. Is not that cleverly done, papa?

Mr. E. It is, indeed. Here are several arts, you see, in this house, which both you and I should be much puzzled to set about. But there are some books, too, I perceive.

Ch. Here is a Bible, and a Testament, and a Prayer-book, and a Spelling-book, and a volume of the Gardener's Dictionary.

Mr. E. And how many of your family can read, my friend?

Jac. All the children, but the two youngest, can read a little, sir; but Meg, there, is the best scholar among us. She reads us a chapter in the Testament every morning, and very well too, though I say it.

Mr. E. Do you hear that, Charles?

Ch. I do, sir. Here's an almanack, too, against the wall; and here are my favourite ballads of the Children in the Wood, and Chevy-Chase.

Jac. I let the children paste them up, sir, and a few more, that have no harm in them. There's Hearts of Oak, Rule Britannia, and Robin Gray.

Mr. E. A very good choice, indeed. I see you have a very pretty garden there, behind the house.

Jac. It is only a little spot, sir; but it serves for some amusement, and use too.

Ch. What beautiful stocks and wall-flowers! We have none so fine in our garden.

Jac. Why, master, to say the truth, we are rather proud of them. I have got a way of cultivating them, that I believe few besides myself are acquainted with; and on Sundays, I have plenty of visitors to come and admire them.

Ch. Pray what is this bush, with narrow, whitish leaves, and blue flowers?

Jac. Don't you know? It is rosemary.

Ch. Is it good for anything?

Jac. We like the smell of it; and then the leaves, mixed with a little balm, make pleasant tea, which we sometimes drink in the afternoon.

Ch. Here are several more plants that I never saw before.

Jac. Some of them are pot-herbs, that we put into our broth or porridge; and others are physic herbs, for we cannot afford to go to a doctor for every trifling ailment.

Ch. But how do you learn the use of these things?

Jac. Why, partly, master, from an old Herbal that I have got; and partly from my good mother, and some old neighbours; for we poor people are obliged to help one another as well as we can. If you were curious about plants, I could go into the fields and show you a great many, that we reckon very fine for several uses, though I suppose we don't call them by the proper names.

Mr. E. You keep your garden very neat, friend, and seem to make the most of every inch of ground.

Jac. Why, sir, we have hands enow, and all of us like to be doing a little in it, when our in-doors work is over. I am in hopes soon to be allowed a bit of land from the waste for a potato-ground, which will be a great help to us. I shall then be able to keep a pig.

Mr. E. I suppose, notwithstanding your industry, you live rather hardly sometimes?

Jac. To be sure, sir, we are somewhat pinched in dear times and hard weather; but, thank God, I have constant work, and my children begin to be some help to us, so that we fare better than some of our neighbours. If I do but keep my health, I don't fear but we shall make a shift to live.

Mr. E. Keep such a contented mind, my friend, and you will have few to envy. Good morning to you, and if any sickness or accident should befal you, remember you have a friend in your neighbour at the hall.

Jac. I will sir, and thank you.

Ch. Good morning to you.

Jac. The same to you, master.

> [*They leave the cottage.*

Mr. E. Well, Charles, what do you think of our visit?

Ch. I am highly pleased with it, sir. I shall have a better opinion of a poor cottager as long as I live.

Mr. E. I am glad of it. You see, when we compare ourselves with this weaver, all the advantage is not on our side. He is possessed of an art, the utility of which secures him a livelihood, whatever may be the changes of the times. All his family are brought up to industry, and show no small ingenuity in their several occupations. They are not without instruction, and especially seem to be in no want of that best of all,—the knowledge of their duty. They understand something of the cultivation and uses of plants, and are capable of receiving enjoyment from the beauties of nature. They partake of the pleasures of home and neighbourhood. Above all, they seem content with their lot, and free from anxious cares and repinings. I view them as truly respectable members of society, acting well the part allotted to them, and that a part most of all necessary to the well-being of the whole. They may, from untoward accidents, be rendered objects of our compassion, but they never can of our contempt.

Ch. Indeed, sir, I am very far from despising them now. But would it not be possible to make them more comfortable than they are at present?

Mr. E. I think it would; and when giving a little from the superfluity of persons in our situation would add so much to the happiness of persons in theirs, I am of opinion that it is unpardonable not to do it. I intend to use my interest to get this poor man the piece of waste land he wants, and he shall have some from my share, rather than go without.

Ch. And suppose, sir, we were to give him some good potatoes to plant it?

Mr. E. We will. Then, you know, we have a fine sow, that never fails to produce a numerous litter twice a year. Suppose we rear one of the next brood, to be ready for him as soon as he has got his potato-ground into bearing?

Ch. O yes! that will be just the thing. But how is he to build a pig-stye?

Mr. E. You may leave that to his own ingenuity; I warrant he can manage such a job as that with the help of a neighbour, at least. Well—I hope both the weaver and you will be the better for the acquaintance we have made to-day: and always remember, that *man, when fulfilling the duties of his station, be that station what it may, is a worthy object of respect to his fellow-men.*

TWENTY-SECOND EVENING.

THE BIRTHDAY GIFT.

THE populous kingdom of Ava, in India beyond the Ganges, was once inhabited by a minor prince, who was brought up in the luxurious indolence of an eastern palace. When he had reached the age of seventeen, which, by the laws of that country, was the period of majority for the crown, all the great men of his court, and the governors of the provinces, according to established custom, laid at his feet presents, consisting of the most costly products of art and nature that they had been able to procure. One offered a casket of the most precious jewels of Golconda; another, a curious piece of clock-work, made by a European artist; another, a piece of the richest silk from the looms of China; another, a Bezoar stone, said to be a sovereign antidote against all poisons and infectious diseases; another, a choice piece of the most fragrant rose-wood in a box of ebony, inlaid with pearls; another, a golden cruse, full of genuine balsam of Mecca; another, a courser of the purest breed of Arabia; and another, a female slave of exquisite beauty. The whole court of the palace was overspread with rarities; and long rows of slaves were continually passing loaded with vessels and utensils of gold and silver, and other articles of high price.

At length an aged magistrate, from a distant province, made his appearance. He was simply clad in a long cotton robe, and his hoary beard waved on his breast. He made his obeisance before the young monarch, and, holding forth an embroidered silken bag, he thus addressed him:—

"Deign, great king, to accept the faithful homage and fervent good wishes of thy servant on this important day, and with them, the small present I hold in my hand. Small, indeed, it is in show, but not so, I trust, in value. Others have offered what may decorate thy person—here is what will impart perpetual grace and lustre to thy features. Others have presented thee with rich perfumes—here is what will make thy name sweet and fragrant to the latest ages. Others have given what may afford pleasure to thine eyes—here is what will nourish a source of never-failing pleasure within thy breast. Others have furnished thee with preservatives against bodily contagion

—here is what will preserve thy better parts uncontaminated. Others have heaped around thee the riches of a temporal kingdom—this will secure thee the treasures of an eternal one."

He said, and drew from the purse a book containing *the Moral Precepts of the sage Zendar*, the wisest and most virtuous man the East had ever beheld. "If," he proceeded, "my gracious sovereign will condescend to make this his constant companion, not an hour will pass in which its perusal may not be a comfort and a blessing. In the arduous duties of thy station, it will prove a faithful guide and counsellor. Amidst the allurements of pleasure and the incitements of passion, it will be an incorruptible monitor, that will never suffer thee to err without warning thee of thy error. It will render thee a blessing to thy people, and blessed in thyself; for what sovereign can be the one without the other?"

He then returned the book to its place, and kneeling gave it into the hands of the king. The young sovereign received it with respect and benignity, and history affirms that the use he made of it corresponded with the wishes of the donor.

ON EARTHS AND STONES.

Tutor—George—Harry.

Harry. I WONDER what all this heap of stones is for.

George. I can tell you—it is for the limekiln; don't you see it just by?

H. O yes, I do. But what is to be done to them there?

G. Why, they are to be burned into lime. Don't you know that?

H. But what is lime, and what are its uses?

G. I can tell you one; they lay it on the fields, for manure. Don't you remember we saw a number of little heaps of it, that we took for sheep at a distance, and wondered they did not move? However, I believe we had better ask our tutor about it. Will you please, sir, to give us some information about lime?

Tutor. Willingly. But suppose, as we talked about all sorts of metals some time ago, I should now give you a lecture about stones and earths of all kinds, which are equally valuable, and much more common, than metals.

G. Pray do, sir.

H. I shall be very glad to hear it.

T. Well, then; in the first place, the ground we tread upon, to as great a depth as it has been dug, consists, for the most part, of matter of various appearance and hardness, called by the general name of *earths.* In common language, indeed, only the soft and powdery substances are so named, while the hard and solid are called *stone* or *rock;* but chemists use the same term for all; as, in fact, earth is only crumbled stone, and stone only consolidated earth.

H. What!—has the mould of my garden ever been stone?

T. The black earth, or mould, which covers the surface wherever plants grow, consists mostly of parts of rotted vegetables, such as stalks, leaves, and roots, mixed with sand or loose clay; but this reaches only a little way; and beneath it you always come to a bed of gravel, or clay, or stone, of some kind. Now these earths and stones are distinguished into several species, but principally into three, the properties of which make them useful to man for very different purposes, and are, therefore, very well worth knowing. As you begin with asking me about lime, I shall first mention that class of earths from which it is obtained. These have derived their name of *calcareous* from this very circumstance, *calx* being lime, in Latin; and lime is got from them all in the same way, by burning them in a strong fire. There are many kinds of calcareous earths. One of them is *marble;* you know what that is?

G. O yes! our parlour chimney-piece and hearth are marble.

H And so are the monuments in the church.

T. True. There are various kinds of it; white, black, yellow, grey, mottled, and veined, with different colours; but all of them are hard and heavy stones, admitting a fine polish, on which account, they are much used in ornamental works.

G. I think statues are made of it.

T. Yes; and where it is plentiful, columns, and porticos, and sometimes whole buildings. Marble is the luxury of architecture.

H. Where does marble come from?

T. From a great many countries. Great Britain produces some, but mostly of inferior kinds. What we use chiefly comes from Italy. The Greek islands yield some fine sorts. That of Paros is of ancient fame for whiteness and purity; and the finest antique statues have been made of Parian marble.

H. I suppose black marble will not burn into white lime?

T. Yes, it will. A violent heat will expel most of the colouring matter of marbles, and make them white. *Chalk* is another kind of calcareous earth. This is of a much softer consistence than marble, being easily cut with a knife, and marking things on which it is rubbed. It is found in great beds in the earth; and, in some parts of England, whole hills are composed of it.

G. Are chalk and whiting the same?

T. Whiting is made of the finer and purer particles of chalk washed out from the rest, and then dried in lumps. This, you know, is quite soft and crumbly. There are, besides, a great variety of stones in the earth, harder than chalk, but softer than marble, which will burn to lime, and are, therefore, called *limestones*. These differ much in colour and other properties, and accordingly furnish lime of different qualities. In general, the harder the limestone is, the firmer the lime made from it. Whole ridges of mountains in various parts are composed of limestone, and it is found plentifully in most of the hilly counties of England, to the great advantage of the inhabitants.

G. Will not oyster-shells burn into lime ?   I think I have heard of oyster-shell lime.

T. They will ; and this is another source of calcareous earth.   The shells of all animals, both land and sea, as oysters, mussels, cockles, crabs, lobsters, snails, and the like, and also egg-shells of all kinds, consist of this earth ; and so does coral, which is formed by insects under the sea, and is very abundant in some countries.   Vast quantities of shells are often found deep in the earth, in the midst of chalk and limestone beds ; whence some have supposed that all calcareous earth is originally an animal production.

H. But where could animals enow ever have lived, to make mountains of their shells ?

T. That, indeed, I cannot answer.   But there are sufficient proofs that our world must long have existed in a very different state from the present.   Well— but, besides these purer calcareous earths, it is very frequently found mingled in different proportions with other earths.   Thus *marl,* which is so much used in manuring land, and of which there are a great many kinds, all consist of calcareous earth, united with clay and sand ; and the more of this earth it contains, the richer manure it generally makes.

G. Is there any way of discovering it, when it is mixed in this manner with other things ?

T. Yes—there is an easy and sure method of discovering the smallest portion of it.   All calcareous earth has the property of dissolving in acids, and effervescing with them ; that is, they bubble and hiss when acids are poured upon them.   You may readily try this at any time with a piece of chalk or an oyster-shell.

G. I will pour some vinegar upon an oyster-shell as soon as I get home.   But, now I think of it, I have often done so in eating oysters, and I never observed it to hiss or bubble.

T. Vinegar is not an acid strong enough to act upon a thing so solid as a shell.   But aqua-fortis, or spirit of salt, will do it at once; and persons, who examine the nature of fossils, always travel with a bottle of one of these acids, by way of a test of calcareous earth. Your vinegar will answer with chalk or whiting. This property of dissolving in acids, and what is called neutralizing them, or taking away their sourness, has caused many of the calcareous earths to be used in medicine. You know that sometimes our food turns very sour upon the stomach, and occasions the pain called heart-burn, and other uneasy symptoms. In these cases, it is common to give chalk or powdered shells, or other things of this kind, which afford relief by destroying the acid.

G. I suppose, then, *magnesia* is something of this sort, for I have often seen it given to my little sister when they said her stomach was out of order?

T. It is; but it has some peculiar properties which distinguish it from other calcareous earths, and, particularly, it will not burn to lime. Magnesia is an artificial production, got from one of the ingredients in sea water, called the bitter, purging salt.

G. Pray, what are the other uses of these earths?

T. Such of them as are hard stone, as the marbles, and many of the limestones, are used for the same purposes as other stones. But their great use is in the form of lime, which is a substance of many curious properties that I will now explain to you. When fresh burnt, it is called *quicklime,* on account of the heat and life, as it were, which it possesses. Have you ever seen a lump put into water?

G. Yes, I have.

T. Were you not much surprised to see it swell and crack to pieces, with a hissing noise, and a great smoke and heat?

G. I was, indeed. But what is the cause of this? how can cold water occasion so much heat?

T. I will tell you. The strong heat to which calcareous earth is exposed in converting it into lime, expels all the water it contained (for all earths, as well as almost everything else, naturally contain water, and also a quantity of air, which was united with it. At the same time, it imbibes a good deal of fire, which remains fixed in its substance, even after it has grown cool to the touch. If water be now added to this quicklime, it is drunk in again with such rapidity, as to crack and break the lime to pieces. At the same time, most of the fire it had imbibed is driven out again, and makes itself sensible by its effects, burning all the things that it touches, and turning the water to steam. This operation is called *slacking* or *slaking* of lime. The water in which lime is slacked dissolves a part of it, and acquires a very pungent, harsh taste; this is used in medicine under the name of lime-water. If, instead of soaking quicklime in water, it is exposed for some time to the air, it attracts moisture slowly, and, by degrees, falls to powder, without much heat or disturbance. But whether lime be slacked in water or air, it does not at first return to the state in which it was before, since it still remains deprived of its air; and on that account is still pungent and caustic. At length, however, it recover this also from the atmosphere, and is then calcareous earth, as at first. Now, it is upon some of these circumstances that the utility of lime depends. In the first place, its burning and corroding quality makes it useful to the tanner, in loosening all the hair from the hides, and destroying the flesh and fat that adhere to them. And so in various other trades it is used as a great cleanser and purifier.

H. I have a thought come into my head. When it is laid upon the ground, I suppose its use must be to burn up the weeds.

T. True—that is part of its use.

G. But it must burn up the good grass and corn, too.

T. Properly objected. But the case is, that the farmer does not sow his seeds till the lime is rendered mild by exposure to the air and weather, and is well mixed with the soil. And even then it is reckoned a hot and forcing manure, chiefly fit for cold and wet lands. The principal use of lime, however, is as an ingredient in *mortar*. This, you know, is the cement by which bricks and stones are held together in building. It is made of fresh-slacked lime and a proportion of sand well mixed together; and generally some chopped hair is put into it. The lime binds with the other ingredients; and, in length of time, the mortar, if well made, becomes as hard, or harder, than stone itself.

G. I have heard of the mortar in very old buildings being harder and stronger than any made at present.

T. That is only on account of its age. Burning of lime, and making of mortar, are as well understood now as ever; but, in order to have it excellent, the lime should be of good quality, and used very fresh. Some sorts of lime have the property of making mortar which will harden under water, whence it is much valued for bridges, locks, wharfs, and the like.

G. Pray, is not plaster of Paris a kind of lime? I know it will become hard by only mixing water with it; for I have used it to make casts of.

T. The powder you call plaster of Paris is made of an earth named *gypsum*, of which there are several kinds. *Alabaster* is a stone of this sort, and hard enough to be used like marble. The gypseous earths are of the calcareous kind, but they have naturally a portion of acid united with them, whence they will not effervesce on having acid poured on them. But they are distinguished by the property, that, after being calcined or burned in the fire, and reduced to powder, they will set into a solid body by the addition of water alone. This makes them very useful for ornamental plasters, that are to receive a form or impression, such as the stucco for the ceiling of rooms.

Well—we have said enough about calcareous earths; now to another class, the *Argillaceous*.

G. I think I know what those are. *Argilla* is Latin for *clay.*

T. True; and they are also called *clayey* earths. In general, these earths are of a soft texture, and a sort of greasy feel; but they are peculiarly distinguished by the property of becoming sticky, on being tempered with water, so that they may be drawn out, and worked into form, like a paste. Have you ever, when you were a little boy, made a clay house?

G. Yes, I have.

T. Then you well know the manner in which clay is tempered, and worked for this purpose.

H. Yes; and I remember helping to make little pots and mugs of clay.

T. Then you imitated the potter's trade; for all utensils of earthenware are made of clays, either pure or mixed. This is one of the oldest arts among mankind, and one of the most useful. They furnish materials for building, too; for bricks and tiles are made of these earths. But, in order to be fit for these purposes, it is necessary that clay should not only be soft and ductile, while it is forming, but capable of being hardened afterwards. And this it is, by the assistance of fire. Pottery-ware and bricks are burned with a strong heat in kilns, by which they acquire a hardness equal to that of the hardest stones.

G. I think I have read of bricks being baked by the sun's heat alone in very hot countries.

T. True; and they may serve for building in climates where rain scarcely ever falls; but heavy showers would wash them away. Fire seems to change the nature of clays; for, after they have undergone its operation, they become incapable of returning again to a soft and ductile state. You might steep brick-dust or powder from pounded pots in water ever so long, without making it hold together in the least.

G. I suppose there are many kinds of clays?

T. There are. Argillaceous earths differ greatly from each other in colour, purity, and other qualities. Some are perfectly white, as that of which tobacco-pipes are made. Others are blue, brown, yellow, and, in short, of all hues; which they owe to mixtures of other earths or metals. Those which burn red contain a portion of iron. No clays are found perfectly pure; but they are mixed with more or less of other earths. The common brick-clays contain a large proportion of sand, which often makes them crumbly and perishable. In general, the finest earthenware is made of the purest and whitest clays; but other matters are mixed, in order to harden and strengthen them. Thus *porcelain*, or *china*, is made with a clayey earth, mixed with a stone of a vitrifiable nature, that is, which may be melted into glass; and the fine pottery, called *queen's ware*, is a mixture of tobacco-pipe clay, and flints burned and powdered. Common stoneware is a coarse mixture of this sort. Some species of pottery are made with mixtures of burned and unburned clay; the former, as I told you before, being incapable of becoming soft again with water like a natural clay.

H. Are clays of no other use than to make pottery of?

T. Yes; the richest soils are those which have a proportion of clay; and marl, which I have already mentioned as a manure, generally contains a good deal of it. Then clay has the property of absorbing oil or grease; whence some kinds of it are used, like soap, for cleaning cloths. The substance called *Fuller's earth* is a mixed earth of the argillaceous kind; and its use in taking out the oil which naturally adheres to wool is so great, that it has been one cause of the superiority of our woollen cloths.

H. Then, I suppose, it is found in England?

T. Yes. There are pits of the best kind of it near Woburn, in Bedfordshire; also at Reigate, in Surrey. A clayey stone, called soap-rock, has exactly the feel and look of soap, and will even lather with water.

The different kinds of slate, too, are stones of the argillaceous class; and very useful ones for covering houses, and other purposes.

H. Are writing-slates like the slates used for covering houses?

T. Yes; but their superior blackness and smoothness make them show better the marks of the pencil.

G. You have mentioned something of sand and flints, but you have not told us what sort of earths they are.

T. I reserved that till I spoke of the third great class of earths. This is the *siliceous* class, so named from *silex*, which is Latin for a flint-stone. They have also been called *vitrifiable* earths; because they are the principal ingredient in glass, named in Latin *vitrum*.

G. I have heard of flint glass.

T. Yes; but neither flint, nor any other of the kind, will make glass, even by the strongest heat, without some addition; but this we will speak of by-and-by. I shall now tell you the principal properties of these earths. They are all very hard, and will strike fire with steel, when in a mass large enough for the stroke. They mostly run into particular shapes, with sharp angles and points, and have a certain degree of transparency; which has made them, also, be called *crystalline* earths. They do not in the least soften with water, like clays; nor are they affected by acids; nor do they burn to lime, like the calcareous earths. As to the different kinds of them, *flint* has already been mentioned. It is a very common production in some parts, and is generally met with in pebbles, or round lumps. What is called the *shingle* on the sea-shore, chiefly consists of it; and the ploughed fields, in some places, are almost entirely covered with flint stones.

H. But do they not hinder the corn from growing?

T. The corn, to be sure, cannot take root upon them; but, I believe, it has been found that the protection they afford to the young plants which grow under them, is more than equal to the harm they do by taking up room. Flints are, also, frequently found imbedded in chalk under the ground. Those used in the Staffordshire potteries chiefly come from the chalk-pits near Gravesend. So much for flints. You have seen white pebbles, which are semi-transparent, and, when broken, resemble white sugarcandy. They are common on the sea-shore, and in beds of rivers.

H. O, yes. We call them fire-stones. When they are rubbed together in the dark, they send out great flashes of light, and have a particular smell.

T. True. The proper name of these is *quartz*. It is found in large quantities in the earth, and the ores of metals are often imbedded in it. Sometimes it is perfectly transparent, and then it is called *crystal*. Some of these crystals shoot into exact mathematical figures; and because many salts do the same, and are also transparent, they are called the *crystals* of such or such a salt.

G. Is not fine glass called crystal, too?

T. It is called so by way of simile; thus we say of a thing, " it is as clear as crystal." But the only true crystal is an earth of the kind I have been describing. Well, now we come to *sand;* for this is properly only quartz in a powdery state. If you examine the grains of sand singly, or look at them with a magnifying-glass, you will find them all either entirely or partly transparent; and, in some of the white shining sands, the grains are all little, bright crystals.

H. But most sand is brown or yellowish.

T. That is owing to some mixture, generally of the metallic kind. I believe I once told you, that all sands were supposed to contain a small portion of gold. It is more certain that many of them contain iron.

G. But what could have brought this quartz and crystal into powder, so as to have produced all the sand in the world?

T. That is not very easy to determine. On the

sea-shore, however, the incessant rolling of the pebbles by the waves, is enough, in time, to grind them to powder, and there is reason to believe that the greatest part of what is now dry land, was once sea, which may account for the vast beds of sand met with inland.

G. I have seen some stone so soft that one might crumble it between one's fingers, and then it seemed to turn to sand.

T. There are several of this kind, more or less solid, which are chiefly composed of sand, conglutinated by some natural cement. Such are called *sand-stone*, or *freestone*, and are used for various purposes, in building, making grindstones, and the like, according to their hardness.

H. Pray what are the common pebbles that the streets are paved with? I am sure they strike fire enough with the horses' shoes.

T. They are stones of the siliceous kind, either pure or mixed with other earths. One of the hardest and best for this purpose is called *granite*, which is of various kinds and colours, but always consists of grains of different siliceous earths cemented together. The streets of London are paved with granite, brought chiefly from Scotland. In some other stones, these bits of different earths dispersed through the cement, are so large, as to look like plums in a pudding, whence they have obtained the name of *pudding-stones.*

G. I think there is a kind of stones that you have not yet mentioned—precious stones?

T. These, too, are all of the siliceous class;—from the opaque or half-transparent, as agate, jasper, cornelian, and the like, to the perfectly clear and brilliant ones, as ruby, emerald, topaz, sapphire, &c.

G. Diamond, no doubt, is one of them?

T. So it has commonly been reckoned, and the purest of all; but experiments have shown, that though it is the hardest body in nature, it may be totally dispersed into smoke and flame, by a strong

fire ; so that mineralogists will now hardly allow it to
be a stone at all, but class it among inflammable substances. The precious stones above mentioned owe
their different colours chiefly to some metallic mixture.
They are in general extremely hard, so as to cut
glass, and one another; but diamonds will cut all the
rest.

G. I suppose they must be very rare.

T. Yes ; and in this rarity consists the greatest part
of their value. They are, indeed, beautiful objects ;
but the figure they make, in proportion to their expense, is so very small, that their high price may be
reckoned one of the principal follies among mankind.
What proportion can there possibly be between the
worth of a glittering stone, as big as a hazel-nut, and
a magnificent house and gardens, or a large tract of
country, covered with noble woods and rich meadows,
and corn-fields ? And as to the mere glitter, a large
lustre of cut glass has an infinitely greater effect on
the eye, than all the jewels of a foreign prince.

G. Will you please to tell us now how glass is
made ?

T. Willingly. The base of it is, as I said before,
some earth of the siliceous class. Those commonly
used are flint and sand. Flint is first burned or calcined, which makes it quite white, like enamel; and
it is then powdered. This is the material sometimes
used for some very white glasses ; but sand is that
commonly preferred, as being already in a powdery
form. The white crystalline sands are used for fine
glass ; the brown or yellow for the common sort. As
these earths will not melt of themselves, the addition
in making glass is something that promotes their
fusion. Various things will do this ; but what is
generally used is an alkaline salt, obtained from the
ashes of burnt vegetables. Of this there are several
kinds, as potash, pearl-ash, barilla, and kelp. The salt
is mixed with the sand in a certain proportion, and the
mixture then exposed in earthen pots to a violent

heat, till it is thoroughly melted. The mass is then taken, while hot and fluid, in such quantities as are wanted, and fashioned by blowing, and the use of shears and other instruments. You must see this done some time, for it is one of the most curious and pleasing of all manufactures; and it is not possible to form an idea of the ease and dexterity with which glass is wrought—blown, cast, or spun—without an actual view.

H. I should like very much to see it, indeed.

G. Where is glass made, in this country?

T. In many places. Some of the finest in London; but the coarser kinds generally where coals are cheap; as at Newcastle and its neighbourhood; in Lancashire, at Stourbridge, Bristol, and in South Wales. I should have told you, however, that in our finest and most brilliant glass, a quantity of the calx of lead is put, which vitrifies with the other ingredients, and gives the glass more firmness and density. The blue, yellow, and red glasses are coloured with the calxes of other metals. As to the common green glass, it is made with an alkali, that has a good deal of calcareous earth remaining with the ashes of the plant. But, to understand all the different circumstances of glass-making, one must have a thorough knowledge of chemistry.

G. I think making of glass is one of the finest inventions of human skill.

T. It is, perhaps, not of that capital importance that some other arts possess; but it has been a great addition to the comfort and pleasure of life in many ways. Nothing makes such clean and agreeable vessels as glass, which has the quality of not being corroded by any sort of liquor, as well as that of showing its contents by its transparency. Hence it is greatly preferable to the most precious metals for drinking out of; and, for the same reasons, it is preferred to every other material for chemical utensils, where the heat to be employed is not strong enough to melt it.

H. Then, glass windows!

T. Ay; they are a very material comfort in a climate like ours,—where we so often wish to let in the light, and keep out the cold wind and rain. What could be more gloomy, than to sit in the dark, or with no other light than came in through small holes, covered with oiled paper or bladder, unable to see anything passing without doors! Yet this must have been the case with the most sumptuous palaces, before the invention of window-glass, which was much later than that of bottles and drinking-glasses.

H. I think looking-glasses are very beautiful.

T. They are, indeed, very elegant pieces of furniture, and very costly, too. The art of casting glass into large plates, big enough to reach from the bottom to the top of a room, was some years ago introduced into this country from France. But the most splendid and brilliant manner of employing glass, is in lustres and chandeliers, hung round with drops, cut so as to reflect the light with all the colours of the rainbow. Some of the shops in London, filled with these articles, appear to realize all the wonders of an enchanted palace, in the Arabian Nights' Entertainments.

G. But are not spectacles, and other optical glasses, more useful than all these?

T. I did not mean to pass them over, I assure you. By the curious invention of optical glasses of various kinds, not only the natural defects of sight have been remedied, and old age has been in some measure lightened of one of its calamities, but the sense of seeing has been wonderfully extended. The telescope has brought distant objects within our view, while the microscope has given us a clear survey of near objects too minute for our unassisted eyes. By means of both, some of the most important discoveries of the moderns have been made; so that glass has proved not less admirable in promoting science, than in contributing to splendour and convenience. Since the recent removal of a heavy impost on the manufacture of glass, great improvements have been effected in the art; and glass is now applied to a thousand domestic and other purposes, for which it was never thought of before. The "Crystal Palace," as it is called, erected in Hyde Park, for the Great Industrial Exhibition of 1851, is in a great measure constructed of glass. Coloured ornamental glass, of various sorts, formerly imported at a heavy cost, is also now manufactured in England.

Well—I don't know that I have anything more at present to say, relative to the class of earths. We have gone through the principal circumstances belonging to their three great divisions, the *calcareous*, *argillaceous*, and *siliceous*. You will remember, however, that most of the earths and stones offered by nature, are not in any one of these kinds perfectly pure, but contain a mixture of one or both the others. There is not a pebble, that you can pick up, which would not exercise the skill of a mineralogist fully to ascertain its properties, and the materials of its composition. So inexhaustible is nature!

TWENTY-THIRD EVENING.

SHOW AND USE; OR, THE TWO PRESENTS.

ONE morning, Lord Richmore, coming down to breakfast, was welcomed with the tidings that his favourite mare, Miss Slim, had brought a foal, and also that a she-ass, kept for his lady's use, as a milker, had dropped a young one. His lordship smiled at the inequality of the presents nature had made him. "As for the foal," said he to the groom, "that, you know, has been long promised to my neighbour, Mr. Scamper. For young Balaam, you may dispose of him as you please." The groom thanked his lordship, and said he would then give him to Isaac, the woodman.

In due time, Miss Slim's foal, which was the son of a noted racer, was taken to Squire Scamper's, who received him with great delight, and out of compliment to the donor, named him Young Peer. He was brought up with at least as much care and tenderness as the Squire's own children—kept in a warm stable, fed with the best of corn and hay, duly dressed, and regularly exercised. As he grew up, he gave tokens of great beauty. His colour was bright bay, with a white star on his forehead; his coat was fine, and shone like silk; and every point about him seemed to promise perfection of shape and make. Everybody admired him, as the completest colt that could be seen.

So fine a creature could not be destined to any common employment. After he had passed his third year, he was sent to Newmarket, to be trained for the turf, and a groom was appointed to the care of him alone. His master, who could not well afford the expense, saved part of it by turning off a domestic tutor, whom he kept for the education of his sons, and was content with sending them to the curate of the parish.

At four years old, Young Peer started for a subscription purse, and came in second out of a number of competitors. Soon after, he won a country plate, and filled his master with joy and triumph. The Squire now turned all his attention to the turf, made matches, betted high, and was at first tolerably successful. At length, having ventured all the money he could raise upon one grand match, Young Peer ran on the wrong side of the post, was distanced, and the Squire ruined.

Meantime, young Balaam went into Isaac's possession, where he had a very different training. He was left to pick up his living as he could, in the lanes and commons; and, on the coldest days in winter, he had no other shelter than the lee-side of the cottage, out of which he was often glad to pluck the thatch for a subsistence. As soon as ever he was able to bear a rider, Isaac's children got upon him, sometimes two or three at once; and, if he did not go to their mind, a broomstick or bunch of furze was freely applied to his hide. Nevertheless, he grew up, as the children themselves did, strong and healthy; and, though he was rather bare on the ribs, his shape was good, and his limbs vigorous.

It was not long before his master thought of putting him to some use; so, taking him to the wood, he fastened a load of fagots on his back, and sent him, with his son Tom, to the next town. Tom sold the fagots, and, mounting upon Balaam, rode him home. As Isaac could get plenty of fagots and chips, he found it a profitable trade to send them for daily sale upon Balaam's back. Having a little garden, which, from the barrenness of the soil, yielded him nothing of value, he bethought him of loading Balaam back from town with dung, for manure. Though all he could bring at once was contained in two small panniers, yet this in time amounted to enough to meet the soil of his whole garden, so that he grew very good cabbages and potatoes, to the great relief of his family. Isaac being now sensible of the value of his ass, began to treat him with more attention. He got a small stack of rushy hay for his winter fodder, and, with his own hands, built him a little shed of boughs and mud, in order to shelter him from the bad weather. He would not suffer any of his family to use Baalam ill, and, after his daily journeys, he was allowed to ramble at pleasure. He was now and then cleaned and dressed, and, upon the whole, made a reputable figure. Isaac took in more land from the waste, so that by degrees he became a little farmer, and kept a horse and cart, a cow, and two or three pigs. This made him quite a rich man, but he had always the gratitude to impute his prosperity to the good services of Balaam, the groom's present; while the Squire cursed Young Peer, as the cause of his ruin, and many a time wished his lordship had kept his dainty gift to himself.

THE CRUCIFORM-FLOWERED PLANTS.

Tutor—George—Harry.

George. How rich yon field looks, with its yellow flowers. I wonder what they can be?

Tutor. Suppose you go and see whether you can ascertain, and bring a stalk of the flowers with you.

G. (*returning*). I know now—they are turnips.

T. I thought you would make it out, when you got near them. These turnips are left to seed, which is the reason why you see them run to flower. Commonly, they are pulled up sooner.

Harry. I should not have thought a turnip had so sweet a flower.

G. I think I have smelt others like them. Pray, sir, what class of plants do they belong to?

T. To a very numerous one, with which it is worth your while to get acquainted. Let us sit down and examine them. The petals, you observe, consist of four flat leaves set opposite to each other, or crosswise. From this circumstance the flowers have been called *cruciform*. As most plants with flowers of this kind bear their seeds in pods, they have also been called the *siliquose* plants, *siliqua* being the Latin for a pod.

G. But the papilionaceous flowers bear pods, too.

T. True; and therefore the name is not a good one. Now, pull off the petals one by one. You see, they are fastened by long claws within the flower-cup. Now count the chives.

H. There are six.

G. But they are not all of the same length—two are much shorter than the rest.

T. Well observed. It is from this that Linnæus has formed a particular class of the whole tribe, which he calls *tetradynamia*, a word implying *four powers*, or the *power of four*, as though the four longer chives were more complete and efficacious than the two shorter; which, however, we do not know to be the case. This superior length of four chives is conspicuous in most plants of this tribe, but not in all. They have, however, other resemblances which are sufficient to constitute them a natural family; and accordingly all botanists have made them such.

The flowers, as I have said, have in all of them four petals placed crosswise. The calyx also consists of four oblong and hollow leaves. There is a single pistil, standing upon a seed-bud, which turns either into a long pod, or a short, round one, called a pouch; and hence are formed the two great branches of the family, the podded and the pouched. The seed-vessel has two valves, or external openings, with a partition between. The seeds are small and roundish, attached alternately to both sutures, or joinings of the valves.

Do you observe all these circumstances?

G. and H. We do.

T. You shall examine them more minutely in a larger plant of the kind. Further, almost all of these plants have somewhat of a biting taste, and also a disagreeable smell in their leaves, especially when decayed. A turnip-field, you know, smells but indifferently; and cabbage, which is one of this class, is apt to be remarkably offensive.

H. Yes—There is nothing more unpleasant than rotten cabbage-leaves.

G. And the very water in which they are boiled is enough to scent a whole house.

T. The flowers, however, of almost all the family are fragrant, and some remarkably so. What do you think of wallflowers and stocks?

H. What, are they of this kind?

T. Yes—and so is candy-tuft, and rocket.

H. Then they are not to be despised.

T. No—and especially as not one of the whole class, I believe, is poisonous; but, on the contrary, many of them afford good food for man and beast. Shall I tell you about the principal of them?

G. Pray do, sir.

T. The pungency of taste which so many of them possess, has caused them to be used for salad herbs. Thus, we have cress, water-cress, and mustard; to which might be added many more, which grow wild; as lady-smock, wild rocket, hedge-mustard, and jack-by-the-hedge, or sauce-alone. Mustard, you know, is also greatly used for its seeds, the powder or flour of which, made into a sort of paste with salt and water, is eaten with many kinds of meat. Rape-seeds are very similar to them; and from both an oil is pressed out, of the mild or tasteless kind, as it is also from cole-seed, another product of this class. Scurvy-grass, which is a pungent plant of this family, growing by the sea-side, has obtained its name from being a remedy for the scurvy. Then there is horse-radish, with the root of which I am sure you are well acquainted, as a companion to roast-beef. Common radish is a plant of this kind, which has considerable pungency. One sort of it has a root like a turnip, which brings it near in quality to the turnip itself. The last-mentioned plant, though affording a sweet and mild nutriment, has naturally a degree of pungency and rankness.

G. That, I suppose, is the reason why turnipy milk and butter have such a strong taste?

T. It is.

H. Then, why do they feed cows with it?

T. In this case, as in many others, quality is sacrificed to quantity. But the better use of turnips to the farmer is to fatten sheep and cattle. By its assistance, he is enabled to keep many more of these animals than he otherwise could find grass or hay for; and the culture of turnips prepares his land for grain as well, or better, than could be done by letting it lie quite fallow. The turnip husbandry, as it is called, is one of the capital modern improvements of agriculture.

G. I think I have heard that Norfolk is famous for it?

T. It is so. That county abounds in light, sandy lands, which are peculiarly suitable to turnips. But they are now grown in many parts of the kingdom besides. Well—but we must say somewhat more about cabbage, an article of food of very long standing. The original species of this is a sea-side plant; but cultivation has produced a great number of varieties, well known in our gardens as white and red cabbage, kale, colewort, broccoli, borecole, and cauliflower.

H. But the flower of cauliflower does not seem at all like that of cabbage or turnip.

T. The white head, called its flower, is not properly so, but consists of a cluster of imperfect buds. If they are left to grow to seed, they throw out some spikes of yellow flowers, like common cabbage. Broccoli-heads are of the same kind. As to the head of white or red cabbage, it consists of a vast number of leaves closing around each other, by which the innermost are prevented from expanding, and remain white, on account of the exclusion of the light and air. This part, you know, is most valued for food. In some countries they cut cabbage-heads into quarters, and make them undergo a sort of acid fermentation; after which, they are salted and preserved for winter food, under the name of sour krout.

G. Cattle, too, are sometimes fed with cabbage, I believe.

T. Yes; and large fields of them are cultivated for that purpose. They succeed best in stiff, clayey soils, where they sometimes grow to an enormous size. They are given to milch-kine, as well as to fattening cattle.

G. Do they not give a bad taste to the milk?

T. They are apt to do so, unless great care is taken to pick off all the decayed leaves.

Coleworts, which are a smaller sort of cabbage, are sometimes grown for feeding sheep and cattle. I think I have now mentioned most of the useful plants of this family, which, you see, are numerous and important. They both yield beef and mutton, and the sauce to them. But many of this species are troublesome weeds. You see how yonder corn is overrun with yellow flowers.

G. Yes. They are as thick as though they had been sown.

T. They are of this family, and called charlock, or wild mustard, or corn kale, which, indeed, are not all exactly the same things, though nearly resembling. These produce such plenty of seeds, that it is very difficult to clear a field of them, if once they are suffered to grow till the seeds ripen. An extremely common weed in gardens, and by road-sides, is shepherd's purse, which is a very good specimen of the pouch-bearing plants of this tribe, its seed-vessels being exactly the figure of a heart. Lady-smock is often so abundant a weed in wet meadows, as to make them all over white with its flowers. Some call this plant cuckoo-flower, because its flowering is about the same time with the first appearance of that bird in the spring.

G. I remember some pretty lines in a song about spring, in which lady-smock is mentioned.

> "When daisies pied, and violets blue,
> And lady-smocks, all silver white ;
> And cuckoo-buds, of yellow hue,
> Do paint the meadows with delight."

T. They are Shakespeare's. You see, he gives the name of cuckoo-bud to some other flower, a yellow one, which appears at the same season. But still earlier than this time, walls and hedge-banks are enlivened by a very small white flower, called whitlew-grass, which is one of this tribe.

H. Is it easy to distinguish the plants of this family from one another ?

T. Not very easy, for the general similarity of the flowers is so great, that little distinction can be drawn from them. The marks of the species are chiefly taken from the form and manner of growth of the seed-vessel, and we will examine some of them by the descriptions in a book of botany. There is one very remarkable seed-vessel, which probably you have observed in the garden. It is a perfectly round, large, flat pouch, which, after it has shed its seed, remains on the stalk, and looks like a thin, white bladder. The plant bearing it is commonly called honesty.

H. O, I know it very well. It is put into winter flower-pots.

T. True. So much, then, for the tetradynamious or cruciform-flowered plants. You cannot well mistake them for any other class, if you remark the six chives, four of them, generally, but not always, longer than the two others; the single pistil changing either into a long pod or a round pouch containing the seeds; the four opposite petals of the flower, and four leaves of the calyx. You may safely make a salad of the young leaves wherever you find them; the worst they can do to you is to bite your tongue.

THE NATIVE VILLAGE.

A DRAMA.

Scene—*A scattered Village, almost hidden with Trees.*
Enter HARFORD *and* BEAUMONT.

Harford. THERE is the place. This is the green on which I played many a day with my companions; there are the tall trees that I have so often climbed for birds' nests; and that is the pond where I used to sail my walnut-shell boats. What a crowd of mixed sensations rush on my mind! What pleasure, and what regret! Yes, there is somewhat in our native soil that affects the mind in a manner different from every other scene in nature.

Beaumont. With you it must be merely the *place;* for I think you can have no attachments of friendship or affection in it, considering your long absence, and the removal of all your family.

Harf. No, I have no family connexions, and, indeed, can scarcely be said ever to have had any; for, as you know, I was almost utterly neglected after the death of my father and mother; and, while all my elder brothers and sisters were dispersed to one part or another, and the little remaining property was disposed of, I was left with the poor people who nursed me, to be brought up just as they thought proper; and the little pension that was paid for me entirely ceased after a few years.

Beaum. Then how were you afterward supported?

Harf. The honest couple, who had the care of me, continued to treat me with the greatest kindness; and, poor as they were, not only maintained me as a child of their own, but did all in their power to procure me advantages more suited to my birth than my deserted situation. With the assistance of the worthy clergyman of the parish, they put me to a day-school in the village, clothed me decently, and being themselves sober, religious persons, took care to keep me from vice. The obligations I am under to them will, I hope, never be effaced from my memory, and it is on their account alone that I have undertaken this journey.

Beaum. How long did you continue with them?

Harf. Till I was thirteen. I then felt an irresistible desire to fight for my country; and, learning by accident that a distant relation of our family was a captain of a man-of-war, I took leave of my worthy benefactors, and set off to the sea-port where he lay, the good people furnishing me, in the best manner they were able, with necessaries for the journey. I shall never forget the tenderness with which they parted with me. It was, if possible, beyond that of the kindest parents. You know my subsequent adventures, from the time of my becoming a midshipman, to my present state of first lieutenant in the *Britannia*. Though it is now fifteen years since my departure, I feel my affection for these good folk stronger than ever, and could not

Y

be easy without taking the first opportunity of seeing them.

Beaum. It is a great chance if they are both living.

Harf. I happened to hear, by a young man of the village, not long since, that they were; but, I believe, much reduced in their circumstances.

Beaum. Whereabouts did they live?

Harf. Just at the turning of this corner. But what's this—I can't find the house. Yet I am sure I have not forgotten the situation. Surely it must be pulled down! Oh, my dear old friends, what can have become of you!

Beaum. You had better ask that little girl.

Harf. Hark ye, my dear!—do you know one John Beech of this place?

Girl. What, old John Beech! O yes, very well, and Mary Beech too.

Harf. Where do they live?

Girl. A little further on in the lane.

Harf. Did they not once live hereabouts?

Girl. Yes, till farmer Tithing pulled the house down, to make his hop-garden.

Harf. Come with me to show me the place, and I'll give you a penny.

Girl. Yes, that I will. (*They walk on.*) There— that low thatched house—and there's Mary spinning at the door.

Harf. There, my dear. (*Gives money, and the girl goes away.*) How my heart beats!—Surely that cannot be my nurse! Yes, I recollect her now; but how very old and sickly she looks!

Beaum. Fifteen years in her life, with care and hardship, must have gone a great way in breaking her down.

Harf. (*Going to the cottage door.*) Good morning, good woman; can you give my companion and me something to drink? We are very thirsty with walking this hot day.

Mary Beech. I have nothing better than water, sir,

but if you please to accept of that, I will bring you
some.

Beaum. Thank you—we will trouble you for some.

Mary. Will you please to walk in out of the sun,
gentlemen; ours is a very poor house, indeed; but I
will find you a seat to sit down on, while I draw the
water.

Harf. (*to Beaumont.*)　The same good creature as
ever! let us go in.

Scene II.—*The Inside of the Cottage.　An old Man sitting by the
Hearth.*

Beaum. We have made bold, friend, to trouble your
wife for a little water.

John Beech. Sit down—sit down, gentlemen.　I
would get up to give you my chair, but I have the
misfortune to be lame, and am almost blind, too.

Harf. Lame and blind! Oh, Beaumont! (*aside.*)

John. Ay, sir, old age will come on! and, God
knows, we have very little means to fence against it.

Beaum. What, have you nothing but your labour
to subsist on?

John. We made that do, sir, as long as we could;
but now I am hardly capable of doing anything, and
my poor wife can earn very little by spinning, so we
have been forced at last to apply to the parish.

Harf. To the parish! well, I hope they consider
the services of your better days, and provide for you
comfortably.

John. Alas, sir! I am not much given to complain;
but what can a shilling a week do, in these hard times?

Harf. Little enough, indeed!　And is that all they
allow you?

John. It is, sir; and we are not to have that much
longer, for they say we must come into the workhouse.

Mary. (*entering with the water.*) Here, gentlemen.
The jug is clean, if you can drink out of it.

Harf. The workhouse, do you say?

Mary. Yes, gentlemen—that makes my poor husband so uneasy—that we should come, in our old days, to die in a workhouse. We have lived better, I assure you—but we were turned out of our little farm by the great farmer near the church; and since that time we have been growing poorer and poorer, and weaker and weaker, so that we have nothing to help ourselves with.

John. (*sobbing.*) To die in a parish workhouse—I can hardly bear the thought of it—but God knows best, and we must submit.

Harf. But, my good people, have you no children or friends to assist you?

John. Our children, sir, are all dead, except one that is settled a long way off, and as poor as we are.

Beaum. But surely, my friends, such decent people as you seem to be must have somebody to protect you.

Mary. No, sir—we know nobody but our neighbours, and they think the workhouse good enough for the poor.

Harf. Pray, was there not a family of Harfords once in this village?

John. Yes, sir, a long while ago—but they are all dead and gone, or else far enough from this place.

Mary. Ay, sir, the youngest of them, and the finest child among them, that I'll say for him, was nursed in our house when we lived in the old spot near the green. He was with us till he was thirteen, and a sweet-behaved boy he was—I loved him as well as ever I did any of my own children.

Harf. What became of him?

John. Why, sir, he was a fine, bold, spirited boy, though the best tempered fellow in the world; so last war he would be a sailor, and fight the French and Spaniards, and away he went, nothing could stop him, and we have never heard a word of him since.

Mary. Ay, he is dead or killed, I warrant; for if he was alive, and in England, I am sure nothing would keep him from coming to see his poor daddy and mammy, as he used to call us. Many a night have I lain awake thinking of him!

Harf. (*to Beaum.*) I can hold no longer!

Beaum. (*to him.*) Restrain yourself awhile. Well, my friends, in return for your kindness, I will tell you some news that will please you. This same Harford, Edward Harford——

Mary. Ay, that was his name—my dear Ned. What of him, sir? Is he living?

John. Let the gentleman speak, my dear.

Beaum. Ned Harford is now alive and well, and a lieutenant in his majesty's navy, and as brave an officer as any in the service.

John. I hope you do not jest with us, sir.

Beaum. I do not, upon my honour.

Mary. O, thank God—thank God! If I could but see him!

John. Ay, I wish for nothing more before I die.

Harf. Here he is—here he is—my dearest, best benefactors! Here I am, to pay some of the great debt of kindness I owe you. (*Clasps Mary round the neck, and kisses her.*)

Mary. What—this gentleman my Ned! Ay, it is, it is—I see it, I see it.

John. O, my old eyes!—but I know his voice now. (*Stretches out his hand, which Harford grasps.*)

Harf. My good old man! O, that you could see me as clearly as I do you!

John. Enough—enough. It is you, and I am contented.

Mary. O, happy day! O, happy day!

Harf. Did you think I could ever forget you?

John. Oh no; I knew you better. But what a long while it is since we parted!

Mary. Fifteen years, come Whitsuntide.

Harf. The first time I set foot in England all this long interval was three weeks ago.

John. How good you were to come to us so soon.

Mary. What a tall, strong man you are grown!—but you have the same sweet smile as ever.

John. I wish I could see him plain. But what

signifies!—he's here, and I hold him by the hand. Where's the other good gentleman?

Beaum. Here—very happy to see such worthy people made so.

Harf. He has been my dearest friend for a great many years, and I am beholden to him almost as much as to you two.

Mary. Has he? God bless him, and reward him!

Harf. I am grieved to think what you must have suffered from hardship and poverty. But that is all at an end; no workhouse now!

John. God bless you! then I shall be happy still. But we must not be burdensome to you.

Harf. Don't talk of that. As long as I have a shilling, it is my duty to give you sixpence of it. Did you not take care of me when all the world forsook me, and treated me as your own child when I had no other parent; and shall I ever forsake you in your old age? Oh, never—never!

Mary. Ay, you had always a kind heart of your own. I always used to think that our dear Ned would, some time or other, prove a blessing to us.

Harf. You must leave this poor hut, that is not fit to keep out the weather, and we must get you a snug cottage, either in this village or some other.

John. Pray, my dear sir, let us die in this town, as we have always lived in it. And as to a house, I believe that where old Richard Carpenter used to live in is empty, if it would not be too good for us.

Harf. What, the white cottage on the green? I remember it—it is just the thing. You shall remove there this very week.

Mary. This is beyond all my hopes and wishes.

Harf. There you shall have a little close to keep a cow—and a girl to milk her, and take care of you both —and a garden, well stocked with herbs and roots— and a little yard for pigs and poultry—and some good, new furniture for your house.

John. O, too much! too much!

Mary. What makes me cry so, when so many good things are coming to us ?

Harf. Who is the landlord of that house ?

John. Our next neighbour, Mr. Wheatfield.

Harf. I'll go and speak about it directly, and then come to you again.   Come, Beaumont.   God bless you both !

John. God in Heaven bless you !

Mary. O, happy day !   O, happy day !

TWENTY-FOURTH EVENING.

PERSEVERANCE AGAINST FORTUNE.

A Story.

THEODORE was a boy of lively parts and engaging manners; but he had the failing of being extremely impatient in his temper, and inclined to extremes. He was ardent in all his pursuits, but could bear no disappointment; and if the least thing went wrong, he threw up what he was about in a pet, and could not be prevailed upon to resume it.   His father, Mr. Carleton, had given him a bed in the garden, which he had cultivated with great delight.   The borders were set with double daisies of different colours, next to which was a row of auriculas and polyanthuses.   Beyond were stocks, and other taller flowers and shrubs; and a beautiful damask rose graced the centre.   This rose was just budding, and Theodore watched its daily progress with great interest.   One unfortunate day, the door of the garden having been left open, a drove of pigs entered, and began to riot on the herbs and flowers.   An alarm being sounded, Theodore and the servant boy rushed upon them, smacking their whips. The whole herd, in affright, took their course across Theodore's flower-bed, on which some of them had before been grazing.   Stocks, daisies, and auriculas were all trampled down, or torn up; and, what was

worst of all, an old sow ran directly over the beautiful
rose-tree, and broke off its stem level with the ground.
When Theodore came up, and beheld all the mischief,
and especially his favourite rose strewed on the soil,
rage and grief choked his utterance. After standing
awhile the picture of despair, he snatched up a spade
that stood near, and with furious haste dug over the
whole bed, and whelmed all the relics of his flowers
deep under the soil. This exertion being ended, he
burst into tears, and silently left the garden.

His father, who had beheld the scene at a distance,
though somewhat diverted at the boy's childish violence,
yet began seriously to reflect on the future conse-
quences of such a temper, if suffered to grow up without restraint. He said nothing to him at the time,
but, in the afternoon, he took him for a walk into a
neighbouring parish. There was a large, wild common,
and at the skirts of it, a neat farm-house, with fields
lying around it, all well fenced, and cultivated in the
best manner. The air was sweetened with the bean-
flower and clover. An orchard of fine young fruit-
trees lay behind the house; and before it a little
garden, gay with all the flowers of the season. A
stand of beehives was on the southern side, sheltered
by a thick hedge of honeysuckle and sweet briar. The
farm-yard was stocked with pigs and poultry. A herd
of cows, with full udders, was just coming home to be
milked. Everything wore the aspect of plenty and
good management. The charms of the scene struck
Theodore very forcibly, and he expressed his pleasure
in the warmest terms. "This place," said his father,
"belongs to a man who is the greatest example I
know of patient fortitude bearing up against misfortune; and all that you see is the reward of his own
perseverance. I am a little acquainted with him, and
we will go in and beg a draught of milk, and try if we
can prevail upon him to tell us his story." Theodore
willingly accompanied his father. They were received
by the farmer with cordial frankness. After they were

seated, " Mr. Hardman," says Mr. Carleton, " I have often heard part of your adventures, but never had a regular account of the whole. If you will favour me and my little boy with the story of them, we shall think ourselves much obliged to you." " Lack-a-day, sir," said he, " there's little in them worth telling of, so far as I know. I have had my ups and downs in the world, to be sure, but so have many men besides. However, if you wish to hear about them, they are at your service ; and I can't say but it gives me pleasure sometimes to talk over old matters, and think how much better things have turned out than might have been expected." " Now, I am of opinion," said Mr. C., " that, from your spirit and perseverance, a good conclusion might have been expected." " You are pleased to compliment, sir," replied the farmer, " but I will begin without more words.

" You may, perhaps, have heard, that my father was a man of good estate. He thought of nothing, poor man ! but how to spend it ; and he had the uncommon luck to spend it twice over. For when he was obliged to sell it the first time, it was bought in by a relation, who left it him again by his will. But my poor father was not a man to take warning. He fell to living as he had lived before, and just made his estate and his life hold out together. He died at the age of five and forty, and left his family beggars. I believe he would not have taken to drinking, as he did, had it not been for his impatient temper, which made him fret and vex himself for every trifle, and then he had nothing for it, but to drown his care in liquor.

" It was my lot to be taken by my mother's brother, who was master of a merchant ship. I served him as an apprentice several years, and underwent a good deal of the usual hardships of a sailor's life. He had just made me his mate, in a voyage up the Mediterranean, when we had the misfortune to be wrecked on the coast of Morocco. The ship struck at some distance from shore, and we lay a long, stormy night, with the waves dashing over us, expecting every moment to perish. My uncle, and several of the crew, died of fatigue and want, and by morning only four of us were left alive. My companions were so disheartened, that they thought of nothing but submitting to their fate. For my part, I considered life still worth struggling for; and the weather having become calmer, I persuaded them to join me in making a sort of raft, by the help of which, with much toil and danger, we reached the land. Here we were seized by the barbarous inhabitants, and carried up the country, for slaves to the emperor. We were employed about some public buildings, made to work very hard, with the whip at our backs, and allowed nothing but water, and a kind of pulse. I have heard persons talk as though there was little in being a slave but the name; but they who have been slaves themselves, I am sure will never make light of slavery in others. A ransom was set on our heads, but so high, that it seemed impossible for poor, friendless creatures like us, ever to pay it. The thought of perpetual servitude, together with the hard treatment we met with, quite overcame my poor companions. They drooped and died, one after another. I still thought it not impossible to mend my condition, and, perhaps, to recover my freedom. We worked about twelve hours in the day, and had one holiday in the week. I employed my leisure time in learning to make mats and flag-baskets in which I soon became so expert, as to have a good many for sale, and thereby got a little money to purchase better food, and several small conveniences. We were afterwards set to work in the emperor's gardens; and here I showed so much good-will and attention, that I got into favour with the overseer. He had a large garden of his own; and he made interest for me to be suffered to work for him alone, on the condition of paying a man to do my duty. I soon became so useful to him, that he treated me more like a hired servant than a slave, and gave me regular wages. I learned the language of the country, and might have passed my time comfortably enough, could I have accommodated myself to their manners and religion, and forgotten my native land. I saved all I could, in order to purchase my freedom; but the ransom was so high, that I had little prospect of being able to do it for some years to come. A circumstance, however, happened which brought it about at once. Some villains one night laid a plot to murder my master, and plunder his house. I slept in a little shed in the garden, where the tools lay; and being awakened by a noise, I saw four men break through the fence, and walk up an alley towards the house. I crept out, with a spade in my hand, and silently followed them. They made a hole with instruments in the house-wall, big enough for a man to enter at. Two of them had got in, and the third was beginning to enter, when I rushed forward, and, with a blow of my spade, clove the skull of one of the robbers, and gave the other such a stroke on the shoulder as disabled him. I then made a loud outcry, to alarm the family. My master and his son, who lay in the house, got up, and having let me in, we secured the two others, after a sharp conflict, in which I received a severe wound with a dagger. My master, who looked upon me as his preserver, had all possible care taken of me; and, as soon as I was cured, made me a present of my liberty. He would fain have kept me with him, but my mind was so much bent on returning to my native country, that I immediately set out to the nearest sea-port, and took my passage in a vessel going to Gibraltar.

"From this place, I returned in the first ship for England. As soon as we arrived in the Downs, and I was rejoicing at the sight of the white cliffs, a man-of-war's boat came on shore, and pressed into the king's service all of us who were seamen. I could not but think it hard that this should be my welcome at home after a long slavery; but there was no remedy. I resolved to do my duty in my station, and leave the rest to Providence. I was abroad during the remainder of the war, and saw many a stout fellow sink under disease and despondence. My knowledge of seamanship got me promoted to the post of a petty officer, and at the peace I was paid off, and received a pretty sum for wages and prize-money. With this, I set off for London. I had experienced too much distress from want, to be inclined to squander away my money, so I put it into a banker's hands, and began to look out for some new way of life.

"Unfortunately, there were some things of which I had no more experience than a child, and the tricks of London were among these. An advertisement, offering extraordinary advantages to a partner in a commercial concern, who could bring a small capital, tempted me to make inquiry about the matter; and I was soon cajoled by a plausible, artful fellow, to venture my whole stock in it. The business was a manufacture, about which I knew nothing at all; but, as I was not afraid of my labour, I set about working as they directed me, with great diligence, and thought all was going on prosperously. One morning, on coming to the office, I found my partners decamped; and the same day I was arrested for a considerable sum due by the partnership. It was in vain for me to think of getting bail, so I was obliged to go to prison. Here I should have been half-starved, but for my Moorish trade of mat-making, by the help of which I bettered my condition for some months; when the creditors, finding that nothing could be got out of me, suffered me to be set at liberty.

"I was now in the wide world without a farthing or a friend, but I thanked God that I had health and limbs left. I did not choose to trust the sea again, but preferred my other new trade of gardening; so I applied to a nurseryman near town, and was received as a day-labourer. I set myself cheerfully to work, taking care to be in the grounds the first man in the morning and the last at night. I acquainted.

my employer with all the practices I had observed in
Morocco, and got him, in return, to instruct me in
his own. In time, I came to be considered as a
skilful workman, and was advanced to higher wages.
My affairs were in a flourishing state. I was well
fed and comfortably lodged, and saved money into
the bargain. About this time, I fell in company with
a young woman at service, very notable and well
behaved, who seemed well qualified for a wife to a
working man. I ventured to make an offer to her,
which proved not disagreeable; and after we had
calculated a little how we were to live, we married.
I took a cottage with an acre or two of land to it,
and my wife's savings furnished our house and bought
a cow. All my leisure time I spent upon my piece
of ground, which I made very productive, and the
profits of my cow, with my wages, supported us very
well. No mortal, I think, could be happier than I
was after a hard day's work, by my own fire side, with
my wife beside me, and our little infant on my knee.

"After this way of life had lasted two or three
years, a gentleman who had dealt largely with my
master for young plants, asked him if he could recommend an honest, industrious man for a tenant,
upon some land that he had lately taken in from the
sea. My master, willing to do me a kindness, mentioned me. I was tempted by the proposal, and
going down to view the premises, I took a farm upon
a lease at a low rent, and removed my family and
goods to it, one hundred and fifty miles from London.
There was ground enough for money, but much was
left to be done for it in draining, manuring, and fenc-
ing. Then it required more stock than I was able to
furnish; so, though unwilling, I was obliged to borrow
some money of my landlord, who let me have it at
moderate interest. I began with a good heart, and
worked late and early to put things into the best condition. My first misfortune was that the place proved
unhealthy to us. I fell into a lingering ague, which

pulled me down much, and hindered my business. My wife got a slow fever, and so did our eldest child (we had now two, and another coming). The poor child died; and what with grief and illness my wife had much ado to recover. Then the rot got among my sheep, and carried off the best part of my stock. I bore up against distress as well as I could; and, by the kindness of my landlord, was enabled to bring things tolerably about again. We regained our health, and began to be seasoned to the climate. As we were cheering ourselves with the prospect of better times, a dreadful storm arose—it was one night in February—I shall never forget it—and drove the spring-tide with such fury against our sea-banks, that they gave way. The water rushed in with such force, that all was presently at sea. Two hours before daylight I was awakened by the noise of the waves dashing against our house, and bursting in at the door. My wife had lain-in about a month, and she and I, and the two children, slept on a ground-floor. We had just time to carry the children up stairs, before all was afloat in the room. When day appeared, we could see nothing from the windows but water. All the out-houses, ricks, and utensils were swept away, and all the cattle and sheep drowned. The sea kept rising, and the force of the current bore so hard against our house, that we thought every moment it must fall. We clasped our babies to our breasts, and expected nothing but present death. At length we spied a boat coming to us. With a good deal of difficulty, it got under our window, and took us in, with a servant-maid and boy. A few clothes was all the property we saved; and we had not left the house half an hour before it fell, and in a minute nothing was to be seen of it. Not only the farm-house, but the farm itself was gone. I was now again a ruined man, and what was worse, I had three partners in my ruin. My wife and I looked at one another, and then at our little ones, and wept. Neither of us had a word of comfort to say. At least, thought I, this country is not Morocco, however. Here are good souls that will pity our case, and perhaps relieve us. Then I have a character, and a pair of hands. Things are bad, but they might have been worse. I took my wife by the hand, and knelt down. She did the same. I thanked God for his mercy in saving our lives, and prayed that he would continue to protect us. We rose up with lightened hearts, and were able to talk calmly about our condition. It was my desire to return to my former master, the nurseryman; but how to convey my family so far without money was the difficulty. Indeed, I was much worse than nothing, for I owed a good deal to my landlord. He came down, upon the news of the misfortune, and though his own losses were heavy, he not only forgave my debt and released me from all obligations, but made me a small present. Some charitable neighbours did the like; but I was most of all affected by the kindness of our late maid-servant, who insisted upon our accepting of a crown which she had saved out of her wages. Poor soul! we had always treated her like one of ourselves, and she felt for us like one.

" As soon as we had got some necessaries, and the weather was tolerable, we set out on our long march. My wife carried her infant in her arms. I took the bigger child on my back, and a bundle of clothes in my hand. We could walk only a few miles a day, but we now and then got a lift in an empty waggon or cart, which was a great help to us. One day we met with a farmer returning with his team from market, who let us ride, and entered into conversation with me. I told him of my adventures, by which he seemed much interested; and learning that I was skilled in managing trees, he acquainted me that a nobleman in his neighbourhood was making great plantations, and would very likely be glad to engage me; and he offered to carry us to the place. As all I was seeking was a living by my labour, I thought the sooner I got it the better; so I thankfully accepted his offer. He took us to the nobleman's steward, and made known our case. The steward wrote to my old master for a character; and receiving a favourable one, he hired me as a principal manager of a new plantation, and settled me and my family in a snug cottage near it. He advanced us somewhat for a little furniture and present subsistence; and we had once more a *home*. O sir! how many blessings are contained in that word to those who have known the want of it!

"I entered upon my new employment with as much satisfaction as though I had been taking possession of an estate. My wife had enough to do in taking care of the house and children; so it lay with me to provide for all, and I may say I was not idle. Besides my weekly pay from the steward, I contrived to make a little money at leisure times by pruning and dressing gentlemen's fruit-trees. I was allowed a piece of waste ground behind the house for a garden, and I spent a good deal of labour in bringing it into order. My old master sent me down, for a present, some choice young trees and flower roots, which I planted, and they throve wonderfully. Things went on almost as well as I could desire. The situation being dry and healthy, my wife recovered her lost bloom, and the children sprang up like my plants. I began to hope that I was almost out of the reach of farther misfortune; but it was not so ordered.

"I had been three years in this situation, and increased my family with another child, when my lord died. He was succeeded by a very dissipated young man, deep in debt, who presently put a stop to the planting and improving of the estate, and sent orders to turn off all the workmen. This was a great blow to me; however, I still hoped to be allowed to keep my little house and garden, and I thought I could then maintain myself as a nurseryman and gardener. But a new steward was sent down, with directions to rack the tenants to the utmost. He asked me as much rent for the place as though I had found the garden ready-made to my hands; and when I told him it was impossible for me to pay it, he gave me notice to quit immediately. He would neither suffer me to take away my trees and plants, nor allow me anything for them. His view, I found, was to put in a favourite of his own, and set him up at my expense. I remonstrated against this cruel injustice, but could obtain nothing but hard words. As I saw it would be the ruin of me to be turned out in that manner, I determined, rather hastily, to go up to London, and plead my cause with my new lord. I took a sorrowful leave of my family, and walking to the next market-town, I got a place on the outside of the stage-coach. When we were within thirty or forty miles of London, the coachman overturned the carriage, and I pitched directly on my head, and was taken up senseless. Nobody knew any thing about me; so I was carried to the next village, where the overseer had me taken to the parish workhouse. Here I lay a fortnight, much neglected, before I came to my senses. As soon as I became sensible of my condition, I was almost distracted in thinking of the distress my poor wife, who was near lying-in, must be under on my account, not hearing anything of me. I lay another fortnight before I was fit to travel; for, besides the hurt on my head, I had a broken collar-bone, and several bruises. My money had somehow all got out of my pocket, and I had no other means of getting away, than by being passed to my own parish. I returned in sad plight indeed, and found my wife very ill in bed. My children were crying about her, and almost starving. We should now have been quite lost, had I not raised a little money by selling our furniture, for I was yet unable to work. As soon as my wife was somewhat recovered, we were forced to quit our house. I cried like a child on leaving my blooming garden and flourishing plantations, and was almost tempted to demolish them, rather than another should unjustly reap the fruit of my labours. But I checked myself, and I am glad I did. We took lodgings in a neighbouring village, and I went round among the gentlemen of the country to see if I could get a little employment. In the mean time, the former steward came down to settle accounts with his successor, and was much concerned to find me in such a situation. He was a very able and honest man, and had been engaged by another nobleman to superintend a large, improveable estate in a distant part of the kingdom. He told me, if I would try my fortune with him once more, he would endeavour to procure me a new settlement. I had nothing to lose, and therefore was willing enough to run any hazard, but I was destitute of means to convey my family to such a distance. My good friend, who was much provoked at the injustice of the new steward, said so much to him, that he brought him to make me an allowance for my garden; and with that I was enabled to make another removal. It was to the place I now inhabit.

"When I came here, sir, all this farm was a naked common, like that you crossed in coming. My lord got an enclosure bill for his part of it, and the steward divided it into different farms, and let it on improving leases to several tenants. A dreary spot, to be sure, it looked at first, enough to sink a man's heart to sit down upon it. I had a little unfinished cottage given me to live in; and, as I had nothing to stock a farm, I was for some years employed as head labourer and planter about the new enclosures. By very hard working and saving, together with a little help, I was at length enabled to take a small part of the ground I now occupy. I had various discouragements, from bad seasons, and other accidents. One year the distemper carried off four out of seven cows that I kept; another year I lost two of my best horses. A high wind once almost entirely destroyed an orchard I had just planted, and blew down my largest barn. But I was too much used to misfortunes to be easily disheartened, and my way always was to set about repairing them in the best manner I could, and leave the rest to Heaven. This method seems to have answered at last. I have now gone on many years in a course of continued prosperity, adding field to field, increasing my stock, and bringing up a numerous family with credit. My dear wife, who was my faithful partner through so much distress, continues to share my prosperous state; and few couples in the kingdom, I believe, have more cause to be thankful for their lot. This, sir, is my history. You see it contains nothing very extraordinary; but if it impress on the mind of this young gentleman the maxim that patience and perseverance will scarcely fail of a good issue in the end, the time you have spent in listening to it will not entirely be lost."

Mr. Carleton thanked the good farmer very heartily for the amusement and instruction he had afforded them, and took leave, with many expressions of regard. Theodore and he walked home, talking, by the way, of what they had heard.

Next morning, Mr. C., looking out of the window, saw Theodore hard at work in his garden. He was carefully disinterring his buried flowers, trimming and cleaning them, and planting them anew. He had got the gardener to cut a slip of the broken rose-tree, and set it in the the middle to give it a chance for growing. By noon, everything was laid smooth, and neat, and the bed was well filled. All its splendour, indeed, was gone for the present, but it seemed in a hopeful way to revive. Theodore looked with pleasure over his work; but his father felt more pleasure in witnessing the first fruits of farmer Hardman's story.

———

THE GOLDFINCH AND LINNET.

A GAUDY Goldfinch, pert and gay
Hopping blithe, from spray to spray,
Full of frolic, full of spring,
With head well plumed, and burnish'd wing,
Spied a sober linnet hen,
   Sitting all alone,
And bow'd, and chirp'd, and bow'd again;
   And, with familiar tone,
He thus the dame address'd,
As to her side he closely press'd:
"I hope, my dear, I don't intrude,
By breaking on your solitude;
But it has always been my passion
To forward pleasant conversation;
And I should be a stupid bird
To pass the fair without a word;
I, who have been for ever noted
To be the sex's most devoted.
Besides, a damsel unattended,
Left unnoticed and unfriended,
Appears (excuse me) so forlorn,
   That I can scarce suppose,
By any she that e'er was born,
   'Twould be the thing she chose.
How happy, then, I'm now at leisure,
To wait upon a lady's pleasure;
And all this morn have nought to do
But pay my duty, love, to you.
"What, silent!—Ah! those looks demure,
And eyes of languor, make me sure
That, in my random, idle chatter,
I quite mistook the matter!
It is not spleen, or contemplation,
   That draws you to the cover;
But 'tis some tender assignation:
   Well!—who's the favour'd lover?

I met, hard by, in quaker suit,
A youth sedately grave and mute ;
And, from the maxim, ' Like to like,'
Perhaps the *sober youth* might strike.
Yes, yes, 'tis he, I'll lay my life,
Who hopes to get you for his wife.
"But, come, my dear, I know you're wise,
Compare and judge, and use your eyes :
No female yet could e'er behold
The lustre of my red and gold,
My ivory bill and jetty crest,
But all was done, and I was blest.
Come, brighten up, and act with spirit,
And take the fortune that you merit."
He ceased : *Linetta* thus replied,
With cool contempt and decent pride :—
"'Tis pity, sir, a youth so sweet,
In form and manner so complete,
Should do an humble maid the honour
To waste his precious time upon her.
A poor, forsaken she, you know,
Can do no credit to a beau ;
And worse would be the case,
    If, meeting one whose faith was plighted,
He should incur the sad disgrace
    Of being slighted.
"Now, sir, the *sober-suited youth*,
Whom you were pleased to mention,
To those small merits, sense and truth,
    And generous love, has some pretension :
And then, to give him all his due,
He sings, sir, full as well as you,
And sometimes can be silent, too.
In short, my taste is so perverse,
    And such my wayward fate,
That it would be my greatest curse
    To have a *Coxcomb* to my mate."
This said, away she scuds,
And leaves *beau Goldfinch* in the suds.

TWENTY-FIFTH EVENING.

THE PRICE OF A VICTORY.

" GOOD news! great news! glorious news!" cried young Oswald, as he entered his father's house. "We have got a complete victory, and have killed, I don't know how many thousands of the enemy; and we are to have bonfires and illuminations."

" And so," said his father, " you think that killing a great many thousands of human creatures is a thing to be very glad about."

Os. No—I do not quite think so, neither; but surely it is right to be glad that our country has gained a great advantage.

F. No doubt, it is right to wish well to our country, as far as its prosperity can be promoted without injuring the rest of mankind. But wars are very seldom to the real advantage of any nation; and when they are ever so useful or necessary, so many dreadful evils attend them, that a humane man will scarcely rejoice in them, if he consider at all on the subject.

Os. But if our enemies would do us a great deal of mischief, and we prevent it by beating them, have we not a right to be glad of it?

F. Alas! we are in general little judges which of the parties may have had the most mischievous intentions. Generally, they are both in the wrong, and success will make either of them unjust and unreasonable. But putting this out of the question, he who rejoices in the event of a battle, rejoices in the misery of many thousands of his species; and the thought of that should make him pause a little. Suppose a surgeon were to come, with a smiling countenance, and tell us triumphantly that he had cut off half-a-dozen legs to day—what would you think of him?

Os. I should think him very hard-hearted.

F. And yet those operations are done for the benefit of the sufferers, and by their own desire. But in a battle, the probability is, that none of those engaged on either side have any interest at all in the cause they are fighting for, and most of them enter into the scene of blood, because they cannot help it. In this battle, that you are so rejoiced about, there have been ten thousand men killed upon the spot, and nearly as many wounded.

Os. On both sides.

F. Yes—but they are *men* on both sides. Consider, now, that the ten thousand sent out of the world in this morning's work, though they are past feeling themselves, have left, probably, two persons each, on an average, to lament their loss, either parents, wives, or children. Here are, then, twenty thousand people made unhappy, at one stroke, on their account. This, however, is hardly so dreadful to think of as the condition of the wounded. At the moment we are talking, eight or ten thousand more are lying in agony, torn with shot or gashed with cuts, their wounds all festering, some hourly to die a most excruciating death, others to linger in torture weeks and months, and many doomed to drag on a miserable existence for the rest of their lives, with diseased and mutilated bodies.

Os. This is shocking to think of, indeed!

F. When you light your candles, then, this evening, *think what they cost.*

Os. But everybody else is glad, and seems to think nothing of these things.

F. True—they do *not* think of them. If they did, I cannot suppose they would be so void of feeling as to enjoy themselves in merriment when so many of their fellow-creatures are made miserable. Do you not remember when poor Dickens had his leg broken to pieces by a loaded waggon, how all the town pitied him?

Os. Yes, very well. I could not sleep the night after, for thinking of him.

F. But here are thousands suffering as much as he, and we scarcely bestow a single thought on them. If any one of these poor creatures were before our eyes, we should probably feel much more than we do now for them altogether. Shall I tell you a story of a soldier's fortune, that came to my own knowledge?

Os. Yes—pray do!

F. In the village where I went to school, there was an honest, industrious weaver and his wife, who had an only son, named Walter, just come to man's estate. Walter was a good and dutiful lad, and a clever workman, so that he was a great help to his parents. One unlucky day, having gone to the next market-town with some work, he met with a companion, who took him to the alehouse, and treated him. As he was coming away, a recruiting serjeant entered the room, and, seeing Walter to be a likely young fellow, had a great mind to entrap him. He persuaded him to sit down again, and take a glass with him; and kept him in talk with fine stories about a soldier's life, till Walter got tipsy before he was aware. The serjeant then clapped a shilling into his hand, to drink his Majesty's health, and told him he was enlisted. He was kept there all night, and next morning he was taken before a magistrate, to be sworn in. Walter had now become sober, and was very sorry for what he had done; but he was told that he could not get off without paying a guinea—smart money. This he knew not how to raise; and, being also afraid and ashamed to face his friends, he took the oath and bounty-money, and marched away with the serjeant, without ever returning home. His poor father and mother, when they heard of the affair, were almost heart-broken; and a young woman in the village, who was his sweetheart, almost went distracted. Walter sent them a line from the first stage, to bid them farewell, and comfort them. He joined his regiment, which soon embarked for Germany, where it continued till the peace. Walter once or twice sent word home of his welfare, but for the last year nothing was heard of him.

Os. Where was he, then?

F. You shall hear. One summer's evening, a man in an old, red coat, hobbling on crutches, was seen to enter the village. His countenance was pale and sickly, his cheeks hollow, and his whole appearance bespoke extreme wretchedness. Several people gathered around him, looking earnestly in his face. Among these, a young woman, having gazed at him awhile, cried out, " My Walter!" and fainted away. Walter fell on the ground beside her. His father and mother being fetched by some of the spectators, came and took him in their arms, weeping bitterly. I saw the whole scene, and shall never forget it. At length, the neighbours helped them into the house, where Walter told them the following story:—

" At the last great battle that our troops gained in Germany, I was among the first engaged, and received a shot that broke my thigh. I fell, and presently after, our regiment was forced to retreat. A squadron of the enemy's horse came galloping down upon us. A trooper making a blow at me with his sabre as I lay, I lifted up my arm to save my head, and got a cut which divided all the sinews at the back of my wrist. Soon after, the enemy was driven back, and came across us again. A horse set his foot on my side, and broke three of my ribs. The action was long and bloody, and the wounded on both sides were left on the field all night. A dreadful night it was to me, you may think! I had fainted through loss of blood, and, when I recovered, I was tormented with thirst, and the cold air made my wounds smart intolerably. About noon next day, waggons came to carry away those who remained alive; and I, with a number of others, was put into one, to be conveyed to the next town. The motion of the carriage was terrible for my broken bones—every jolt went to my heart. We were taken to an hospital, which was crammed as full as it could hold; and we should all have been suffocated with the heat and stench, had not a fever broke out, which soon thinned our numbers. I took it, and was twice given over; however, I struggled through. But my wounds proved so difficult to heal, that it was almost a twelvemonth before I could be discharged. A great deal of the bone in my thigh came away in splinters, and left the limb crooked and useless, as you see. I entirely lost the use of three fingers of my right hand; and my broken ribs made me spit blood a long time, and have left a cough and difficulty of breathing, which I believe will bring me to my grave. I was sent home, and discharged from the army, and I have begged my way hither as well as I could. I am told that the peace has left the affairs of my country just as they were before; but who will restore me my health and limbs? I am put on the list for a Chelsea pensioner, which will support me, if I live to receive it, without being a burden to my friends. That is all that remains for Walter now."

Os. Poor Walter! What became of him afterwards?

F. The wound in his thigh broke out afresh, and discharged more splinters, after a great deal of pain and fever. As winter came on, his cough increased. He wasted to a skeleton, and died the next spring. The young woman, his sweetheart, sat up with him every night to the last; and, soon after his death, she fell into a consumption, and followed him. The old people, deprived of the stay and comfort of their age, fell into despair and poverty, and were taken into the workhouse, where they ended their days.

This was the history of *Walter the Soldier*. It has been that of thousands more; and will be that of many a poor fellow over whose fate you are now rejoicing. Such is the *price of a victory.*

GOOD COMPANY.

" BE sure, Frederick, always keep *good company*,"
was the final admonition of Mr. Lofty, on dismissing
his son to the University.

" I entreat you, Henry, always to choose *good company*," said Mr. Manly, on parting with his son to an
apprenticeship in a neighbouring town.

But it is impossible for two people to mean more
differently by the same words.

In Mr. Lofty's idea, good company was that of
persons superior to ourselves in rank and fortune.
By this alone he estimated it; and the degrees of
comparison, better and best, were made exactly to
correspond to such a scale. Thus, if an esquire were
good company, a baronet was *better*, and a lord *best of
all*, provided he were not a *poor* lord, for, in that case,
a rich gentleman might be at least as good. For as,
according to Mr. Lofty's maxim, the great purpose for
which companions were to be chosen was to advance a
young man in the world, by their credit and interest,
they were to be preferred who afforded the best prospects in this respect.

Mr. Manly, on the other hand, understood by *good*
company that which was improving to the morals and
understanding; and by the *best*, that which, to a high
degree of these qualities, added true politeness of
manners. As superior advantages in education to a
certain point accompany superiority of condition, he
wished his son to prefer as companions those whose
situation in life had afforded them the opportunity of
being well educated; but he was far from desiring
him to shun connexions with worth and talents,
wherever he should find them.

Mr. Lofty had an utter aversion to *low company*, by
which he meant inferiors, people of no fashion and
figure, shabby fellows, whom nobody knows.

Mr. Manly equally disliked *low company*, understanding by it persons of mean habits and vulgar conversation.

A great part of Mr. Manly's good company, was Mr. Lofty's low company; and not a few of Mr. Lofty's very best company, were Mr. Manly's very worst.

Each of the sons understood his father's meaning, and followed his advice.

Frederick, from the time of his entrance at the University, commenced what is called a *Tuft-hunter*, from the tuft in the cap worn by young noblemen. He took pains to insinuate himself into the good graces of all the young men of high fashion in his college, and became a constant companion in their schemes of frolic and dissipation. They treated him with an insolent familiarity, often bordering upon contempt; but, following another maxim of his father's, "One must stoop to rise," he took it all in good part. He totally neglected study, as unnecessary, and, indeed, inconsistent with his plan. He spent a great deal of money, with which his father, finding that it went in *good company*, at first supplied him freely. In time, however, his expenses amounted to so much, that Mr. Lofty, who keep good company too, found it difficult to answer his demands. A considerable sum that he lost at play with one of his noble friends, increased the difficulty. If it were not paid, the disgrace of not having discharged a *debt of honour* would lose him all the favour he had acquired; yet the money could not be raised without greatly embarrassing his father's affairs.

In the midst of this perplexity, Mr. Lofty died, leaving behind him a large family and very little property. Frederick came up to town, and soon dissipated in *good company* the scanty portion that came to his share. Having neither industry, knowledge, nor reputation, he was then obliged to become an humble dependant on the great, flattering all their follies, and

ministering to their vices, treated by them with mortifying neglect, and equally despised and detested by
the rest of the world.

Henry, in the mean time, entered with spirit into
the business of his new profession, and employed his
leisure in cultivating an acquaintance with a few select
friends. These were partly young men in a situation
similar to his own, partly persons already settled in
life, but all distinguished by propriety of conduct, and
improved understandings. From all of them he
learned somewhat valuable; but he was more particularly indebted to two of them, who were in a station
of life inferior to that of the rest. One was a watch-
maker, an excellent mechanic, and tolerable mathe-
matician, and well acquainted with the construction
and use of all the instruments employed in experi-
mental philosophy. The other was a young druggist,
who had a good knowledge of chemistry, and frequently
employed himself in chemical operations and experiments. Both of them were men of very decent
manners, and took a pleasure in communicating their
knowledge to such as showed a taste for similar studies.
Henry frequently visited them, and derived much
useful information from their instructions, for which
he ever expressed great thankfulness. These various
occupations and good examples effectually preserved
him from the errors of youth, and he passed his time
with credit and satisfaction. He had the same misfortune with Frederick, just as he was ready to come
out into the world, of losing his father, upon whom the
support of the family chiefly depended; but in the
character he had established, and the knowledge he
had acquired, he found an effectual resource. One of
his young friends proposed to him a partnership in a
manufactory he had just set up at considerable expense,
requiring for his share only the exertion of his talents
and industry. Henry accepted the offer, and made
such good use of the skill in mechanics and chemistry
he had acquired, that he introduced many improve-

ments into the manufactory, and rendered it a very
profitable concern. He lived prosperously and independent, and retained in manhood all the friendships
of his youth.

THE WANDERER'S RETURN.

It was a délightful evening, about the end of August
he sun, setting in a pure sky, illuminated the tops of
the western hills, and tipped the opposite trees with a
yellow lustre.

A traveller, with sun-burnt cheeks and dusty feet,
strong and active, having a knapsack at his back, had
gained the summit of a steep ascent, and stood gazing
on the plain below.

This was a wide tract of champaign country,
chequered with villages, whose towers and spires
peeped above the trees in which they were embosomed.
The space between them was chiefly arable land, from
which the last products of the harvest were busily
carrying away.

A rivulet wound through the plain, its course
marked with grey willows. On its banks were verdant
meadows, covered with lowing herds, moving slowly
to the milkmaids, who came tripping along with pails
on their heads. A thick wood clothed the side of a
gentle eminence rising from the water, crowned with
the ruins of an ancient castle.

Edward (that was the traveller's name) dropped on
one knee, and clasping his hands, exclaimed, " Welcome, welcome, my dear, native land! Many a sweet
spot have I seen since I left thee, but none so sweet
as thou! Never has thy dear image been out of my
memory; and now, with what transport do I retrace
all thy charms! O, receive me again, never more to
quit thee!" So saying, he threw himself on the
turf, and having kissed it, arose, and proceeded on his
journey.

As he descended into the plain, he overtook a little
group of children, merrily walking along the path,

and stopping now and then to gather berries in the hedge.

"Where are you going, my dears?" said Edward.

"We are going home," they all replied.

"And where is that?"

"Why, to Summerton, that town there among the trees, just before us. Don't you see it?"

"I see it well," answered Edward, the tear standing in his eye.

"And what is your name—and yours—and yours?"

The little innocents told their names. Edward's heart leaped at the well-known sounds.

"And what is *your* name, my dear?" said he to a pretty girl, somewhat older than the rest, who hung back shyly, and held the hand of a ruddy, white-headed boy, just breeched.

"It is Rose Walsingham, and this is my younger brother, Roger."

"*Walsingham!*" Edward clasped the girl round the neck, and surprised her with two or three very close kisses. He then lifted up little Roger, and almost devoured him. Roger seemed as though he wanted to be set down again, but Edward told him he would carry him home.

"And can you show me the house you live at, Rose?" said Edward.

"Yes; it is just there, beside the pond, with the great barn before it, and the orchard behind."

"And will you take me home with you, Rose?"

"If you please," answered Rose, hesitatingly.

They walked on. Edward said but little, for his heart was full, but he frequently kissed little Roger.

Coming at length to a stile, from which a path led across a little close. "This is the way to our house," said Rose.

The other children parted. Edward set down Roger, and got over the stile. He still, however, kept hold of the boy's hand. He trembled, and looked wildly around him.

When they approached the house, an old mastiff

came running to meet the children. He looked up at
Edward rather sourly, and gave a little growl, when
all at once his countenance changed; he leaped upon
him, licked his hand, wagged his tail, murmured in a
soft voice, and seemed quite overcome with joy.
Edward stooped down, patted his head, and cried,
" Poor Captain, what, are you alive yet ?" Rose was
surprised that the stranger and their dog should know
one another.

They all entered the house together. A good-
looking, middle-aged woman was busied in preparing
articles of cookery, assisted by her grown-up daughter.
She spoke to the children as they came in, and casting
a look of some surprise on Edward, asked him what
his business was ?

Edward was some time silent; at length, with a
faltering voice, he cried, " Have you forgotten me,
mother ?"

" Edward! my son Edward!" exclaimed the good
woman. And they were instantly locked in each
other's arms.

" My brother Edward!" said Mary; and took her
turn for an embrace, as soon as her mother gave her
room.

" Are you my brother?" said Rose. " That I am,"
replied Edward, with another kiss. Little Roger
looked hard at him, but said nothing.

News of Edward's arrival soon flew across the yard,
and in came from the barn his father, his next brother,
Thomas, and the third, William. The father fell on
his neck, and sobbed out his welcome and blessing.
Edward had not hands enow for them all to shake.

An aged, white-headed labourer came in, and held
out his shrivelled hand. Edward gave it a hearty
squeeze. " Good bless you," said old Isaac; " this is
the best day I have seen this many a year."

" And where have you been this long while ?"
cried the father. " Eight years and more," added the
mother.

*"My brother Edward!" said Mary; and took her turn for an
embrace.*   P. 352.

His elder brother took off his knapsack; and Mary drew him a chair. Edward seated himself, and they all gathered around him. The old dog got within the circle, and lay at his feet.

"O, how glad I am to see you all again!" were Edward's first words. "How well you look, mother! but father's grown thinner. As for the rest, I should have known none of you, unless it were Thomas and old Isaac."

"What a sun-burnt face you have got—but you look brave and hearty," cried his mother.

"Ay, mother, I have been enough in the sun, I assure you. From seventeen to five-and-twenty I have been a wanderer upon the face of the earth, and I have seen more in that time than most men in the course of their lives.

"Our young landlord, you know, took such a liking to me at school, that he would have me go with him on his travels. We went through most of the countries of Europe, and at last to Naples, where my poor master took a fever and died. I never knew what grief was till then; and I believe the thoughts of leaving me in a strange country went as much to his heart as his illness. An intimate acquaintance of his, a rich young West Indian, seeing my distress, engaged me to go with him, in a voyage he was about to take to Jamaica. We were too short a time in England before we sailed for me to come and see you first, but I wrote you a letter from the Downs."

"We never received it," said his father.

"That was a pity," returned Edward; "for you must have concluded I was either dead or had forgotten you. Well—we arrived safe in the West Indies, and there I stayed till I buried that master too; for young men die fast in that country. I was very well treated, but I could never like the place; and yet Jamaica is a very fine island, and has many good people in it. But for me, used to see freemen work cheerfully along with their masters—to behold nothing

2 A

but droves of black slaves in the fields, toiling in the burning sun, under the constant dread of the lash of hard-hearted task-masters;—it was what I could not bring myself to bear; and though I might have been made an overseer of a plantation, I chose rather to live in a town, and follow some domestic occupation. I could soon have got rich there; but I fell into a bad state of health, and people were dying all around me of the yellow fever; so I collected my little property, and, though a war had broken out, I ventured to embark with it for England.

"The ship was taken and carried into the Havanna, and I lost my all, and my liberty besides. However, I had the good fortune to ingratiate myself with a Spanish merchant whom I had known at Jamaica, and he took me with him to the continent of South America. I visited great part of this country, once possessed by flourishing and independent nations, but now groaning under the severe yoke of their haughty conquerors. I saw those famous gold and silver mines, where the poor natives work naked, for ever shut out from the light of day, in order that the wealth of their unhappy land may go to spread luxury and corruption throughout the remotest regions of Europe.

"I accompanied my master across the great southern ocean, a voyage of some months, without the sight of anything but water and sky. We came to the rich city of Manilla, the capital of the Spanish settlements in those parts. There I had my liberty restored, along with a handsome reward for my services. I got thence to China, and from China to the English settlements in the East Indies, where the sight of my countrymen, and the sounds of my native tongue, made me fancy myself almost at home again, though still separated by half the globe.

"Here I saw a delightful country, swarming with industrious inhabitants, some cultivating the land, others employed in manufactures, but of so gentle and effeminate a disposition, that they have always fallen under the yoke of their invaders. Here, how was I forced to blush for my countrymen, whose avarice and rapacity so often have laid waste this fair land, and brought on it all the horrors of famine and desolation! I have seen human creatures quarrelling like dogs for bare bones thrown upon a dunghill. I have seen fathers selling their families for a little rice, and mothers entreating strangers to take their children for slaves, that they might not die of hunger. In the midst of such scenes, I saw pomp and luxury of which our country affords no examples.

"Having remained here a considerable time, I gladly, at length, set my face homewards, and joined a company, who undertook the long and perilous journey to Europe overland. We crossed vast tracts, both desert and cultivated; sandy plains parched with heat and drought, and infested with bands of ferocious plunderers. I have seen a well of muddy water more valued than ten camel-loads of treasure; and a few half-naked horsemen strike more terror than a king with all his guards. At length, after numberless hardships and dangers, we arrived at civilized Europe, and forgot all we had suffered. As I came nearer my native land, I grew more and more impatient to reach it; and, when I had set foot on it, I was still more restless, till I could see again my beloved home.

"Here I am at last—happy in bringing back a sound constitution and a clear conscience. I have also brought enough of the relics of my honest gains to furnish a little farm in the neighbourhood, where I mean to sit down and spend my days in the midst of those whom I love better than all the world besides."

When Edward had finished, kisses and kind shakes of the hand were again repeated, and his mother brought out a large slice of harvest cake, with a bottle of her nicest currant wine, to refresh him after his day's march. "You are come," said his father,

" at a lucky time, for this is our harvest supper. We shall have some of our neighbours to make merry with us, who will be almost as glad to see you as we are—for you were always a favourite among them."

It was not long before the visitors arrived. The young folk ran out to meet them, crying, " Our Edward's come back—our Edward's come home! Here he is—this is he;" and so, without ceremony, they introduced them. " Welcome!—welcome! God bless you!" sounded on all sides. Edward knew all the elderly ones at first sight, but the young people puzzled him for a while. At length he recollected this to have been his schoolfellow, and that his companion in driving the plough; and he was not long in finding out his favourite and playfellow Sally, of the next farm-house, whom he left a romping girl of fifteen, and now saw a blooming, full-formed young woman of three-and-twenty. He contrived in the evening to get next her; and, though she was somewhat reserved at first, they had pretty well renewed their intimacy before the company broke up.

" Health to Edward, and a happy settlement among us!" was the parting toast. When all were retired, the *Returned Wanderer* went to rest in the very room in which he was born, having first paid fervent thanks to Heaven for preserving him to enjoy a blessing the dearest to his heart.

TWENTY-SIXTH EVENING.

DIFFERENCE AND AGREEMENT;
OR, SUNDAY MORNING.

It was Sunday morning. All the bells were ringing for church, and the streets were filled with people moving in all directions.

Here, numbers of well-dressed persons, and a long train of charity children, were thronging in at the wide doors of a large handsome church. There, a smaller number, almost equally gay in dress, were entering an elegant meeting-house. Up one alley, a Roman Catholic congregation was turning into their retired chapel, every one crossing himself with a finger dipped in holy water as he went in. The opposite side of the street was covered with a train of Quakers, distinguished by their plain and neat attire and sedate aspect, who walked without ceremony into a room as plain as themselves, and took their seats, the men on one side and the women on the other, in silence. A spacious building was filled with an overflowing crowd of Methodists, most of them meanly habited, but decent and serious in demeanour; while a small society of Baptists in the neighbourhood quietly occupied their humble place of assembly.

Presently the different services began. The church resounded with the solemn organ, and with the indistinct murmurs of a large body of people following the minister in responsive prayers. From the meeting were heard the slow psalm, and the single voice of the leader of their devotions. The Roman Catholic chapel was enlivened by strains of music, the tinkling of a small bell, and a perpetual change of service and ceremonial. A profound silence and unvarying look and posture announced the self-recollection and mental devotion of the Quakers.

Mr. Ambrose led his son Edwin round all these different assemblies as a spectator. Edwin viewed everything with great attention, and was often impatient to inquire of his father the meaning of what he saw; but Mr. Ambrose would not suffer him to disturb any of the congregations even by a whisper. When they had gone through the whole, Edwin found a great number of questions to put to his father, who explained everything to him in the best manner he could. At length says Edwin,

"But why cannot all these people agree to go to the same place, and worship God the same way?"

" And why should they agree ?" replied his father.
" Do not you see that people differ in a hundred other
things ? Do they all dress alike, and eat and drink
alike, and keep the same hours, and use the same
diversions ?"

" Ay—but those are things in which they have a
right to do as they please."

" And they have a right, too, to worship God as they
please. It is their own business, and concerns none
but themselves."

" But has not God ordered particular ways of wor-
shipping him ?"

" He has directed the mind and spirit with which
he is to be worshipped, but not the particular form
and manner. That is left for every one to choose,
according as suits his temper and opinions. All these
people like their own way best, and why should they
leave it for the choice of another ? Religion is one of
the things in which *mankind were made to differ.*"

The several congregations now began to be dismissed, and the street was again overspread with
persons of all the different sects, going promiscuously to their respective homes. It chanced that a
poor man fell down in the street in a fit of apoplexy,
and lay for dead. His wife and children stood around
him, crying and lamenting in the bitterest distress.
The beholders immediately flocked around, and, with
looks and expressions of the warmest compassion, gave
their help. A Churchman raised the man from the
ground by lifting him under the arms, while a Dis-
senter held his head and wiped his face with his handkerchief. A Roman Catholic lady took out her smell-
ing-bottle, and assiduously applied it to his nose. A
Methodist ran for a doctor. A Quaker supported and
comforted the woman, and a Baptist took care of the
children.

Edwin and his father were among the spectators.
Here (said Mr. Ambrose) is a thing in which *mankind
were made to agree.*

THE LANDLORD'S VISIT.

A DRAMA.

Scene.—*A Room in a Farm-house.* Betty, *the farmer's wife;* Fanny, *a young woman grown up;* Children, *of various ages, differently employed.*

Enter LANDLORD.

Landl. GOOD morning to you, Betty.

Betty. Ah! is it your honour? How do you do, sir? How are madam and all the good family?

Landl. Very well, thank you; and how are you, and all yours?

Betty. Thank your honour—all pretty well. Will you please to sit down? Ours is but a little crowded place, but there is a clean corner. Set out the chair for his honour, Mary.

Landl. I think everything is very clean. What, John's in the field, I suppose?

Betty. Yes, sir, with his two eldest sons, sowing and harrowing.

Landl. Well—and here are two, three, four, six; all the rest of your stock, I suppose. All as busy as bees!

Betty. Ay, your honour! These are not times to be idle in. John and I have always worked hard, and we bring up our children to work too. There's none of them, except the youngest, but can do something.

Landl. You do very rightly. With industry and sobriety there is no fear of their getting a living, come what may. I wish many gentlemen's children had as good a chance.

Betty. Lord, sir! if they have fortunes ready got for them, what need they care?

Landl. But fortunes are easier to spend than to get; and when they are at the bottom of the purse, what must they do to fill it again?

Betty. Nay, that's true, sir; and we have reason enough to be thankful that we are able and willing to work, and have a good landlord to live under.

Landl. Good tenants deserve good landlords; and I have been long acquainted with your value. Come, little folk, I have brought something for you.

[*Takes out cakes.*

Betty. Why don't you thank his honour?

Landl. I did not think you had a daughter so old as that young woman.

Betty. No more I have, sir. She is not my own daughter, though she is as good as one to me.

Landl. Some relation, then, I suppose?

Betty. No, sir, none at all.

Land. Who is she, then?

Betty (*whispering*). When she is gone out I will tell your honour.—(*Loud.*) Go, Fanny, and take some milk to the young calf in the stable. [*Exit* FANNY.

Landl. A pretty, modest-looking young woman, on my word!

Betty. Ay, sir, and as good as she is pretty. You must know, sir, that this young woman is a stranger, from a great way off. She came here quite by accident, and has lived with us above a twelvemonth. I'll tell your honour all about it, if you choose.

Landl. Pray do,—I am curious to hear it. But first favour me with a draught of your whey.

Betty. I beg your pardon, sir, for not offering it. Run, Mary, and fetch his honour some fresh whey in a clean basin. [MARY *goes.*

Landl. Now pray begin your story.

Betty. Well, sir, as our John was coming from work one evening, he saw at some distance on the road a carrier's waggon overturned. He ran up to help, and found a poor old gentlewoman lying on the bank much hurt, and this girl sitting beside her, crying. My good man, after he had helped in setting the waggon to rights, went to them, and with a good deal of difficulty got the gentlewoman into the waggon again, and walked by the side of it to our house. He called me out, and we got something comfortable for her; but she was so ill that she could not bear to be carried farther. So, after consulting awhile, we took her into the house, and put her to bed. Her head was sadly hurt, and she seemed to grow worse instead of better. We got a doctor to her, and did our best to nurse her, but all would not do, and we soon found that she was likely to die. Poor Fanny, her grand-daughter, never left her day or night; and it would have gone to your honour's heart to hear the pitiful moan she made over her. She was the only friend she had in the world, she said; and what would become of her if she were to lose her? Fanny's father and mother were both dead, and she was going with her grandmother into the north, where the old gentlewoman came from, to live cheap, and try to find out some relations. Well, to make my story short, in a few days the poor woman died. There was little more money about her than would serve to pay the doctor and bury her. Fanny was in sad trouble indeed. I thought she would never have left her grandmother's grave. She cried and wrung her hands most bitterly. But I tire your honour.

Landl. O no! I am much interested in your story.

Betty. We comforted her as well as we could; but all her cry was, " What will become of me?" " Where must I go?" " Who will take care of me?" So, after a while, said I to John, " Poor creature! my heart grieves for her. Perhaps she would like to stay with us; though she seems to have been brought up in a way of living different from ours, too; but what can she do, left to herself in the wide world?" So my husband agreed that I should ask her. When I mentioned it to her, poor thing! how her countenance altered. " O," said she, " I wish for nothing so much as to stay and live with you! I am afraid I can do but little to serve you, but, indeed, I will learn and do my best." Said I, " Do no more than you like; you are welcome to stay and partake with us as long as you please." Well, sir! she stayed with us; and set about learning to do all kind of our work with such good will, and so handily, that she soon became my best helper. And she is so sweet tempered, and so fond of us and the children, that I love her as well as though she were my own child. She has been well brought up, I am sure. She can read and write, and work with her needle, a great deal better than we can, and when work is over she teaches the children. Then she is extraordinarily well-behaved, so as to be admired by all that see her.—So your honour has now the story of our Fanny.

Landl. I thank you heartily for it, my good Betty! It does much credit both to you and Fanny. But, pray what is her surname?

Betty. It is—let me see—I think it is Welford.

Landl. Welford! that is a name I am acquainted with. I should be glad to talk with her a little.

Betty. I will call her in then.

Enter FANNY.

Landl. Come hither, young woman; I have heard your story, and been much interested by it. You are an orphan, I find.

Fanny. Yes, sir; a poor orphan.

Landl. Your name is Welford?

Fan. It is, sir.

Landl. Where did your parents live?

Fan. In London, sir; but they died when I was very young, and I went to my grandmother's, in Surrey.

Landl. Was she your father's mother? You will excuse my questions. I do not ask from idle curiosity.

Fan. She was, sir; and had been long a widow.

Landl. Do you know what her maiden name was?

Fan. It was Borrowdale, sir.

Landl. Borrowdale!—And pray whither were you going when the unfortunate accident happened?

Fan. To Kendal in Westmoreland, sir, near which my grandmother was born.

Landl. Ah! 'tis the very same—every circumstance corresponds! My dear Fanny (*taking her hand*), you have found a relation when you little thought of it. I am your kinsman. My mother was a Borrowdale of Westmoreland, and half-sister to your grandmother. I have heard of all your parentage; and I remember the death of your poor father, who was a very honest ingenious artist; and of your mother soon after, of a broken heart. I could never discover what family they left, nor what had become of my kinswoman. But I heartily rejoice I have found you out in this extraordinary manner. You must come and live with me. My wife and daughters will be very glad to receive one whose conduct has done her so much credit.

Fan. I am much obliged to you, sir, for your kindness; but I am too mean a person to live as a relation in a family like yours.

Landl. O no! you will not find us of that sort who despise worthy people for being low in the world; and your language and actions show that you have been well brought up.

Fan. My poor grandmother, sir, was so kind as to give me all the education in her power; and if I have not somewhat benefited by her example and instructions, it must have been my own fault.

Landl. You speak very well, and I feel more attached to you the more I hear you. Well—you must prepare to come home with me. I will take care to make proper acknowledgments to the good people here, who have been so kind to you.

Betty. My dear Fanny, I am heartily glad of your good fortune, but we shall all be sorry to part with you.

Fan. I am sure, my dear friend and mistress, I shall be sorry too. You received me when I had no other friend in the world, and have treated me like your own child. I can never forget what I owe you.

Enter JOHN, *and his eldest son* THOMAS.

John. Is your honour here?

Landl. Yes, John, and I have found somewhat worth coming for.

John. What is that, sir?

Land. A relation, John. This young woman, whom you have so kindly entertained, is my kinswoman.

John. What—our Fanny?

Thomas. Fanny!

Landl. Yes, indeed. And after thanking you for your kindness to her and her poor grandmother, I mean to take her home for a companion to my wife and daughters.

John. This is wonderful news indeed! Well, Fanny, I am very glad you have got such a home to go to—you are worthy of it—but we shall miss you much here.

Betty. So I have been telling her.

Thomas (aside to FANNY). What, will you leave us, Fanny? Must we part?

Fan. (aside to him). What can I do, Thomas?

Landl. There seems some unwillingness to part, I see, on more sides than one.

Betty. Indeed, sir, I believe there is. We have lived very happily together.

Thomas (aside to FANNY). I see we must part with you, but I hope—Surely you won't quite forget us?

Fan. (to him). You distress me, Thomas. Forget you! O no!

Landl. Come, I see there is something between the young folk that ought to be spoken about plainly. Do you explain it, Betty.

Betty. Why, your honour knows we could not tell that Fanny was your relation. So, as my son Thomas and she seemed to take a liking to one another, and she was such a good clever girl, we did not object to their thinking about making a match of it, as soon as he should be settled in a farm.

John. But that must be over now.

Thomas. Why so, father?

John. Why you can't think of his honour's kins-woman.

Landl. Come, Fanny, do you decide this affair.

Fan. Sir, Thomas offered me his service when he thought me a poor friendless girl, and I might think myself favoured by his notice. He gained my good-will, which no change of circumstances can make me withdraw. It is my determination to join my lot with his, be it what it may.

Thomas. My dearest Fanny. [*Taking her hand.*

Landl. You act nobly, my dear girl, and make me proud of my relation. You shall have my free consent and something handsome into the bargain.

Betty. Heaven bless your honour! I know it would have been a heart-breaking to my poor boy to have parted with her. Dear Fanny! [*Kisses her.*

Landl. I have a farm just now vacant. Thomas shall take it, and Fanny's portion shall stock it for him.

Thomas. I humbly thank your honour.

John. I thank you too, sir, for us all.

Fan. Sir, since you have been so indulgent in this matter, give me leave to request you to be satisfied with my paying my duty to the ladies, without going to live in a way so different from what I have been used to, and must live in hereafter. I think I can be nowhere better than with my friends and future parents here.

Landl. Your request, Fanny, has so much propriety and good sense in it, that I cannot refuse it. However, you must suffer us to improve our acquaintance. I assure you it will give me particular pleasure.

Fan. Sir, you will always command my most grateful obedience.

Landl. Well—let Thomas bring you to my house this afternoon, and I will introduce you to your relations, and we will talk over matters. Farewell, my dear! Nay, I must have a kiss.

Fan. I will wait on you, sir. [*Exit* Landlord.

Betty. My dear Fanny—daughter I may now call you—you cannot think how much I feel obliged to you.

Thomas. But who is so much obliged as I am?

Fan. Do you not all deserve everything from me?

John. Well, who could have thought when I went to help up the waggon, that it could have brought so much good luck to us?

Betty. A good deed is never lost, they say.

Fan. It shall be the business of my life to prove that this has not been lost.

ON EMBLEMS.

" PRAY, papa," said CECILIA, " what is an *emblem*? I have met with the word in my lesson to-day, and I do not quite understand it."

" An emblem, my dear," replied he, " is a visible image of an invisible thing."

C. A visible image of—I can hardly comprehend—

P. Well, I will explain it more at length. There are certain notions that we form in our minds without the help of our eyes, or any of our senses. Thus, Virtue, Vice, Honour, Disgrace, Time, Death, and the like, are not sensible objects, but ideas of the understanding.

C. Yes, we cannot feel them or see them, but we can think about them.

P. True. Now it sometimes happens that we wish to represent one of these in a visible form ; that is, to offer something to the sight that shall raise a similar notion in the minds of the beholders. In order to do this, we must take some action or circumstance belonging to it, capable of being expressed by painting or sculpture ; and this is called a *type* or *emblem*.

C. But how can this be done?

P. I will tell you by an example. You know the Sessions-house where trials are held. It would be easy to write over the door, in order to distinguish it, "This is the Sessions-house;" but it is a more ingenious and elegant way of pointing it out, to place upon the building a figure representing the purpose for which it was erected, namely, to distribute *justice*. For this end the notion of justice is to be *personified*, that is, changing from an idea of the understanding into one of the sight. A human figure is therefore made, distinguished by tokens which bear a relation to the character of that virtue. Justice carefully *weighs* both sides of a cause; she is therefore represented as holding a *pair of scales*. It is her office to *punish* crimes; she therefore bears a *sword*. This is then an *emblematical figure*, and the sword and scales are *emblems*.

C. I understand this very well. But why is she blindfolded?

P. To denote her impartiality—that she decides only from the merits of the case, and not from a view of the parties.

C. How can she weigh anything, though, when her eyes are blinded?

P. Well objected. These are two inconsistent emblems; each proper in itself, but when used together, making a contradictory action. An artist of judgment will therefore drop one of them; and accordingly the best modern figures of Justice have the balance and sword, without the bandage over the eyes.

C. Is there not the same fault in making Cupid blindfolded, and yet putting a bow and arrow into his hands?

P. There is. It is a gross absurdity, and not countenanced by the ancient descriptions of Cupid, who is represented as the surest of all archers.

C. I have a figure of *Death* in my fable-book. I suppose that is emblematical?

P. Certainly, or you could not know that it meant Death. How is he represented ?

C. He is nothing but bones, and he holds a scythe in one hand and an hour-glass in the other.

P. Well, how do you interpret these emblems ?

C. I suppose he is all bones, because nothing but bones are left after a dead body has lain long in the grave.

P. True. This, however, is not so properly an emblem, as the real and visible effect of death. But the scythe ?

C. Is not that because death mows down every thing ?

P. It is. No instrument could so properly represent the wide wasting sway of death, which sweeps down the race of animals, like flowers falling under the hand of the mower. It is a simile used in the Scriptures.

C. The hour-glass, I suppose, is to show people their time is come ?

P. Right. In the hour-glass that Death holds, all the sand is run out from the upper to the lower part. Have you never observed upon a monument an old figure, with wings, and a scythe, and with his head bald all but a single lock before ?

C. O yes; and I have been told it is *Time.*

P. Well—and what do you make of it ? Why is he old ?

C. O ! because time has lasted a long while.

P. And why has he wings ?

C. Because time is swift, and flies away.

P. What does his scythe mean ?

C. I suppose that is, because he destroys and cuts down everything, like Death.

P. True. I think, however, a weapon rather slower in its operation, as a pick-axe, would have been more suitable to the gradual action of time. But what is his single lock of hair for ?

C. I have been thinking, and cannot make it out.

P. I thought that would puzzle you. It relates to time as giving *opportunity* for doing anything. It is to be seized as it presents itself, or it will escape, and cannot be recovered. Thus the proverb says, "Take Time by the forelock." Well—now you understand what emblems are ?

C. Yes, I think I do. I suppose the painted sugar-loaves over the grocer's shop, and the mortar over the apothecary's, are emblems too ?

P. Not so properly. They are only the pictures of things which are themselves the objects of sight, as the real sugar-loaf in the shop of the grocer, and the real mortar in that of the apothecary. However, an implement belonging to a particular rank or profession, is commonly used as an emblem to point out the man exercising that rank or profession. Thus a crown is considered as an emblem of a king ; a sword or spear, of a soldier ; an anchor, of a sailor ; and the like.

C. I remember Captain Heartwell, when he came to see us, had the figure of an anchor on all his buttons.

P. He had. That was the emblem or badge of his belonging to the navy.

C. But you told me that an emblem was a visible sign of an invisible thing ; yet a sea-captain is not an invisible thing.

P. He is not invisible as a man, but his profession is invisible.

C. I do not well understand that.

P. Profession is a *quality*, belonging equally to a number of individuals, howsoever different they may be in external form and appearance. It may be added or taken away without any visible change. Thus, if Captain Heartwell were to give up his commission, he would appear to you the same man as before. It is plain, therefore, that what in that case he had lost, namely, his profession, was a thing invisible. It is one of those ideas of the understanding which I before mentioned to you, as different from a sensible idea.

2 B

C. I comprehend it now.

P. I have got here a few emblematical pictures. Suppose you try whether you can find out their meaning.

C. Oh, yes—I should like that very well.

P. Here is a man standing on the summit of a steep cliff, and going to ascend a ladder which he has planted against a cloud.

C. Let me see!—that must be *Ambition*, I think.

P. How do you explain it?

C. He has got very high already, but he wants to be still higher: so he ventures up the ladder, though it is supported only by a cloud, and hangs over a precipice.

P. Very right. Here is now another man, hood-winked, who is crossing a raging torrent upon step-ping stones.

C. Then he will certainly fall in. I suppose he is one that runs into danger without considering whither he is going.

P. Yes; and you may call him *Fool-hardiness.* Do you see this hand coming out of a black cloud, and putting an extinguisher upon a lamp?

C. I do. If that lamp be the lamp of life, the hand that extinguishes it must be *Death.*

P. Very just. Here is an old half-ruined building, supported by props; and the figure of Time is sawing through one of the props.

C. That must be *Old age*, surely.

P. It is. The next is a man leaning upon a break-ing crutch.

C. I don't well know what to make of that.

P. It is intended for *Instability;* however, it might also stand for *False Confidence.* Here is a man poring over a sun-dial, with a candle in his hand.

C. I am at a loss for that too.

P. Consider—a sun-dial is made only to tell the hour by the light of the sun.

C. Then this man must know nothing about it.

P. True· and his name is therefore *Ignorance.*

Here is a walking-stick, the lower part of which is set in the water, and it appears crooked. What does that denote?

C. Is the stick really crooked?

P. No; but it is the property of water to give that appearance.

C. Then it must signify *Deception*.

P. It does. I dare say you will at once know this fellow who is running as fast as his legs will carry him, and looking back at his shadow.

C. He must be *Fear* or *Terror*, I fancy.

P. Yes; you may call him which you please. But who is this sower, that scatters seed in the ground?

C. Let me consider. I think there is a parable in the Bible about seed sown, and it there signifies something like *Instruction*.

P. True; but it may also represent *Hope*, for no one would sow without hoping to reap the fruit. What do you think of this candle held before a mirror, in which its figure is exactly reflected?

C. I do not know what it means.

P. It represents *Truth;* the essence of which consists in the fidelity with which objects are received and reflected back by our minds. The object is here a luminous one, to show the clearness and brightness of Truth. Here is next an upright column, the perfect straightness of which is shown by a plumb-line hanging from its summit, and exactly parallel to the side of the column.

C. I suppose that must represent *Uprightness*.

P. Yes — or, in other words, *Rectitude*. The strength and stability of the pillar also denote the security produced by this virtue. You see here a woman disentangling and reeling off a very perplexed skein of thread.

C. She must have a great deal of patience.

P. True. She is *Patience* herself. The brooding hen, sitting beside her, is another emblem of the same quality that aids the interpretation. Whom do you

2 B 2

think this pleasing female is, that looks with such kindness upon the drooping plant she is watering.

C. That must be *Charity*, I believe.

P. It is; or you may call her *Benignity*, which is nearly the same thing. Here is a lady sitting demurely, with one finger on her lip, while she holds a bridle in her other hand.

C. The finger on the lip, I suppose, denotes Silence. The bridle must mean confinement. I should almost fancy her to be a school-mistress.

P. Ha! ha! I hope, indeed, many school-mistresses are endued with her spirit, for she is *Prudence* or *Discretion*. Well—we have now got to the end of our pictures, and upon the whole you have interpreted them very prettily.

C. But I have one question to ask you, papa! In these pictures, and others that I have seen of the same sort, almost all the *good* qualities are represented in the form of *women*. What is the reason of that?

P. It is certainly a compliment, my dear, either to woman's person or mind. The inventor either chose the figure of a female to clothe his agreeable quality in, because he thought that the more agreeable form, and therefore best suited it; or he meant to imply that the female character is really the more virtuous and amiable. I rather believe that the former was his intention, but I shall not object to your taking it in the light of the latter.

C. But is it true—is it true?

P. Why, I can give you very good authority for the preference of the female sex in a moral view. One Ledyard, a great traveller, who had walked through almost all the countries of Europe, and at last died in an expedition to explore the internal parts of Africa, gave a most decisive and pleasing testimony in favour of the superior character of women, whether savage or civilized. I was so much pleased with it, that I put great part of it into verse; and if it will

not make you vain, I will give you a copy of my
lines.

C. O, pray do!

P. Here they are. Read them.

LEDYARD'S PRAISE OF WOMEN.

THROUGH many a land and clime a ranger,
   With toilsome steps I've held my way,
A lonely unprotected stranger,
   To all the stranger's ills a prey.

While steering thus my course precarious,
   My fortune still has been to find
Men's hearts and dispositions various,
   But gentle Woman ever kind.

Alive to every tender feeling,
   To deeds of mercy ever prone;
The wounds of pain and sorrow healing,
   With soft compassion's sweetest tone.

No proud delay, no dark suspicion,
   Stints the free bounty of their heart;
They turn not from the sad petition,
   But cheerful aid at once impart.

Form'd in benevolence of nature,
   Obliging, modest, gay, and mild,
Woman's the same endearing creature
   In courtly town and savage wild.

When parched with thirst, with hunger wasted,
   Her friendly hand refreshment gave;
How sweet the coarsest food has tasted!
   What cordial in the simple wave!

Her courteous looks, her words caressing,
   Shed comfort on the fainting soul:
Woman's the stranger's general blessing
   From sultry India to the Pole.

TWENTY-SEVENTH EVENING.

GENEROUS REVENGE.

AT the period when the Republic of Genoa was divided between the factions of the nobles and the people, Uberto, a man of low origin, but of an elevated mind, and superior talents, and enriched by commerce, having raised himself to be head of the popular party, maintained for a considerable time a democratical form of government.

The nobles at length, uniting all their efforts, succeeded in subverting this state of things, and regained their former supremacy. They used their victory with considerable rigour; and in particular, having imprisoned Uberto, proceeded against him as a traitor, and thought they displayed sufficient lenity in passing a sentence upon him of perpetual banishment, and the confiscation of all his property. Adorno, who was then possessed of the first magistracy, a man haughty in temper, and proud of ancient nobility, though otherwise not void of generous sentiments, in pronouncing the sentence on Uberto, aggravated its severity, by the insolent terms in which he conveyed it. " You," said he,—" you, the son of a base mechanic, who have dared to trample upon the nobles of Genoa—you, by their clemency, are only doomed to shrink again into the nothing whence you sprang."

Uberto received his condemnation with respectful submission to the court; yet stung by the manner in which it was expressed, he could not forbear saying to Adorno, "that perhaps he might hereafter find cause to repent the language he had used to a man capable of sentiments as elevated as his own." He then made his obeisance, and retired; and, after taking leave of his friends, embarked in a vessel bound for Naples, and quitted his native country without a tear.

He collected some debts due to him in the Neapolitan dominions, and with the wreck of his fortune, went to settle on one of the islands in the Archipelago, belonging to the state of Venice. Here his industry and capacity in mercantile pursuits raised him in a course of years to greater wealth than he had possessed in his most prosperous days at Genoa; and his reputation for honour and generosity equalled his fortune.

Among other places which he frequently visited as a merchant, was the city of Tunis, at that time in friendship with the Venetians, though hostile to most of the other Italian states, and especially to Genoa. As Uberto was on a visit to one of the first men of that place, at his country-house, he saw a young Christian slave at work in irons, whose appearance excited his attention. The youth seemed oppressed with labour, to which his delicate frame had not been accustomed; and while he leaned at intervals upon the instrument with which he was working, a sigh burst from his full heart, and a tear stole down his cheek. Uberto eyed him with tender compassion, and addressed him in Italian. The youth eagerly caught the sounds of his native tongue, and replying to his inquiries, informed him that he was a Genoese. " And what is your name, young man?" said Uberto. " You need not be afraid of confessing to *me* your birth and condition." " Alas!" he answered, " I fear my captors already suspect enough to demand a large ransom. My father is, indeed, one of the first men in Genoa. His name is Adorno, and I am his only son." " Adorno!" Uberto checked himself from uttering more aloud, but to himself he cried, " Thank heaven! then I shall be nobly revenged."

He took leave of the youth and immediately went to inquire after the corsair captain, who claimed a right in young Adorno, and having found him, demanded the price of his ransom. He learned that he was considered as a captive of value, and that less than two thousand crowns would not be accepted. Uberto paid the sum; and causing his servant to follow him with a horse, and a complete suit of handsome apparel, he returned to the youth, who was working as before, and told him he was free. With his own hands he took off his fetters, and helped him to change his dress, and mount on horseback. The youth was tempted to think it all a dream, and the flutter of emotion almost deprived him of the power of returning thanks to his generous benefactor. He was soon, however, convinced of the reality of his good fortune, by sharing the lodging and table of Uberto.

After a stay of some days at Tunis, to despatch the remainder of his business, Uberto departed homewards, accompanied by young Adorno, who, by his pleasing manners, had highly ingratiated himself with him. Uberto kept him some time at his house, treating him with all the respect and affection he could have shown for the son of his dearest friend. At length, having a safe opportunity of sending him to Genoa, he gave him a faithful servant for a conductor, fitted him out with every convenience, slipped a purse of gold into one hand, and a letter into the other, and thus addressed him :—

" My dear youth, I could with much pleasure detain you longer in my humble mansion, but I feel your impatience to revisit your friends, and I am sensible that it would be cruelty to deprive them longer than necessary, of the joy they will receive in recovering you. Deign to accept this provision for your voyage, and deliver this letter to your father. *He* probably may recollect somewhat of me, though you are too young to do so. Farewell! I shall not soon forget you, and I will hope you will not forget me." Adorno poured out the effusions of a grateful and affectionate heart, and they parted with mutual tears and embraces.

The young man had a prosperous voyage home; and the transport with which he was again beheld by his almost heart-broken parents may more easily be conceived than described. After learning that he had been a captive in Tunis (for it was supposed that the ship in which he sailed had foundered at sea), "And to whom," said old Adorno, "am I indebted for the inestimable benefit of restoring you to my arms?" "This letter," said his son, "will inform you." He opened it, and read as follows:—

"That son of a vile mechanic, who told you, that one day you might repent the scorn with which you treated him, has the satisfaction of seeing his prediction accomplished. For know, proud noble! that the deliverer of your only son from slavery is

"*The banished Uberto.*"

Adorno dropped the letter, and covered his face with his hand, while his son was displaying in the warmest language of gratitude, the virtues of Uberto, and the truly paternal kindness he had experienced from him. As the debt could not be cancelled, Adorno resolved, if possible, to repay it. He made such powerful intercession with the other nobles, that the sentence pronounced on Uberto was reversed, and full permission given him to return to Genoa. In apprising him of this event, Adorno expressed his sense of the obligations he lay under to him, acknowledged the genuine nobleness of his character, and requested his friendship. Uberto returned to his country, and closed his days in peace, with the universal esteem of his fellow-citizens.

THE POWER OF HABIT.

WILLIAM was one day reading in a book of travels to his father, when he came to the following relation:—

"The Andes, in South America, are the highest ridge of mountains in the known world. There is a road over them, on which, about half way between the summit and the foot, is a house of entertainment, where it is common for travellers in their ascent and descent to meet. The difference in their feelings upon the same spot is very remarkable. They who are descending the mountain are melting with heat; so that they can scarcely bear any clothes upon them; while they who are ascending, shiver with cold, and wrap themselves up in the warmest garments they have."

"How strange this is," cried William. "What can be the reason of it?"

"It is," replied his father, "a striking instance of the *power of habit* over the body. The cold is so intense on the tops of these mountains, that it is as much as travellers can do to keep themselves from being frozen to death. Their bodies, therefore, become so habituated to the sensation of cold, that every diminution of it as they descend seems to them a degree of actual heat; and when they have got half way down, they feel as though they were quite in a sultry climate. On the other hand, the valleys at the foot of the mountains are so excessively hot, that the body becomes relaxed, and sensible to the slightest degree of cold; so that when a traveller ascends from them towards the hills, the middle regions seem quite inclement from their coldness."

"And is the same change," rejoined William, "always perceptible in crossing high mountains?"

"It is," returned his father, "in a degree proportioned to their height, and the time taken in crossing them. Indeed, a short time is sufficient to produce similar effects. Let one boy have been playing at rolling snowballs, and another have been roasting himself before a great fire, and let them meet in the porch of the house;—if you ask them how they feel, I will answer for it you will find them as different in their accounts as the travellers on the Andes. But this is only one example of the operation of a universal principle belonging to human nature; for the power of habit is the same thing, whatever be the circumstance which calls it forth, whether relating to the mind or the body.

"You may consider the story you have been reading as a sort of simile or parable. The central station on the mountain may be resembled to *middle life*. With what different feelings is this regarded by those who bask in the sunshine of opulence, and those who shrink under the cold blasts of penury!

"Suppose the wealthy duke, our neighbour, were suddenly obliged to descend to our level, and live as we do—to part with all his carriages, sell his coach-horses and hunters, quit his noble seat with its fine park and gardens, dismiss all his train of servants except two or three, and take a house like ours. What a dreadful fall would it seem to him! how wretched would it probably make him, and how much would he be pitied by the world!

"On the other hand, suppose the labourer who lives in the next cottage were unexpectedly to fall heir to an estate of a few hundreds a year, and in consequence to get around him all the comforts and conveniences that we possess—a commodious house to inhabit, good clothes to wear, plenty of wholesome food and firing, servants to do all the drudgery of the family, and the like;—how all his acquaintance would congratulate him, and what a paradise would he seem to himself to be got into! Yet he, and the duke, and ourselves, are equally *men*, made liable by nature to the same desires and necessities, and perhaps all equally strong in constitution, and equally capable of supporting hardships. Is not this fully as wonderful a difference in feeling as that on crossing the Andes?"

"Indeed it is," said William.

"And the cause of it must be exactly the same—the influence of habit."

"I think so."

"Of what importance, then, must it be towards a happy life, to regulate our habits so that in the possible changes of this world we may be more likely to be gainers than losers!"

"But how can this be done? Would it be right for the duke to live like us, or us like the labourer?"

" Certainly not. But to apply the case to persons of our middle condition, I would have us use our advantages in so frugal a manner, as to make them as little as possible essential to our happiness, should fortune sink us to a lower station. For as to the chance of rising to a higher, there is no need to prepare our habits for that—we should readily enough accommodate our feelings to such a change. To be pleased and satisfied with simple food, to accustom ourselves not to shrink from the inclemencies of the seasons, to avoid indolence, and take delight in some useful employment of the mind or body, to do as much as we can for ourselves, and not expect to be waited upon on every small occasion—these are the habits which will make us in some measure independent of fortune, and secure us a moderate degree of enjoyment under every change short of absolute want. I will tell you a story to this purpose.

" A London merchant had two sons, James and Richard. James from a boy accustomed himself to every indulgence in his power, and when he grew up was quite a fine gentleman. He dressed expensively, frequented public diversions, kept his hunter at a livery stable, and was a member of several convivial clubs. At home, it was almost a footman's sole business to wait on him. He would have thought it greatly beneath him to buckle or tie his own shoes; to pull on his boots, without assistance; and if he wanted anything at the other end of the room, he would ring the bell, and bring a servant up two pair of stairs, rather than rise from his chair to fetch it. He did a little business in the counting-house on forenoons, but devoted all his time after dinner to indolence and amusement.

" Richard was a very different character. He was plain in his appearance, and domestic in his way of life. He gave as little trouble as possible, and would have been ashamed to ask assistance in doing what he could easily do for himself. He was assiduous in business, and employed his leisure hours chiefly in reading and acquiring useful knowledge.

"Both were still young and unsettled when their father died, leaving behind him very little property. As the young men had not capital sufficient to follow the same line of mercantile business in which he had been engaged, they were obliged to look out for a new plan of maintenance; and a great reduction of expense was the first thing requisite. This was a severe stroke to James, who found himself at once cut off from all the pleasures and indulgences to which he was so habituated, that he thought life of no value without them. He grew melancholy and dejected, hazarded all his little property in lottery tickets, and was quite beggared. Still unable to think of retrieving himself by industry and frugality, he accepted a commission in a newly-raised regiment ordered for the West Indies, where, soon after his arrival, he caught a fever and died.

"Richard, in the mean time, whose comforts were little impaired by this change of situation, preserved his cheerfulness, and found no difficulty in accommodating himself to his fortune. He engaged himself as clerk in a house his father had been connected with, and lived as frugally as possible upon his salary. It furnished him with decent board, lodging, and clothing, which was all he required, and his hours of leisure were nearly as many as before. A book or a sober friend always sufficed to procure him an agreeable evening. He gradually rose in the confidence of his employers, who increased from time to time his salary and emoluments. Every increase was a source of gratification to him, because he was able to enjoy pleasures which, however, habit had not made necessary to his comfort. In process of time he was enabled to settle for himself, and passed through life in the enjoyment of that modest competence which best suited his disposition."

THE COST OF A WAR.

" You may remember, Oswald," said Mr. B. to his son, "that I gave you some time ago a notion of *the price of a victory* to the poor souls engaged in it."

" I shall not soon forget it, I assure you, sir," replied Oswald.

Father. Very well. I mean now to give you some idea of *the cost of a war* to the people among whom it is carried on. This may serve to abate something of the admiration with which historians are apt to inspire us for great warriors and conquerors. You have heard, I doubt not, of Louis the Fourteenth, King of France ?

Os. O yes !

F. He was entitled by his subjects *Louis le Grand,* and was compared by them to the Alexanders and Cæsars of antiquity ; and with some justice as to the extent of his power, and the use he made of it. He was the most potent prince of his time ; commanded mighty and victorious armies, and enlarged the limits of his hereditary dominions. Louis was not naturally a hard-hearted man ; but having been taught from his cradle that everything ought to give way to the interests of his glory, and that this glory consisted in domineering over his neighbours, and making conquests, he grew to be insensible to all the miseries brought on his own and other people in pursuit of what he thought this noble design. Moreover, he was plunged in dissolute pleasures, and the delights of pomp and splendour from his youth ; and he was ever surrounded by a tribe of abject flatterers, who made him believe that he had a full right in all cases to do as he pleased. Conquest abroad and pleasure at home were therefore the chief business of his life.

One evening, his minister, Louvois, came to him and said, " Sire, it is absolutely necessary to make a desert of the *Palatinate.*"

This is a country in Germany, on the banks of the Rhine, one of the most populous and best cultivated districts in that empire, filled with towns and villages, and industrious inhabitants.

"I should be sorry to do it," replied the King, "for you know how much odium was cast upon us throughout Europe when a part of it was laid waste some time ago, under Marshal Turenne."

"It cannot be helped, sire," returned Louvois. "All the damage he did has been repaired, and the country is as flourishing as ever. If we leave it in its present state, it will afford quarters to your Majesty's enemies, and endanger your conquests. It must be entirely ruined—the good of the service will not permit it to be otherwise."

"Well, then," answered Louis, "if it must be so, you are to give orders accordingly." So saying, he left the cabinet, and went to assist at a magnificent festival given in honour of his favourite mistress by a prince of the blood.

The pitiless Louvois lost no time; but despatched a courier that very night, with positive orders to the French generals in the Palatinate to carry fire and desolation through the whole country—not to leave a house or a tree standing—and to expel all the inhabitants.

It was the midst of a rigorous winter.

Os. Oh, horrible! But surely the generals would not obey such orders?

F. What! a general disobey the commands of his sovereign! that would be contrary to every maxim of the *trade*. Right and wrong are no considerations to a military man. He is only to do as he is bidden. The French generals who were upon the spot, and must see with their own eyes all that was done, probably felt somewhat like men on the occasion; but the sacrifice to their duty as soldiers was so much the greater. The commands were peremptory, and they were obeyed to a tittle. Towns and villages were burnt to the ground; vineyards and orchards were cut down and rooted up; sheep and cattle were killed; all the fair works of ages were destroyed in a moment; and the smiling face of culture was turned to a dreary waste.

The poor inhabitants were driven from their warm and comfortable habitations into the open fields, to confront all the inclemencies of the season. Their furniture was burnt or pillaged, and nothing was left them but the clothes on their backs, and the few necessaries they could carry with them. The roads were covered with trembling fugitives, going they knew not whither, shivering with cold, and pinched with hunger. Here an old man, dropping with fatigue, lay down to die—there a woman, with a new-born infant, sank perishing on the snow, while her husband hung over them in all the horror of despair.

Os. Oh, what a scene! Poor creatures! what became of them at last?

F. Such of them as did not perish on the road got to the neighbouring towns, where they were received with all the hospitality that such calamitous times would afford; but they were beggared for life. Meantime, their country, for many a league around, displayed no other sight than that of black, smoking ruins, in the midst of silence and desolation.

Os. I hope, however, that such things do not often happen in war.

F. Not often, perhaps, to the same extent; but, in some degree, they must take place in every war. A village which would afford a favourable post to the enemy is always burnt without hesitation. A country which can no longer be maintained, is cleared of all its provision and forage before it is abandoned, lest the enemy should have the advantage of them; and the poor inhabitants are left to subsist as they can. Crops of corn are trampled down by armies in their march, or devoured while green, as fodder for their horses. Pillage, robbery, and murder are always going on in the outskirts of even the best disciplined camp. Then, consider what must happen in every siege. On the first approach of the enemy, all the buildings in the suburbs of a town are demolished, and all the trees in gardens and public walks are cut down, lest they should afford shelter to the besiegers. As the siege goes on, bombs, hot balls, and cannon-shot are continually flying about, by which the greater part of a town is ruined or laid in ashes, and many of the innocent people are killed or maimed. If the resistance be obstinate, famine and pestilence are sure to occur; and if the garrison hold out to the last, and the town be taken by storm, it is generally given up to be pillaged by the enraged and licentious soldiery.

It would be easy to bring too many examples of cruelty exercised upon a conquered country, even in very late times, when war is said to be carried on with so much humanity; but, indeed, how can it be otherwise? The art of war is essentially that of destruction, and it is impossible there should be a mild and merciful way of murdering and ruining one's fellow-creatures. Soldiers, as men, are often humane; but war must ever be cruel. Though Homer has filled his Iliad with the exploits of fighting heroes, yet he makes Jupiter address Mars, the God of War, in terms of the utmost abhorrence.

> " Of all the gods who tread the spangled skies,
> Thou most unjust, most odious in our eyes!
> Inhuman discord is thy dire delight,
> The waste of slaughter, and the rage of fight;
> No bound, no law, thy fiery temper quells."—*Pope.*

Os. Surely, as war is so bad a thing, there might be some way of preventing it.

F. Alas! I fear mankind have been too long accustomed to it, and it is too agreeable to their bad passions, easily to be laid aside, whatever miseries it may bring upon them. But, in the meantime, let us correct our own ideas of the matter, and no longer, lavish admiration upon such a pest of the human race as a *Conqueror*, how brilliant soever his qualities may be; nor ever think that a profession which binds a man to be the servile instrument of cruelty and injustice is an *honourable* calling. War is defensible only when opposed to the aggression of an enemy by whom our country and all that is dear to us might be enslaved or destroyed.

TWENTY-EIGHTH EVENING.

GREAT MEN.

"I WILL show you a *great man*," said Mr. C. one day to his son, at the time the Duke of Bridgewater's canal was making. He accordingly took him to a place where a number of workmen were employed in raising a prodigious mound, on the top of which the canal was to be carried across a deep valley. In the midst of them was a very plainly dressed man, awkward in his gestures, uncouth in his appearance, and rather heavy in his countenance—in short, a mere countryman like the rest. He had a plan in his hand, and was giving directions to the people round him, and surveying the whole labour with profound attention. "This Arthur," said Mr. C. " is the *great* Mr. Brindley."

"What," cried Arthur, in surprise. "is that a *great man ?*"

Mr. C. Yes, a very great man. Why are you surprised?

A. I don't know, but I should have expected a great man to look very differently.

Mr. C. It matters little how a man may look, if he can perform great things. That person, without any advantages of education, has become, by the force of his own genius, the first engineer of the age. He is doing things that were never done, or even thought of, in this country before. He pierces hills, builds bridges over valleys, makes aqueducts across navigable rivers, and in short is likely to change the whole face of the country, and to introduce improvements the value of which cannot be calculated. When at a loss how to bring about any of his designs, he does not go to other people for assistance, but he consults the wonderful faculties of his own mind, and finds a way to overcome his difficulties. He looks like a rustic, it is true, but he has a soul of the first order, such as is not granted to one out of millions of the human race.

A. But are all men of extraordinary abilities, properly *great men?*

Mr. C. The word has been variously used; but I would call every one a great man *who does great things by means of his own powers.* Great abilities are often employed about trifles, or indolently wasted without any considerable exertion at all. To make a great man, the object pursued should be large and important, and vigour and perseverance should be employed in the pursuit.

A. All the great men I remember to have read about were kings, or generals, or prime ministers, or in some high station or other.

Mr. C. It is natural they should stand foremost in the list of great men, because the sphere in which they act is an extensive one, and what they do has a powerful influence over numbers of mankind. Yet those who invent useful arts, or discover important truths which may promote the comfort and happiness of unborn generations in the most distant parts of the world, act a still more important part; and their claim to merit is generally more undoubted than that of the former, because what they do is more certainly their own.

In order to estimate the real share a man in a high station has had in the great events which have been attributed to him, strip him, in your imagination, of all the external advantages of rank and power, and see what a figure he would have made without them—or

2 c 2

fancy a common man put in his place, and judge whether affairs would have gone on in the same track. Augustus Cæsar and Louis XIV. of France, have both been called great princes; but deprive them of their crowns, and they will both dwindle into obscure and trivial characters. But no change of circumstances could reduce Alfred the Great to the level of a common man. The two former could sink into their graves, and yield their power to a successor, and scarcely be missed; but Alfred's death changed the fate of his kingdom. Thus with Epaminondas fell all the glory and greatness of the Theban state. He first raised it to consequence, and it could not survive him.

A. Was not Czar Peter a great man?

Mr. C. I am not sure that he deserves that title. Being a despotic prince, at the head of a vast empire, he could put into execution whatever plans he was led to adopt, and these plans in general were grand and beneficial to his country. But the means he used were such as the master of the lives and fortunes of millions could easily employ, and there was more of brute force than of skill and judgment in the manner in which he pursued his designs. Still he was an *extraordinary* man; and the resolution of leaving his throne, in order to acquire in foreign countries the knowledge necessary to rescue his own from barbarism, was a feature of greatness. A truly great prince, however, would have employed himself better than in learning to build ships at Saardam or at Deptford. Allowance, however, must be made for the age in which he lived.

A. What was Alexander the Great?

Mr. C. A great conqueror, but not a great man. It was easy for him, with the well-disciplined army of Greeks, which he received from his father Philip, to overrun the unwarlike kingdoms of Asia, and defeat the Great King, as the king of Persia was called; but though he showed some marks of an elevated mind, he seems to have possessed few qualities which could have raised him to distinction had he been born in an humble station. Compare his fugitive grandeur, supported by able ministers and generals, to the power which his tutor, the great Aristotle, merely through the force of his own genius, exercised over men's minds throughout the most civilized part of the world for two thousand years after his death. Compare also the part which has been acted in the world by the Spanish monarchs, the masters of immense possessions in Europe and America, to that by Christopher Columbus, the Genoese navigator, who could have it inscribed on his tomb-stone, that he *gave* a new world to the kingdoms of Castile and Aragon. These comparisons will teach you to distinguish between greatness of character and greatness of station, which are too often confounded. He who governs a great country may in one sense be called a great king; but this is no more than an appellation belonging to rank, like that of the Great Mogul, or the Grand Seignior, and infers no more personal grandeur than the title of Mr. Such-a-one, as the Great Grocer or Great Brewer.

A. Must not great men be good men, too ?

Mr. C. If that man be great who does great things, it will not follow that goodness must necessarily be one of his qualities, since that chiefly refers to the end and intention of actions. Julius Cæsar, and Cromwell, for example, were men capable of the greatest exploits; but directing them not to the public good, but to the purposes of their own ambition, in pursuit of which they violated all the duties of morality, they have obtained the title of *great bad men*. A person, however, cannot be great at all without possessing many virtues. He must be firm, steady, and diligent, superior to difficulties and dangers, and equally superior to the allurements of ease and pleasure. For want of these moral qualities, many persons of exalted minds and great talents have failed to deserve the title of great men. It is in vain that the French poets and historians have decorated Henry the Fourth with the appellation of Great; his facility of disposition and uncontrollable love of pleasure have caused him to forfeit his claim to it in the estimation of impartial judges. As power is essential to greatness, a man cannot be great without *power over himself*, which is the highest kind of power.

A. After all, is it not better to be a good man than a great one?

Mr. C. There is more merit in being a good man, because it is what we make ourselves, whereas, the talents that produce greatness are the gift of nature; though they may be improved by our own efforts, they cannot be acquired. But if goodness be the proper object of our love and esteem, greatness deserves our high admiration and respect. This Mr. Brindley before us is, by all accounts, a worthy man, but it is not for this reason I have brought you to see him. I wish you to look upon him as one of those sublime and uncommon objects of nature, which fill the mind with a certain awe and astonishment. Next to being great oneself, it is desirable to have a true relish for greatness.

THE FOUR SISTERS.

I AM one of four sisters; and having some reason to think myself not well used either by them or by the world, I beg leave to lay before you a sketch of our history and characters. You will not wonder there should be frequent bickerings amongst us, when I tell you, that in our infancy we were continually fighting; and so great were the noise, and din, and confusion, in our continual struggles to get uppermost, that it was impossible for anybody to live amongst us, in such a scene of tumult and disorder. These brawls, however, by a powerful interposition, were put an end to; our proper place was assigned to each of us, and we had strict orders not to encroach on the limits of each other's property, but to join our common offices for the good of the whole family.

My first sister (I call her the first, because we have generally allowed her the precedence in rank) is, I must acknowledge, of a very active, sprightly disposition; quick and lively, and has more brilliancy than either of us; but she is hot: everything serves for fuel to her fury, when it is once raised to a certain degree, and she is so mischievous whenever she gets the upper hand, that, notwithstanding her aspiring disposition, if I may freely speak my mind, she is calculated to make a good servant, but a very bad mistress.

I am almost ashamed to mention, that, notwithstanding her seeming delicacy, she has a most voracious appetite, and devours every thing that comes in her way; though, like other eager, thin people, she does no credit to her keeping. Many a time has she consumed the product of my barns and storehouses, but it is all lost upon her. She has even been known to get into an oil-shop, or tallow-chandler's, when every body was asleep, and lick up, with the utmost greediness, whatever she found there. Indeed, all prudent people are aware of her tricks, and though she is admitted into the best families, they take care to watch her very narrowly. I should not forget to mention, that my sister was once in a country where she was treated with uncommon respect; she was lodged in a sumptuous building, and had a number of young women of the best families to attend on her, and feed her, and watch over her health: in short, she was looked upon as something more than a common mortal. But she always behaved with great severity to her maids, and if any of them were negligent of their duty, or made a slip in their own conduct, nothing would serve her but burying the poor girls alive. I have myself had some dark hints and intimations from the most respectable authority, that she will, some time or other, make an end of me. You need not wonder, therefore, if I am jealous of her motions.

The next sister I shall mention to you, has so far the appearance of Modesty and Humility, that she generally seeks the lowest place. She is, indeed, of a very yielding, easy temper, generally cool, and often wears a sweet, placid smile upon her countenance; but she is easily ruffled, and when worked up, as she often is, by another sister, whom I shall mention to you by and by, she becomes a perfect fury. Indeed, she is so apt to swell with sudden gusts of passion, that she is suspected at times to be a little lunatic. Between her and my first mentioned sister, there is a more settled antipathy than between the Theban pair, and they never meet without making efforts to destroy one another. With me she is always ready to form the most intimate union, but it is not always to my advantage. There goes a story in our family, that when we were all young, she once attempted to drown me. She actually kept me under a considerable time, and though at length I got my head above water, my constitution is generally thought to have been essentially injured by it ever since. From that time she has made no such atrocious attempt, but she is continually making encroachments upon my property, and even when she appears most gentle, she is very insidious, and has such an undermining way with her, that her insinuating arts are as much to be dreaded as open violence. I might, indeed, remonstrate, but it is a known part of her character, that nothing makes any lasting impression upon her.

As to my third sister, I have already mentioned the ill offices she does me with my last-mentioned one, who is entirely under her influence. She is, besides, of a very uncertain, variable temper, sometimes hot, and sometimes cold, nobody knows where to have her. Her lightness is even proverbial, and she has nothing to give those who live with her more substantial than the smiles of courtiers. I must add, that she keeps in her service three or four rough blustering bullies, with puffed cheeks, who, when they are let loose, think they have nothing to do but drive the world before them. She sometimes joins with my first sister, and their violence occasionally throws me into such a trembling, though naturally of a firm constitution, I shake as though I were in an ague fit.

As to myself, I am of a steady, solid temper, not shining, indeed, but kind and liberal; quite a Lady Bountiful. Every one tastes of my beneficence, and I am of so grateful a disposition, that I have been known to return a hundred-fold for any present that has been made me. I feed and clothe all my children, and afford a welcome home to the wretch who has no other. I bear with unrepining patience all manner of ill usage: I am trampled upon; I am torn and wounded with the most cutting strokes; I am pillaged of the treasures hidden in my most secret chambers; notwithstanding which, I am always ready to return good for evil, and am continually subservient to the pleasure or advantage of others; yet, so ungrateful is the world, that because I do not possess all the airiness and activity of my sisters, I am stigmatized as dull and heavy. Every sordid, miserable fellow is called, by way of derision, one of *my* children; and if a person, on entering the room, do but turn his eyes upon me, he is thought stupid and mean, and not fit for good company. I have the satisfaction, however, of finding that people always incline towards me as they grow older; and that they who seemed proudly to disdain any affinity with me, are content to sink at last into my bosom. You will, probably, wish to have some account of my person. I am not a regular beauty; some of my features are rather harsh and prominent, when viewed separately; but my countenance has so much variety of expression, and so many different attitudes of elegance, that they who study my face with attention, find out continually new charms; and it may be truly said of me, what Titus says of his mistress, and for a much longer space,

"Pendant cinq ans entières tous les jours je la vois,
Et crois toujours la voir pour la première fois."

"For five whole years each day she meets my view,
Yet every day I seem to see her new."

Though I have been so long a mother, I have still a surprising air of youth and freshness, which is assisted by all the advantages of well-chosen ornament, for I dress well, and according to the season.

This is what I have chiefly to say of myself and my sisters. To a person of your sagacity it will be unnecessary for me to sign my name. Indeed, one who becomes acquainted with any one of the family, cannot be at a loss to discover the rest, notwithstanding the difference in our features and characters.

THE GAIN OF A LOSS.

PHILANDER possessed a considerable place about the court, which obliged him to live in a style of show and expense. He kept high company, made frequent entertainments, and brought up a family of several daughters, in all the luxurious elegance which his situation and prospects seemed to justify. His wife had balls and routs at her own house, and frequented all the places of fashionable amusement. After some years passed in this manner, a sudden change of parties threw Philander out of his employment, and at once ruined all his plans of future advancement. Though his place had been lucrative, the expense it led him into more than counterbalanced the profits; so that, instead of saving anything, he had involved himself considerably in debt. His creditors, on hearing of the change in his affairs, became so importunate, that, in order to satisfy them, he was compelled to sell a moderate paternal estate in a remote county, reserving nothing out of it but one small farm. Philander had strength of mind sufficient to enable him at once to decide on the best plan to be followed in his present circumstances; instead, therefore, of wasting his time and remaining property in fruitless attempts to interest his town friends in his favour, he sold off his fine furniture, and without delay carried down his whole family to the little spot he could still call his own, where he commenced a life of industry and strict frugality in the capacity of a small farmer. It was long before the female part of his household could accommodate themselves to a mode of living so new to them, and so destitute of all that they had been accustomed to regard as essential to their very existence. At length, however, mutual affection and natural good sense, and above all, necessity, brought them to acquiesce tolerably in their situation, and to engage in earnest in its duties. Occasional regrets, however, could not but remain; and the silent sigh would tell whither their thoughts had fled.

Philander perceived it, but took care never to embitter their feelings by harsh chidings or untimely admonitions. But on the anniversary of their taking possession of the farm-house, he assembled them under a spreading tree that grew before their little garden, and while the summer's sun gilded all the objects around, he thus addressed them :—

"My dear partners in every fortune, if the revolution of a year have had the effect on your mind that it has on mine, I may congratulate you on your condition. I am now able, with a firm tone, to ask myself, What have I lost? and I feel so much more to be pleased with than to regret, that the question gives me rather comfort than sorrow. Look at yon splendid luminary, and tell me if its gradual appearance above the horizon on a fine morning, shedding light and joy over the wide creation, be not a grander as well as a more heart-cheering spectacle than that of the most magnificent saloon, illuminated with dazzling lustres. Is not the spirit of the wholesome breeze, fresh from the mountain, and perfumed with wild flowers, infinitely more invigorating to the senses than the air of the crowded drawing-room, laden with scented powder and essences? Did we relish so well the disguised dishes with which a French cook strove to whet our sickly appetites, as we do our draught of new milk, our home-made loaf, and the other articles of our simple fare? Was our sleep so sweet after midnight suppers and the long vigils of cards, as it is now, that early rising and the exercises of the day prepare us for closing our eyes as soon as night has covered everything with her friendly veil? Shall we complain that our clothes at present answer only the purpose of keeping us warm, when we recollect all the care and pains it cost us to keep pace with the fashion, and the mortification we underwent at being outshone by our superiors in fortune? Did not the vexation of insolent and unfaithful servants overbalance the trouble we now find in waiting on ourselves? We may regret the loss of society; but, alas! what was the society of a crowd of visitors, who regarded us merely as the keepers of a place of public resort, and whom we visited with similar sensations? If we formerly could command leisure to cultivate our minds, and acquire polite accomplishments, did we, in reality, apply much leisure to these purposes, and is not our time now filled more to our satisfaction by employments of which we cannot doubt the usefulness?—not to say, that the moral virtues we are now called upon to exercise, afford the truest cultivation to our minds. What, then, have we lost? In improved health, the charms of a beautiful country, a decent supply of all real wants, and the love and kind offices of each other, do we not still possess enough for worldly happiness? We have lost, indeed, a certain rank and station in life; but have we not acquired another as truly respectable? We are debarred the prospects of future advancement; but if our present condition be a good one, why need we lament that it is likely to be lasting? The next anniversary will find us more in harmony with our situation than even the present. Look forward, then, cheerily. The storm is past. We have been shipwrecked, but we have only exchanged a cumbrous vessel for a light pinnace, and we are again on our course. Much of our cargo has been thrown overboard, but no one loses what he does not miss."

Thus saying, Philander tenderly embraced his wife and daughters. The tear stood in their eyes, but consolation beamed on their hearts.

WISE MEN.

" You may remember, Arthur," said Mr. C. to his son, " that some time ago, I endeavoured to give you a notion of what a *great man* was. Suppose we now talk a little about *wise men ?*"

" With all my heart, sir," replied Arthur.

Mr. C. A wise man, then, is *he who pursues the best ends by the properest means.* But as this definition may be rather too abstract to give you a clear comprehension of the thing, I shall open it to you by examples. What do you think is the best end a man can pursue in life ?

A. I suppose, to make himself happy.

Mr. C. True. And as we are so constituted that we cannot be happy ourselves without making others happy, the best end of living is to produce as much general happiness as lies in our power.

A. But that is *goodness*, is it not ?

Mr. C. It is ; and therefore wisdom includes goodness. The wise man always intends what is good, and employs skill or judgment in attaining it. If he were to pursue the best things weakly, he could not be wise, any more than though he were to pursue bad or indifferent things judiciously. One of the wisest men I know is our neighbour, Mr. Freeland.

A. What, the Justice ?

Mr. C. Yes. Few men have succeeded more perfectly in securing their own happiness, and promoting that of those around them. Born to a competent estate, he early settled upon it, and began to improve it. He reduced all his expenses within his income, and indulged no tastes that could lead him into excesses of any kind. At the same time he did not refuse any proper and innocent pleasures that came in his way ; and his house has always been distinguished for decent cheerfulness and hospitality. He applied himself with diligence to amending the morals and improving the condition of his dependants. He studied attentively the laws of his country, and qualified himself for administering justice with skill and fidelity. No one sooner discovers where the right lies, or takes surer means to enforce it. He is the person to whom the neighbours of all degrees apply for counsel in their difficulties. His conduct is always consistent and uniform—never violent—never rash, never in extremes, but always deliberating before he acts, and then acting with firmness and vigour. The peace and good order of the whole neighbourhood materially depend upon him; and upon every emergency his opinion is the first thing inquired after. He enjoys the respect of the rich, the confidence of the poor, and the good will of both.

A. But I have heard some people reckon old Harpy as wise a man as he.

Mr. C. It is a great abuse of words to call Harpy a wise man. He is of another species—a *cunning man*—who is to a wise man what an ape is to a human creature—a bad and contemptible resemblance.

A. He is very clever, though; is he not?

Mr. C. Harpy has a good natural understanding, a clear head, and a cool temper; but his only end in life has been to raise a fortune by base and dishonest means. Being thoroughly acquainted with all the tricks and artifices of the law, he employed his knowledge to take undue advantages of all who intrusted him with the management of their affairs; and under colour of assisting them, he contrived to get possession of all their property. Thus he has become extremely rich, lives in a great house with a number of servants, is even visited by persons of rank, yet is universally detested and despised, and has not a friend in the world. He is conscious of this, and is wretched. Suspicion and remorse continually prey upon his mind. Of all whom he has cheated, he has deceived himself the most; and has proved himself as much a fool in the end he has pursued, as a knave in the means.

A. Are not men of great learning and knowledge wise men ?

Mr. C. They are so, if that knowledge and learning are employed to make them happier and more useful. But it too often happens that their speculations are of a kind beneficial neither to themselves nor to others ; and they often neglect to regulate their tempers while they improve their understandings. Some men of great learning have been the most arrogant and quarrelsome of mortals, and as foolish and absurd in their conduct, as the most untaught of their species.

A. But is not a philosopher and a wise man the same thing ?

Mr. C. A philosopher is properly *a lover of wisdom ;* and if he search after it with a right disposition, he will probably find it oftener than other men. But he must practise as well as know, in order to be truly wise.

A. I have read of the seven wise men of Greece. What were they ?

Mr. C. They were men distinguished for their knowledge and talents, and some of them for their virtue too. But a wiser than them all was Socrates, whose chief praise it was that he turned philosophy from vain and fruitless disputation to the regulation of life and manners, and that he was himself a great example of the wisdom he taught.

A. Have we had any person lately very remarkable for wisdom ?

Mr. C. In my opinion, few wiser men have ever existed than the late Dr. Franklin, the American. From the low station of a journeyman printer, to the elevated one of ambassador plenipotentiary from his country to the court of France, he always distinguished himself by sagacity in discovering, and good sense in practising, what was most beneficial to himself and others. He was a great natural philosopher, and made some very brilliant discoveries; but it was ever his favourite purpose to turn everything to use, and to extract some practical advantage from his speculations. He thoroughly understood *common life*, and all that conduces to its comfort; and he has left behind him treasures of domestic wisdom, superior, perhaps, to any of the boasted maxims of antiquity. He never let slip any opportunity of improving his knowledge, whether of great things or of small; and was equally ready to converse with a day-labourer and a prime-minister upon topics from which he might derive instruction. He rose to wealth, but obtained it by honourable means. He prolonged his life by temperance to a great age, and enjoyed it to the last. Few men knew more than he, and none employed knowledge to better purposes. [There are those, however, who consider, and upon strong grounds, that Franklin was cold and calculating, selfish and heartless, in his general intercourse with mankind.—EDITOR.]

A. A man, then, I suppose, cannot be wise without knowing a great deal?

Mr. C. If a man be acquainted with everything belonging to his station, it is wisdom enough; and a peasant may be as truly wise in his place as a statesman or legislator. You remember that fable of Gay, in which a shepherd gives lessons of wisdom to a philosopher.

A. O yes—it begins

" Remote from cities lived a swain."

Mr. C. True. He is represented as drawing all his maxims of conduct from observation of brute animals, and they, indeed, have universally that character of wisdom, of pursuing the ends best suited to them by the properest means. But this is owing to the impulse of unerring instinct. Man has reason for his guide, and his wisdom can only be the consequence of the right use of his reason. This will lead him to virtue. Thus the fable we have been mentioning rightly concludes with

> " Thy fame is just, the sage replies,
> Thy *virtue* proves thee *truly wise.*"

TWENTY-NINTH EVENING.

A FRIEND IN NEED.

GEORGE CORNISH, a native of London, was brought up to the sea. After making several voyages to the East Indies in the capacity of mate, he obtained the command of a ship in the country trade there, and passed many years of his life in sailing from one port to another of the Company's different settlements, and residing at intervals on shore with the superintendents of their commercial concerns. Having by these means raised a moderate fortune, and being now beyond the meridian of life, he felt a strong desire of returning to his native country, and seeing his family and friends, concerning whom he had received no tidings for a long time. He realized his property, settled his affairs, and taking his passage for England, arrived in the Downs after an absence of sixteen years.

He immediately repaired to London, and went to the house of an only brother, whom he had left respectably established in a public office. He found that his brother was dead, and the family broken up; and he was directed to the house of one of his nieces, who was married and settled at a small distance from town. On making himself known, he was received with great respect and affection by the married niece, and a single sister, who resided with her. To this good reception, the idea of his bringing back with him a large fortune did not a little contribute. They pressed him in the most urgent manner to take up his abode there, and omitted nothing that could testify their dutiful regard to so near a relation. On his part, he was sincerely glad to see them, and presented them with some valuable Indian commodities which he had brought with him. They soon fell into conversation concerning the family events that had taken place during his long absence. Mutual condolences passed on the death of the father; the mother had been dead long before. The captain, in the warmth of his heart, declared his intention of befriending the survivors of the family, and his wishes of seeing the second sister as comfortably settled in the world as the first seemed to be.

"But," said he, "are you two the only ones left? What is become of my little smiling playfellow, Amelia? I remember her as though it were yesterday, coming behind my chair, and giving me a sly pull, and then running away that I might follow her for a kiss. I should be sorry if anything had happened to her."

"Alas! sir," said the elder niece, "she has been the cause of an infinite deal of trouble to her friends! She was always a giddy girl, and her misconduct has proved her ruin. It would be an advantage if we could all forget her!"

"What, then," said the uncle, "has she dishonoured herself? Poor creature!"

"I cannot say," replied the niece, "that she has done so in the worst sense of the word; but she has disgraced herself and her family by a hasty, foolish match with one beneath her, and it has ended, as might have been expected, in poverty and wretchedness."

"I am glad," returned the captain, "that it is no worse; for, though I much disapprove of improper matches, yet young girls may fall into still greater evils, and where there is no crime, there can be no irreparable disgrace. But who was the man, and what did my brother say to it?"

"Why, sir, I cannot say, but it was partly my father's own fault; for he took a sort of liking to the young man, who was a drawing-master employed in the family, and would not forbid him the house after we had informed him of the danger of an attachment between Amelia and him. So, when it was too late, he fell into a violent passion about it, which had no other effect than to drive the girl directly into her lover's arms. They married, and soon fell into difficulties. My father, of course, would do nothing for them; and when he died, he not only disinherited her, but made us promise no longer to look upon her as a sister."

"And you *did* make that promise?" said the captain, in a tone of surprise and displeasure.

"We could not disobey our parent," replied the other sister; "but we have several times sent her relief in her necessities, though it was improper for us to see her."

"And pray, what is become of her at last—where is she now?"

"Really, she and her husband have shifted their lodgings so often, that it is some time since we heard anything about them."

"Some time! how long?"

"Perhaps half a year, or more."

"Poor outcast!" cried the captain, in a sort of muttered half voice. "I have made no promise, however, to renounce thee. Be pleased, madam," he continued, addressing himself gravely to the married niece, "to favour me with the *last* direction you had to this unfortunate sister."

She blushed, and looked confused; and at length, after a good deal of searching, presented it to her uncle. "But, my dear sir," said she, "you will not think of leaving us to-day. My servant shall make all the inquiries you choose, and save you the trouble ; and to-morrow you can ride to town, and do as you think proper."

"My good niece," said the captain, "I am but an indifferent sleeper, and I am afraid things would run in my head, and keep me awake. Besides, I am naturally impatient, and love to do my business myself. You will excuse me." So saying, he took up his hat, and, without much ceremony, went out of the house, and took the road to town on foot, leaving his two nieces somewhat disconcerted.

When he arrived, he went without delay to the place mentioned, which was a by-street, near Soho. The people who kept the lodgings informed him that the persons he inquired after had left them several months, and they did not know what had become of them. This threw the captain into great perplexity ; but while he was considering what he should do next, the woman of the house recollected that Mr. Bland (that was the drawing-master's name) had been employed at a certain school, where information about him might possibly be obtained. Captain Cornish hastened away to the place, and was informed by the master of the school that such a person had, indeed, been engaged there, but had ceased to attend for some time past.

"He was a very well-behaved, industrious young man," added the master, "but in distressed circumstances, which prevented him from making that respectable appearance which we expect in all who attend our school; so I was obliged to dismiss him. It was a great force upon my *feelings*, I assure you, sir, to do so ; but you know the thing could not be helped."

The captain eyed him with indignant contempt, and said, "I suppose, then, sir, your *feelings* never suffered you to inquire where this poor creature lodged, or what became of him afterwards !"

"As to that," replied the master, " every man

knows his own business best, and my time is fully taken up with my own concerns; but I believe I have a note of the lodgings he then occupied—here it is."

The captain took it, and, turning on his heel, withdrew in silence.

He posted away to the place, but there, too, had the mortification of learning that he was too late. The people, however, told him that they believed he might find the family he was seeking in a neighbouring alley, at a lodging up three pair of stairs. The captain's heart sank within him; however, taking a boy as a guide, he proceeded immediately to the spot. On going up the narrow, creaking staircase, he met a man coming down with a bed on his shoulders. At the top of the landing stood another with a bundle of blankets and sheets. A woman, with a child in her arms, was expostulating with him, and he heard her exclaim, "Cruel! not to leave me *one* bed for myself and my poor children!"

"Stop," said the captain to the man, "set down those things." The man hesitated. The captain renewed his command in a peremptory tone; and then advanced towards the woman. They looked earnestly at each other. Through her pale and emaciated features, he saw something of his little smiler; and at length, in a faint voice, he addressed her,—

"Are you Amelia Cornish?"

"That *was* my name," she replied.

"I am your uncle," he cried, clasping her in his arms, and sobbing as though his heart would break.

"My uncle!" said she, and fainted.

He was just able to set her down on the only remaining chair, and take her child from her. Two other young children came running up, and began to scream with terror. Amelia recovered herself.

"Oh, sir, what a situation you see me in!"

"A situation, indeed!" said he. "Poor forsaken creature! but you have *one* friend left!"

He then asked what had become of her husband. She told him, that having fatigued himself with walking every day to a great distance, for a little employment, that scarcely afforded them bread, he had fallen ill, and was now in an hospital, and that, after having been obliged to sell most of their little furniture and clothes for present subsistence, their landlord had just seized their only remaining bed, for some arrears of rent. The captain immediately discharged the debt, and causing the bed to be brought up again, dismissed the man. He then entered into a conversation with his niece, about the events that had befallen her.

"Alas! sir," said she, "I am sensible I was greatly to blame in disobeying my father, and leaving his roof as I did; but, perhaps something might be alleged in my excuse—at least, years of calamity and distress may be an expiation. As to my husband, however, he has never given me the least cause of complaint—he has ever been kind and good, and what we have suffered has been through misfortune, and not fault. To be sure, when we married, we did not consider how a family was to be maintained. His was a poor employment, and sickness and other accidents soon brought us to a state of poverty, from which we could never retrieve ourselves. He, poor man! was never idle when he could help it, and denied himself every indulgence, in order to provide for the wants of his wife and the children. I did my part, too, as well as I was able. But my father's unrelenting severity made me quite heart-broken; and though my sisters two or three times gave us a little relief in our pressing necessities—for nothing else could have made me ask it in the manner I did,—yet they would never permit me to see them, and for some time past have entirely abandoned us. I thought heaven had abandoned us too.

The hour of extreme distress was come ; but *you* have been sent for our comfort."

"And your comfort, please God! I will be," cried the captain, with energy. "You are my own dear child, and your little ones shall be mine too. Dry up your tears—better days, I hope, are approaching."

Evening was now coming on, and it was too late to think of changing lodgings. The captain procured a neighbour to go out for some provisions and other necessaries, and then took his leave, with a promise of being with his niece early the next morning. Indeed, as he proposed going to pay a visit to her husband, she was far from wishing to detain him longer. He went directly from thence to the hospital, and having got access to the medical man in attendance, begged to be informed of the real state of his patient Bland. The gentleman told him that he laboured under a slow fever, attended with extreme dejection of spirits, but that there were no signs of urgent danger.

"If you will allow me to see him," said the captain, "I believe I shall be able to administer a cordial, more effectual, perhaps, than all your medicines."

He was shown up to the ward where the poor man lay, and seated himself by his bedside.

"Mr. Bland," said he, "I am a stranger to you, but I come to bring you some news of your family."

The sick man aroused himself, as it were, from a stupor, and fixed his eyes in silence on the captain.

He proceeded—"Perhaps you may have heard of an uncle that your wife had in the East Indies—he is come home, and—and—I am he."

Upon this he eagerly stretched out his hand, and taking that of Bland, which was thrust out of the bedclothes to meet it, gave it a cordial shake. The sick man's eyes glistened—he grasped the captain's hand, with all his remaining strength, and drawing it to his mouth, kissed it with fervour. All he could say, was, " God bless you!—be kind to poor Amelia !"

" I will—I will," cried the captain—" I will be a father to you all. Cheer up—keep up your spirits— all will be well!" He then, with a kind look, and another shake of the hand, wished him a good night, and left the poor man lightened at once of half his disease.

The captain went home to the coffee-house where he lodged, got a light supper, and went early to bed. After meditating some time with heartfelt satisfaction on the work of the day, he fell into a sweet sleep, which lasted till day-break. The next morning early he arose and sallied forth in search of furnished lodgings. After some inquiry, he met with a commodious set, in a pleasant airy situation, for which he agreed. He then drove to Amelia, and found her and her children neat and clean, and as well dressed as their poor wardrobe would admit. He embraced them with the utmost affection, and rejoiced Amelia's heart with a favourable account of her husband. He then told them to prepare for a ride with him. The children were overjoyed at the proposal, and they accompanied him down to the coach in high spirits. Amelia scarcely knew what to think or expect. They drove first to a warehouse for ready-made linen, where the captain made Amelia furnish herself with a complete set of everything necessary for present use, for the children and herself, not forgetting some shirts for her husband. Thence they went to a clothes-shop, where the little boy was supplied with a jacket and trowsers, a hat and great coat, and the girl with another great coat and a bonnet—both were made as happy as happy could be. They were next all furnished with new shoes. In short, they had not proceeded far, before the mother and three children were all in complete new habiliments, decent but not fine ; while the old ones were all tied up in a great bundle, and destined for some family still poorer than they had been.

The captain then drove to the lodgings he had taken, and which he had directed to be put in thorough order. He led Amelia up stairs, who knew not whither she was going. He brought her into a handsome room, and seated her in a chair.

"This, my dear," said he, "is your home. I hope you will let me now and then come and see you in it."

Amelia turned pale, and could not speak. At length a flood of tears came to her relief, and she suddenly threw herself at her uncle's feet, and poured out thanks and blessings in a broken voice.

He raised her, and kindly kissing her and her children, slipped a purse of gold into her hand, and hurried down stairs.

He next went to the hospital, and found Mr. Bland sitting up in bed, and taking some food with apparent pleasure. He sat down by him.

"God bless you, sir!" said Bland, "I see now it is all a reality, and not a dream. Your figure has been haunting me all night, and I have scarcely been able to satisfy myself whether I had really seen and spoken to you, or whether it were a fit of delirium. Yet my spirits have been lightened, and I have now been eating with a relish I have not experienced for many days past. But may I ask, how is my poor Amelia, and my little ones?"

"They are well and happy, my good friend," said the captain; "and I hope you will soon be so along with them."

The medical gentleman came up, and felt his patient's pulse.

"You are a skilful doctor, indeed, sir," said he to Captain Cornish; "you have cured the poor man of his fever. His pulse is as calm as my own."

The captain consulted him about the safety of removing him ; and he said he thought there would be no hazard in the removal that very day. The captain awaited the arrival of the physician, who confirmed that opinion. A sedan chair was procured, and full directions being obtained for his future treatment, with the physician's promise to look after him, the captain walked before the chair to the new lodgings. On the knock at the door, Amelia looked out of the window, and seeing the chair, ran down, and met her uncle and husband in the passage. The poor man, not knowing where he was, and gazing wildly around him, was carried up stairs, and placed upon a good bed, while his wife and children assembled round it. A glass of wine restored him to his recollection, when a most tender scene ensued, which the uncle closed as soon as he could, for fear of too much agitating the yet feeble organs of the sick man.

By Amelia's constant attention, assisted by proper help, Mr. Bland shortly recovered ; and the whole family lost their sickly, emaciated appearance, and became healthy and happy. The kind uncle was never long absent from them, and was always received with looks of pleasure and gratitude that penetrated his very soul. He obtained for Mr. Bland a good engagement in the exercise of his profession, and took Amelia and her children into his special care. As to his other nieces, though he did not entirely break off his connection with them, but, on the contrary, showed them occasional marks of the kindness of a relation, yet he could never look upon them with true cordiality. And as they had so well kept their promise to their father of never treating Amelia as a sister, while in her afflicted state, he took care not to tempt them to break it, now she was in a favoured and prosperous condition.

MASTER AND SLAVE.

Master. Now, villain! what have you to say for this second attempt to run away? Is there any punishment that you do not deserve?

Slave. I well know that nothing I can say will avail. I submit to my fate.

M. But are you not a base fellow, a hardened and ungrateful rascal?

S. I am a *slave*. That is answer enough.

M. I am not content with that answer. I thought I discerned in you some tokens of a mind superior to your condition. I treated you accordingly. You have been comfortably fed and lodged, not overworked, and attended with the most humane care when you were sick. And is this the return?

S. Since you condescend to talk with me as man to man, I will reply. What have you done—what can you do for me, that will compensate for the liberty which you have taken away?

M. I did not take it away. You were a slave when I fairly purchased you.

S. Did I give my consent to the purchase?

M. You had no consent to give. You had already lost the right of disposing of yourself.

S. I had lost the *power;* but how the *right?* I was treacherously kidnapped in my own country when following an honest occupation. I was put in chains, sold to one of your countrymen, carried by force on board his ship, brought hither and exposed to sale like a beast in the market, where you bought me. What step in all this progress of violence and injustice can give a *right?* Was it in the villain who stole me, in the slave-merchant who tempted him to do so, or in you who encouraged the slave-merchant to bring his cargo of human cattle to cultivate your lands?

M. It is in the order of providence that one man should become subservient to another. It ever has been so, and ever will be. I found the custom, and did not make it.

S. You cannot but be sensible that the robber who puts a pistol to your breast may make just the same plea. Providence gives him a power over your life and property; it gave my enemies a power over my liberty. But it has also given me legs to escape with; and what should prevent me from using them? Nay, what should restrain me from retaliating the wrongs I have suffered, if a favourable occasion should offer?

M. Gratitude, I repeat,—gratitude! Have I not endeavoured ever since I possessed you to alleviate your misfortunes by kind treatment, and does that confer no obligation? Consider how much worse your condition might have been under another master?

S. You have done nothing for me more than for your working cattle. Are they not well fed and tended? do you work them harder than your slaves? is not the rule of treating both, only your own advantage? You treat both your men and beast slaves better than some of your neighbours, because you are more prudent and wealthy than they.

M. You might add, more *humane* too.

S. Humane! Does it deserve that appellation to keep your fellow-men in forced subjection, deprived of all exercise of their free-will, liable to all the injuries that your own caprice, or the brutality of your overseers, may heap on them, and devoted, soul and body, only to your pleasure and emolument? Can gratitude take place from creatures in such a state, towards the tyrant who holds them in it? Look at these limbs— are they not those of a man? Think that I have the spirit of a man, too.

M. But it was my intention not only to make your life tolerably comfortable at present, but to provide for you in your old age.

S. Alas ! is a life like mine, torn from country, friends, and all I held dear, and compelled to toil under the burning sun for a master, worth thinking about for old age ? No—the sooner it ends, the sooner I shall obtain that relief for which my soul pants.

M. Is it impossible, then, to hold you by any ties but those of constraint and severity ?

S. It is impossible to make one who has felt the value of freedom, acquiesce in being a slave.

M. Suppose I were to restore you to your liberty— would you reckon that a favour ?

S. The greatest ; for although it would only be un- doing a wrong, I know too well how few among man- kind are capable of sacrificing interest to justice, not to prize the exertion when it is made.

M. I do it, then ;—be free.

S. Now I am indeed your servant, though not your slave. And as the first return I can make for your kindness, I will tell you freely the condition in which you live. You are surrounded with implacable foes, who long for a safe opportunity to revenge upon you and the other planters all the miseries they have en- dured. The more generous their natures, the more indignant they feel against that cruel injustice which has dragged them hither, and doomed them to perpe- tual servitude. You can rely on no kindness on your part to soften the obduracy of their resentment. You have reduced them to the state of brute beasts, and if they have not the stupidity of beasts of burden, they must have the ferocity of beasts of prey. Superior force alone can give you security. As soon as that fails, you are at the mercy of the merciless. Such is the social bond between *master* and *slave*.

THIRTIETH EVENING.

EARTH AND HER CHILDREN.

In a certain district of the globe, things one year went on so ill, that almost the whole race of living beings, animals and vegetables, carried their lamentations and complaints to their common mother, *the Earth.*

First came *Man.* "O Earth," said he, "how can you behold unmoved the intolerable calamities of your favourite offspring! Heaven shuts up all the sources of its benignity to us, and showers plagues and pestilence on our heads—storms tear to pieces all the works of human labour—the elements of fire and water seem let loose to devour us—and in the midst of all these evils, some demon possesses us with a rage of destroying one another; so that the whole species seems doomed to perish. O, intercede in our behalf, or else receive us again into your maternal bosom, and hide us from the sight of these accumulated distresses!"

The other animals then spoke by their deputies, the horse, the ox, and the sheep. "O pity, mother Earth, those of your children that repose on your breast, and derive their subsistence from your fruitful bosom! We are parched with drought, we are scorched by lightning, we are beaten by pitiless tempests, salubrious vegetables refuse to nourish us, we languish under disease, and the race of men treat us with unusual rigour. Never, without speedy succour, can we survive to another year."

The vegetables next, those which form the verdant carpet of the earth, that cover the waving fields of harvest, and that spread their lofty branches in the air, sent forth their complaint. "O, our general mother, to whose breast we cleave, and whose vital juices we drain, have compassion upon us! See how we wither and droop under the baleful gales that sweep over us—how we thirst in vain for the gentle dew of heaven—how immense tribes of noxious insects pierce and devour us—how the famishing flocks and herds tear us up by the roots—and how men, through mutual spite, lay waste and destroy us while yet immature. Already whole nations of us are desolated, and, unless you save us, another year will witness our total destruction."

"My children," said Earth, "I have now existed some thousand years; and scarcely one of them has passed in which similar complaints have not arisen from one quarter or another. Nevertheless, everything has remained in nearly the same state, and no species of created beings has been finally lost. The injuries of one year are repaired by the succeeding. The growing vegetables may be blasted, but the seeds of others lie secure in my bosom, ready to receive the vital influence of more favourable seasons. Animals may be thinned by want and disease, but a remnant is always left, in whom survives the principle of future increase. As to man, who suffers not only from natural causes, but from the effects of his own follies and vices, his miseries arouse within him the latent powers of remedy, and bring him to his reason again; while experience continually goes along with him to improve his means of happiness, if he will but listen to its dictates. Have patience, then, my children! You were born to suffer, as well as to enjoy, and you must submit to your lot. But console yourselves with the thought that you have a kind master above, who created you for benevolent purposes, and will not withhold his protection when you stand most in need of it."

A SECRET CHARACTER UNVEILED.

AT a small house in one of the old squares in London, there lived, for a number of years, a person rather advanced in life, whose household consisted of one male and one female servant. His person was slender, and rather above the middle size; he had a grave and pensive aspect; his dress was neat and plain, but seldom varied, being generally black, which in make, was never affected by the change of fashion. He wore his own hair, which had become thin and gray; in his appearance and simplicity of manner he much resembled a Quaker, though without the peculiarities of that sect. He kept up no intercourse with his neighbours, and for a long period was known to them only by sight. He was very regular in his habits, and was observed to go out and come in almost always on foot, and even in the worst weather, and a stranger was never observed to visit at his house. His servants paid ready money for every article they required. If there were a collection in the parish for any charitable object, he always contributed fully as much as was expected of him. His sentiments on religion and politics were entirely unknown, though he was regularly observed to leave his house on Sunday a full half-hour before the church service commenced, from which it was conjectured that he was a regular attendant at some church in a distant part of the town. His manner commanded the respect of his neighbours, and he always returned the salutation of the hat to those who gave it him; but in any conversation he might be led into by them he never exceeded a few words. Many were curious to know the name and employment of such a regular and inoffensive man—but, after all their inquiries, they were only able to obtain his name, which, by the parish-books, appeared to be Moreland.

Though there were many conjectures as to his circumstances, the general supposition appeared to be, that in early life he had been unfortunate in business, and had been reduced to live retired on a small annuity which had been settled on him by a friend.

After he had thus lived a number of years, a train of circumstances occurred within a short time which fully displayed his real character.

In a narrow lane, at a little distance, there lived a poor widow, who had five children, the eldest a beautiful girl of nineteen. The mother had been very industrious, and supported her family by taking in sewing, in which she was assisted by her two eldest daughters. It happened that one of the children, and at length herself, fell ill of a violent fever, which reduced them to very great distress. Her two daughters did all in their power, but they were unable to earn beyond a few shillings a week, so that they were obliged to part with the greater portion of their goods for present subsistence. On the recovery of the poor widow and her child, a half-year's rent was due, which she was unable to pay. The cruel landlord threatened to seize the remainder of her effects, and turn her and her children into the street. The youth and beauty of the eldest girl had so excited his passion, that he unfeelingly informed the mother that it was in the power of her daughter to prevent his severity; but that pure virtue which frequently dwells in the heart of many that are reduced to distress, treated his proposal with disdain. The girl had a faithful lover, a journeyman shoemaker, who, during the illness of her family, had worked very hard, and divided his weekly earnings with them, and now, by his promises, endeavoured to soften the severity of the landlord, but to no purpose. As he was going one night to pay his accustomed

2 E

visit to the distressed family, he perceived Mr. Moreland passing down the lane, whom he had known for several years (his master having supplied him with shoes). When he entered the door, all the suspicions natural to a lover induced him to follow, when he observed him stealing up the stairs to the widow's lodging, and open the door. The poor family showed some surprise at the entrance of the stranger, and still more when, after a short conversation, he put a purse of money into the hand of the mother, and immediately went away. "What messenger from heaven," cried the poor widow, "has brought me this relief? Run, daughter, and thank him on your knees!" She ran, but he had got down stairs into the lane. "I know him," cried her lover (now making his appearance); "it is Mr. Moreland."

The officers of justice had for some time been employed in attempting to discover the retreat of a gang of venders of base coin, who were at last traced to a house in an obscure part of the town. A poor, lame fellow, who had lived in an adjoining room, being unable to give a satisfactory account of his manner of procuring a livelihood, was brought along with the rest for examination. "Well," said one of the justices, "who are you?"

"Please your worship, I am a poor man, having lost the use of my limbs for several years."

"And how have you been able to support yourself all this time?"

"Why, sir, I might have starved long ago, having no parish settlement, as the masters for whom I worked would not interest themselves for me, though I lost the use of my limbs in their service; but a good gentleman has been so very kind as to give me five shillings a week for these six years past."

"Ay! you were very fortunate, indeed; pray who is that gentleman?"

"Why, please your worship, I don't know."

" No ! 'Tis very strange you do not know the name of the person who supports you: but where does he live ?"

" I know nothing at all of him, but the good he has done for me."

" Then how did you first become acquainted with him ?"

" I was in the hospital, and just going to be turned out of it incurable, and was thinking that I had nothing for it but to beg or starve, when the gentleman, who visited the hospital, learned my story; after I had been discharged, he came to my poor lodging and gave me a guinea to buy some necessaries, and told me, that if I would do all that I was capable of to maintain myself, he would take care that I should never want. From the serious and kind manner in which he spoke, I believed that he would do something for me, and ever since he or his man-servant has brought me five shillings a week."

" This story will hardly pass; but tell me what trade you worked at before you lost the use of your limbs ?"

" I was an engraver."

" O ho ! then you understand working in metals ! Circumstances are very suspicious—you must be kept until further information is obtained of you."

The poor man in vain protested that he had no connexion with the party in the adjoining room, and that every word he stated was true. He offered to bring proof of his honesty and regular life from among his neighbours; but that could not be received, and he was remanded for further examination. The officers were leading him to prison, when he perceived his benefactor crossing the street. He called aloud, and desired them to stop him; and then, in a piteous tone, told him his story, entreating that he would go back with him to the justices, and bear witness in his behalf. This he could not refuse. They were ad-

2 E 2

mitted into the crowded hall, and the officers related
the cause of their return. All eyes were turned upon
the gentleman, when he was desired to give his name.
"It is Moreland," said he. He then in a few words
stated that, some years ago, having become acquainted
with the character and distress of this poor man, he
had since regularly assisted him.

"'Tis enough, sir," said a gentleman upon the
bench; "I have the honour of being a neighbour of
yours; but until now I did not know what a neighbour
I had." Mr. Moreland thanked him, and retired: the
poor fellow was discharged.

A very worthy tradesman, who, by a variety of
unforeseen circumstances, was reduced from respectability to poverty, at last died of a broken heart, leaving two maiden daughters altogether unprovided for.

Shortly after his death, one evening a person
knocked at the door of their lodging, which was on a
third floor, and delivered into their hands a parcel,
containing four ten-pound bank-notes, with a slip of
paper, on which was written, "To be continued, but
no inquiry to be made." This sum they regularly received twice a year for several years; by which means,
and their own industry, they were able to live in considerable comfort, without knowing to whom they were
indebted.

Though many were their conjectures on this subject, they never arrived at any probability, and they
were restrained from making any inquiry by the in-
junction given. Perhaps they never would have become acquainted with their benefactor had not an
accident led to the discovery. The person who came
as usual to deliver the packet of notes, hastily turning
round to depart, fell from the top of the stairs to the
bottom. The lady shrieked out, and, running down,
found the man lying bleeding and senseless: a surgeon was immediately sent for, who, by bleeding and
other remedies, restored him to his senses. He was

too unwell to be sent home that night, but in the morning he requested the surgeon to permit him to be moved to his master's.—"Who is your master?" inquired the surgeon. "Mr. Moreland, of ——— Square."—"What!" exclaimed the elder of the ladies, "Mr. Moreland, my poor father's greatest creditor— is it he to whom we have been so much indebted for everything?" The servant made a sign for her to be silent, which she understood. He was sent away in a coach, accompanied by the surgeon. They arrived at Mr. Moreland's, where, after the confusion occasioned by the accident had subsided, the surgeon discovered that the faces of both master and man were familiar to him. "I am sure," said he, "that you are the gentleman who has so charitably assisted the poor family in this neighbourhood and the man with the sore limbs, and so willingly paid me my fees for attendance." Mr. Moreland admitted that he was the same person. At this discovery, the surgeon, on taking his leave, could not refrain from expressing his veneration for the humanity he had shown.

About the same time many other private acts of benevolence of this good man became known. In the neighbourhood where Mr. Moreland resided was a tailor's shop, kept by a man who had a wife and six children. He was a very industrious person, and being assisted in his trade by his wife, they were, with great exertions, just able to maintain themselves and family in a decent manner. Conjointly with a friend, he had become security to the amount of three hundred pounds for a younger brother, who had obtained a situation in one of the government offices. The brother fell into bad company, and at length absconded. The tailor was called upon to pay his part of the bond; but on account of several bad debts, and having lately paid his rent and made some small purchases of cloth, he was unable to meet this unexpected demand. He was, in consequence, sent to prison. The distress which this brought upon the family was greatly increased by his wife being at that time confined. He had been almost four weeks in prison, without any prospect of release, his friends and relations having been tried and found unable to assist him, when one evening the keeper of the prison came up to him and said, " You are free." The poor man scarcely could believe what he heard: his surprise and joy were so great that he nearly fainted away. Before leaving the prison, he was anxious to know his generous benefactor; but all he could learn was, that the debt and all expenses had been paid by a gentleman whose name was unknown to them, but whose face was familiar, as he had often before been there on similar business. " O," cried the tailor, " that I knew him, that I and my family might thank him!" He hurried home, where his unexpected appearance almost overcame his poor family. On talking over the matter with his wife, she informed him that the servant of Mr. Moreland had called a few days before, and was very particular in his inquiries. This naturally led them to conjecture that it was to him they were indebted, which was confirmed by the keeper of the prison, who had learned the name, from Mr. Moreland having appeared in behalf of the lame man taken up on suspicion.

The tailor was overjoyed at this intelligence, but was still at a loss to know in what manner he ought to express his gratitude. He was afraid to offend Mr. Moreland; but it was necessary to give vent to the fulness of his heart. He took his wife and two of his children and called at his house, desiring to speak with him. When admitted, he was unable to give utterance to the expressions of gratitude he had prepared, and bursting into a fit of crying, he fell on his knees, seizing one hand of his benefactor, which he kissed with the utmost fervency; while his wife and children fell also on their knees, lifted up their hands, and implored a blessing upon him. Mr. Moreland was much affected, and after remaining silent for some time, "It is too much! too much!" he cried. "Go home, my good people! God bless you all."

Now that Mr. Moreland's character became known, it would be impossible to relate all the private acts of benevolence that were discovered to have proceeded from him.

An old clergyman from the country came up to town on business about this time, and paid a visit to an intimate friend. After mutual congratulations, he informed him that his parish had undergone a blessed alteration since he had last visited him. "The principal estate was sold some years ago to a gentleman in London, who is one of those few who are never weary in well-doing. He built, in the first place, twelve neat cottages where all the industrious poor who were unfit for labour, are comfortably maintained at his expense. He has endowed a school in the parish for the instruction of the children in reading, writing, and accounts, and placed it upon such a footing that the fees of the master will never be felt by the parents. He orders the baker of the village to deliver twice a week a large loaf to each of the poor people's houses; during the severity of winter he also supplies them with fuel at a cheap rate: he has, besides, frequently remitted his rents to poor people in bad seasons, and, indeed, the good deeds he has done cannot be enumerated. I myself have been much indebted to him, and I am also informed that he contributes largely to the support of a dissenting minister in the neighbourhood. But what is surprising, he is very shy of being seen, nor do we know anything of his profession or of his town residence, and I really believe we should not have known his name, had it not been made public when he purchased the property. It is Moreland."

"Why," said his friend, "I have a parishioner of

that name; and from what I have lately heard of him, I suspect he is the same person."

"Could not I get a sight of him?" replied the first.

"Probably you may," said the other; and presently seeing him cross the court, he pointed him out.

"Ah! that is the truly charitable man!" exclaimed the old clergyman in a rapture. And running up to him, he seized him by the hand and expressed the most affectionate wishes for his welfare.

Mr. Moreland now became well known; and though many were desirous to become acquainted with so good a man, he always avoided any intercourse that would bring himself into notice. It was not till after his death that an old friend thought fit to gratify the world with an account of his private history.

Mr. Moreland was the youngest son of a country gentleman, and came to London at an early age to be educated for commercial life. In this, by diligence and attention, he succeeded so well, that after having passed through the different gradations of clerk, he was admitted a partner in the house, which was one of the first respectability. In this situation he acquired a considerable fortune, and sustained the character of one of the leading merchants of the day. In early life he married an amiable and accomplished lady, who brought him two children: both died in their infancy, and the death of their mother, which followed in a few years, made such an impression on his mind that he gradually withdrew from business. The common pleasures of the world grew daily less interesting to his mind, and he found a vacancy which could only be filled up by reading and contemplation. The liberality of his mind led him to take an interest in the various conditions of society; and in order to extend his knowledge, he visited the different governments of the continent, travelling chiefly on foot, avoiding common routes, that he might have an opportunity of mingling with the mass of the people.

He saw abroad, as well as at home, a great deal of misery; he saw wretchedness everywhere close in the train of splendour. He lamented the evils of the world; but whatever might be their original source, he saw that man had within himself the power of remedying many of them. And it occurred to him that in exercising this power, all duty, all virtue, seemed to consist; and from that time he resolved to direct his attention to the best means of benefiting society.

Full of these meditations, he returned; and convinced that the great inequality of rank and property is one principal cause (though a necessary one) of the ills of life, he resolved, as much as it lay in his power, to counteract it. " How few things," thought he, " are necessary to my external comfort! wholesome food, warm clothing, clean lodging, a little waiting upon, and a few books. Anything else would be superfluous. In what manner, then, ought the remainder to be applied?"

That he might at once get rid of the craving and burdensome demands which opinion imposes, he took a house in a distant part of the town, where his name was unknown; and of all his former acquaintances he only reserved one or two confidential friends. He selected out of the number of his former domestics one of each sex, steady and confidential, whose lives he made as comfortable as his own. After all the expenses of his household were defrayed, there remained two-thirds of his income, which he applied in secretly relieving the distresses of others.

He chose that his charities should be secret, not only as being utterly averse to all ostentation, but also to avoid those importunities which are often made by unworthy objects. He wished personally to become acquainted with the real circumstances of every case; and it was his chief employment to mingle amongst the people, and to inquire into the private history of

those individuals who came under his observation.   If
he discovered that their distress proceeded from misfortune, and not from crime, he never failed in adopt-
ing a plan to give permanent relief.

His philanthropy was general; but it was his greatest
delight to assist those who, by unforeseen circumstances,
had been reduced to poverty.   Hence the sums which
he bestowed were often so considerable as at once to
retrieve the affairs of the sufferer; nor did he withdraw
support so long as it was necessary.

In his opi ns on general subjects he was liberal
and free from bigotry, and if they chanced to differ
from those recognized in society, he refrained from
expressing them.

So he lived, so he died! injuring no one, benefiting
many, bearing with pious resignation the evils that
fell to his own lot, continually endeavouring to alleviate
those of others—and hoping to behold a state in which
all evil shall be abolished.

THIRTY-FIRST EVENING.

A GLOBE LECTURE.

Papa—Lucy.

Papa. You may remember, Lucy, that I talked to
you some time ago about the earth's motion round
the sun.

Lucy. Yes, papa; and you then said you would
tell me another time somewhat about the other
planets.

P. I mean some day to take you to the lecture of an
ingenious philosopher, who has contrived a machine
that will give you a better notion of these things in
an hour, than I could by mere talking in a week.   But

it is now my intention to make you better acquainted with this globe which we inhabit, and which, indeed, is the most important to us. Cast your eyes upon this little ball. You see it is a representation of the earth, being covered with a coloured map of the world. This map is crossed with lines in various directions; but all you have to observe, relative to what I am going to talk about, is the great line across the middle, called the *equator*, or *equinoctial line*, and the two points at top and bottom, called the *poles*, of which the uppermost is the northern, the lowermost the southern.

L. I see them.

P. Now, the sun, which illuminates all the parts of this globe by turns as they roll round before it, shines directly upon the equator, but darts its rays aslant towards the poles; and this is the cause of the great heat perceived in the middle regions of the earth, and of its gradual diminution as you proceed from them on either side towards the extremities. To use a vulgar illustration, it is like a piece of meat roasting before a fire, the middle part of which is liable to be overdone, while the two ends are raw.

L. I can comprehend that.

P. From this simple circumstance, some of the greatest differences on the surface of the earth, with respect to man, other animals, and vegetables, proceed; for heat is the great principle of life and vegetation; and where it most prevails, provided it be accompanied with due moisture, nature is most replenished with all sorts of living and growing things. In general, then, the countries lying on each side about the equator, and forming a broad belt around the globe, called the *tropics*, or *torrid zone*, are rich and exuberant in their products to a degree much superior to what we see in our climates. Trees, and other plants, shoot to a vast size, and are clothed in perpetual verdure, and loaded with flowers of the gayest colours and sweetest fragrance, succeeded by fruits of high flavour or abundant nutriment. The insect tribe is multiplied so as to fill all the air, and many of them astonish by their size and extraordinary forms, and the splendour of their hues. The ground is all alive with reptiles, some harmless, some armed with deadly poisons.

L. O, but I should not like that at all.

P. The birds, however, decked in the gayest plumage conceivable, must give unmixed delight; and a tropical forest, filled with parrots, macaws, and peacocks, and enlivened with the gambols of monkeys and other nimble quadrupeds, must be a very amusing spectacle. The largest of quadrupeds, too, the elephant, the rhinoceros, and the hippopotamus, are natives of these regions; and not only those sublime and harmless animals, but the terrible lion, the cruel tiger, and all the most ravenous beasts of prey, are here found in their greatest bulk and fierceness.

L. That would be worse than the insects and reptiles.

P. The sea, also, is filled with inhabitants of an immense variety of size and figure; not only fishes, but tortoises, and all the shelly tribes. The shores are spread with shells of a beauty unknown to our coasts; for it would seem as though the influence of the solar heat penetrated into the farthest recesses of nature.

L. How I should like to ramble on the sea-side there!

P. But the elements, too, are there upon a grand and terrific scale. The sky either blazes with intolerable beams, or pours down rain in irresistible torrents. The winds swell to furious hurricanes, which often desolate the whole face of nature in a day. Earthquakes rock the ground, and sometimes open it in chasms, which swallow up entire cities. Storms raise the waves of the ocean into mountains, and drive them in a deluge to the land.

L. Ah! that would spoil my shell-gathering. These countries may be very fine, but I don't like them.

P. Well, then; we will turn from them to the *temperate* regions. You will observe, on looking at the map, that these chiefly lie on the northern side of the tropics; for, on the southern side, the space is almost wholly occupied by sea. Though geographers have drawn a boundary-line between the torrid and temperate zones, yet nature has made none; and, for a considerable space on the borders, the diminution or heat is so gradual, as to produce little difference in the appearance of nature. But, in general, the temperate *zones*, or *belts*, form the most desirable districts on the face of the earth. Their products are extremely various, and abound in beauty and utility. Corn, wine, and oil, are among their vegetable stores: the horse, the ox, and the sheep, graze their verdant pastures. Their seasons have the pleasing vicissitudes of summer and winter, spring and autumn. Though, in some parts, they are subject to excess of heat, and in others of cold, yet they deserve the general praise of a mild temperature, compared to the rest of the globe.

L. They are the countries for me, then.

P. You *do* live in one of them, though our island is situated so far to the north, that it ranks rather among the cold countries than the warm ones. However, we have the good fortune to be a long way removed from those dreary and comfortless tracts of the globe which lie about the poles, and are called the *frigid zones.* In these, the cheering influence of the sun gradually becomes extinct, and perpetual frost and snow take possession of the earth. Trees and plants diminish in number and size, till at length no vegetables are found but some mosses, and a few stunted herbs. Land animals are reduced to three or four species; reindeer, white bears, arctic foxes, and snow-birds. The sea, however, as far as it remains free from ice, is all

alive with the finny tribe. Enormous whales spout
and gambol among the floating ice-islands, and herds
of seals pursue the shoals of smaller fish, and harbour
in the caverns of the rocky coasts.

L. Then I suppose these creatures have not much
to do with the sun ?

P. Nature has given them powers of enduring cold
beyond those of many other animals; and then, the
water is always warmer than the land in cold climates;
nay, at a certain depth, it is equally warm in all parts
of the globe.

L. Well, but as I cannot go to the bottom of the
sea, I desire to have nothing to do with these dismal
countries.   But do any men live there ?

P. It is one of the wonderful things belonging to
man, that he is capable of living in all parts of the globe
where any other animals live. And as nothing relative
to this earth is so important to us as the condition of
human creatures in it, suppose we take a general survey of the different races of men who inhabit all the
tracts we have been speaking of ?

L. Blacks, and whites, and all colours ?

P. Surely. If a black dog be as much a dog as a
white one, why should not a black man be as much a
man ? I know nothing that colour has to do with
mind. Well, then—to go back to the equator. The
middle or tropical girdle of the earth, which, by the
ancients, was concluded to be uninhabitable, from its
extreme heat, has been found by modern discoveries
to be as well filled with men as it is with other living
creatures. And no wonder; for life is maintained
here at less cost than elsewhere. Clothes and fuel are
scarcely at all necessary. A shed of bamboo, covered
with palm-leaves, serves for a house; and food is
almost the spontaneous product of nature. The bread-
fruit, the cocoa, the banana, and the plantain, offer
their stores freely to the gatherer; and, if he take the
additional pains to plant a few yams, or sow a little

Indian corn, he is furnished with never-failing plenty. Hence the inhabitants of many tropical countries live nearly in what is called a state of nature, without care or labour, using the gifts of Providence like the animals around them. The naked Indian, stretched at ease under the shade of a lofty tree, passes his hours in indolent repose, unless aroused to temporary exertion by the passion of the chase, or the love of dancing and other social sports.

L. Well—that would be a charming life!

P. So the poet Thomson seemed to think, when he burst out in a rapturous description of the beauties and pleasures afforded by these favoured regions. Perhaps you can remember some of his lines?

L. I will try.

> ——" Thrown at gayer ease, on some fair brow,
> Let me behold, by breezy murmurs cool'd,
> Broad o'er my head the verdant cedar wave,
> And high palmettos lift their graceful shade.
> Or stretch'd amid these orchards of the sun,
> Give me to drain the cocoa's milky bowl,
> And from the palm to draw its freshening wine!"

P. Delightful! Think, however, at what price they purchase this indolent enjoyment of life. In the first place, all the work that is done is thrown upon the women, who are always most tyrannized over, the nearer a people approach to a state of nature.

L. Oh, horrible! I am glad I do not live there.

P. Then, the mind not having that spur to exertion which necessity alone can give, moulders in inaction, and becomes incapable of those advances in knowledge and vigour which raise and dignify the human character.

L. But that is the same with lazy people everywhere.

P. True. The excessive heat, however, of these countries seems of itself to relax the mind, and unfit it for its noblest exertions. And I question if a single instance could be produced of an original inhabitant of the tropics, who has attained to eminence in the higher walks of science. It is their general character to be gay, volatile, and thoughtless, subject to violent passions, but commonly mild and gentle, fond of society and amusements, ingenious in little arts, but incapable of great or long-continued efforts. They form a large portion of the human race, and probably not the least happy. You see what vast tracts of land lie within this division; most of Africa and South America; all the great islands of Asia, and two of its large peninsulas. Of these, the Asiatic part is the most populous and civilized; indeed, many of its nations are as far removed from a state of nature as we are, and their constitutional indolence has been completely overcome by necessity. The clothing of those who are in a civilized state is mostly made of cotton, which is a natural product of those climates. Their food is chiefly of the vegetable kind; and besides the articles already mentioned, consists much of rice.

L. Are the people all black?

P. Yes; entirely, or nearly so.

L. I suppose that is owing to the heat of the sun?

P. Undoubtedly; for we find all the shades from jet black to tawny, and at length white, as we proceed from the equator towards the poles. The African negroes, however, from their curled woolly air, and their flat features, have been supposed an originally distinct race of mankind. The East-Indian blacks, though under an equally hot climate, have long flowing hair, and features not very different from those of their fairer neighbours. Almost all of these nations are subject to despotic governments. In religion they are mostly pagans, with a mixture of Mahometans.

L. I think we have had enough about these people.

P. Well, then, look again on the globe to the northern side of the tropics, and see what a tour we shall take you among the inhabitants of the north temperate zone. Here are all the most famous places on the earth; rich populous countries, renowned at different periods for arts and arms. Here is the greater part of Asia, a little of Africa, all Europe, and North America.

L. I suppose, however, there must be great differences both in the climate and the way of life, in so many countries?

P. Extremely great. The southern parts partake a good deal of the character of the tropical regions. The heat is still excessive, and renders exertion painful; whence the people have in general been reckoned soft, effeminate, and voluptuous. Let us, however, look at them a little closer. Here is the mighty empire of China, swarming with people to such a degree, that, notwithstanding its size and fertility, the inhabitants are obliged to exert the greatest industry to procure the necessaries of life. Nearly in a line with it are the Mogul's empire, the kingdom of Persia, and the Turkish dominions in Asia; all warm climates, abounding in products of use and beauty, and inhabited by numerous and civilized people. Here stretches out the great peninsula of Arabia, for the most part a dry and desert land, overspread with burning sands, to be crossed only by the patient camel. Wild and ferocious tribes of men wander over it, subsisted chiefly by their herds and flocks, and by the trade of robbery, which they exercise on all travellers that fall in their way. A tract somewhat similar, though in a colder climate, is the vast country of Tartary, stretching like a belt from east to west across the middle of Asia; over the immense plains and deserts of which, a number of independent tribes continually roam, fixing their moveable habitations in one part or another, according as they afford pasture to their herds of cattle and horses. These men have for many ages lived in the same simple

2 F

state, unacquainted as well with the arts, as the vices, of civilized nations.

L. Well, I think it must be a very pleasant life to ramble about from place to place, and change one's abode according to the season.

P. The Tartars think so; for the worst wish they can find for a man is, that he may live in a house and work like a Russian. Now, look at Europe. See what a small figure it makes on the surface of the globe as to size; and yet it has for many years held the first place in knowledge, activity, civilization, and all the qualities that elevate man among his fellows. For this it is much indebted to that temperature of climate which calls forth all the faculties of man in order to render life comfortable, yet affords enough of the beauties of nature to warm the heart and exalt the imagination. Men here earn their bread by the sweat of their brow. Nature does not drop her fruits into their mouths, but offers them as the price of labour. Human wants are many. Clothes, food, lodging, are all objects of much care and contrivance, but the human powers, fully exerted, are equal to the demand; and nowhere are enjoyments so various and multiplied. What the land does not yield itself, its inhabitants, by their active industry, procure from the remotest parts of the globe. When we drink tea, we sweeten the infusion of a Chinese herb with the juice of a West-India cane; and your common dress is composed of materials collected from the equator to the frigid zone. Europeans render all countries and climates familiar to them; and everywhere they assume a superiority over the less enlightened or less industrious natives.

L. Then Europe for me, after all. But is not America as good?

P. That part of North America which has been settled by Europeans, is only another Europe in manners and civilization. But the original inhabitants of that extensive country were bold and hardy barbarians, and many of them continue so to this day. So much for the temperate zone, which contains the prime of mankind. They differ extremely, however, in governments, laws, customs, and religions. The Christian religion has the credit of reckoning among its votaries all the civilized people of Europe and America. The Mahometan possesses all the nearer parts of Asia and the north of Africa; but China, Japan, and most of the circumjacent countries, profess different forms of paganism. The east, in general, is enslaved to despotism; but the nobler west enjoys, in most of its states, more or less of freedom.

As to the frigid zone, its few inhabitants can but just sustain a life little better than that of the brutes. Their faculties are benumbed by the climate. Their chief employment is the fishery or the chase, by which they procure their food. The tending of herds of reindeer in some parts varies their occupations and diet. They pass their long winters in holes dug under-ground, where they doze out most of their time in stupid repose.

L. I wonder any people should stay in such miserable places.

P. Yet none of the inhabitants of the globe seem more attached to their country and way of life. Nor do they, indeed, want powers to render their situation tolerably comfortable. Their canoes, and fishing and hunting tackle, are made with great ingenuity; and their clothing is admirably adapted to fence against the rigours of cold. They are not without some amusements to cheer the gloom of their condition; but they are abjectly superstitious, and given to fear and melancholy.

L. If I had my choice, I would rather go to a warmer than a colder country.

P. Perhaps the warmer countries are pleasanter; but there are few advantages which are not balanced by some inconveniences; and it is the truest wisdom to be contented with our lot, and endeavour to make the best of it. One great lesson, however, I wish you to derive from this *globe-lecture*. You see that no part of the world is void of our human brethren, who, amidst all the diversities of character and condition, are yet all *men*, filling the station in which their Creator has placed them. We are too apt to look at the differences of mankind, and to undervalue all those who do not agree with us in matters that we think of high importance. But who are we—and what cause have we to think ourselves right, and all others wrong? Can we imagine that hundreds of millions of our species in other parts of the world are left destitute of what is essential to their well-being, while a favoured few, like ourselves, are the only ones who possess it? Having all a common nature, we must necessarily agree in more things than we differ. The road to virtue and happiness is alike open to all. The mode of pursuit is various; the end is the same.

ENVY AND EMULATION.

At one of the celebrated schools of painting in Italy, a young man, named Guidotto, produced a piece so excellent, that it was the admiration of the masters in the art, who all declared it to be their opinion, that he could not fail of rising to the summit of his profession, should he proceed as he had begun.

This performance was looked upon with very different eyes by two of his fellow-scholars. Brunello, the elder of them, who had himself acquired some reputation in his studies, was mortified in the highest degree at this superiority of Guidotto; and regarding all the honour his rival had acquired, as so much taken from himself, he conceived the most rancorous dislike of him, and longed for nothing so much as to see him lose the credit he had gained. Afraid openly to decry the merit of a work which had obtained the approbation of the best judges, he threw out secret insinuations that Guidotto had been assisted in it by one or other of his masters; and he affected to represent it as a sort of lucky hit, which the reputed author would probably never equal.

Not so Lorenzo. Though a very young proficient in the art, he comprehended in its full extent the excellence of Guidotto's performance, and became one of the sincerest of his admirers. Fired with the praises he saw him receive on all sides, he ardently longed one day to deserve the like. He placed him before his eyes as a fair model, which it was his highest ambition to arrive at equalling—for as to excelling him, he could not as yet conceive the possibility of it. He never spoke of him but with rapture, and could not bear to hear the detractions of Brunello.

But Lorenzo did not content himself with words. He entered with his whole soul into the career of improvement—was first and last of all the scholars in the designing-room—and devoted to practice at home those hours which the other youths passed in amusement. It was long before he could please himself with any of his attempts, and he was continually repeating over them, " Alas! how far distant is this from Guidotto's!" At length, however, he had the satisfaction of becoming sensible of progress; and, having received considerable applause on account of one of his performances, he ventured to say to himself, " And why may not I too become a Guidotto ?"

Meanwhile, Guidotto continued to bear away the palm from all competitors. Brunello struggled a while to contest with him, but at length gave up the point, and consoled himself under his inferiority, by ill-natured sarcasm and petulant criticism. Lorenzo worked away in silence, and it was long before his modesty would suffer him to place any piece of his in view at the same time with one of Guidotto's.

There was a certain day in the year in which it was

customary for all the scholars to exhibit their best performance in a public hall, where their merit was solemnly judged by a number of select examiners, and a prize of value was awarded to the most excellent. Guidotto had prepared for this anniversary, a piece which was to excel all he had before executed. He had just finished it on the evening before the exhibition, and nothing remained but to heighten the colouring, by means of a transparent varnish. The malignant Brunello contrived artfully to convey into the phial, containing this varnish, some drops of a caustic preparation, the effect of which would be entirely to destroy the beauty and splendour of the piece. Guidotto laid it on by candlelight, and then with great satisfaction hung up his picture in the public room against the morrow.

Lorenzo, too, with beating heart, had prepared himself for the day. With vast application he had finished a piece which he humbly hoped might appear not greatly inferior to some of Guidotto's earlier performances.

The important day was now arrived. The company assembled, and were introduced into the great room, where the light had just been fully admitted by drawing up a curtain. All went up with raised expectations to Guidotto's picture, when behold! instead of the brilliant beauty they had conceived, there was nothing but a dead surface of confused and blotched colours. "Surely," they cried, "this cannot be Guidotto's!" The unfortunate youth himself came up, and on beholding the dismal change of his favourite piece, burst out into an agony of grief, and exclaimed that he was betrayed and undone. The vile Brunello in a corner was enjoying his distress. But Lorenzo was little less affected than Guidotto himself. "Trick! knavery!" he cried. "Indeed, gentlemen, this is not Guidotto's work. I saw it when only half-finished, and it was a most charming performance. Look at the outline, and judge what it must have been before it was so basely injured."

The spectators were all struck with Lorenzo's generous warmth, and sympathized in the disgrace of Guidotto; but it was impossible to adjudge the prize to his picture in the state in which they beheld it. They examined all the others attentively, and that of Lorenzo, till then an unknown artist to them, gained a great majority of suffrages. The prize was therefore awarded to him; but Lorenzo, on receiving it, went up to Guidotto, and presenting it to him, said, "Take what merit would undoubtedly have acquired for you, had not the basest malice and envy defrauded you of it. To me it is honour enough to be accounted your second. If hereafter I may aspire to equal you, it shall be by means of fair competition, not by the aid of treachery."

Lorenzo's nobleness of conduct excited the warmest encomiums among the judges, who at length determined, that for this time there should be two equal prizes distributed; for that, if Guidotto had deserved the prize of painting, Lorenzo was entitled to that of virtue.

PROVIDENCE; OR, THE SHIPWRECK.

It was a dreadful storm. The wind blowing full on the sea-shore, rolled tremendous waves on the beach, while the half-sunk rocks at the entrance of the bay were enveloped in a mist of white foam. A ship appeared in the offing, driving impetuously under her bare poles to land; now tilting aloft on the surging waves, now plunging into the intervening hollows. Presently she rushed among the rocks and there struck, the billows beating over her deck, and climbing up her shattered rigging. "Mercy! mercy!" exclaimed an ancient Solitary, as he viewed from a cliff the dismal scene. It was in vain. The ship fell on her side, and was seen no more.

Soon, however, a small, dark object appeared coming from the rocks towards the shore; at first dimly descried through the foam, then quite plain as it rode on the summit of a wave, then for a time totally lost. It approached, and showed itself to be a boat, with men in it rowing for their lives. The Solitary hastened down to the beach, and in all the agonizing vicissitudes of hope and fear watched its advance. At length, after the most imminent hazards, the boat was thrown violently on the shore, and the dripping, half-dead mariners crawled out to the dry land.

" Heaven be praised!" cried the Solitary; " what a providential escape!" And he led the poor men to his cell, where, kindling a good fire, and bringing out his little store of provision, he restored them to health and spirits. " And are you six men the only ones saved?" said he. " That we are," answered one of them. " Threescore and fifteen men, women, and children, were in the ship when she struck. You may think what a clamour and confusion there was : women clinging to their husbands' necks, and children hanging about their clothes, all shrieking, crying, and praying! There was no time to be lost. We got out the small boat in a twinkling; jumped in, without staying for our captain, who was fool enough to be minding the passengers; cut the rope, and pushed away, just time enough to be clear of the ship as she went down; and here we are, all alive and merry!" An oath concluded his speech. The Solitary was shocked, and could not help secretly wishing that it had pleased Providence to have saved some of the innocent passengers rather than these reprobates.

The sailors having got what they could, departed, scarcely thanking their benefactor, and marched up the country. Night came on. They descried a light at some distance, and made up to it. It proceeded

from the window of a good-looking house, surrounded
with a farm-yard and garden. They knocked at the
door, and, in a supplicating tone, made known their
distress, and begged relief. They were admitted, and
treated with compassion and hospitality. In the house
were the mistress, her children, and women-servants,
an old man, and a boy: the master was abroad. The
sailors, sitting round the kitchen fire, whispered to
each other, that here was an opportunity of making a
booty, that would amply compensate for the loss of
clothes and wages. They settled their plan, and on
the old man's coming with logs to the fire, one of them
broke his skull with the poker, and laid him dead.
Another took up a knife, which had been brought with
the loaf and cheese, and running after the boy, who
was making his escape out of the house, stabbed him
to the heart. The rest locked the doors, and after
tying all the women and children, began to ransack
the house. One of the children, continuing to make
loud exclamations, a fellow went and strangled it.
They had nearly finished packing up such of the most
valuable things as they could carry off, when the master
of the house came home. He was a smuggler as well
as a farmer, and had just returned from an expedition,
leaving his companions, with their goods, at a neighbouring public-house. Surprised at finding the doors
locked, and at seeing lights moving about in the
chambers, he suspected somewhat amiss; and, upon
listening, he heard strange voices, and saw some of the
sailors through the windows. He hastened back to
his companions, and brought them with him just as
the robbers opened the door, and were coming out
with their pillage, having first set fire to the house, in
order to conceal what they had done. The smuggler
and his friends let fly their blunderbusses in the
midst of them, and then rushing forwards, seized the
survivors and secured them. Perceiving flames in the
house, they ran and extinguished them. The villains

were next day led to prison amidst the curses of the neighbourhood.

The good Solitary, on hearing of the event, at first exclaimed, "What a wonderful interference of Providence to punish guilt and protect innocence!" Pausing a while, he added, "Yet had Providence thought fit to have drowned these sailors in their passage from the ship, where they left so many better people to perish, the lives of three innocent persons would have been saved, and these wretches would have died without such accumulated guilt and ignominy. On the other hand, had the master of the house been at home, instead of following a lawless and desperate trade, he would perhaps have perished with all his family, and the villains have escaped with their booty. What am I to think of all this?" Thus pensive and perplexed, he laid him down to rest, and after some time spent in gloomy reflections, fell asleep.

In his dream he fancied himself seated on the top of a high mountain, where he was accosted by a venerable figure in long white garments, who asked him the cause of the melancholy expressed on his countenance. "It is," said he, "because I am unable to reconcile the decrees of Providence with my ideas of wisdom and justice." "That," replied the stranger, "is probably because thy notions of Providence are narrow and erroneous. Thou seekest it in *particular events*, and dost not raise thy survey to the *great whole*. Every occurrence in the universe is *providential*, because it is the consequence of those laws which divine wisdom has established as most productive of the general good. But to select individual facts as more directed by the hand of Providence than others, because we think we see a particular good purpose answered by them, is an infallible inlet to error and superstition. Follow me to the edge of this cliff." He seemed to follow.

"Now look down," said the stranger, "and tell me what thou seest." "I see," replied the Solitary, "a hawk darting amidst a flock of small birds, one of which he has caught, while the others escape." "And canst thou think," rejoined the stranger, "that the single bird, made a prey of by the hawk, lies under any particular doom of Providence, or that those which fly away are more the objects of divine favour than it? Hawks, by nature, were made to feed upon living prey, and were endowed with strength and swiftness to enable them to overtake and master it. Thus life is sacrificed to the support of life. But to this destruction limits are set. The small birds are much more numerous and prolific than the birds of prey; and though they cannot resist his force, they have dexterity and nimbleness of flight sufficient in general to elude his pursuit. It is in this *balance* that the wisdom of Providence is seen; and what can be a greater proof of it than that both species, the destroyer and his prey, have subsisted together from their first creation. Now look again, and tell me what thou seest."

"I see," said the Solitary, "a thick black cloud gathering in the sky. I hear the thunder rolling from side to side of the vault of heaven. I behold the red lightning darting from the bosom of darkness. Now it has fallen on a stately tree, and shattered it to pieces, striking to the ground an ox sheltered at its foot. Now it falls again in the midst of a flock of timorous sheep, and several of them are left on the plain;—and see! the shepherd himself lies extended by their side. Now it strikes a lofty spire, and at the same time sets in a blaze an humble cottage beneath. It is an awful and terrible sight!"

"It is so," returned the stranger; "but what dost thou conclude from it? Dost thou not know, that from the genial heat, which gives life to plants and animals, and ripens the fruits of the earth, proceeds this electrical fire, which, ascending to the clouds, and charging them beyond what they are able to contain, is launched again in burning bolts to the earth ? Must it leave its direct course to strike the tree rather than the dome of worship, or to spend its fury on the herd rather than the herdsman ? Millions of millions of living creatures have owed their birth to this active element ; and shall we think it strange if a few meet their deaths from it ? Thus the mountain torrent that rushes down to fertilize the plain, in its course may sweep away the works of human industry, and man himself with them ; but could its benefits be purchased at another price ? "

" All this," said the Solitary, " I tolerably comprehend ; but may I presume to ask, whence have proceeded the *moral evils* of the painful scenes of yesterday ? What good end is answered by making man the scourge of man, and preserving the guilty at the cost of the innocent ? "

" That, too," replied the venerable stranger, " is a consequence of the same wise laws of Providence." If it were right to make man a creature of habit, and render those things easy to him with which he is most familiar, the sailor must, of course, be better able to shift for himself in a shipwreck than the passenger ; while that self-love, which is essential to the preservation of life, must, in general, cause him to consult his own safety in preference to that of others. The same force of habit, in a way of life full of peril and hardship, must conduce to form a rough, bold, and unfeeling character. This, under the direction of principle, will make a brave man ; without it, a robber and a murderer. In the latter case, human laws step in to remove the evil which they have not been able to prevent. Wickedness meets with the fate which, sooner or later, always awaits it; and innocence, though occasionally a sufferer, is proved in the end to be the surest path to happiness."

" But," resumed the Solitary, " can it be said that

the lot of innocence is *always* preferable to that of guilt in this world?"

"If it cannot," replied the other, "thinkest thou that the Almighty is unable to make retribution in a future world? Dismiss, then, from thy mind the care of *single events*, secure that the *great whole* is ordered for the best. Expect not a particular interposition of Heaven, because such an interposition would seem to thee seasonable. Thou, perhaps, wouldst stop the vast machine of the universe to save a fly from being crushed under its wheels. But innumerable flies and men are crushed every day, yet the grand motion goes on, and will go on, to fulfil the benevolent intentions of its Author."

He ceased, and sleep on a sudden left the eyelids of the Solitary. He looked abroad from his cell, and beheld all nature smiling around him. The rising sun shone in a clear sky. Birds were sporting in the air, and fish glancing on the surface of the waters. Fleets were pursuing their steady course, gently wafted by the pleasant breeze. Light, fleecy clouds were sailing over the blue expanse of heaven. His soul sympathized with the scene, and peace and joy filled his bosom.

EPILOGUE.

AND now, so many *Evenings* past,
Our *Budget's* fairly out, at last;
Exhausted all its various store,
Nor like to be replenish'd more.
Then, youthful friends, farewell! my heart
Shall speak a blessing as we part.
   May wisdom's seeds in every mind
Fit soil and careful culture find;
Each generous plant with vigour shoot,
And kindly ripen into fruit!

Hope of the world, the *rising race*,
May Heaven, with fostering love embrace,
And, turning to a whiter page,
Commence with them a *better age!*
An age of light and joy, which we,
Alas! in promise only see.

ROUTLEDGE'S JUVENILE BOOKS.

Price **3s. 6d.** each.

The greatest care has been taken in the production of this series to render them the cheapest and best set of Books of the kind that can be anywhere obtained. All have been carefully revised by competent editors. The Illustrations are designed by the best artists, and the whole series well printed and bound elegantly in emblematical cloth bindings.

CLASS I.—BOOKS OF ADVENTURE.

In fcap. 8vo, 3s. 6d. each, cloth gilt ; or with gilt edges, **4s.**,

THE WILD MAN OF THE WEST. By R. M. BALLANTYNE. With Illustrations by ZWECKER.

LAND AND SEA TALES. By THE OLD SAILOR. With Eight Illustrations.

THE RED ERIC ; or, The Whaler's Last Cruise. By R. M. BALLANTYNE. With Illustrations by W. S. COLEMAN.

THE BEAR HUNTERS OF THE ROCKY MOUNTAINS. By ANNE BOWMAN. Illustrated by ZWECKER.

"Miss Bowman's style is simple, pleasing, and judicious, her language graceful though familiar, and the subjects on which she treats are presented to the reader in a most intelligible and fascinating aspect."—*Morning Herald.*

THE CASTAWAYS ; or, Adventures of a Family in the Wilds of Africa. By ANNE BOWMAN. With Eight Illustrations by HARRISON WEIR.

Is a most interesting work, containing the adventures of a family in the wilds of Africa, with many thrilling, perilous, and amusing incidents. The hunting adventures are related with great spirit.

ESPERANZA ; or, The Home of the Wanderers. By ANNE BOWMAN. With Eight Illustrations by BIRKET FOSTER.

THE KANGAROO HUNTERS ; or Adventures of a Family in the Bush and Plains of Australia. By ANNE BOWMAN. With Illustrations by HARRISON WEIR.

THE YOUNG EXILES. A Boy's Book of Adventure amongst the Wild Tribes of the North. By ANNE BOWMAN. With Eight Illustrations by HARRISON WEIR.

THE BOY VOYAGERS. By ANNE BOWMAN. Illustrated By HARRISON WEIR.

ROBINSON CRUSOE; including His Further Adventures. By DANIEL DEFOE. Illustrated by PHIZ.

"The passing delightful story of many generations, the always entertaining book, and the subject of copy to all ages."

SWISS FAMILY ROBINSON; or, Adventures on a Desert Island. Complete Edition. Revised and Improved. With Sixteen Large Engravings by JOHN GILBERT.

THE ISLAND HOME; being the Adventures of Six Young Crusoes, cast on a Desolate Island. With Illustrations.

THE WAR TRAIL; or, The Hunt of the Wild Horse. By Captain MAYNE REID. With Eight Illustrations by W. HARVEY.

THE QUADROON; or, Adventures in the Far West. By Captain MAYNE REID. With Eight Illustrations by W. HARVEY.

Price 3s. 6d. each. Bevelled boards, extra gilt sides and edges,

VOYAGE AND VENTURE; or Perils by Sea and Land. Selected from the Works of the most celebrated Travellers in Modern Times. With Illustrations by JOHN GILBERT.

THE LITTLE WHALER. By F. GERSTAECKER. With Eight Illustrations by HARRISON WEIR.

"Gerstaecker is the most popular writer of the day with the young. He has seen what he describes, and shared in the adventures which he relates. Hence his books are truthful pictures of the busy scenes of active life."

FRANK WILDMAN'S ADVENTURES by WATER and LAND. By FREDERICK GERSTAECKER. Translated from the German. With Illustrations by HARRISON WEIR.

"We have perused the adventures of the hero of the story with much pleasure, and can recommend it without hesitation; the descriptions of men and things are sketched off with apparently a practised hand."—*Morning Chronicle.*

WILD SPORTS IN THE FAR WEST. By FREDERICK GERSTAECKER. With Eight Illustrations by HARRISON WEIR.

CLASS II. — ENTERTAINING AND USEFUL KNOWLEDGE.

In fcap., price 3s. 6d. each, cloth gilt ; or with gilt edges, 4s.,

THE BOYHOOD OF GREAT MEN. Intended as an example to youth. By JOHN G. EDGAR. Illustrated by BIRKET FOSTER.

FOOTPRINTS OF FAMOUS MEN : Biography for Boys.

CELEBRATED CHILDREN OF ALL AGES AND NATIONS. By M. MASSON. With Illustrations, from Designs by ABSOLON.

HISTORY FOR BOYS; or, Annals of the Nations of Modern Europe. By JOHN G. EDGAR. With Eight Illustrations.

THE BOY'S OWN NATURAL HISTORY BOOK. By the Rev. J. G. WOOD. With 350 Illustrations by HARVEY.

" A condensation of the Illustrated Natural History."

SKETCHES AND ANECDOTES OF ANIMAL LIFE By the Rev. J. G. WOOD, M.A., F.L.S., &c. With Eight Illustrations by HARRISON WEIR.

" A fresh spirit pervades the book, as well in the narratives as the descriptive account of the nature and habits of the animals."—*Spectator*.

ANIMAL TRAITS AND CHARACTERISTICS. Comprising Anecdotes of Animals not included in the above. By the Rev. J. G. WOOD, M.A., F.L.S., &c. With Illustrations by HARRISON WEIR.

MY FEATHERED FRIENDS. Containing Anecdotes of Bird-life, more especially Eagles, Vultures, Hawks, Magpies, Rooks, Crows, Ravens, Parrots, Humming Birds, Ostriches, &c., &c. By the Rev. J. G. WOOD. With Illustrations by HARRISON WEIR.

WHITE'S NATURAL HISTORY OF SELBORNE. With Notes by the Rev. J. G. WOOD, M.A. With 150 Illustrations.

FOREST LIFE IN NORWAY AND SWEDEN; being Extracts from the Journal of a Fisherman. By the Rev. HENRY NEWLAND. With Eight Illustrations.

Price **3s. 6d.** each, bevelled boards, extra gilt,

THE ANCIENT CITIES OF THE WORLD, in their Glory and their Desolation. By the Rev. T. A. BUCKLEY, M.A. Illustrated with numerous Engravings. The Third Edition.

THE GREAT CITIES OF THE MIDDLE AGES: their Rise and Progress. A Companion Volume to "The Ancient Cities." By the Rev. T. A. BUCKLEY, M.A., F.S.A. With Eight Illustrations from Designs by WILLIAM HARVEY.

JOHN RAILTON; or, Read and Think. By WILLIAM ROBSON, Author of "The Life of Richelieu," &c.

"If a parent be desirous of placing a really instructive book into the hands of his children, we can recommend to him no volume better calculated to improve the disposition and elevate the mind than this."—*Bell's Messenger.*

CLASS III.—TALES ILLUSTRATING MORAL AND RELIGIOUS SENTIMENTS.

In fcap. 8vo, price **3s. 6d.** each, cloth gilt; or with gilt edges, **4s.**,

SCHOOL-BOY HONOUR: a Tale of Halminster. By the Rev. H. C. ADAMS, Author of "The Cherry Stones," "The First of June." With Illustrations by PORTCH.

"Full of incitements to good deeds and perseverance, and written in such a manner as to interest and captivate, while it inculcates, by examples, useful moral lessons."—*Observer.*

TALES OF CHARLTON SCHOOL; containing "The Cherry Stones," and "The First of June." By the Rev. H. C. ADAMS. With Illustrations by ABSOLON.

THROUGH LIFE AND FOR LIFE. By D. RICHMOND, Author of "Annie Maitland." With Illustrations by J. D. WATSON.

"The great charm of this story consists in its simplicity. The rules of right and wrong are most admirably set forth, and show how discipline, rightly directed, succeeds in bringing about happiness and prosperity."—*Bell's Messenger.*

NEW GIRL'S BOOK.

MERVYN. By MISS BOWMAN. With Eight Illustrations.
[*Just ready.*

HOW TO MAKE THE BEST OF IT. A Domestic Tale for young Ladies. By Miss BOWMAN. With Illustrations by ABSOLON.

"It is, like Miss Bowman's other tales, marked by a union of good sense and love of adventure."—*Globe.*

In fcap. 8vo, price **3s. 6d.** each, cloth gilt ; or with gilt edges, **4s.**,

THE FOUR SISTERS: Patience, Humility, Hope, and Love. Illustrated by the Stories of Little Patience, Robert Eyre, Ruth Benson, and Rachael Dunn ; with Eight Engravings from Designs by ABSOLON.

THE GOLDEN RULE; or Stories illustrative of the Ten Commandments. By the Author of "A Trap to catch a Sunbeam," &c. With 8 Illustrations.

BOYS AT HOME. By C. ADAMS, Author of "Edgar Clifton," &c. The Third Edition. Illustrated by JOHN GILBERT.

INFLUENCE. By the Author of "A Trap to catch a Sunbeam." With beautiful Engravings by JOHN GILBERT.

SANDFORD AND MERTON. By THOMAS DAY. Newly Revised and Edited. With Illustrations.

EVENINGS AT HOME; or, The Juvenile Budget Opened. By LUCY AIKEN and Mrs. BARBAULD. With eight finely executed Engravings.

GUIZOT'S (Madame) MORAL TALES FOR YOUNG PEOPLE. Translated from the Latest French Edition, by Mrs. L. BURKE. The Fourth Edition. Illustrated by O. R. CAMPBELL.

LILLIESLEA; or, Lost and Found. A New Book for Girls. By MARY HOWITT. Illustrated by ABSOLON.

THE PARENT'S ASSISTANT; or, Stories for Children. By MARIA EDGEWORTH. Illustrated by PHIZ.

EARLY LESSONS. By MARIA EDGEWORTH. Illustrated by BIRKET FOSTER.

MORAL TALES. By MARIA EDGEWORTH. Illustrated by JOHN ABSOLON.

POPULAR TALES. By MARIA EDGEWORTH. Illustrated by DALZIEL.

H

In fcap. 8vo, price 3s. 6d., cloth gilt ; or with gilt edges, 4s.,

THE WIDE, WIDE WORLD. By ELIZABETH WETHERELL.
With Eight Illustrations.

Price 3s. 6d. each, bevelled boards, extra gilt,

MATILDA LONSDALE. By CHARLOTTE ADAMS, Author
of "Edgar Clifton." With Eight Illustrations by BIRKET FOSTER.

EDGAR CLIFTON ; or, Right and Wrong. A Story of
School Life. By CHARLOTTE ADAMS, Author of "Boys at Home."
With 8 Illustrations by BIRKET FOSTER.

STRAY LEAVES FROM SHADY PLACES. By Mrs.
NEWTON CROSLAND (late CAMILLA TOULMIN). With Eight Illustrations from Designs by JOHN GILBERT.

HILDRED THE DAUGHTER. By Mrs. NEWTON CROS-
LAND (late CAMILLA TOULMIN). Illustrated by JOHN GILBERT.

HEROINES OF DOMESTIC LIFE. By Mrs. OWEN,
Authoress of "The Heroines of History." With beautiful Illustrations by J. D. WATSON.

CLASS IV.—FAIRY TALES AND FABLES.

"*It would be hard to estimate the amount of gentleness and mercy that has made
its way among us through the channels of Fairy Tales. Forbearance, courtesy,
consideration for the poor and aged, kind treatment of animals, the love of nature,
abhorrence of tyranny and brute force—many such good things have been nourished
in the child's heart by this powerful aid.*"—Charles Dickens's Household Words.

In fcap. 8vo, price 3s. 6d. each, cloth gilt ; or with gilt edges, 4s.,

HANS ANDERSEN'S FAIRY TALES AND LEGENDS.
Translated by Madame DE CHATELAIN, and Illustrated by HENRY
WARREN.

"Hans Andersen's delightful mode of conveying moral instruction has contributed to render his works universal favourites."

WOLFF'S FAIRY TALES. Edited by K. R. MACKENZIE,
and Illustrated by HARVEY.

"Wolff's reputation in Germany as a writer of Fairy Stories is only equalled
by Hans Andersen or the Brothers Grimm."

ORIENTAL FAIRY TALES. An Original Translation.
Illustrated by W. HARVEY.
"One of the prettiest books that has been published for a long time. The
tales are quite equal to those of the far-famed Hans Andersen."

In fcap. 8vo, price **3s. 6d.** each, cloth gilt ; or with gilt edges, **4s.**,

GRIMM'S HOME STORIES FOR THE YOUNG. Newly Translated by M. L. DAVIS, and Illustrated by GEORGE THOMPSON.

"The tales throughout will entertain children, little and big. while the many lessons they contain of love, charity and generosity, are calculated to win a way to their hearts. The volume will be a most acceptable gift to all boys and girls."—*The Press.*

OLD TALES FOR THE YOUNG. Newly Written by PALMER, and Illustrated by ALFRED CROWQUILL.

"This volume consists of the most popular Nursery Tales in the language—newly written and illustrated."

ALFRED CROWQUILL'S FAIRY TALES, comprising The Giant and the Dwarf, Peter and his Goose, The Giant Hand, Tiny and her Vanity, The Selfish Man, Patty and her Pitcher. With 96 Illustrations by ALFRED CROWQUILL.

*** The same with the Plates Coloured, price **6s.**, cloth, gilt edges.

AUNT MAVOR'S PICTURE STORY-BOOKS.
In royal 8vo, price **3s. 6d.** each, bound in cloth,

NURSERY TALES FOR GOOD LITTLE BOYS. Comprising—

THE HISTORY OF TOM THUMB.	THE CHERRY ORCHARD.
THE THREE BEARS.	DICK WHITTINGTON AND HIS CAT.
LITTLE DOG TRUSTY.	PUNCH AND JUDY.

With Large Coloured Illustrations.

A PRESENT FOR A GOOD LITTLE BOY. Comprising—

A-APPLE PIE—B-BIT IT, &c.	SINBAD THE SAILOR.
THE HISTORY OF JOHN GILPIN.	JACK AND THE BEAN STALK.
THE HISTORY OF BLUE BEARD.	THE HOUSE THAT JACK BUILT.

With Large Coloured Illustrations.

THE GOOD LITTLE BOY'S BOOK. Comprising—

TOM THUMB'S ALPHABET.	CHERRY ORCHARD.
BARON MUNCHAUSEN.	PUNCH AND JUDY
LITTLE DOG TRUSTY.	THE CAT'S TEA PARTY.

With Large Coloured Illustrations.

A STORY BOOK FOR A GOOD LITTLE GIRL. Comprising—

LITTLE RED RIDING HOOD.	LITTLE TOTTY.
THE HISTORY OF OUR PETS.	COCK ROBIN AND JENNY WREN.
OLD MOTHER HUBBARD.	THE OLD WOMAN AND HER PIG.

With Large Coloured Illustrations.

H 2

AUNT MAVOR'S PICTURE STORY-BOOKS—*continued.*

THE NURSERY STORY BOOK.   Comprising—

The Nursery Alphabet.	The Three Bears.
Tom Thumb.	Beauty and the Beast.
Cinderella.	Aladdin.

With Large Coloured Illustrations.

AUNT MAVOR'S TOY BOOK.   Comprising—

Nursery Alphabet.	Hop o' my Thumb.
Willie's Holiday.	Jack the Giant Killer.
Aladdin.	The Butterfly's Ball.

With Large Coloured Illustrations.

THE EVERLASTING TOY BOOK FOR CHILDREN.
Comprising—

The Victoria Alphabet.	Uncle Hugh's Country House.
Little Polly's Doll's House.	Master Bunch's Evening Party.

Printed on Linen, with Large Coloured Illustrations.

In oblong boards, price 3s. 6d.,

THE BOOK OF NONSENSE.   By Edward Lear.
Sixth Edition, with upwards of 100 full-page Illustrations.

ROUTLEDGE'S HALF-A-CROWN REWARDS.

Fcap. cloth gilt, or with gilt edges, 3s.,

"We hardly know how to speak in terms of sufficient admiration and approbation of these beautiful books, so well adapted for the youth of both sexes, and for which the publishers have become so honourably known, and established so wide and enviable a reputation."—*Weekly Dispatch.*

EILDON MANOR.   A Book for Girls.   By the Author of
"The Four Sisters."   Illustrated by J. D. Watson.

"A very excellent story enforcing an admirable thought thus expressed by Mr. Kingsley:
'Be good, sweet maid, and let who will be clever;
Do noble things, not dream them, all day long.'"
Morning Herald.

THE MAZE OF LIFE; its Flowers and Thorns.   By the
Author of "The Four Sisters."   With Illustrations by J. D. Watson.

"'The Maze of Life' is thoroughly good.   It has honest pathos, honest humour, and honest teaching in it."—*Illustrated Times.*

ARBELL: A Tale for Young People.   By Jane Winnard
Hooper, Author of "Recollections of Mrs. Anderson's School."
With Illustrations by James Godwin.

Fcap. cloth gilt, price **2s. 6d.** ; or with gilt edges, **3s.,**

EDA MORTON, and her Cousins. By M. BELL, Author of "Deeds, not Words." With Illustrations by BIRKET FOSTER.

MINNA RAYMOND ; or, Self-Sacrifice. With Illustrations by BIRKET FOSTER and JOHN GILBERT.

HELENA BERTRAM : A Tale for the Young. By the Author of "The Four Sisters." With Illustrations.

SUNSHINE AND CLOUDS IN THE MORNING OF LIFE. By MISS BOWMAN, Author of "Esperanza," Castaways," &c. With Illustrations by ZWECKER.

THE OCEAN CHILD ; or, Showers and Sunshine. A Tale of Girlhood. By Mrs. HARRIET MYRTLE. With Eight Illustrations. by BIRKET FOSTER.

THE LUCKY PENNY, and other Tales. By Mrs. S. C. HALL, Author of "Tales of Woman's Trials," &c., &c.
*** Fifteen of Mrs. S. C. Hall's Best Tales or Stories are embodied in this Volume.

GILBERT THE ADVENTURER. Edited by PETER PARLEY. With Two Illustrations by DALZIEL. A revised Edition.

"Every young person who has any taste for good books will brighten up at the name of Peter Parley. "Gilbert the Adventurer" travels over the best part of the world by land and sea. When he comes home he has plenty of stories to relate about the wonders he has seen abroad, and in such a delightful manner that it almost makes you feel as if you had actually seen the curiosities he talks about."

KALOOLAH ; or, African Wanderings. Edited by Dr. MAYO. With Four Illustrations.

Robinson Crusoe and Baron Munchausen well mixed together—adventure without end—is the staple of "Kaloolah."

THE YOUNG GOLD DIGGER ; or, A Boy's Adventures in the Gold Regions. By F. GERSTAECKER. With Four Illustrations by HARRISON WEIR.

"Gerstaecker is one of the most popular writers of the day with the young. He has seen what he describes, and shared in the adventures which he relates. Hence his books are truthful pictures of the busy scenes of active life, and merit the very wide circulation they have obtained."—*The Nonconformist.*

THE ARCTIC REGIONS, AND POLAR DISCOVERIES DURING THE NINETEENTH CENTURY ; with the Discoveries made by Captain McClintock as to the fate of the Franklin Expedition. By P. L. SIMMONDS, F.R.G.S. Ninth Edition.

Fcap. cloth gilt, price **2s. 6d.** ; or with gilt edges, **3s.**,

THE STORY OF CERVANTES. By AMELIA B. EDWARDS. With Six Illustrations.

THE PLAYGROUND; or, The Boy's Book of Games. By GEORGE FORREST, Esq., M.A. With many Illustrations.

"Mr. Forrest, himself a schoolmaster, well knows the use of recreative sports; and he has not considered it beneath him to write a little volume descriptive of them for the information of the young generation."—*Civil Service Gazette.*

" An excellent book for boys."—*Literary Gazette.*

HEROES OF THE LABORATORY AND THE WORK-SHOP. By C. L. BRIGHTWELL. With Four Illustrations by ABSOLON.

BIBLE HISTORY: for the Use of Children and Young Persons. With Descriptive Explanations. Illustrated with Wood Engravings and Maps.

In post 8vo, price **2s. 6d.** cloth limp,

NORTHCOTE'S FABLES. Original and Selected. With 275 Illustrations, Drawn and engraved by the First Artists, and Splendidly Printed by CLAY on Tinted Paper.

In fcap. 4to, price **2s. 6d.** each, cloth gilt,

THE ADVENTURES OF A BEAR, and a Great Bear Too. By ALFRED ELWES. With Eight Coloured Illustrations by HARRISON WEIR.

THE ADVENTURES OF A CAT, and a Fine Cat Too. By ALFRED ELWES. With Eight Coloured Illustrations by HARRISON WEIR.

THE ADVENTURES OF A DOG, and a Good Dog Too. By ALFRED ELWES. With Eight Coloured Illustrations by HARRISON WEIR.

Square 16mo, price **2s. 6d.** cloth gilt,

SUMMER SONGS OF COUNTRY LIFE, A Child's Poetry Book. With 40 Coloured Illustrations.

⁎ The same with Plain Plates, Stiff Cover, **1s.**